Really?

Really?

JEREMY CLARKSON

MICHAEL JOSEPH
an imprint of
PENGUIN BOOKS

MICHAEL JOSEPH

UK | USA | Canada | Ireland | Australia
India | New Zealand | South Africa

Michael Joseph is part of the Penguin Random House group of companies
whose addresses can be found at global.penguinrandomhouse.com

First published 2019
001

Copyright © Jeremy Clarkson, 2019

The moral right of the author has been asserted

Set in 13.5/16pt Garamond MT Std
Typeset by Jouve (UK), Milton Keynes
Printed and bound in Great Britain by Clays Ltd, Elcograf S.p.A.

A CIP catalogue record for this book is available from the British Library

HARDBACK ISBN: 978–0–241–36677–6
OM PAPERBACK ISBN: 978–0–241–36678–3

The contents of this book first appeared in Jeremy Clarkson's *Sunday Times* column. Read more about the world according to Clarkson every week in the *Sunday Times*.

Contents

Who cares if it's slow? It's got more toys than Hamleys

Lexus NX 300h Premier

When a new Mercedes comes along, you know before you've even opened the door what it will be like. All Mercs feel broadly similar until the company changes direction, which happens about once every 4,000 years, and then, ever so slowly, they all start to feel slightly different.

It's the same story with BMW. Its cars were all fast and light for a long time, and then they all became heavy and a bit terrible, and now they're all as good as cars can be (except the X3, obviously).

With Lexus, you never know what you're going to get. It's not swings and roundabouts; it's rollercoasters and big buckets full of steaming excrement. Some Lexuses are so brilliant that you have to bite the back of your hand to stop yourself crying out. Others are so bad that you consider driving at full speed into a tree to end the misery. And then you have those that are beautifully made but a bit forgettable. I can't recall their names at the moment.

Only recently, I tried the new RC F, which is a four-seat, two-door sports coupé priced and powered to compete with the BMW M4. And despite what my colleague said last week, it misses the target by about 217 miles, partly because it weighs more than the Atlantic Ocean and partly because you drive around everywhere in a wail of dreary understeer.

So what of the new NX? Hmm. There are lots of letters

that work well in a car's name. T, for example, or S or R – R's very popular right now. R says a lot about a man. It says nearly as much as Z. But N? No. N doesn't work. It's like U.

To make matters worse, it's one of those crossover SUV thingies, which are popular because they are perceived to be more robust and safer than ordinary hatchbacks. They're not. But they are more expensive, more wasteful and needlessly enormous.

What's more, if you peel away the premium-brand badging, the NX is essentially a Toyota RAV4. So you can think of it as a sweatshop jumper with a Ralph Lauren horse on the front.

Oh, and here's the clincher. It's a hybrid. It says so on the side, so that cyclists will not be tempted to bang on your roof as they pedal by. Yes, you're driving a large car, but it's kind to the environment so that's OK. No, it isn't. It's unkind and daft. A hybrid may produce fewer carbon dioxides from its tailpipe than a normal car, but the cost to the planet of making the damn things with all those motors and batteries is immense. Anyone who buys a hybrid for ecological reasons is telling the world that they are an idiot.

So, a crossover hybrid with an N in its name and low-rent underpinnings from a company that's capable of turning out a howler from time to time. This is not looking good. But here's the thing: it does. At first you think it's all too complicated and fussy, but it's actually very well proportioned and full of genuinely lovely touches. It's one of those cars that compel you to turn round for another look after you've locked them up for the night.

And it's even better on the inside. The driving position is good, the dials look as if they were designed by the International Watch Company, the quality of the materials is way better than you have a right to expect for this price and there are many toys to play with. And just when you think you've played with them all, you find another bank of switches and off you go again. I especially liked the touchpad that steers the arrow around the satnav screen.

And I amused myself for hours with the head-up display system, moving it up the windscreen to its highest point and then wondering what shape a driver would have to be to want it there. Another game was pushing buttons and guessing what you'd done. Half the time, nothing seemed to happen.

This is because, behind the scenes, the Lexus is phenomenally complicated. There's a normal 4-cylinder 2.5-litre petrol engine that produces 153bhp, but then there are other motors too, doing all sorts of trickery. There's even one in the back to power the rear wheels when you are in a field.

And they are all linked together by sorcery. It feels, when you put your foot down, as if it's fitted with one of those awful cones-and-belt continuously variable gearboxes – technology that fills me with such rage that my hair starts to move about and my teeth begin to itch. But further investigation reveals that, although the transmission system is called eCVT, it's different from traditional versions: all the units send their power into what in essence is a differential, and this sends the motive force to the wheels.

So you start the engine and nothing happens. You set off in electric silence, and then when you want to go faster you push the accelerator and the petrol engine zooms up to a certain point in the rev band and stays there until you decide you've had enough. I don't like it at all and I cannot believe it's the most economical solution. But the NX 300h is not aimed at me. It's aimed at, um, people who don't really care what the rev counter's doing.

This is not a fast car. It's not even on nodding terms with the concept of speed. Time and again, I found myself driving along with a huge queue of cars in my wake, wondering why everyone was being so aggressive and sporty all of a sudden. But they weren't. It was me. I've never driven so slowly in all my life. I actually had to speed up for the cameras.

Which is fine because in this day and age lots of people just want to get home at night. And it's good at that. Very good. It is extremely comfortable and remarkably quiet. There's even an EV mode button that puts it in a pure electric motor setting, which would make it quieter still, but every time I pushed it I was told the system was temporarily unavailable. I therefore went back to playing with the head-up display.

It's strange. The Lexus is sold as a hybrid, and it has two different power sources, so, technically, it is. But it can't really run on batteries alone. So if you are looking for a car to save the polar bear, you'd be better off with a McLaren P1 or a Porsche 918 Spyder.

However, if you are normal, the Lexus is pretty good. It worked in a field, the boot is huge, the back is spacious and the air of good quality is all-pervading. The handling also is good for a car this tall and heavy – it's really heavy – but despite its bulk, you can do hundreds of miles on a single tank of fuel. I enjoyed my time with it and would recommend it to anyone who for some reason doesn't want a Range Rover Evoque.

I can't for the life of me work out what that reason might be, but if you have one, then the NX, despite all the evidence to the contrary, is your answer.

4 January 2015

Dear Deidre, I had a fling with my first love. She's lost it

Volkswagen Scirocco

Thirty-five years ago, having achieved 110 words a minute in my shorthand exam – by cheating – I became a qualified journalist and immediately went to work for my parents as a travelling sales rep flogging Paddington Bears. This is because they were offering me a company car.

I agonized for many months over what that car should be, because this was 1980, a period of great change. Most of my friends had Triumph Dolomite Sprints and Ford Escort RS2000s, and those certainly had a great deal of appeal. But the hot hatchback had just been born and, I dunno, that seemed to be even better somehow.

And then there was the Vauxhall Chevette HS, which, despite its rear-wheel-drive, rally-bred layout, wasn't an old-school car, but then it wasn't a hot hatchback either. And, as I recall, it could do 0 to 60mph in 7.9 seconds, which was 0.2 of a second faster than the Volkswagen Golf GTI. Which in turn was 0.1 of a second faster than a Ford Escort XR3. This sort of thing mattered then, more than almost anything else.

Eventually, Volkswagen came to the rescue by announcing that it would be fitting the engine from the Golf GTI into its Scirocco to create a hot coupé. I went for a fetching gold paint job that I teamed with brown velour seats and a brown dashboard.

Then, having bought the car, I immediately ruined it by

fitting gigantic 205/60 white-walled tyres that filled the arches very well and looked extremely snazzy. But they made the steering wheel feel as though it had been set in concrete. Reversing into a tight space took about an hour and burnt 4,000 calories.

This is why there were no gyms back then. In the days before power steering we didn't need them. We'd get a full upper-body workout every time we wanted to go round a corner.

However, despite the enormous effort required to drive my Scirocco, I loved it more than life itself, and in one year we did 54,000 miles together. I would drive to the pub and not drink for five hours so that I could have the pleasure of driving it home again. I'd go all the way to Wales to see a shopkeeper I didn't like, who wouldn't buy any bears, because it meant I could spend a whole day in my Volkswagen.

And when I wasn't driving it I was talking about it, sometimes to girls, who would listen for a while to see if I might start talking about something else and then wander off when they realized I wouldn't. But mostly to other men, who thought that because my car had front-wheel drive I might be a bit hairdresserish. I'd then pass them on the way home standing by their upside-down rear-wheel-drive cars and laugh.

I was born with a love of cars, a love that was ignited by the Maserati in my *Ladybird Book of Motor Cars* and nurtured by my first serious relationship, with a Ford Cortina 1600E. But it was cemented in place by that Scirocco.

Which is why I was delighted several years ago when VW said it would use exactly the same recipe to make a new Scirocco. It would simply take a Golf and give it a new, sleeker and more attractive body.

The trouble was that the body it selected wasn't sleek or

attractive. It looked sort of broken and fat at the back. And why would you pay a premium to buy a car that looked even worse than the hatchback on which it was based?

VW came up with another reason for not buying one when it brought out the diesel version. Because there we had a car that didn't look as good as the hatchback, was based on the previous generation anyway and had an engine entirely unsuited to coupé motoring.

When it came along, James May and I tried to make some television commercials about it on *Top Gear*, and I seem to recall we managed to spark fury in the process. Mostly, I guess, on the part of Volkswagen, which was probably not best pleased to have its car and its excellent advertising ridiculed in a series of casually offensive jokes about Germans.

Truth be told, I didn't really want to drive this car for all the reasons that you read about on the Dear Deidre page in the *Sun*. You know how it goes. You enjoy a year-long relationship thirty-five years ago. You hook up again, thanks to Facebook. And she has turned into a moose. Nobody wants that in their lives. Better to keep love from the past as a memory.

But then in the run-up to Christmas I went to retrieve my Mercedes from the garage and it had been in there for such a long time that it wouldn't start. It was right on the edge. The starter motor clicked and there were many whirring noises, but despite a great deal of pleading from me, and a lot of counting to ten before trying again, there simply wasn't enough juice in the battery to prod the V8 into life.

I needed four wheels and a seat. And a boot for all the presents. And all that I could get my hands on in the time available was the Scirocco diesel.

It still doesn't look right and it still makes all the wrong noises when you start the engine, and there's no getting round the fact that you are driving a car based on the Golf Mk 6, not the current and much better Mk 7. Oh, and you can't see anything out of the rear-view mirror. And what's this? Yes. It's stalled.

It stalls a lot. Doubtless for reasons that have a lot to do with the polar bear, this diesel engine needs a bootful of revs before you can even think about setting off. And then, when you do, you think something is broken because there simply isn't enough oomph.

On top of the dashboard are three dials in a raised binnacle. They tell you nothing you need to know but they look good. They look sporty. They tell you that you are a man in a hurry, but here's hoping you aren't, because this is not a fast car.

And the gearing's weird. Time and again when cruising along the motorway I'd try to change up from sixth. And third is so high that in town it's never really an option. Probably the polar bears again.

Yes, it's priced well, and, yes, the Scirocco badge still carries a bit of kudos, thanks entirely to the Mk 1 that I fell in love with. It's also beautifully made and blessed with some lovely touches – pillarless doors being the standout feature on this front.

But as an overall package it did nothing all week except remind me how much I wanted a Golf GTI. A modern version of the Scirocco, but with a better-looking body and the sort of engine you expect in a car such as this.

Volkswagen, then, has got it the wrong way round. It has built a coupé that forces you to buy the hatchback instead. I hope it addresses this when the time comes for a replacement.

11 January 2015

Sorry, sir, you can't take that machine-gun in hand luggage

Audi TT

I was extremely drunk at the launch of the original Audi TT and can't recall much about anything that happened. It was staged in Italy, or maybe France, and I seem to recall that one of the guests, whom I met there for the first time, was a spectacular pedant called James May.

In the interminable press conference, which went on for about two days, the German engineers droned on and on about every single nut and every single bolt, and all of that is a grey fog, but I distinctly remember one of them saying the styling was very Bauhaus.

This sounded important, so when I reviewed the car on the early incarnation of *Top Gear* I thought it would be a good plan to mention it. So I pulled a serious face and said: 'The styling is very Bauhaus.'

Other motoring correspondents, including the pedant who went on to become James May, did much the same thing. Everyone did. And soon everyone in the land of petrol and noise was talking about this wondrous new Audi: 'I love the Bauhaus styling,' they all said, even though no one had the first clue what Bauhaus was.

Plainly, it means 'looks that appeal to air hostesses', because they very quickly became the TT's core market. Seriously, have a look next time you're out and about. Every single TT you see is being driven down the M23 by a woman with a raffish scarf and orange skin.

It's slightly weird. Audi had made a sports car. It was turbo-charged and four-wheel-drive and sleek and dynamic and Bauhaus, and it could zoom along at more than 150mph, and yet it was bought by people who drove it to the staff car park at Gatwick and left it there while they flew to Miami for a spot of light sex with the co-pilot.

With the power of hindsight, I can see why. It was curvy. And curvy cars such as the Nissan Micra and Lexus SC 430 don't appeal to men. They come across as friendly and Noddyish. Curves are not aggressive and as a result have no place in a man's straight-line world of guns and fighter planes and nineteenth-century former public-school boys drawing up African borders. The main reason men don't eat lettuce is that it's too curvy. We prefer chips, and KitKats, which aren't.

Plainly, Audi has now arrived at the same conclusion, and as a result the new TT has lost the rounded edges. There are sharp creases and acute angles all over it, and I think it looks absolutely terrific. Inside, it's even better. With the exception of the Lexus LFA's, this is probably the best car interior I've encountered. The seats in my test vehicle were made from quilted leather such as you get in a Bentley – a £1,390 option – and I liked that a lot.

But what I liked even more was the instrument binnacle, because you can set it up to be whatever you want it to be. Speedo and rev counter. Or a satnav map, or a radio tuner. It makes an iPad look like a Victorian's typewriter.

And because all the information is presented right where you are looking, space on the rest of the dash is freed up for big knobs, clear read-outs and yet more dinky styling touches.

That's before we get to the indicator stalks. Normally, an indicator stalk is a sort of cylinder, but in Audi's attempts to get rid of all the curves it's now sharp-edged, so when you want to turn left or right it's as if you're signalling your intentions with a beautifully crafted hunting knife.

Now I would love at this point to tell you that the TT is not much fun to drive and that it rides like every other Audi: not very well. But I'm afraid I can't, because it's sublime.

I want to start with the brakes, which completely redefine the concept of how good such components can be. They won't stop you any more quickly than the ones in any other car, but the feel through the pedal is extraordinary. It's as though every equation about deceleration and trajectory and distance is fed directly to your mind each time you want to slow down. Frankly, the TT's brakes make those in every other car feel like anchors made from trifle and iron filings.

And there's a similar leap forwards with the button that changes how the car feels. Many cars have a facility such as this these days, and, if I'm honest, in most it's pointless. In some the button makes absolutely no difference at all. In others it simply makes the vehicle extremely uncomfortable. But in the TT it's a tool you'll want to use a lot.

On a motorway you put it in Comfort mode, and the car becomes just that. In a town you put it in the Efficiency setting and it consumes fuel like an Edwardian sipping tea at a beetle drive, and on an A-road you put it in Dynamic and the exhaust starts to make farty noises during gear changes. And you go faster, and the faster you go, the faster you'll want to go, because everything feels just right.

The steering, the turn-in, the ride, the acceleration and the brakes – oh, those brakes – give you the encouragement to be Daniel Ricciardo, and the TT is so good you will feel you've succeeded. It's fabulous.

And yet here is a car that has two back seats into which any normal person could fit, provided they had no legs or head, and a boot that is genuinely useful. It's practical and economical and safe, and quiet and unruffled, and it's an Audi, which means it's a Volkswagen, and that means everything is screwed together properly.

This, then, is Audi's best car in decades, and yet I couldn't actually buy one because . . . well, let me put it this way. Imagine Agent Provocateur putting a Y-shaped front on to its latest line of thongs and marketing them at men. You still wouldn't, would you?

Such an undergarment might be practical and finished in a fabric that appealed to your inner testosterone but you couldn't go round telling people that you were wearing Agent Provocateur underwear.

And there's another issue. By fitting the new model with sharp edges and the sort of tech you normally find on one of Tom Clancy's stealth destroyers, Audi runs the risk of making the nation's air hostesses think the car's become a bit unnecessary. A bit stormtrooperish.

And that's a problem. It's a machinegun in a dress. A car with a badge that appeals to BA's cabin crew and dynamics that will go down well on the nation's automotive web forums. Which means Audi has ended up with a brilliant car . . . that no one is going to buy.

25 January 2015

It's drizzling, I'm doing 2mph . . . and all's well with the world

Ferrari California T

A recent report suggested that people who use Apple iPhones are more intelligent, more successful and, of course, better-looking than those who use telephones made by other companies. But I'm not sure this is accurate.

I have an Apple iPhone and I'm well aware that it is riddled with faults. The map feature doesn't work, the battery life is woeful, its camera is up there in quality with a Zenit SLR from 1973 and the screen smashes whenever there's a light breeze. And I can't update to the latest model because experts tell me it's all bendy.

There's more. I recently bought a new laptop and loading it with all my data was a nightmare simply and only because of Apple, which wanted my password seven times before announcing that I'd entered it all wrong and that I'd have to come up with a new one that must feature a capital letter, a number, a cave drawing, a fully working model of the Tirpitz and three letters from my mother's middle name.

Then, when I'd come up with something it liked, I was told not to write it down anywhere. Which I didn't. Which meant I'm now in a bit of a pickle because all my other devices won't work unless I remember what it was. By Thursday I was wishing Steve Jobs had never been born.

But I will not switch to another brand because I simply cannot be bothered to learn how it all works.

We see this with everything. I have a PlayStation and won't entertain the idea of an Xbox because it all seems to be the wrong way round. I have a Gaggia coffee machine that is utterly and completely useless but I can't change to one of George Clooney's Nespressos because I don't have enough hours in the day to work out what its buttons do.

Car firms plainly understand this, which is why they all use completely different command and control software. After you've spent a year learning how to turn the bossy sat-nav voice off, you are not very inclined to switch to another brand and learn all over again.

And it's not just the satnav. Turning the heated seats on, shutting down the traction control, tightening the suspension, adjusting the dashboard brightness, choosing a radio station: in every single car every single thing you do is different.

All of which brings me on to the new Ferrari California T. This is the cheapest, or should I say least expensive, Ferrari and is the company's first foray into the mainstream market. It's a cruising car, a convertible 2+2 (yeah, right) in the mould of the Mercedes SL.

This means it will be used every day by people who play golf and live in suburbia. So it needs to be a Ferrari, or else what's the point? And yet at the same time it needs to be benign and easy. And if it's going to appeal to the Bobby Ewings of this world, it needs all the toys you get in a Mercedes, all the hi-techery.

As a result, the California comes with the Apple CarPlay system, which pairs the vehicle with every single thing on your iPhone. This means you can, for example, speak a text and the car sends it.

And here's the most amazing thing. It works. Not once

did it mistakenly send the head of the army a message saying, 'Send three and fourpence – we're going to a dance.'

However, the rest of the electronic systems were an unfathomable tangle of swearwords and frustration. I couldn't make the satnav work at all. I can get my head round the system in a Subaru, which takes a while, and even the one in a Jeep, which was set up by a madman, but this flummoxed me, and I don't know why. I can't work out whether it's Ferrari just being obtuse or whether it was suffering from some kind of electronic hiccup. This seems unlikely, though, in a car from the country that invented electricity . . . he said, with just a hint of a smile.

There's another issue too. The California comes with the same sort of steering wheel as the 458 Italia. That is definitely Ferrari being obtuse, because it must know by now that putting the buttons for the indicators, headlamps and windscreen wipers on the wheel – which moves about – is galactically idiotic. And yet Ferrari continues to insist it isn't. I would not buy a Ferrari these days simply because of this.

And because of the beeping. It beeps when you are reversing. It beeps when it thinks you are too close to another car. It beeps when you haven't done up your seatbelts. It beeps constantly.

And we haven't even got on to the sheer size of the thing. It's a problem that affects all Ferraris these days – the F12 is about the same size as a Canadian combine – and in London it's a menace. After a couple of days I gave up using the narrow rat runs, because I'd spent most of the time reversing.

Which meant I'd had to suffer the beeping. I know I'm going backwards, for God's sake. I am a sentient being. And as a result I know I wouldn't have to go backwards if this bloody car weren't so bloody wide.

So there is much to annoy you in a California T. And only some of it is down to the fact that I'm trying to judge its systems while on the inevitable learning curve. And yet . . .

Every week I have to drive to the *Top Gear* test track in Surrey. It's always rush hour. It's always drizzling. The traffic's always awful. There are roadworks every few yards, so it takes fifty minutes to cover the 2 miles from Holland Park to Hammersmith Bridge and, frankly, this is motoring at its worst.

In a normal Ferrari life in these circumstances is intolerable, and I usually end up looking longingly at people on buses. But in the California I was quite content just to sit there listening to the radio. It wasn't uncomfortable or noisy or show-offy in any way.

Later, it sat on the A3 at a steady 50mph, and it didn't feel as if I was having to hold back some kind of deranged stallion.

On the face of it, then, what we have here is a car that's like a Mercedes SL, only a bit harder to live with because of its size and the complexity of its controls. And a bit more expensive.

Yes, but underneath it all it's still a Ferrari. Oh, sure, the engine is turbocharged now to meet emissions regulations, but you don't notice that. What you do notice is the feel through the steering and the immediacy of the gear changes. No Mercedes feels quite so − what's the word? − sharp. And no Mercedes comes with an adjustable speed limiter.

If you've always hankered after a Ferrari and you really can't afford to buy a second car for driving round town in the rain, the California T is a godsend. Yes, its command and control stuff is bonkers and the steering wheel is so stupid I'm not tempted. But I quite understand if you are.

1 February 2015

With this many 911s, they were bound to make a good one

Porsche 911 Carrera 4 GTS

A colleague of mine noted recently that there are 154 options you can have on a Porsche 911, and as a result there are a staggering 9.6 trillion possible combinations. That, said my meticulous friend, works out at 1,371 versions of the car for every man, woman and child on earth.

But he's wrong. It's way more than that. And it gets worse, because the options list is only the beginning. Before that you have to choose what sort of 911 you want. There are many. You can have a 993 series or a 997 or a 991. You can have two-wheel drive, or a two-wheel-drive with more power, and you can have either of those with a hard roof, with a Targa roof or as a cabriolet. Then you can have the exact same set of choices with the four-wheel-drive option. Or you can have a GT3. Or a GT3 RS. Or a Turbo with four-wheel drive or two-wheel drive and a choice of roof arrangements.

It's all completely mad because all of them look pretty much exactly the same and all of them have broadly the same engine and all of them are driven by people whose penises are about to break.

As I may have mentioned about 200 times over the years, I've never been a fan of the 911, whichever one of the 270 million models you happen to be talking about. My prejudice was born back in the early 1990s, when I wasn't much of a helmsman.

Back then the 911 was a pig. It would understeer when you turned into a corner and, as I didn't really know what I was doing, I'd take my foot off the accelerator as quickly as possible, which would then cause the car to start oversteering. Which meant I had to undo my seatbelt and cower in the back until it hit something and stopped.

And what really used to annoy me was that on the next lap you'd do pretty much the exact same thing at pretty much the exact same speed and it would respond in a completely different way.

More experienced colleagues would tell me that this was because the 911 was engineered and designed for people who knew what they were doing, and that minute adjustments to the steering and the throttle would cause it to behave in a completely different way: just what the serious opposite-locksmith wants, they would argue. Since then, of course, I've had a lot of practice at driving round corners too quickly and now the 911 doesn't frighten me at all. I can handle it and its silly little foible with ease.

'Yes,' say the experts, in their annoying adenoidal way, 'but that's because it doesn't have any foibles any more. It's been softened.' The engine, which used to sit right at the back, where it would act as a pendulum in extreme circumstances, has been moved forwards, and it is now cooled with water rather than air. And the steering is now done with electricity rather than hydraulics. And because of all this the 911 is a big pussycat. This is seen in adenoid-land as the end of days.

Not to you and me it isn't. Because the 911 stands out as a very real way of experiencing a little bit of genuine sports motoring for a fraction of the cost of buying a Ferrari and with far fewer histrionics. And, these days, less of a tendency to end up in a hedge.

But which model should you choose? Well, to make life even more difficult, Porsche has now introduced a new version called the GTS. It sits in the range between the Carrera S and the GT3. Yes, I know. I didn't realize there was a gap there either, but apparently there was and the GTS has filled it.

The idea is simple. You get more horsepower than you do from the Carrera S, and a wider body, but it's less raw than the GT3 and cheaper. It's good value because, unusually for a Porsche, it comes with quite a bit of kit as standard.

If I were in the market for a 911 – and if I hadn't been quite so vocal about its awfulness over the past few years, I might be – I'd go for a two-wheel-drive GTS. It seems to offer the best of all worlds. Sadly, though, the car I drove last week was the four-wheel-drive alternative.

I know that a four-wheel-drive 911 is less pure than a model that is driven only from the rear, but as I set off on a long rush-hour journey from London to Rugby I didn't really care about that. And I was positively grateful when just past Northampton it started to snow.

There was something else to be grateful for too. Every car has a cruising speed, a speed at which it settles when you are on a quiet motorway and you're thinking about other stuff. This has something to do with resonance and noise and gearing. In a Mini it's a worrying 110mph, which means that with the new speed cameras you could lose your licence – twice – in one lap of the M25.

In the GTS it's 59mph. I have no idea why, but I think the throttle pedal is to blame. It has quite a strong spring, so to go any faster you have to make a conscious effort with your foot. This is a small point, but it's important because, if you're daydreaming, you at least know you won't get nicked.

I'm not going to beat about the bush. This is an excellent

car. It is fast without being stupid, even if you're running it in Sport Plus mode, which makes it uncomfortable, noisy and uneconomical. Best to leave that facility alone.

It's not as though you're short of other things to play with. The satnav system is as good as anything you'll find in any car, and there's a computer that tells you all sorts of things, such as how much G-force you are generating and when you will arrive at your destination. It's German. It knows this stuff.

And then there's the driving position. Ooh, it's good. Nearly as good, in fact, as the flappy-paddle gearbox. The only trouble is that, while I liked the GTS a lot, and marvelled at its ability to be fast, sensible, comfy and quiet all at the same time, I couldn't really love it. At no point did I think, 'I have got to get me one of these.'

There's a magazine called *Autocar* that provides us *Top Gear* boys with a massive laugh every Wednesday because its road testers always look so serious when they're driving a car. When we are power-sliding a Lamborghini round a hairpin bend in the Alps we bounce around and squeak like schoolboys – well, two of us do – but at *Autocar* they always look as if they're in a meeting.

And that's the face you find yourself pulling in a Porsche. You never think, 'Wow.' It's all very – what's the word? Clinical. But if you're going to buy a 911, the GTS is definitely the version to go for.

8 February 2015

Perfect for Jimi's hairdo, but no good for crosstown traffic

Land Rover Discovery Sport

Upon returning from my holidays earlier this year, I decided that I should become less fat. So I made some inquiries and discovered there were two ways of doing this. And since one was 'doing exercise', there was in fact only one way of doing this: not drinking any more.

The effects have been remarkable. In just a month I've lost six chins and can get into my suit again. But there has been a downside: instead of using taxis when I go out in the evening I now use the car.

In some ways it's a joy. You feel when you're driving in London at night that you can jump red lights, break the speed limit and knock down anyone who gets in your way, because if you are stopped by the police, you can put your hand on your heart and say, 'Nope. I haven't even had a sniff.' And they'll be forced to let you go with a cheery wave.

But it doesn't work out quite like that, because what you actually do when you take the car is sit in a traffic jam, and then, when you arrive, an hour late, spend an hour looking for somewhere to park. I realize that sobriety will add many years to my life, but I'm wasting so much time in traffic these days I wonder if the maths adds up.

Last week, for instance, I had to go from Holland Park to something called Bloomsbury, and London was in a bad mood. Every single road was a tangle of frayed tempers, red lights and the sirens of stuck ambulances. So I wiggled about the back streets and was doing quite well until a diversion put me on a collision course with the Crossrail works at the bottom of Tottenham Court Road.

These have been snarling up the capital since 1951 and there seems to be no sign of progress. Hoardings around the site tell us that one day the scheme will bring an extra 1.5 million people within forty-five minutes of central London, but as you sit in the endless jam, with all the Humbers and Hill-mans that have been queuing there since the road was closed, you can't help wondering if more people is quite what London wants.

The traffic lights go from red to green endlessly and nothing moves because everyone at the head of the queue died in 1973. And still the workmen dig, creating an underground superhighway that will link west London, where people live and work, to the east, where there are a few fishmongers and that's about it. They may as well build a tunnel from Hull to Dogger Bank.

Then you have the roadworks on the New King's Road that turn SW6 into an island every time Chelsea play at home. The Fulham Road is closed as well. I'd like to meet the man who thought this was an acceptable plan. Perhaps someone could send me the address of the home where he's living and the name of his nurse.

What's made all this congestion worse is that I've been trying to get about in Land Rover's new Discovery Sport, which feels a great deal bigger than it actually is. This is because it has a vast amount of headroom. Jimi Hendrix would be able to drive this car – if he were still alive, obviously – without flattening his hairdo at all. It's like sitting in a cathedral. And when you are in St Paul's you don't even attempt to drive through gaps that actually are easily wide enough.

It's a strange car, this: billed as a replacement for the solid, no-nonsense Freelander, it is badged as a Discovery and sits on the same running gear as a Range Rover Evoque. Confused? Mmm. I was too. So let me put it to you this way. It's a seven-seat alternative to the rather too mumsy Volvo XC90. And a better-looking alternative to the standard Discovery, which, as we know, is mostly driven by murderers.

It's also very comfortable. Around town it isolates you from roads that have been mended by people who think 'good enough' is pedantry, and on a motorway it glides along like a hovercraft. Only with better steering. And it's not just the suspension that warrants praise. The seats are comfortable too, and if you push the back bench backwards there is acres of space for kids. I haven't seen so much legroom in the back of a car since Citroën stopped making the CX Prestige.

Yes, the seats that rise up out of the boot floor are not ideal for the aged, the infirm, the fat or even the fully formed, but for a short school run it's better to have them than not. Even if it does mean you have to do without a full-sized spare wheel.

All of this – the nice ride, the school-run stuff and indeed the extremely sharp and precise steering – would lead us to think Land Rover had given up with its core values and that the Disco Sport would be flummoxed by any sort of weather or rough terrain. But no. It still comes with all the fancy off-road programs. You tell it what sort of ground you want to cover – mud, sand, a bog or whatever – and it sorts out its differentials and its four-wheel-drive system for you.

So far, then, everything is good. And it gets better, because at long last Land Rover has updated its satellite navigation and central command system. It's still touchscreen, which is the wrong way of doing things, especially when the display in question is a hell of a stretch even for me, but it's much better than it was.

However, things go a bit wrong with the engine. Only one is on offer and – how can I put this? – it's a bit old now, and a bit tractory. The power it produces is fine – it'll get the car from 0 to 62mph in 8.9 seconds, which is brisk – but I couldn't really live with the roughness.

I hear Land Rover is currently working on a new power-plant that will be ready and available in the Discovery Sport later this year, so if the car appeals, best to wait until then.

And start saving, because it's not cheap. The basic price of the version I tested is £42,995 and, yes, this is quite good compared with the price of a Volvo XC90. It's quite good also for a luxurious, attractive and spacious seven-seater. And yet . . .

I dunno. It's hard to get your head round a price such as this for a car that is billed as a replacement for the much cheaper Freelander.

And then there's the biggest problem of them all. It's going to get nicked. Land Rovers and Range Rovers are popular with gangs that ship them out to Africa before you've even noticed they've gone. And I'm told that, to make matters worse, the keyless entry system, which is on higher-spec versions of the Discovery Sport, is not that hard to crack. In certain parts of London now, new Range Rovers are routinely stopped by the police because there's a good chance the driver won't be the actual owner.

That's not such a problem for me, of course, because I'm not drinking. You, on the other hand . . .

22 February 2015

No need for Supercar when Clutch Kent's here

Ford Fiesta Zetec S Red Edition

I wonder if in the First World we have all become mad. Because when we are buying something we always choose the most expensive option. Rather than the best. We have somehow got it into our heads that a £200 set of kitchen knives will last longer and do more cutting than a £100 set of kitchen knives. We think that a £4 million house will suit us better than a house for £250,000. We assume the food in a restaurant with big numbers on the menu is bound to be better and tastier and nicer than a Big Mac meal. But is any of this true?

Well, it's probably not true with the McMeal and it's definitely not true when it comes to cars. I know this because I have spent yet another week with the Volkswagen Golf GTI and it's completely perfect. You can spend ten times more on a car and it will be worse. This is a fact. There is no room for debate.

You may think that Volkswagen puts its brightest and its best engineers into the boutique, high-profile companies that it owns: Bugatti, Lamborghini and Bentley. But it doesn't. It uses its absolute geniuses on the Golf, because that's the bread and butter of its operations. The Golf has to be right.

And it is right. I drive a lot of cars and every single one of them does at least one little thing that is annoying. The Golf doesn't. The way the seats slide about, the feel of the buttons, the weight of the steering, everything: it's all absolutely spot on. As long as you ignore the dashboard 'eco driving' tips.

And then, sitting on top of this nest of perfection, we have the GTI version, which comes with more power than you were expecting – a lot more – and an amusing gear knob in the shape of a golf ball. Das ist fun, ja?

I drove a Porsche 911 GTS the other day and I thought it was pretty damn good. I was also very taken with the Bentley Continental GT V8 S. But the Yorkshireman in me says, 'What's the point?' Because neither of those cars is better in any way than the GTI.

Sure, they have more power, but, come on, be realistic. When does that do anything apart from use more fuel? Most versions of the GTI will average more than 40mpg and you'd have to be extremely committed in your Porsche or your Bentley to get away from it on anything other than a road through Monument Valley.

On a Welsh mountain road, in the rain, the VW would be faster. Much faster. So the conclusion is this. No matter what you can afford, buy a Golf GTI instead. It's that simple.

Or is it? Because for about £9,000 less than a Golf GTI you could have a Ford Fiesta ST, which, if anything, is even more fun to drive. It's more fun to drive, in fact, than almost anything that's been fitted with four wheels. It's a little gem, that car.

Of course, it's a little smaller than a Golf, but how often does that matter? Do you really go everywhere with a couple of prop forwards in the back, and a St Bernard in the boot? No. For most of the time, a small, unpretentious car such as this is handier than a bigger, flashier one.

If you have a Bentley, the day will come when you say, 'If only this damn thing were a bit smaller, I'd be able to fit into that parking space, but now I've got to waste a further hour of my life looking for another.'

It's the same story with the Porsche 911. There will come a day when you come out of a meeting to find some worthless layabout has keyed the flanks and carved rude words into the roof. Then you will think, 'If only I'd bought something a bit less showy.'

I cannot think of a single thing, however, that would cause the owner of a Ford Fiesta ST to say, 'If only'. Unless, of course, they happen to try out the Fiesta Zetec S Red Edition that I took for a spin last week. Then they are going to say, 'If only I had one of these.'

On the face of it, it's a ridiculous car. It's called Red because it's red. There's a black one called the Black Edition. I know. Mad. And it gets sillier because it costs only £1,250 less than the super-fast ST but comes with a 3-cylinder 1-litre engine that's so small it could easily be mistaken for a pencil sharpener. The block – and this is a true fact – would sit comfortably on a piece of A4 paper.

Do not imagine, however, that because it's physically small, it is weedy. Because as any flyweight boxer will tell you, that's a mistake. In fact, this little engine produces 138bhp. That's not a misprint. Ford has managed to extract 138 brake horsepower from an engine that has the same capacity as two cans of beer.

I remember the song and dance Daihatsu made when it developed a 1-litre engine for the Charade GTti that developed 100bhp. 'We have made a hundred horsepower from just 1 litre,' the company said at the launch, moments before I stuffed its test car into a ditch and knocked the front off.

And now Ford has upped that to 138bhp. You might imagine that it's a mass of turbo lag and torque holes and strange noises. But no. It makes a sort of 'brrrrr' noise and is like having a West Highland terrier under the bonnet. I completely loved it. I loved the speed as well. It gets from 0 to 60mph in nine seconds and will eventually reach 125mph. And yet because it's a 1-litre car the insurance is cheap and it is said you'll get more than 60mpg.

I haven't even got to the best bit yet: it's a Fiesta, which means it has an absolutely stupendous chassis. Maybe the chassis in a Porsche 918 Spyder is a bit better. And there's no doubt the Ferrari 458 Italia has a peach too. But the little Ford is in the same league – it really is.

It absorbs bumps as though they're not there, it has a tenaciously grippy front and a waggly tail, and above all it makes you feel – even at half-speed – very happy. It is a car filled with joy, and that's a rare thing these days.

Maybe the controls are fiddly, and if you specify some of the electronic extras, you will find them extremely complicated to use, but you can solve that by not bothering. Who needs DAB radio anyway? Only those who enjoy long and sustained periods of silence.

The only real problem with this car is where you live, which is in Britain. Because if you sell your Audi or your Bentley or your Ferrari to buy one – which, if you had any sense, you would – all your friends and neighbours would assume that things were going badly in your life and not talk to you any more.

That's because we live in the First World. And we're all mad.

1 March 2015

The Hottest Hatch Bar None Streaks out of the Last Chintz Saloon

Mercedes GLA AMG 4Matic

As we know, there are far fewer blockbuster films being made these days than at any time in cinema's peacetime history. When I was growing up, there was a constant supply, and they were varied. There were westerns and historical dramas and war films and huge, sweeping epics involving Julie Christie. I'd see *Lawrence of Arabia* one weekend, *Where Eagles Dare* the next and *Young Winston* after that.

Then I'd see *Young Winston* again because it was the first time I'd copped a pair of breasts on the silver screen. Then I'd claim I'd lost my bus fare home and watch it again.

Today, it's a very different story. You have *Iron Man*, *Iron Man 2* and *Iron Man 3*. Then you have *Iron Man* teaming up with *Captain America* and *Thor*, and *Wolverine* versus *Jaws*.

It's the same story with monsters. You had *Alien* and *Aliens*, and *Predator* and *Predator 2*. And later you had *Alien* versus *Predator*. And soon you just know it will be *Alien* and *Predator* versus *Iron Man* and *Wolverine* and an Old Etonian in a cape, or a suit, or a spaceship – or maybe an Old Harrovian. Whatever; it'll definitely be some kind of thin-lipped Brit.

I don't really mind any of this. I like Robert Downey Jr, I loved *Avengers Assemble* and I'll watch almost anything if it features Scarlett Johansson in a pair of rather too tight trousers. But I am a bit sad that every single big-bucks film these days is about someone with metal bones or a massive hammer.

We see pretty much the same sort of thing going on with cars. It's not that we've lost brands such as Humber and Wolseley and Hillman; that happened back in the mists of time. No, it's that what's left is all a bit samey.

The Škoda Octavia is a VW Golf. So's the Audi A3 and so is the Seat Leon. And anything that isn't a Golf is either a VW Polo or a Fiat 500. Except the Fiat 500X, which is an Alfa Romeo.

Rolls-Royce has done a magnificent job with the Ghost of disguising the fact that, underneath, it shares many components with the BMW 7-series. You absolutely cannot tell, but you know. And that spoils the experience a bit.

It's the same story with the Bentley Continental GT. As I may have mentioned about 700 times in the past few months, I currently have a big fan-boy crush on that car. But if I were to own one, I'd always know, every time I climbed into it, that, actually, I was climbing into a Volkswagen Phaeton.

You might imagine that the solution to all this is to buy a Mercedes-Benz, because what you're getting underneath is a Mercedes-Benz. Unfortunately, Mercedes has gone completely bonkers in the past couple of years, which means that the Mercedes you buy could well be based on a Mercedes you don't like.

There was a time when the company's range was very simple. You had medium-sized cars, large cars and very large cars. All of them were functional, restrained, beautifully made and tasteful. But Mercedes has gone all Hollywood and is now making a million versions of the same thing. There is now a Mercedes for every single person on the planet.

And all of them are a bit – how can I put this tactfully? – chintzy. Mercs used to be styled by a man called Brown Bag. I'm not joking. That was his name. Oh, he said it in Italian to make it sound more interesting, but there's no getting round the fact that Bruno Sacco means Brown Bag.

Anyway, Brown Bag was brilliant. He had no time for jewellery and glitter. But he's gone, and in his place is the sort of man who would describe Elton John's spectacles as a bit understated. Just look at the front of a Merc these days. It has about a million styling details. It's a sensory overload. A Cheshire IT man's front room with headlamp washers.

All of which brings me on to the car I've been using for the past week. It's the Mercedes GLA 45 AMG 4Matic, which means it's a four-wheel-drive A-class that's been slightly raised to give it a bit of off-road credibility and then lowered again to make it sporty. The end result is a car that's just 3 inches taller than the standard hatchback but includes roof bars. So really it's not taller at all.

And then we get to the styling, and, ooh, there's a lot of it. At the back there are vents and kick plates picked out in aluminium, plus there's a spoiler, and if you want, there's the option of having another spoiler mounted over the one that's already there. There are also many chromed badges, plus lights that look as if they belong on top of an American police car, and the net effect is: there's more stuff here than you would find in your granny's sitting room.

Look at the front for too long and you start to go cross-eyed. Then you have power bulges on the bonnet – obviously – and picked out on the front wings the legend 'turbo'.

You don't need to be reminded of it because, crikey, this thing is fast. Lots of hot hatches have a 2-litre turbocharged engine, but none produces quite so much get-up-and-go as

Merc's one. Put your foot down hard and 4.8 seconds later you're doing 62mph.

The Golf R is often cited as the best and the fastest of the hot hatches, but in a drag race with this Merc the VW wouldn't know where it had gone. Well, it would. Because you can see the glare of all the chrome from space. But you know what I mean. So it's very, very fast and it handles nicely too. Even when it's raining and the roads are slippery, you can bomb along, allowing the four-wheel-drive system to keep you on the tarmac.

Inside are some lovely touches. You get brilliant seats and a seatbelt that works out how fat you are by strangling you before you set off – it's surprisingly reassuring in a BDSM kind of way. You also get a very Germanic satnav system that knows – precisely – where the jams are. Because of this I saved myself a two-hour hold-up outside Guildford last week.

The only real drawback to the way this car works is the throttle. It's a problem with all GLA cars. The accelerator doesn't send a request for more power from the engine until about a second after you've asked for it, which on a busy roundabout is an age.

That would drive me a bit potty. But not as potty as the styling. I simply couldn't live with it. And I'm not even sure what this car is supposed to be: a high-riding hot hatch? A low-riding SUV? A crossover with attitude?

In all honesty, I wouldn't bother working it out. I'd simply save my money and buy the standard A-class instead.

8 March 2015

Persuasion's perfect, Miss Austen. Don't go trying Perversion

Ford Mondeo EcoBoost 1.5 Titanium

Given the choice of buying a BMW or a Ford, almost everyone would choose a BMW, which makes everything I'm going to say in this article wearisomely irrelevant. I could tell you that if you buy the Ford you get free myrrh for life and an evening out with the dealer's extremely accommodating young wife, and you'd still say, 'Nah. I'll take the Bee Em, thanks.'

Working for Ford must be a bit like being Jeffrey Archer. You slave for years and years on a project, and you're proud of it, and it's very good, but when it emerges into the marketplace, everyone says, 'Yes. But you're Jeffrey Archer.'

Or working in public relations for Blackpool Pleasure Beach. 'Yes, very nice. But it's not Disney World, is it?'

When I first started writing about cars, Ford had developed a cunning solution to the problem of badge snobbery. It worked out that for £20,000 BMW would sell you four wheels and a seat. Everything else was a very expensive option. 'Oh, you'd like a windscreen? Well, that'll be £17 million, sir.'

So a £20,000 Ford came with absolutely everything as standard. I remember once driving a Ford Granada estate and it was kitted out with electric seats, an electric sunroof, air-conditioning and a million other things that would have made a BMW cost more than a house on Venice Beach.

This trinketry was a bit like filling an average book with a sex scene every few pages. You get a couple of pudendas here and some buttocks like ostrich eggs there, and pretty soon people begin to forget that the plot's a bit shaky and the characters aren't fully formed. Except, you know, down there.

Unfortunately, this doesn't work any more, because today BMW is filling its cars with sex scenes as well. They are no longer boxes with wind-down windows. They come with climate control and satnavs and electric windows as standard.

Which means Ford has had to go mad, and explains why the Ford Mondeo EcoBoost Titanium I've been testing for the past week came with more standard equipment than you would find on the bridge of a Nimitz-class aircraft carrier. The steering wheel was festooned with buttons, and woe betide anyone who delved into the submenus on the central command and control system. Let me put it this way. It comes with voice-activated texting. As standard.

So let me say this loud and clear. This is a big car, a five-seater with a truly gigantic boot. It is fitted with every conceivable luxury. And it costs £22,245. I cannot think of any car yet made that offers better value for money than that.

Frankly, it wouldn't matter if it had the engine from a cement mixer and suspension made from scaffolding: £22,245 for a car this size and this well equipped is crazily low. It is the McMeal of motoring.

Let's look first of all at the drawbacks. Perhaps because it was developed mainly in America, it is wilfully unsporty. Ford of Europe is responsible for some of the sportiest cars built: the Escort Mexico, the Escort RS Cosworth, the Sierra RS Cosworth, the Fiesta XR2, the Lotus Cortina, the Escort RS2000 . . . the list goes on and on.

Ford in America is different. It did the Mustang, which came with leaf-spring suspension and a live rear axle such as you would find on an ox cart, and that's it. It has the same sporting heritage as I do.

Ford of Europe spent three years trying to fix the American car. It had to make the suspension function and fit an interior trim that didn't look like it had been made from melted-down cassette boxes. But you can take the boy out of Texas, send him to Eton and dress him up in tweed and you'll still be able to tell that he's not from round here.

So it goes with the Mondeo. It's not slow, by any means. Its 1.5-litre engine will zoom you to 62mph in less than ten seconds and propel you on a wave of pleasant noises to a top speed in the region of 140mph. It's got nicely weighted steering too, and my test car had a sweet, six-speed manual gearbox that felt very old-school. But the suspension is set up, to the exclusion of everything else, for comfort.

It's not what I was expecting but it could be quite a clever idea. There are many cars that offer a sporty, taut and connected-to-the-road feel, but very few that offer a comfy place to sit down after a long day at work. If that's what you want, then you'll be wanting the Mondeo.

Just don't drive it at night. Recent research suggests that the average driver uses full beam for only 2 per cent of the time behind the wheel, but this is no excuse for fitting glowworms instead of actual lightbulbs. Because when it's dark and you're on a country lane you really can't see where you're going. I bloody nearly piled into a car that was parked at the side of the road.

Also, don't bother trying to use some of the more exotic toys. Because they don't really work. You push the voice-activation button and say in your best RP, 'Radio 4'. And the one thing you can guarantee is that what happens next will not be the selection of Radio 4.

This makes me worry a little bit about the inflatable seat-belts that are fitted in the back. The idea is that, if you crash, the belt turns into a bouncy castle and spreads the impact over a much wider area of your children's fragile bodies. In theory, it sounds a very good idea. But will it work like the voice activation? Or the full-beam headlights? My children elected not to find out.

It sounds here as if I'm having a downer on this car, and I'm really not. As the week crawled by in a tangle of dreary journeys from London to Guildford and a Saturday-afternoon trudge up the M1, I really did start to appreciate the Mondeo's extraordinary comfort. And there's no getting away from the fact that it is extremely large and extremely good value for money.

So, really, who cares if the voice activation is a bit wonky? Jane Austen's sex scenes aren't much cop either, but every-one seems to like her books.

And I liked the Mondeo. Maybe the diesel version would be better – its economy would be – but the model that intrigues me most comes with a 3-cylinder 1-litre petrol engine. I shall try it as soon as possible and report back.

In the meantime, you go and buy yourself a BMW. It'll hurt your back and won't come with inflatable rear seatbelts so it might end up hurting your children as well. But, hey, the most important thing is impressing the neighbours and, on that score, the Ford won't do at all.

15 March 2015

We can't go on like this. You're beautiful but a control freak

Mercedes S 63 AMG Coupé

We have been told many times in recent months that driver-less cars are now being developed, and we're all dimly aware, if we are paying attention, that there are many issues to be addressed before they are allowed on to the roads. Quite apart from the technical hurdles, which are legion, there are ethical conundrums too. For example, what will a driverless car do when, in an emergency, it is presented with a choice of whom to kill? You, its owner? Or the bus queue into which it must plough if it is to save your life?

And then there's the biggest question of them all: what's the point? You send your driverless car into town, it finds a parking space, slots in neatly without scraping itself against anything and . . . and . . . and then what? It can't go into a shop and pick up some milk, can it?

For a driverless car to be useful, it must, first and foremost, be a car. And if it's going to be a car, which is a personal trans-portation device, you may as well do the driving. Because driving is not taxing or difficult. You just have to sit there and miss stuff.

I had a taste of driverless-car motoring last week when I spent the week with a Mercedes S 63 AMG coupé. This car had the lot. It could steer down a road with no input from me. It could sense an impending accident and lock its brakes to activate the seatbelt pre-tensioners; it could also identify pedestrians on the pavement and anticipate what they would do next, and then take avoiding action to miss them. My job was simply to get out at the other end, looking as relaxed as that smug chap from the old Rothmans adverts.

But I never did because, actually, the cleverest electronics are not as clever as even the stupidest human.

Let us take the humble parking sensor as an example. In any city-centre parking manoeuvre, they start wailing and barking when they are 3 feet away from an obstacle. This is no use at all. You're always 3 feet from something when you're parking. You need a reminder when the gap's down to 3 millimetres.

This is the problem that blights the Mercedes. Yes, it's very clever that it can 'read' the speed of the car in front and maintain a constant gap. But how does the driver of the car in front know you want to overtake when you are being stationed by electricity 3 miles off his rear end?

And then there was the last-minute change of direction that I needed to make to avoid one of the nutty paps who remain on my tail. I had seen the car on my near side and I knew for sure I could nip in front, but the Mercedes decided it knew best and took control of the steering and the brakes.

I blame the world's lawyers for all of this. Mercedes knows that it could bring the tolerances down to reasonable levels but, if it did so, and there was a crash, any QC worth his considerable weight could summon a galactic bout of mock-incredulity in a courtroom. 'Do you expect us to believe that this car could steer through a gap with just' – snort – '3 millimetres to spare?'

I'm afraid that after just a couple of days I turned off all of the drive-by-wire stuff and just used the Mercedes as a car.

There has always been a coupé version of the S-class and

it's always been called the CL. But for reasons that are entirely unclear to everyone outside the Mercedes marketing department this is called the S-class coupé. That may be technically correct, but I can assure you it sure as hell neither looks nor feels like a two-door version of the big Berlin taxi.

It looks wondrous. My test car had silly red brake callipers and optional Swarovski crystals in both its daytime running lights and its indicators but, these aside, it was a menacing blend of power bulges, skirts and the sort of brushed-zinc look that you find in those million-pounds-a-yard kitchen shops on Holland Park Avenue in west London.

Inside, there was quilted leather and a sense that you were in the first-class cabin of a Far Eastern airline. It's the sort of car in which you say, 'Mmm,' as you settle down and close the door. The seatbelt is even handed to you by a butler. He never brought any nuts, though. Black mark, that.

Eventually, though, when you've stopped going, 'Mmm,' and turning all the electronic paranoia off, it's time to go for a drive – and it's exactly what you'd imagine. 'Cadderberry luggzury' (as the chocolate ads used to say) with a hint of chilli pepper.

Of course, there are buttons to make the whole car uncomfortable – you even get one that makes it lean the wrong way in corners – but if you leave all this alone, you get a fast, comfy coupé that rumbles when you give it the beans and hums when you don't. It's nice.

Apart from the steering. There's nothing wrong with it, naturally. It doesn't suddenly stop working and the wheel doesn't abruptly become red hot. But just occasionally you do wonder if it's connected up as well as it could be. I have a similar issue with the mildly hesitant throttle.

But here's the main problem I have. For quite a lot less you can have a BMW M6 Gran Coupé, which is even better-looking and comes with two more doors. It doesn't have the driverless toys, but you don't want them anyway. And it won't cruise quite as well but, on the upside, it is much, much more exciting.

If that's not what you want, fair enough, but that's where the Bentley Continental GT enters stage left. This has the Merc's luggzury and the quilted leather and, if you go for the V8, the exhaust bark as well. Plus, it is a Bentley, and that counts for more than a Mercedes badge.

All three cars are good-looking, fast two-seaters with space in the back for very small people on very short journeys. And all will depreciate like a chest of drawers falling out of a tower block.

If you really do like driving – and if you've read this far into a motoring column, I have to suppose you do – then the BMW is the obvious choice. It is magnificent and snarly and balanced and all the things you crave. On a dirt road in Australia last year, with the sun going down after a long, hot, beautiful day, it provided me with what I think was the nicest drive of my life.

As a driver's car, the Bentley is not – quite – in the same league as the BMW, but what you lose in cornering and braking and acceleration, you gain in the 'Ooh, that feels nice' moment when you close the door.

Which leaves us with the Merc. It is stuck between a rock and a soft place. And I'm not sure that's a very sensible place to be.

29 March 2015

Cancel the Uber car – I'll catch a Crazy Horse cab

Mercedes-AMG GT S

Have you ever tried to send a text from the back of a London cab? The suspension is so catastrophically hard that it's just about impossible. And even if by some miracle you do manage to write vaguely what you had in mind, you will go over a speed bump as you're sending it, which means it'll go to completely the wrong person.

Life is a lot more smooth in the new four-wheel-steer Mercedes Vito Taxi vans, but these too come with a drawback. The windows don't go down, so after half a mile on a hot day you start to feel like Alec Guinness in that box.

Of course, life is a lot more comfortable – and cheaper – if you use Uber, and yet somehow I just can't bring myself to make the change. I don't know why. I'm not the sort of person who won't have a mobile phone because 'there's nothing wrong with a good old-fashioned red phone box' and I'm not writing this on a typewriter. But there's something about Uber that feels wrong.

Maybe it's the name. Nobody likes a word that begins with U. Or maybe it's the way Uber cars are driven: I follow them sometimes and it's as though the driver has just ingested a litre of pethidine. And then there's the smell. It's an aroma that comes with its own mass and just a hint of gravity. It's revolting.

There's another thing too. I wonder what damage Uber is

doing to the Mercedes-Benz brand. Because nobody is going to get out of an Uber E-class and think, 'Mmmm, yes, I have got to get one of those.' The suspension is invariably worn out, the upholstery always has at least one worrying stain and the dash is always festooned with wires to power the driver's satnav, which, after you've made sixteen left turns on the trot, you notice is programmed to work only in Kampala.

I know Mercs aren't like that in real life. I know they are beautifully made and sensibly equipped and strong. But you don't. To you, the Uber customer, Mercs are vomitous and horrid.

Which brings me neatly on to the problem you have if you are in the market for a six-figure GT car. It's a nice problem, the sort of thing you could sort out in your head while lying on your back on a summer's day in a field full of wild flowers. It's this: there are now many GT cars costing six figures – or thereabouts – and they're all very, very good.

There's the Aston Martin Vantage, the Jaguar F-type, the Porsche 911 Carrera GTS, the Bentley Continental GT V8 S, the BMW M6 and, for rather less, the Nissan GT-R and the Chevrolet Corvette. Don't laugh. The last model was excellent and the new one is even better.

And now, to make the decision even harder, there's the AMG GT S. Which is not billed as a Mercedes because this has nothing to do with the diesel E-class in which you came home last night. Can we be clear on that? Good. So let's move on.

In the beginning was the SLS AMG, a silly-money quasi-supercar that I completely loved. It was fast only in theory because, in practice, it simply spun its rear wheels and went sideways. Really, it should have had wipers on the side windows.

What it had instead were gull-wing doors, and I'll let you into a little secret. No one has ever watched anyone climbing from a car with up-and-over doors and thought, 'Crikey. I bet that bloke is intelligent and blessed with a gigantic penis.' Things that have never been said to someone climbing from under a gull-wing door include, 'Thank you for coming, Your Holiness.'

The SLS AMG, then, was a stupid car for stupid show-offs, which probably explains why I liked it so much. I certainly liked the noise. You may remember it was used as the Formula One safety car and, even when the racers didn't sound like vacuum cleaners, you could still hear it – a thundering baritone to the wailing treble.

Anyway, the new car sits on the same basic chassis as the SLS but costs, for reasons that are not entirely clear, almost £50,000 less. Sure, you don't get gull-wing doors – which is a good thing – and you don't get the old 6.2-litre V8. But that's not the end of the world either, because what you do get is a wondrous 4-litre dry-sump V8 twin turbo.

It's clever too. The turbos sit in the middle of the V, which makes the engine incredibly small. And that means it can be located low down and behind the front axle, for a lower centre of gravity and better weight distribution.

There's more racy stuff, too, because the seven-speed insta-shift flappy-paddle gearbox sits at the back of the car, being fed by a carbon-fibre prop shaft.

The GT S weighs just over 1.5 tons, which is light for a car of this size, and it feels it – it's almost unnerving. Because from behind the wheel it feels as if you are sitting at the back of a supertanker. The bonnet is so vast that, if it arrives on time, you will be twenty minutes late. It's not just long either. It's so wide that someone could land a medium-sized helicopter on it and you wouldn't even notice.

It's odd, then. Because here is a car with many track-oriented features and many buttons that will turn it from a cruiser into a Nürburgring barnstormer. And yet it has a bonnet that's 7 miles longer than necessary.

I think I know why. Behind all the racing paraphernalia and the Mercedes suede and silicone, this is a modern-day muscle car. It's Merc's Mustang. You sense this when you drive it. The GT S feels as though there's very little rubber in the bushes and only the smallest amount of insulation between you and the oily bits. It feels raw. Much more raw than any other Mercedes and any of the other cars that you can buy for this sort of money. It feels – how can I put this? – extremely exciting.

It looks extremely exciting as well. I'm not going to say it's pretty, because it isn't. The windscreen is wilfully upright and the back just sort of tapers away to a sea of nothingness. But, ooh, it has presence. You get one of these in your rear-view mirror and you will get out of the way.

On a day-to-day basis, it's swings and roundabouts. The hatchback at the rear is good and the boot's big. But the width means it won't fit in a standard London parking bay. And you should definitely avoid the optional carbon ceramic brakes, which work like a switch. One minute you're going along and the next you have a broken nose.

Inside? It's close to faultless, really. Maybe the gear lever is too far back and maybe the satnav screen looks a bit of an afterthought, but it has everything you could want and a few things you don't. Why, for instance, would you want to make the exhausts louder?

In a silly car for silly show-offs, that sort of thing would work well. But this isn't a silly car at all. Of all the vehicles in this bit of the market, it'd almost certainly be my choice.

Because, as I said at the start, I don't use Uber. So Mercs are still all right in my book. And this isn't a Mercedes anyway.

26 April 2015

If you don't buy one, at least watch the crashes on the Web

Lamborghini Huracán LP 610-4

In the olden days, when Raymond Baxter was on the television and you had to have two O-levels to be a policeman, a family saloon took about twenty seconds to reach 60 miles per hour, which then turned out to be its top speed. Whereas a supercar such as the Ferrari 308 GTB would get to 60mph in a dizzying 6.7 seconds and then keep on accelerating all the way to an almost unbelievable 155mph.

Today, however, family saloon cars can do 155mph, and so, to keep ahead of the pack, supercars are now so fast that if you keep your foot hard down on the throttle in second, third or fourth gear for more than about three seconds you will lose control and crash into a tree. This is a fact. And if you don't believe me, put 'supercar crash' into Google. You'll get more than 1.3 million hits.

It's not simply the speed and the power that cause these crashes, either. It's the fact that, today, supercars are no harder to operate than a knife and fork. In a seventies Lamborghini you really had to work for a living. The clutch pedal felt as if it was set in concrete, the interior was as hot as the middle of a star, the steering was heavier than dark matter and usually you died of heat exhaustion from reversing out of your garage.

A modern supercar doesn't feel like that at all. Even the Bugatti Veyron is no more dramatic to drive than a Volkswagen

Golf. This lulls people into a false sense of security. They think they can handle the savagery that lives under the bonnet. So with a big grin they shout, 'Watch this!' to their passenger, and stamp on the throttle – which means three seconds later they are going through the Pearly Gates, backwards, in a cloud of fire and screaming.

When I drove the McLaren P1 around the Spa-Francorchamps racetrack in Belgium recently, it was raining and I didn't use full throttle once. But of course you know that, because I'm still here, writing this.

It was much the same story with the Ferrari F12berlinetta that I drove over a Cairngorm in the snow a couple of years ago. I think I may have used full power once, for about a two-hundredth of a second. But I was in seventh gear at the time, doing 24mph. And still a bit of poo came out.

I love that these idiotic cars exist. And I love that we live in a world where all you need to buy one is some money. The government doesn't insist on any special training; it simply says, 'Can you reverse round a corner?' If you demonstrate that you can, then you are allowed to buy a car that can do 250mph. That's fantastic when you think about it.

However, while I will applaud the people who buy these vehicles, I wouldn't – because what's the point of buying a car so scary-fast you don't dare use more than half of what's available?

Much better, if you want a snazzy mid-engined rocketship, is to come down a peg or two and buy something from the Little League. The new Ferrari 488 GTB looks as though it might be quite interesting, and there's always the McLaren [insert whatever name it is using today] – that's a good car as well.

But come on: you aren't really buying a supercar for the

speed, are you? It's because you like the way it looks. Yes it is. Be honest.

And if that's the case, then really the one-stop shop has always been Lamborghini, purveyor through history of motor-cars that are demonstrably worse than the equivalent Ferrari but that look sen-bleeding-sational.

Let us examine the case of the recently departed Gallardo. It was not as nice to drive as the Ferrari 458 Italia. And yet more than 14,000 people bought one. Me included. And Richard Hammond. Why? Because it was – and will remain – one of the best-looking cars ever made.

All of which brings me on to the Gallardo's replacement. The Huracán. Sounds good, yes? As though it's named after the most cataclysmic weather event known to man? Yes, but it isn't. Like almost all Lamborghinis, it's named after a stabbed cow.

And straight away there's a problem. It is striking, for sure, but is it as striking as a Lamborghini should be? This is a descendant of the mad Countach and the bonkers Diablo. What you want from Lambo is a *Game of Thrones* assault on the senses, and, I dunno, the Huracán is a bit *Wolf Hall*. And, whisper this, I don't even think it's particularly good-looking. Look at it from directly behind and it has the exact same silhouette as a loaf of bread. This is not a good thing.

Don't be too disheartened, though, because beneath the Hovis styling you get four-wheel drive, a carbon-fibre and aluminium chassis that is light and easy to fix, a snappy flappy-paddle gearbox (manual isn't available) and, joy of joys, a normally aspirated 5.2-litre V10.

It's fitted with a stop–start system for city driving, but don't be fooled: a motor such as this runs on baby polar bears and causes extreme weather events. And it sounds completely wonderful.

I have heard it said there's too much understeer when you really open the taps, but I didn't notice any of that. I thought it was a joyous car to drive. In Road (Strada) mode, it's extremely comfortable, and if you go for Track (Corsa) or Sport on the Soul button on the steering wheel, it is fast. But not so fast you actually soil yourself. (Although there is a tremendous Huracán crash on the internet, during which both occupants almost certainly had a bit of a trouser accident.)

Apart from the lack of a cup-holder, this is a car you could and would use every day. It's not so big that it's hopeless in town, the dashboard is wonderful to behold, and it's comforting to know that behind the scenes everything is made by Audi. The next R8, in fact, will be a Huracán with Lamborghini crossed out and the word Audi written on, in crayon.

There is, however, one problem that drove me mad. Italy's motor industry finally mastered the art of making a decent driving position a few years ago, yet now Lamborghini has forgotten and mounted the seat far too high.

This means you sort of look down on the interior rather than across it, but worse, because the windscreen is a long way away and there's a lot of roof between you and it, it's as if you're driving round in a preposterous peaked cap. And that means when you are waiting at a set of lights, you can't see when they go green. You only know you have to set off when the chap behind starts beeping.

Oh, and I have to mention the steering-wheel-mounted switches for the indicators and wipers. No, Lamborghini. Just no. I know Ferrari did it first, but as my teachers used to say when I'd been caught copying, 'If Wilkins jumped off a cliff, would you jump off one too?'

Niggles aside, though, this is an interesting car because it's an other-way-round Lamborghini. It doesn't look very exciting, but it's tremendous to drive. Really tremendous, actually. Around something called 'the *Top Gear* test track' it was faster, apparently, than its big brother, the Aventador.

3 May 2015

Hold the high fives, Hank, till someone figures out how to drive it

Chevrolet Corvette Z06

In the past few weeks, as you might imagine, I've spent quite a lot of time on the telephone to various people in California, and I must admit it's been rather enjoyable. Talking to an American about stuff is like talking to a child who's going to the zoo. There's no irony, no self-deprecation and none of the barely fathomable subtlety you get when talking to a Britisher. It's a non-stop rollercoaster of primary-coloured enthusiasm.

We see exactly the same sort of thing in the online blurb Chevrolet has created for its new Corvette Z06. It's billed as a 'world-class supercar' and a 'triumph of design and engineering'. There's even a quote from Tadge Juechter, the chief engineer who worked on the car: 'Its aerodynamic downforce performance is massive and unlike anything we've ever tested in any street car.'

Here in Europe we scoff at this sort of thing. We read it and think, 'Yeah, well, you would say that. You designed it, so you're hardly likely to say it's a bit crap.' Whereas an American would read the quote and think, 'Wow. The new Z06's aerodynamic downforce performance is massive and unlike anything Chevrolet has ever tested in any street car.'

There's more. Chevrolet tells us the Z06 sits 'at the intersection of Le Mans and the autobahn', which to me means it sits in the French village of Bar-sur-Seine, just to the southeast of Troyes. But it wasn't sitting there at all. It was sitting in the pits at the Thruxton racing circuit, in Hampshire, on a very windy and extremely cold May day last week.

There is nothing on God's green earth that is quite as depressing as a second-division British racing circuit: the metal window frames on the mildewy portable buildings, the boarded-up burger vans, the cock-eyed signs saying, 'Marshal camping'. And there in the middle of it all was what appeared to be a child's toy, an egg-yellow Corvette. It cheered the place up in the way a pair of bright curtains can make a squat feel like home.

Before we begin, I should explain that I like the 2015 Corvette a very lot. Only recently, I told you that the Stingray convertible version was good-looking, fast, adroit in the corners and excellent value for money. If it weren't for the scrap-metal-dealer image and the fact the steering wheel is on the left whether you like it or not, the new Corvette is a car I would very much like to own.

Or would I? Because the latest incarnation of the new 'Vette, the Z06, a car that sits at the intersection of Le Mans and the autobahn and has better downforce performance than any other street car ever made by anyone ever.

It certainly has plenty of grunt because the company has added a supercharger to the 6.2-litre V8 engine. And in round numbers this means 650bhp and 650 torques. Which in turn means that in a drag race – and I know this because I tested it – it has the same performance as a Porsche 911 Turbo.

In the olden days this would have been enough. Hank and Bud and Tadge would have looked at the straight-line speed and, after a bout of high-fiving, put the car on sale. But that is not the way in Kentucky these days. So the Corvette has a carbon-fibre bonnet for a lower centre of gravity, along with titanium intake valves and composite floor panels, plus the option of carbon ceramic brakes.

And you get a dial on the centre console that can turn your relatively benign road car into a screaming track monster. Although when I say 'screaming', I mean 'bellowing'. And even that doesn't quite cover it. When the Z06 leaves the line in a full-bore racing start, the noise from its four centrally mounted tailpipes is painful. Ever heard a Harrier hover? Well, it's like that.

Except it's louder. Once, I was taken to watch NASA test a 37-million-plus-horsepower Space Shuttle rocket engine in a place called Stennis, in Mississippi. I told the man I didn't need ear defenders because I'd seen The Who, but it turned out I did. It was a genuinely awesome and awful experience, that sound. And even that wasn't as loud as the 'Vette. It's a sound that has a mass. It has gravity. I shouldn't be at all surprised to hear that it can kill.

Of course, inside the car, you are several yards in front of the noise and, anyway, you've got more important things on your mind, such as: 'I'm going to crash soon.' It's hard in the cockpit to work out what's wrong, there's just so much going on, but having given the matter some thought since I came home and lay in the bath shaking, I think I have found the problem. Chevrolet has fitted titanium this and ceramic that because these words look good in a brochure. And they give an owner good boasting rights at the golf club and the shooting range. But don't be fooled into thinking they make the car easier to drive and easier to manage. Because they don't.

This car is evil. You turn into a corner and there's some quite pronounced understeer. You give it a dab of power to solve the problem but, because there's so much torque, the back end doesn't start to come loose. It lets go completely.

So now you're sideways and in real trouble. Because Hank and Bud and Tadge have heard that a racing car needs quick steering, they've gone mad and given the Z06 a rack that would be deemed twitchy on a PlayStation. And semi-slick tyres. And nowhere near enough lock. So now you've spun.

On the next lap you know not to exceed the levels of grip, but because the steering is so twitchy and because the power is so grunty, it's hard to stay below the point of no return. The only solution is to drive very slowly indeed.

Let me put it this way. If this car is supposed to sit at the intersection of Le Mans and the autobahn, and if all that titanium and carbon-fibre stuff is there for a reason other than marketing, why is it available only with a manual gear-box or the dim-witted automatic that was in my test car? Why would it not have blink-of-an-eye flappy paddles?

That's the giveaway, really. This car was built to look good in a brochure. The numbers and ingredients are tantalizing, but this car is not a serious player in the European theatre of war. It may be able to out-accelerate just about everything, and on a skid pan the size of Texas, where there's nothing to hit if you overstep the mark, it can generate some extraordinary lateral G. But it's not nice to drive.

So if you want a serious car, buy one from the continent that gave the world Shakespeare, Monet and Emerson, Lake & Palmer. Europe does serious well. It does substance. It does brilliant. America does Disney. And what we have with the Z06 is Disney trying to do a hard-hitting documentary about Africa's civil wars.

Naturally, it hasn't really worked.

10 May 2015

Lower suspension, faster cornering but still no Italian starlet

Porsche Cayman GTS

Soon almost no one will want to buy a car. You may think the industry is vibrant and full of many exciting things, but the truth is: cars are enjoying their last hurrah, burning brightly, as suns do just before they fizzle out.

The problem is simple. Apart from a few friendless weirdos, today's young people are simply not interested in cars at all. When I turned seventeen, and this is probably true of you too, I became consumed with the need to get on the road as quickly as possible. I wanted a car, not just for the freedom that such a thing would afford, but for the sheer joy of being able to drive a ton of machinery at 100 miles an hour.

My son is very different. He's nineteen and has not bothered to take his driving test. His argument is a simple one. There's a coach that stops right outside his flat in London and it takes him, in a blizzard of wi-fi, to and from Oxford. For £11.

If he wants to go somewhere else, he can use a train or something called 'a bus'. An Uber cab is never more than a few clicks away, and there's always a Boris bike for short trips on level ground when it's not too cold or hot or wet. He can move about without worrying about breath tests or speeding fines or parking tickets or no-claims bonuses. My son therefore thinks he's free simply because he doesn't have a car.

And there's no point going on about the open road and the wind in your hair and the snarl of a straight six because he just doesn't see cars this way. With good reason. When he was little he spent two hours a day on the school run strapped into a primary-coloured child's seat, in the back of a Volvo, in an endless jam. There's no way this was going to engender any motoring-related dreams. He wasn't sitting there in a goo of expectation, thinking, 'Hmm, when I'm big I will do this as well.'

There's more. When I was a boy, we had *Grandstand* and *World of Sport* on the television, bringing us all the action from the country's racetracks. We had rallycross, and we had Minis going wheel to wheel with Ford Cortinas and enormous American muscle cars. And Formula One had no stewards in Pringle jumpers making sure that on the circuit there were no overtaking moves at all.

But look at what we have today. F1 is so boring that the television companies have to show replays of a pit stop. They do. In Barcelona last week they showed us a car having its wheels changed and then they showed it to us again, as though we might be interested. My son certainly wasn't. So we turned it off and went to watch some football.

In the olden days there was even a car show on the television. There were Lamborghinis whizzing hither and thither and McLarens at full chat in Italian motorway tunnels. But that's gone, too, now, and when it comes back you can be fairly sure it'll be full of handy eco-Milibandy hints on how to get more miles to the gallon from your hybrid.

Then we have car advertising. Where are the burning cornfields and the shots of pretty women hanging their fur coats on parking meters? Gone. And in their stead we have £9.99 win free save international zoom-zoom nonsense full of palindromic numberplates with a bouncy Europop beat. They're selling cars as though they're fridges.

And if you sell something as a practical proposition, it had better actually be practical. Which, as we've established, a car isn't. Nor is a fridge, for that matter, since you have a supermarket on every street corner now that can keep everything chilled until you need it. Free up the space in your kitchen. Get rid. And free up the space in your garage while you're at it. Because you don't need a car. Not really. Not these days.

My generation, we see the car as an Alfa Romeo drophead on the Amalfi coast with a French playboy at the wheel and Claudia Cardinale in a headscarf in the passenger seat. Today's generation sees the car as a Toyota Prius, in a jam, on a wet Tuesday, with a Syrian accountant at the wheel and a broken TomTom on the passenger seat.

The tragedy is that car-makers don't seem to have noticed that this is going on. That there's nothing – absolutely nothing – out there selling the idea of a car as a dream.

Jaguar, for example, makes a sporty car and then two weeks later brings out a new version that is sportier still. But it is chasing an audience that is getting older and dying. Most people just want a bit of peace and quiet and 40 miles to the gallon. And the new generation doesn't want a car at all. And certainly not a car that can do 180mph.

There's a similar problem at Porsche. I tested the Cayman S not long ago and thought it was pretty much spot on, an almost perfect sports car for the fiftysomething chap whose automotive love affair began long before the thought police arrived with their Gatsos and their parking-by-phone nonsense.

So what does Porsche do? Well, it brings out a new model called the GTS, which is lower and gruntier and more sporty.

Hmm. Does Porsche think the world is full of people saying, 'Wow. There's a new Cayman out that is 10 millimetres closer to the ground for better cornering'? Because it isn't.

Still, that's its problem. Not mine. Mine is reviewing a car that's a bit odd because it is not, as you might expect, a follow-up to the 2011 Cayman R. That came with no equipment at all and was designed for track-day enthusiasts. The GTS comes with all the usual appurtenances of gracious living. But is actually more powerful and faster than the R was. Odd.

And it gets odder because, if you buy a normal Cayman S and fit all the stuff that the GTS has as standard, the two cars cost as near as dammit the same.

I'd stick with the S because, while the GTS is a lovely thing to drive on the sort of deserted road that doesn't exist any more, really, apart from in Wales (where I was, luckily), you'd need a stopwatch to tell it apart from the S. Both are beautiful to hustle through bends, both go well and both ride nicely apart from on bumpy city-centre streets, where they are both a bit crashy. The GTS especially so.

I had only two criticisms of the S. I didn't like its flappy paddle box and its seats were deeply uncomfortable. Well, the GTS I tried had a manual, which was sharper, even if it did feel very old-fashioned to be doing so much work, and seats that felt better.

But were they? I only ask because after a week with the car I had to visit a massage person. I'm not saying the two things are connected. But it seems likely.

So I don't see the point of this car. If Porsche wants to give us a lower ride height and slightly higher cornering speeds, it's got to start reselling the dream of the car. It's got to forget G-forces and think about the G-spot.

We need more glamour. We need more Italian starlets in headscarves. We need a new James Dean, because he sold more cars by dying in one than a million engineers will shift in a lifetime.

17 May 2015

Be gone, crazy creature. The ecstasy I feel is not enough

Alfa Romeo 4C Coupé

A number of years ago a writer on the hysterically earnest motoring magazine *Autocar* wrote in a review of some supercar or other that it caused 'absolute mayhem' when he parked it in a supermarket car park.

Hmm. I'm not sure his definition of 'absolute mayhem' is quite the same as mine. Because in my quite extensive experience no supercar causes people to run screaming for their lives, or to throw a milk bottle full of petrol at a policeman. And no. Not even the lowest, yellowest, loudest Lamborghini makes people rush into a petrol station kiosk and start helping themselves to the sweets, before killing the cashier and burning it down.

In Italy, a small crowd of admirers may gather, but elsewhere, and especially in Britain, the only reaction you get is from small boys, who clutch excitedly at their tinkles. That's not absolute mayhem in my book.

But it must be said that the Alfa Romeo 4C coupé did cause something of a stir. In London, where most people wouldn't even look twice if Harrison Ford bounced down the middle of the road on a space hopper, women from offices would stop halfway across zebra crossings for a better look. Bus passengers would reach for their cameraphones.

Other motorists would applaud. It was a long way from absolute mayhem but I can tell you this: I've never driven any mainstream road car that generated quite such an outpouring of affection. Not ever. It was like I was whizzing about in a reincarnated blend of Gandhi and Diana, Princess of Wales.

The reason people like it is simple: it's sporty and interesting and different but it's not even slightly threatening. Think of it as a Ferrari puppy. Sadly, however, there are a few issues with the actual car. Where do I start? With the steering wheel, which would be dismissed as 'too plasticky' by the makers of those penny-in-the-slot cars you find outside suburban chemist shops?

How about the problem of getting out after you've parked? Put simply, it's like being calved. Or maybe I should major on the width. This car is so wide it won't even fit in a standard parking bay. And even if you do shoehorn it into a space, you will then only be able to open the doors the merest crack, which makes getting out even more difficult. Realistically, you'll get into this car once, and then that'll be that.

Other things. Well, the boot lid won't stay up by itself. There is almost no rear visibility at all. The switchgear is so flimsy it makes the steering wheel look like a Fabergé egg. There's a draught from the bottom of the doors as you drive along, and it's as luxuriously appointed as a Presbyterian beach hut.

'Aha,' I hear you say, 'but I bet it's an absolute joy to drive.' Nope. It may have a carbon-fibre tub, the sort of thing you find in a Formula One car or a McLaren P1, and it may be so light as a result that it can make do with a tiny turbocharged 1742cc engine, but the steering is inert, and not power assisted, and the brakes lack any feel at all. You have to use muscle memory to decide how quickly you want to stop.

And then there's the noise. Oh my God. Around town it's fun. It snuffles and roars and farts, but last Saturday I had to drive up the M1 to the Midlands and, by the time I reached

Watford, I'd had enough. I think my ears were actually bleeding. Manfully, I reached 70mph, at which point I started to understand how General Noriega must have felt when the Americans bombarded him with volume. I just wanted to get out. But as we know, that's not possible.

I didn't think life could be any more miserable. But then in Northamptonshire I hit the 700-mile roadworks that are monitored by average-speed cameras to make sure everyone does 50mph. There was a sign showing a middle-aged woman in a hard hat and a hi-vis jacket that asked drivers to be careful by saying: 'My mum works on this site.'

Don't be so bloody daft. Of course she doesn't work on the site. No one does, or they'd have finished whatever it is they were supposed to be doing two years ago.

Anyway, the joy of being forced to drive at 50mph – at which speed the sound is roughly akin to the noise generated by the Grateful Dead – was short-lived because a new problem had reared its head: tramlining.

I have driven the 4C before in Italy and was assured that its alarming tendency to follow the camber would be solved in the UK by smaller wheels. Well, it wasn't. Holy cow, it's frightening. You're trundling along, minding your own business, when suddenly the car will turn left. Or right. There's no warning at all, and unless you are an actual Terminator with an ability to know the future, there's nothing you can do to stop it happening.

And to make matters worse, it really was causing absolute mayhem. The occupants of every other car were swarming around it, trying to take pictures, and there was nothing I could do. If I slowed down, they slowed down, causing people behind to jam on their brakes, and I couldn't speed up or I'd get three points on my licence. The mandatory

50mph limit is already one of the most dangerous aspects of driving in Britain because it causes bunching and frayed tempers. But in an Alfa it's borderline lethal.

And so there we are. It's a terrible car, riddled with the sort of faults that every other motoring manufacturer had addressed by about 1972. And yet I completely adored it. Every other vehicle, with its perfect refinement and its perfect electrics and its perfectly adjustable suspension, cannot help but feel like a machine. Whereas the Alfa, with its flaws and its tendency to go where it wants, feels human.

Will it go wrong? Probably. But so will your girlfriend from time to time. And you're not going to swap her for a librarian, are you?

I may not have enjoyed getting out of the Alfa very much but I loved getting into it because it's just so exciting to drive a car that has a mind of its own. I've driven a few vehicles over the years that made me happy but none of them even gets close to this. It's a wonderful little package of deep, deep joy.

The problem is that I cannot realistically advise you to buy one. And worse, I could not even buy one myself. Yes, it's everything a true petrolhead wants in a car, but the noise and the veering about and the veterinary operation that's necessary every time you need to get out would drive me insane.

I wish Alfa would call because I'm not busy at the moment and I really do have a few ideas that would keep the wild-child spirit but sandpaper away just a couple of the really rough edges.

As it is, I'm left with a problem. Because, as a car, it gets two stars; one for having a fabulously clever stereo system and one for being very economical. But as a thing, I'd give it six.

31 May 2015

Usually, they send a Bluebeard. This time I got a blue rinse

VW Passat 2.0 TDI SE Business

Motor industry press officers are no fools. If a journalist asks to borrow a car to test, he is sent an all-singing, all-dancing, four-wheel-drive, top-of-the-range super-turbocharged model that has been fitted with every conceivable extra.

The reasoning is simple. The journalist will be so impressed by the 250mph top speed and the fold-away ski jump in the boot, he won't realize that the suspension is made from milk-bottle tops and that the dashboard consists of recycled video-cassette boxes. And nor will he notice that, while the range starts at a headline-grabbing £15,000, the car he's testing would cost more than a Gulfstream GV.

Volkswagen, however, is different. The Jetta I borrowed recently was in full rental-car spec, with wipe-down seats, wind-down windows and the sort of engine that you would normally find in a motorized pencil sharpener.

Asking me to review a car such as that is like asking a food critic to review a tablespoonful of rice or a political correspondent to report on a meeting where absolutely nothing of any interest happened.

This is not because the Volkswagen PR man is an idiot. Quite the reverse. He is one of the few people in the motor industry whom I actually know and he has a delicious wicked streak about 6 miles wide. He sent the Jetta round in Oxfam trim because he would enjoy watching me struggle to review it.

And now he's done it again. Many car journalists who have reviewed the new Passat have tested the 4 × 4 SCR R-Line version, with central heating, a marble bath the shape of a carp's head and seats upholstered in whale foreskin. Not me, though.

The model he sent round to my house was the 2.0 turbo-diesel saloon. In SE Business spec. And don't muddle that up with business class. 'Business spec' in Volks-speak means it's designed for the rental market and Tommy the taxi driver. It means you get four wheels and a seat.

Now at this point Paul – the VW PR man in question – is sitting at his kitchen table wearing the smug expression of a man who's boxed me in. He's thinking, 'You've been waffling away for a while now, sunshine, but you still have a thousand words to go. Let's see what you've got . . .'

But Paul has made a mistake. Because the car he sent round had been painted in one of the most delightful colours I've seen in many, many, many years. It was very, very, very lovely. Really lovely. I'd like to describe it as a sort of dusky cornflower blue, or maybe the colour of a clear tropical sky just after the sun has done that green flash trick and slipped behind the western horizon. But neither of these things is quite right.

It could be described as the colour of cyanosis, the bluey colour that fingertips become when they've been starved of oxygen, but actually it's closer really to the hue of the powdery flowers that blossom at this time of year on a *Ceanothus thyrsiflorus* bush.

White is now the most commonly chosen colour by motorists in Britain, and I'm not sure why, because while I am not in the least bit practically minded, white really looks good only when it's clean. Which means, of course, that if you do go down the white route, you will have to spend your weekends on the drive with a bucketful of soapy water, a hosepipe and a faux chamois leather that cost just £2.75 and appeared to be a bargain, right up to the moment when you discovered it had the exact same ability to absorb water as steel.

There's another issue too. Anyone who has a clean car is saying to the world that they have a tiny mind. People who wash their cars are telling passers-by that, in the house, visitors are expected to leave their shoes in the front hall and that dogs are not allowed on the furniture. Furthermore, they are saying they don't like or have sex because of the mess it makes.

In continental Europe, where people have a very great deal of sex and there are goats and rabbits on all the furniture, the most popular colour appears to be grey. I was in Paris last week and in every single street, every single car without exception was the colour of a prep-school boy's shorts. It's the same story in Rome.

Part of the problem comes from the car-makers, which, at best, offer a range of ten colours. I don't understand this. Farrow & Ball can offer every colour you've ever thought of, but BMW and Mercedes and Land Rover, and so on, seem to think that cars can be painted only in colours that were used by Charlie Chaplin. 'Red, sir? What, like a dog's penis? Crikey, no.'

Bentley does a nice range, but my favourite – since Škoda dropped the Cotswold-windowsill green it offered a few years ago – is Mazda's candy-apple red. That said, though, VW's *Ceanothus thyrsiflorus* blue is right up there.

The car manufacturer calls it Harvard Blue, but it is wrong because the colour of Harvard University is in fact crimson.

If it isn't to your taste, you are rather stuck, because the only other colours that are available are grey, grey, grey, grey, white, black, brown and placenta red. Inside, there are nine options for the colour of the interior trim. These are: grey, grey, grey, grey, grey, grey, beige, beige and beige.

I realize at this point that I now have only about 250 words left to cover the all-new Volkswagen Passat, but that's fine. I'm not panicking because that's more than enough. A point proved beautifully by the verse from Corinthians about love.

Love is patient, love is kind.
It does not envy, it does not boast, it is not proud.
It is not rude, it is not self-seeking, it is not easily angered, it keeps no record of wrongs.
Love does not delight in evil but rejoices with the truth.
It always protects, always trusts, always hopes, always perseveres.
Love never fails.

That's love covered in just 60 words, so you can see 250 words is easily enough to cover the Volkswagen Passat SE Business saloon with the 148bhp 2-litre turbodiesel engine and six-speed manual gearbox.

So here goes. Ready? Good. Then we shall begin. It's a very handsome car that handles nicely, uses little fuel and is extremely quiet and comfortable. Inside, everything is screwed together beautifully and everything is where you expect it to be. If ever I'm at an airport and the rental company gives me the keys to a car like this, I shall be very pleased.

There are now just thirty words left, which is enough to say that no petrol-powered versions are currently available but that an estate is.

There you go, Paul. I managed it. But next time I try one of your cars, can it please have a bit of angel dust?

7 June 2015

Does this Spanish fly? No, it's a homage to catatonia

Seat Leon

This is one of the most important reviews I have yet written. Because, since I started testing cars thirty-one years ago, I have never once driven a Seat. The company has never offered and I've never asked because I really couldn't see the point.

Unlike Jaguar or Honda or Chevrolet, Seat wasn't created by one man with a vision and a passion for speed, beauty and power. It was created because at the time Spain was emerging from its Third World status and the government didn't want its people squandering their beads and their chickens, or whatever currency they used at the time, on high-value imports such as cars.

So it did what all emerging nations do: set up a factory on home turf that made cheap little run-abouts and then put huge taxes on imported cars. The choice for Spanish consumers was simple: buy a Seat for £2.75 or a Volkswagen for £856 billion.

This may seem sound economic thinking but the fact is that, when you are making a car for people who are trading up from a mule, and there's no competition and the bean-counters are all civil servants, it's not going to be very good.

The government didn't even bother giving it a decent name. It's all very well coming up with a statist acronym for the Spanish Car Company, but did it not think, 'Wait a minute. If we sell this thing in the English-speaking world, Seat is going to look a bit silly'?

At least it didn't go for Spanish High Industry Technology.

When I first started to notice Seat, it was making Fiat Pandas under licence and I didn't bother driving one because why would I care about an Italian car made by a bunch of people who the week before had been shooting one another and stabbing cows?

Eventually, the deal with Fiat fell apart and Seat had a bash at going it alone. Do you remember what it came up with? Nope. Me neither. But it can't have been much of a success because pretty soon its bosses were standing outside Volkswagen's headquarters, hoping for assistance.

Today, Seat makes Volkswagens. They don't look like Volkswagens, but if you examine every piece, by which I mean the engines, the gearboxes and all the switches, you will find they are identical to the engines, gearboxes and switches that you find in a Golf.

So why would you buy the Seat version? Who would choose to have his car made by Spaniards, who are good at fishing off Cornwall, when he could have the exact same thing made by Germans, who, let's be frank, are good at making cars?

The answer is simple. Seat's Golf – the Leon – is cheaper than VW's Golf. But again, there's a problem. Because if you want a cheaper Golf, you can buy a Škoda Octavia. Which is made by Czechs, who are also good at making cars.

The idea is, though, that if you buy a Seat you get a cheaper Golf with a bit of Mediterranean flair and pizzazz. A bit of that Barcelona angel dust. Which raises a couple of questions about the Seat Leon X-Perience SE Technology that was sent round to my house last week.

What Mediterranean flair? What pizzazz? What Barcelona angel dust?

Yes, I agree, it had very snazzy door mirrors, but apart from this it was easily the most nondescript waste of metal, glass and plastic since Microsoft's Kin phone. And it was brown.

Seat tries to jazz this up by saying it's actually Adventure Brown, but there's no such thing. Adventure colours are purple and lime green. You never see a brown Hobie Cat or a brown jet ski or a woman in brown underwear. Unless she's, like, ninety.

This car is supposed to put us in the middle of Barcelona, sitting in a fun little restaurant on a sunny day, watching the crowds go past that Middle Earthy cathedral, but in fact it's as far removed from that as a monster truck is from the gurgle of a newborn baby. I tried as I drove along to imagine who on earth would want to buy such a thing.

But I couldn't. Because I can't think of anyone I've ever met, seen or heard about who would sit down with the calculator and say: 'Right. I want a cheap Volkswagen, but it must be built by Spaniards, not Czechs.'

I assume, though, such a person must exist. So, for the benefit of the nurse who must read this out to him after she's mashed his breakfast, here goes . . .

The car I tried is fitted with a 148 brake horsepower turbo-diesel engine that has been tuned to deliver as many miles to the gallon as possible. A million times a second it takes note of where your foot is on the accelerator, what gear you've chosen, the barometric pressure, the ambient temperature and the engine temperature, before deciding – precisely – how much fuel should be delivered to the cylinders. And the result is: unless you give it a bootful of revs when setting off, you'll stall.

Also, any attempt to use second for a low-speed man-oeuvre means you will judder to a halt and people will point and laugh and you will feel foolish. I haven't stalled so much since I last drove a Golf diesel, which, of course, has exactly the same engine.

Speaking of which. The X-Perience tag tells us that this car is an estate and has the four-wheel-drive system used in the Golf Alltrack and the Škoda Octavia Scout. And not only do you get the benefit of all-wheel drive, but it rides higher than the basic Leon, and some of the more vulnerable panels are shrouded in plastic. It might not be a bad farm car, this. Apart from the stalling. And the fact that an almost identical Škoda is cheaper. Certainly, the boot is huge.

Further forwards, you get a Golf steering wheel, a Golf satnav system, Golf climate control and Golf dials, all for only a fraction more than you pay for exactly the same stuff in a Škoda.

I liked the vast electric glass sunshine roof. But further investigation revealed it to be a £1,060 option. In fact, most of the stuff on my test car was an option. God knows what you get on the £26,905 basic Leon X-Perience SE Technology. Four wheels and a seat, probably.

To drive, however, it feels like a Lamborghini Aventador. I'm lying. I just wanted to think of something different to say because, actually, it feels like a Golf or an Octavia, and I bet you're getting a bit fed up with that observation now. I know I am.

So let's conclude. I'm grateful to Seat for lending me this car because it reinforces every belief I've held about Seat's cars. They're a waste of time.

If they were bright and funky, ran on Rioja and had uphol-stery made from prawn shells, then I could see the point. They would offer an upbeat, flamenco alternative to a humourless Volkswagen.

But they don't. The car I drove was boring. And brown. And you can buy an Octavia Scout, which is the same car, only better-looking, for £1,500 less.

14 June 2015

The Rangie Rolex: it's big, it's daft and your man can't afford one

Range Rover Sport SVR

As my parents dropped me off at boarding school my dad reached into his pocket and presented me with a small box. In it was an Omega Genève Dynamic, and I welled up a bit. Partly because I was very frightened about what boarding school would be like, but mostly because I had never seen such a wondrous thing. A whole watch. Of my very own.

As the years dragged by, I suffered many terrible things. I was thrown on an hourly basis into the icy plunge pool, dragged from my bed in the middle of the night and beaten, made to lick the lavatories clean and all the usual humiliations that public school used back then to turn a small boy into a gibbering, sobbing suicidal wreck.

In the first two years the older boys broke pretty much everything I owned. They glued my records together, snapped my compass, ate my biscuits, defecated in my tuck box and cut my trousers in half with a pair of garden shears, but I made sure when I heard them coming that my watch was safely locked away.

Today, the Genève Dynamic has become something of a classic. James May recently bought one and took it to work, showing it off to everyone. 'Look,' he said, like an excited Eeyore. 'Isn't it beautiful?' An opinion he held right up to the moment I said, 'Oh, yeah. I've got one of those.'

I really have. Sometimes I take it out and wind it up and remind myself that, no matter how awful life might be, it was, from 1973 to 1975, one hell of a lot worse.

I would like to start wearing the Genève again. But there's a problem. Since those days, watches have stopped being an heirloom that was presented by fathers to sons on important days and worn for life. And have become symbols of God knows what.

I fear that if I wore what is obviously a seventies watch, people might think I was being postmodern or ironic or some such nonsense. And I'd hate that, because as a general rule I pretty much despise anyone whose watch face is deliberately interesting. Which in certain circles today is: pretty much everyone. I saw a man the other day wearing a watch that was a) electric blue and b) about the same size as his face. I don't doubt for one minute that it had cost about £60,000 an acre, and, boy, did he want you to know it.

I'd also like to bet that in a special mahogany box in his dressing room there were several other watches, and that raises a question: why? Owning two watches is like owning two irons, or two tumble dryers. It's totally unnecessary.

Why would you buy a watch when the one you are currently using still works? They don't – and I won't take any argument on this – go out of fashion. And there has been no big technological breakthrough that means they are now able to keep time more efficiently than they did in the past.

I like a nice watch. I look with great attention at all the 200-page features about them in *GQ* magazine and I have been known to pause for several moments to look in a jeweller's window. But I wouldn't actually buy one, because what's the point? My current Omega Seamaster is still going strong and I don't doubt for a moment that the only thing that will stop it will be the incinerator into which they put me when I'm dead.

I'm going on a bit here so I'll come to the point. When did Rolexes become naff? There must have been a time when they were elegant and beautiful and worn by people with taste and discretion. But then one day they became the time-piece of choice for people called Steve. And now I think it's fair to say the only thing in the world that's worse than a fake Rolex is a real one.

I don't doubt for a moment that they are well engineered and designed to survive a nuclear holocaust, but you only ever see them sticking out from the cuff of a suit that's a bit too shiny, wrapped round the tattooed wrist of an arm that's a bit too thick.

And that brings me neatly on to the Range Rover. Not that long ago Range Rovers were the very embodiment of quiet good taste. And underneath the raffish, stately exterior they were extremely capable. You could buy a BMW or a Mercedes, but you would end up needing a new wing after you'd crashed in slow motion into a gatepost, having failed to traverse a muddy field. On the correct tyres a Range Rover has always been miles and miles better than anything else. It's been a world-class car. A gem. An all-time classic.

But now something is going wrong because Range Rovers are becoming like Rolexes: a bit naff. I think I know why. They have always been extremely expensive, which meant that everybody who couldn't afford one had to buy some-thing else. But now things have changed because there's a Range Rover Sport and a Range Rover Evoque and the Land Rover Discovery Sport, which looks like a cross between the Range Rover Evoque and the Range Rover Sport.

And that means every Steve in the land is now running around in one, with his ridiculously thick tattooed arm hanging out of the window.

It's as though it has suddenly become possible for the mildly well-off to buy themselves a title. And what it means is: the really well-off who would ordinarily buy the big, proper version of the Range Rover with the split, folding tailgate are thinking, 'Oh, Lord. I can't drive the same car as my plumber. I must get something else.'

But what? There is nothing else. Unlike Rolex, which has competition from about a thousand other brands, there is no alternative to a Range Rover. You can get machines that work as well in the fields and you can get machines that work as well on the road. But you cannot get one car that can do both things quite so well as the King of Solihull.

And now, finally, we arrive at the car I'm supposed to have been reviewing. The new Range Rover Sport SVR. It's ridiculous in every way. It's ridiculously expensive and ridiculously unnecessary. And it has a supercharged 5-litre V8, so it is ridiculously thirsty and ridiculously fast.

I mean, if you want a car that goes from 0 to 62mph in about a millionth of a second and has a top speed of several thousand mph, why buy something with the frontal area of a house and the fuel consumption an of an oil-rig disaster?

Yes, it handles extremely well for something that's bigger than a Scottish island but, if that's what you want, why not buy a Jaguar, which has roughly the same engine, uses less fuel, goes even more speedily and costs less?

It gets worse because the ride in the Sport SVR is woefully abrupt. It's the price you pay for its ability to lap the Nürburgring in two seconds dead.

It is a stupid car and I loved it very much indeed. Because this is a Range Rover you can buy knowing with absolute certainty that the man who comes to service your electric gates won't have one as well.

21 June 2015

Common sense, pah. Look at this tasty Porsche pudding

Porsche 911 Targa 4 GTS

Anyone who buys anything for practical reasons is almost certainly a bore with a cardigan, a no-feet-on-the-furniture rule and so much time on their hands they can spend an entire afternoon reading online reviews of dishwashers.

Who can be bothered to write an online review of a dishwasher? They're all the same. They're white and boxy, and after they've finished making your dishes clean they issue a succession of beeps, telling you they must be emptied instantly, even if you are watching *Game of Thrones* and someone's just got their kit off.

I hate *Which?* magazine. I hate every single thing it does and every single thing it stands for. I hate having to share a planet with people whose job is to test kettles. And I hate, even more, people who read their findings before deciding what sort to buy. It's an effing kettle, for God's sake. Just buy the blue one.

I keep being told there are now better phones on the market than an iPhone, and I'm not interested. Yes, they may have better cameras and battery life and they may sort pictures by where they were taken rather than when (which is idiotic), but an iPhone looks nicer and that's the most important thing. I hate people who don't have iPhones.

I also hate people who buy Kias, because they did not use any emotion at all when making their purchasing decision.

They read road tests, doubtless in *Which?* magazine. They looked at online reliability surveys. And possibly even made comparative resale charts on the kitchen table. People such as this should be sent to prison.

There's nothing wrong with a Kia. They're good cars. But nobody's buying them because they're good. They're buying them because of some finance deal or some extended-warranty package. Which is why, whenever I'm pulling up behind a Kia at a set of red traffic lights, I'm tempted to run into the back of it on purpose. To punish the chap behind the wheel. Who will then have to spend the next two months of his life researching injury lawyers to find what firm would be best at convincing a judge that he really does have whiplash.

All of which brings me on to yet another review of the Porsche 911. There are many models in the current range, and if you ask a 911 enthusiast to talk you through the subtle differences between each, you can be sure that by the end of the conversation one of you will be dead. Because either you will kill him to shut him up, or you will kill yourself.

All you need to know is this. If you have any common sense at all, you will buy the Carrera S, because if you buy anything more exotic than that you are wasting your money. Happily, from Porsche's point of view, most of its customers don't have any common sense and almost all of them think their lives will be enriched if they buy a 911 with no roof, or with four-wheel drive, or with a turbo or with some scaffolding in the back.

The result: Porsche made more money last year from selling almost 190,000 cars than its parent company, Volkswagen, made from selling more than 4.5 million.

Do you really think it costs £401 to paint the instrument dials yellow, or £170 to make the key fob the same colour as the car? Do you think it costs £5,787 to fit ceramic brake discs? Well, it doesn't. And if you tick that box on the order form, you are being milked.

And good for you. Because when you spend a silly amount of money on a silly, trivial thing that will help you not one jot, you are demonstrating that you have a soul and a heart and that you are the sort of person who has no time for *Which?* magazine because you were up till three the previous night enjoying 'just one more bottle'.

All of which brings me back to the car I'm reviewing. It's called the 911 Targa 4 GTS. Which means that it comes with unnecessary four-wheel drive, a massively complicated sun-roof and wheels that can be removed only by someone with a degree in engineering. Not that you'll ever need to remove them, because there's no spare.

The GTS badge means this car is fitted with a collection of options that are available individually on the normal Car-rera Targa 4. And if you had all the time in the world, and a calculator, you could work out whether or not they represent good value. Knowing Porsche, I have a hunch they don't.

To drive? Hmm. Well, because of the massively compli-cated sunroof, this car is quite heavy, a point that becomes obvious shortly after you've put the exhaust in Sport mode, said to your passenger, 'Watch this,' and put your foot down. There is acceleration, for sure, and anyone from the 1970s would describe it as vivid. But today? It feels a bit lacklustre, to be honest.

It's much the same story in the corners. Because the Targa is more softly sprung than other 911s, and because this one has four-wheel drive, it's not quite as exciting as you might imagine. It's a long, long way from spongy, but it's pointing in that direction.

There's more, I'm afraid. When you want to open the sunroof, it's like a scene from *Thunderbirds*. The whole car splits in half, palm trees lie flat, swimming pools fold away and, after a little while, everything goes back together again. Except now the bit of canvas that was above your head is stowed behind what are laughably called the rear seats.

Not since the BMW Z1 with its drop-down doors have I seen such a complex solution to such a simple problem. And to make matters worse, as with all Targas, the noise and the buffeting when you drive along with the roof stowed is, shall we say, noticeable. No, let's not. Let's be honest and say horrid.

And I don't care. I like the idea of the GTS because GTS sounds good. And I like the Targa because it looks fabulous. The back window with that brushed-aluminium hoop is style at its best. Yes, it makes the car heavy, puddingy, slow and noisy, but those are things that trouble only the weak and the foolish.

Put it this way. You can go skiing in Aviemore, which is close by and the locals speak an approximation of English. Or you can go to St Moritz. You can fill yourself up when you're hungry with a cheese sandwich, or you can eat out. You can live in Huddersfield, or you can live in San Francisco. Why not live as well as you can?

And why allow practicalities to stick their awkward noses into the equation? If you do, you won't buy a 911 Targa. It has too many drawbacks. But if you don't, you end up with a car that looks nice.

Let me put it this way: when you buy a painting, do you go for something that fits in a particular space? Or one you like looking at?

28 June 2015

Let me introduce the latest member of the 500 family: Uncle Fester

Fiat 500X 1.4 MultiAir Cross

I think I wouldn't enjoy working in marketing very much because, when you go home after a hard day's thinking, you have absolutely no idea whether your endeavours were successful or not.

You may have dreamed up the most brilliant sponsorship deal or an extremely clever bit of product placement, but did it have any effect at all on sales? There's no way of knowing.

I bet you any money that the man in the polo-necked jumper and thin glasses was given an immediate pay rise and keys to the executive lavatory after he managed to do the deal for the Philips logo to crop up time and again in various James Bond films. It was on the stereo in Timothy Dalton's Aston Martin in *The Living Daylights*, and on the keyring finder he used to kill a villain in Tangiers. But did that have an impact on sales? Not in my house, it didn't.

Or what about Robinsons Barley Water? If it were removed from the umpire's chair on Wimbledon's Centre Court, would there be gallons of the stuff sitting around undrunk in warehouses? And if there were, could the slump have happened anyway, because kids prefer Coca-Cola?

We see a lot of marketing in the world of cars and we have no idea whether it works or not. Take Audi's *Vorsprung durch Technik* campaign. It was hailed as a triumph, but since it stopped being read out at the end of the TV ads, sales of the brand have skyrocketed. It's much the same story at Ford. In the olden days, Ford spent a fortune on Formula One and rallying and, as a result, it dominated the sales charts. And today it does much less motor sport, which means, er . . . it still dominates the sales charts.

Enzo Ferrari used to say that if you win a race on a Sunday afternoon, you make a sale on a Monday morning. And everyone nodded sagely. But if that were true, Ferrari wouldn't have sold a single car for two years, and, let's see now, it has sold loads. Mostly to James May.

All of which brings me to Fiat. Several years ago it made a cheeky little homage to the original 500 and decided – after a great deal of market research, I should imagine – to call it the 500. It sold like hot cakes. In Britain alone, 200,000 estate agents have bought one.

Ford obviously thought this runaway success had something to do with the actual car, so it launched its own version of it – the second-generation Ka. And nobody wanted one. This must have caused Fiat to think that the success of its 500 had something to do with the name it had given it. So when it decided to make a people carrier, it called that the 500 as well.

Then it decided to make a trendy, city-based European version of the rugged, all-American Jeep Renegade. So what would it call this, do you suppose? Well, after many meetings and a lot of espresso, Fiat has decided that it should be called the 500 as well.

There was a time when Fiat gave all the cars it made different names. You had the Panda, the Strada, the Stilo, the Croma, the X1/9, and so on. But it has decided that's very old-school. So now, to keep things simple, everything is called the 500, whether it's a hatchback, a lorry, a sports car or an off-roader. I wonder how long will it be before La Stampa, the Fiat-owned newspaper, is relaunched as La 500.

Anyway, back to the latest 500, which is badged with an X. This is an internationally recognized symbol to tell onlookers the car has four-wheel drive. But in the 500X that isn't necessarily so. All-wheel drive is just an option. So it's not a 500 and it's not a 500X either.

Several trim levels are available. In the 'Off-Road Look' versions of the car there's Cross and Cross Plus. And in the 'City Look' there's Pop (coming later this month), Pop Star and Lounge. I am not making the last one up. I am aware, of course, that 'lounge' these days is supposed to conjure up an image of some chill-out music wafting through calico drapes on a perfect Ibiza morning. But to me it's the horse-brass-festooned front room in a Cheshire semi.

It's probably best we strip away all the marketing nonsense and concentrate on the car. It shares its basic architecture with the Jeep, but the two cars are very dissimilar. The Renegade may have grown up a bit, but it's still the only car that actually shows up on a man's gaydar. The Fiat, on the other hand, is aimed at estate agents who've met a client, got married and had children. So they need something with a bit of space in the back and a proper boot.

Hmm. And why would these thirtysomething bods and boddesses buy a Fiat that is made by Italians out of American components, rather than, say, a nice'n'sensible Nissan or Škoda?

Well, here's something strange. In recent years Fiats seem to have stopped grinding to a halt in a cloud of steam when they are three minutes old. New figures suggest they are pretty reliable. That's one thing. The next is: it doesn't feel even remotely as though it's made out of George Michael's chaps.

In essence, it's a five-door hatchback that looks quite good, in an unthreatening way. It's also good value when you look at the long list of equipment that's provided as standard.

And yet I didn't like it very much. Part of the problem was that I was driving around in a car that was called a 500 but so plainly wasn't. That's a bit like me deciding to call myself Brad Pitt. I could, but you wouldn't be fooled for very long.

Then there's my natural aversion to this sort of car. The Mini Countryman, the Nissan Kumquat, and so on. I can't see why you would need the ground clearance or the extra headroom. And why pay a premium for something you don't need? Why not just buy a normal hatchback? A Volkswagen Golf, say.

The main reason I didn't much care for the Fiat, though, was: it was deeply uninspiring to drive. The ride was poor, the steering was loose, the clutch was sudden and the brakes were so sharp that pulling up gently was nigh on impossible.

Then there was a switch on the centre console that made everything worse. Turn it to the left and the steering got heavier, which seemed fairly pointless. Turn it to the right and the car pulled away from a junction as though it had suddenly become a tortoise with some kind of cannabis addiction.

As I said, I would never recommend any car of this type, unless you have a farm and need the ground clearance and the headroom for your horse. And if you have your heart set on such a thing, I still can't really recommend the Fiat.

If you really want to say at parties you drive a 500, there's a better plan. Buy a Škoda Yeti, then simply remove the badge and screw a Fiat logo to the boot instead.

5 July 2015

Put a forged Monet in the boot and you'd have a real bounder's Jag

Jaguar XE

No one has yet said to me: 'I'm thinking of buying a new Jaguar. What do you reckon?' People ask me about BMWs and Mercedes and Range Rovers all the time, but Jags? No. It's as though they've dropped off the businessman's radar completely.

We keep being told Jaguar is building another factory and taking on another billion or so employees, and that's true. It is. But only so it can build more Range Rovers. Jag sales are – how can I put this kindly? – a bit Betamax.

The problem is simple, really. Why would you buy a big XJ when for the same sort of money you could have a BMW 7-series or an S-class Mercedes or one of those Audis that take Cara Delevingne to film premieres? Answer? Anyone? Anyone?

In the days of Terry-Thomas and of John Steed in *The Avengers*, Jags were rather caddish and wonderful. They were driven by charmers and chancers who always had a dodgy Monet in the boot and a 'spot of bother' with the mortgage company, so 'Would it be OK if I crashed at your place for a few nights, old boy?'

I know Jaguar worried about the Arthur Daley connection, but that was foolish, because people liked Arthur Daley. Even today, people like a loveable rogue – someone who can charm his way into a woman's knickers even though he always leaves his wallet at home 'by mistake'. It's why we're always happy to have a drive tarmacked by someone who we know has nicked the ingredients from the council. It's why we buy rugs if we think they've fallen off the back of a lorry.

Jaguar should have worked hard to develop this market. The cars themselves should have been sold from behind the railway arches and fitted as standard with a cubbyhole for shooters in the boot. But instead it went with vodka-bar lighting and rorty oversteer handling, and the moment was lost. It's a pity.

As soon as you step into the new XE, you feel the disappointment. There in the middle of the steering wheel is the Jaguar badge, which suggests you should be waist-deep in Wilton carpet, looking at your own raffish reflection in the highly polished walnut dashboard. But no. It's just a car in there. So, as with all vehicles in this price bracket, it feels as if you're sitting in a man's washbag.

There's more, I'm afraid. There's less space in the back than in the BMW 3-series and C-class Mercedes, and you get a smaller boot. And while clever new petrol engines are on the way, they haven't arrived yet. So the 2-litre turbo in my test car is an old Ford unit that first saw the light of day in the Mondeo. There's nothing wrong with it. It's refined and economical, but you'd always know as you bimbled about that the heart of the machine was from the wrong side of the tracks.

It's all a bit lacklustre, really, until you get to the eight-speed automatic gearbox, which isn't lacklustre at all. It's dreadful. You might imagine that, no matter what the situation, an eight-speed box would always have the right ratio to ensure you had the punch to get-up-and-go. I'm afraid not.

Quite the reverse, in fact. It has been programmed to make sure that the engine is using as little fuel as possible at all times. This is to keep the EU emissions Nazis happy. So when you put your foot down to exploit a gap at a round-about, the gearbox immediately forms a committee to decide how best to balance your request for power with its mission priority, which is: save the polar bear.

As a result, not much happens. So you ask for more power, which causes the committee to have a bit of a panicky wob-ble. Now it's like the Terminator in that scene in the new film when it has been told to kill John Connor and save him. It hasn't a clue what to do, so it just gives you random gears in no particular order until finally you mash the pedal to the metal, at which point it has a temper tantrum and throws a saucepan at your head.

Happily, there is a solution. You keep the gear selector in the Sport position, which tells the on-board computer that you literally couldn't give a pig's arse about the polar bear. You just want to be able to pull on to a roundabout without being T-boned by an oncoming lorry.

Maybe these issues will be addressed when the latest pet-rol engines come on stream next year. But that doesn't really help if you're looking for a new car now.

This might, though. I was on the M40 – a road I know so well that I've given all the cat's eyes names – when I suddenly realized that the XE is extremely comfortable. Oh, there are buttons that ruin that by making it bumpier, but in Normal mode it is fabulous.

And it's not just the ride either. It has a refinement that is far beyond anything you could reasonably expect in this area of the market. In short, it feels noticeably more expensive than its German rivals. Even when you're going round Hammersmith roundabout, in west London, which is basically a ploughed field these days, it feels as though you're on a magic carpet.

Maybe this is down to the integral-link rear suspension, which is heavier than the set-up everyone else uses but is better at its job. Or maybe the all-new platform, which one day will be used to make the Range Rover Evoque, is just inherently excellent. Or maybe it's a combination of things. But the XE feels like a £100,000 car. It drives well too.

And then it gets better because it is also extremely good-looking. It doesn't stand up and shout, 'Look at me,' but when you do, you will be mesmerized by its beauty. It's a minx with windscreen wipers.

I have no doubt at all that if you leave this car's gearbox in Sport mode, switching back to 'D' only when you're on a motorway, it's a better buy than anything BMW, Audi or Mercedes will sell you for the same money. It's definitely the one I'd choose.

There is just one thing, though, before I close. In the fullness of time, Jaguar will launch a fast XE. It'll have a V8, and everyone will rush around clutching their tinkles, saying that it's as good as a BMW M3. But no one will actually buy it, because if you want an M3, you'll buy one, not something that's just pretending.

So how's this for a plan? Jaguar should launch a Terry-Thomas special edition with lots of wood and tweed and possibly a decanter in the centre armrest. Sell it with a mildly forged Monet in the boot and the number of a good lawyer programmed into the phone.

Because anyone who's old enough to be able to afford a Jaguar will want that from his car, not an ability to leave 300 yards of black stripes down the road every time he sets off.

12 July 2015

Sven and Thor's safety car now comes with insomnia control

Volvo XC90

At the turn of the century Volvo's engineers hit on an amazing idea. Sitting in the sauna one day, as naked as the day he was born, Thor turned to Sven and said: 'Sven. After you have whipped me with some twigs and I have leapt for no reason into a freezing-cold lake, why don't we design a big family car that might actually suit a big family?'

Land Rover had tried this with the seven-seat Discovery. But of course Land Rover was run back then by people who were only interested in how a car performed on a very muddy slope in Wales. They didn't understand children. Many, I suspect, weren't even quite sure where they came from.

As a result, the Discovery had seats in the boot that could be accessed only by someone with a degree in engineering. Certainly, they could not be folded down unless you were some kind of Indian god with six arms. And to make matters worse, there was no space in the boot for even the thinnest dog.

Sven and Thor had had a better idea. Their car would not be particularly good on a muddy slope in Wales. And it would not be able to spin its wheels when leaving the traffic lights. Nürburgring lap times? They weren't interested at all.

However, it would have the cool, raised splendour of a big 4 × 4 and it would have buttons that could be operated by someone wearing gloves. The seats could be moved about and folded away easily, even by a harassed mum who had six bags of shopping and a child who'd run off to jump in puddles.

They called their new car the XC90 and, in 2002, showed it off to the public at an American motor show. Nobody paid it much attention. Why would they, when the rest of the hall was full of cars that could growl and generate so much G in the bends that your face would come off? At a motor show, nobody is interested in harassed mums or seats that can be folded down with one hand.

Despite the wall of silence that greeted the new car, Sven and Thor went ahead and put it on sale. They obviously weren't expecting much. Because they'd geared up to make only about forty-two in the first year.

But the world went mad for the XC90. It soon became Volvo's bestselling model and, because demand way outstripped supply, second-hand values were off the charts. It won award after award as people began to realize that the Swedes had pretty much reinvented the wheel. A 4×4 for people who don't answer to the name of Ranulph or Sir Stirling.

I first saw an XC90 at the Donington Park racetrack. I can't remember why it, or I, was there, but as the father of three young children I knew straight away that I had to have one. And a few years later I bought a second. And then a third. And then a couple of months ago a fourth.

This may strike you as odd, because why would you buy one of the last of the old models when you knew a new one was due to be launched in a matter of weeks? Simple. Back when the original XC90 was launched, Volvo was owned by Ford. It was a big player with deep pockets. But today Volvo is owned by a Chinese operation called Geely and, from what

I can gather, its pockets are now a bit more like those flaps you get in a pair of Levi's. To put it simply, I figured the new car would have been designed on a bit of a shoestring.

When the second-generation XC90 was brought round to my gaff recently, I thought I'd made the right decision. It's not really much of a looker any more. The deeply sculpted sides are now more slabby and, my God, it's big. Really big.

But the bigness pays dividends on the inside, where you now get a boot and seating for seven adults. Not five adults and a lot of moaning from the teenagers who have been put in the very back.

And there's more, because, ooh, it's a nice place to sit. The dials, the textures, the air-cooled subwoofer and the sheer design of everything is absolutely wonderful.

It's so simple too. There are only eight buttons on the dash – not counting the diamond-cut starter button – because everything is controlled by what isn't an iPad but sure as hell looks like one.

There is a bit of a drawback, though. Have you seen a child's iPad after he's had some sticky buns for tea? Well, that's what the screen in the Volvo looked like after I'd played with it for five minutes. Oh, and the satnav idea where you pinch the screen to zoom? That doesn't work at all. But these are niggles compared with the feature that had driven me mad before I'd even reversed out of my drive . . .

The problem is that, back in 2012, Sven and Thor had another idea. They said that, by 2020, no one should be killed or injured in a new Volvo. That's obviously preposterous, because what if you drove one off Beachy Head? No safety feature is going to save you then.

But, having made the claim, they are now working flat-out to realize it, and as a result the XC90 is festooned with systems that become hysterical if they think you are about to bump into even a rose bush.

Manoeuvring this car in a tight spot is like being at a rave. You have flashing lights, sirens and whistles, and there's no point diving into the iPad thingy to turn everything off because that's smeared with fingerprints and is invisible.

Later, on the motorway, the car did its best to stop me changing lanes – by which I mean it took control of the steering – and it applied the brakes if it thought I was too close to the car in front.

Every fibre of my being was stretched to a teeth-bared grimace by all this, but then I started to think: 'Hang on – just go with the flow. Let it do its thing and you are less likely to have a crash.' And when you start to think that way, the new XC90 starts to make sense.

It becomes quite relaxing. Very relaxing, in fact. Because the 2-litre engine is now far quieter than it was in the old model, and the ride – mostly – is pretty good too. It's so soothing, you could nod off. And you'd be fine because it'd wake you up if anything was going wrong.

In the course of a week I drove this car around my farm, around London when the Tubes were on strike and on various motorways, and after seven days I was pretty much in a coma.

So, yes, I made a mistake by buying the old one. This new car is very good; so good, in fact, that it'd be ideal for those who find the current offerings from Land Rover a bit – how can I put this? – pratty.

26 July 2015

You did have one excuse not to buy a 3-series. Not any more

BMW 3-Series 320d xDrive SE

I have been much amused in recent weeks by various earnest BBC news reporters telling us that people these days decide which car to buy on the basis of how much damage it will cause to the environment.

Of course, this is entirely true inside the BBC, which is why many of the staff go to work on fold-away bicycles. But in the actual world, where women shave their armpits and see Jeremy Corbyn as a humorous throwback, people couldn't give a stuff about emissions or any of that PC nonsense. You could use slave labour to build a car that ran on a mixture of cyanide and potassium and, if it had free mud flaps and a five-year warranty, you'd sell it by the shipload.

Value for money matters. Fuel economy matters, too, along with comfort, zest and reliability. What comes out of the poo chute is irrelevant. And so, too, weirdly, is styling.

It's odd. Nobody would choose to have ugly children and nobody would deliberately fill their house with furniture that they found displeasing to the eye. And yet, every year, thousands and thousands of people buy a car that has the aesthetic appeal of a gaping wound.

I don't think there's been a time in automotive history when the market has been so awash with ugly cars. Skinny-wheeled, ungainly monstrosities crammed with unnecessary styling features and roof lines that seem to have been designed so people in the back can wear stovepipe hats.

I look at the Citroën Cactus and wonder: 'What's that all about? Why's it got bubble wrap down the side?' But, plainly, lots of people think differently because the damn things are everywhere. It's the same with that new Lexus NX. Why did they allow a four-year-old with a space-laser fixation to do the styling?

Then you have the Mini Countryman and, oh, I nearly forgot, the new Jeep Cherokee. That's astonishing. Because what they've done is taken the old Pontiac Aztec and blended it with a wide-mouthed frog.

However, there are a few manufacturers that are swimming against the ugly tide. Kia is one. And BMW is another. Of course, the German giant can sell you an X3 that is terrible, but its saloons and coupés are magnificent, their lines spoilt only by the curse of familiarity. The 5-series in particular is a masterpiece.

And the 3-series that I was using last week is not far behind. You look at it and you think: 'Why on earth would someone choose to buy an Audi or a Mercedes or a Lexus instead?'

One of the reasons, of course, is that, in winter, BMWs are famously hopeless. In fact, the main reason the country grinds to a halt every time there's a light dusting of snow or a mild frost is that every road in the land is blocked by a BMW, its big fat rear wheels spinning uselessly and its panicking driver filling in insurance forms, knowing that, although the accident hasn't happened yet, it will.

Well, with the BMW I've been driving, those days are gone, because it has four-wheel drive. Such a car has been available on the Continent for almost a decade, but until recently BMW's designers never really saw the point of engineering all-wheel drive into right-hand-drive models. They probably thought that in Britain, where the weather is rarely very bad, we could cope. Yeah, right.

We are told this winter will be very bad and, doubtless, if it is, the BBC will blame Volkswagen. But in your sparkly new 320d with xDrive you'll be fine.

There are, however, some downsides on the days when it's not snowing. First of all, there's a premium to pay. That's reasonable. There are a lot of extra cogs and stuff. But the premium is £1,500, and that's what economists call 'a lot'.

There's more. The space between the centre console and the wheel arch is quite tight, which means that every time you want to go faster you hit the brake and come to a halt.

More importantly, the fuel consumption is hit hard. The four-wheel-drive car does 5.3 fewer miles to the gallon than its rear-drive sister. And it's slower. I suppose, in case someone from the BBC is reading this – highly unlikely, I know – I should also mention that it produces ten more carbon dioxides.

So, there's a heavy price to pay for the ability to get out of your drive on that chilly February morning when you wake to find Jack Frost has been round in the night. And in all probability, you won't be going anywhere anyway, because your neighbour will have slithered into a lamppost in his two-wheel-drive 3-series and blocked the road.

Really, then, it's up to you whether you choose xDrive or not. Only you know whether you need it enough to make the penalties worthwhile.

Either way, you do get a lovely car. Wheel-arch intrusion aside, the driving position is sublime and the thickness and texture of the steering wheel are perfect.

In the early days, BMW's iDrive command and control system was a jumble of unintelligible submenus and nonsense, but today it's the standard-bearer of common sense and logic, twin features that you find throughout the car. Rear-seat space, the size of the boot, the way everything operates and the ride: it's all how it would be if you'd designed it yourself.

Naturally, I do have a couple of niggles. The steering – electric these days, rather than hydraulic – is a bit 50p-piecey, if you know what I mean. It doesn't have the fluidity that used to be a hallmark of BMW when it billed itself as the maker of the ultimate driving machine. And the parking sensors are stupidly pessimistic. 'You're going to crash! You're going to crash!!!!' they wail hysterically when you are still yards from the car behind.

Oh, and then there's the diesel engine. Two years ago eco-loonies were telling everyone diesel was the fuel to use. But then they woke up one day and decided that, no, diesel was not the fuel to use. Because it will cause global warming that will cool the planet. Or something.

It's hard to be sure with these nutters who say they can predict what the weather will be in 1,000 years, even though the Met Office's giant computers can't even work out what it will be doing tomorrow afternoon. So I shall ignore them and tell you that BMW's diesel engine is fine. It sounds rather good, it has immense torque and it settles down to a muted hum on the motorway.

Plus, you'll be doing many more miles to the gallon than you would be with a petrol-powered alternative. Which, as we established at the beginning, matters a great deal more than how many nitrogens are being left in your wake.

4 October 2015

And on this bombshell, I can officially declare: we're back

McLaren P1

On Wednesday morning I climbed behind the wheel of a McLaren P1, fired up its massive engine, eased it into Drive and set off in a blizzard of noise and wheelspin to start filming Amazon Prime's new motoring show.

On one side of me was James May in a Ferrari. On the other was Richard Hammond in a Porsche 918 Spyder. And in front, hanging from the back of a Land Rover Discovery, was the big, bushy beard of Ben the cameraman. The band was back together and I was very excited. But, ooh, getting it to this point had not been easy.

When the BBC bigwig Alan Yentob called back in April to say my contract would not be renewed as a result of the 'fracas', I really didn't know what I was going to do. A large part of me considered the appealing option of 'nothing at all'. A smaller part thought I should change tack and do a programme on farming.

I had no idea what James and Richard were planning. When we spoke, they made supportive noises but, unlike the US marines, the three of us have always operated under the rule that we do leave a man behind. Put simply, they had themselves to look after and the BBC was making all sorts of coo-coo noises while dribbling warm honey into their heads.

Of course, you all now know that they decided to leave Auntie and come with me to look for a new home. To find one, we decided to get an American agent, which meant doing conference calls with people who dressed up like the Borg and communicated by barking. 'Woof, woof,' they all went, into their face-mounted microphones. James May in particular looked very distressed.

Eventually, though, we found a chap who said that the three of us and our executive producer, Andy Wilman, suddenly becoming available was a huge opportunity for any broadcaster. Or at least that's what we thought he said – it came across as a series of dog sounds.

He was true to his word, however, and soon the offers started pouring in. All of a sudden we were up to our scrotums in the dizzying world of modern narrowcasting, in which you can upload a programme when it's ready, not necessarily at 7 p.m. on a Tuesday.

And you can say what you want, because out there, in the free world, there's no Ofsted. There's no finger-wagging. Kevin Spacey spat on Jesus and no one batted an eyelid. Because the internet, let's face it, is also showing a gentleman and a lady making sweet love in extreme detail.

The problem was that standing between us and all this freedom was an impenetrable layer of legal gobbledy-gook. James May gave up and disappeared. And I wanted to do the same because, while I could tell that the words being used in meetings were English, they made no sense at all.

And then, riding over the horizon on a white charger, in a brown cardboard envelope, came Amazon. It took us to its London headquarters and showed us the tech it had lined up for the very near future, made us an offer in English – well, it was in American, actually, but that's close enough – and that was that. We had a new home.

All we needed to do, then, was come up with the new show. All of the previous ingredients – the Stig, the Star in a Reasonably Priced Car and the Cool Wall – belonged to the BBC, so we'd have to start from scratch.

It forced us to get creative. To do what we'd never dared to do in the past: to change what we knew worked. We have, though. It's going to be all new. New name. New segments. New ideas. Everything is different. Apart from James May, obviously, who is still in 1953. And Richard Hammond, who still doesn't quite understand anything. And me, who thinks everything can be solved with a hammer.

Oh, and we will still be testing cars. And once we'd decided to keep on doing that rather than switching to icebreakers or handbags, it was pretty obvious where we'd begin.

Which is why, last week, I arrived in a part of Portugal that smells faintly of sewage and is full of people I meet at drinks parties in Oxfordshire and friends of Prince Andrew enjoying the last of the summer sunshine.

Why Portugal? Well, because it's home to the extremely brilliant International Racetrack of the Algarve. A racetrack Ferrari, Porsche and McLaren, all agreed would be ideal to sort out the question that has vexed the world's motoring enthusiasts for nearly a year: which is best, the Ferrari, the Porsche 918 or the McLaren P1?

We knew before we set off that other people from the internet have now tested these cars to see which is the fastest, and so on. And we wondered whether we should start our new show by gorging on sloppy seconds, but then we thought: 'People will hopefully want to know what we think.' And so we got on the plane and came.

I'm here now, and I've spent the day in the McLaren and I still can't quite believe that the thing's for real. I'll admit the

Ferrari is extremely pretty and that the Porsche grips like an especially clingy and nervous barnacle, but for sheer 'Oh my God', sweaty-pawed, heart-racing, wide-eyed, hair-on-end, ball-shrinking terror, you simply can't beat the P1.

It doesn't accelerate in the conventional sense. The throttle pedal is more a sort of portal to a wormhole. You press it and instantly 903 brake horsepower of electricity and petrol working together puts you somewhere else.

I am still slightly amazed – and thrilled – that we live in a world where a car as fast as this can be made. And that if someone has the money, they can drive it on any road they like. Even if they are only seventeen years old.

It's not the best-looking car in the world, but it has a sinister presence. Like the fold-away stock on an AK-47, it's functional, and its function is to terrify.

But the looks and the speed are nothing compared with the noises it makes. Because it's a hybrid, there's a little bit of everything in there. You have the whirrings of a milk float, the chirps of the wastegates, the bellow of the V8 and the roar of the exhaust, all of which come together to make the sort of sound you would normally associate only with a dramatic and sudden movement of tectonic plates.

Inside, there are many dials and read-outs and there are buttons that make it go even faster. But you have no time for any of this because you are going so bloody fast and your eyes are full of sweat and you're getting to a corner and you're doing a million miles an hour and you have to trust that the invisible elephant sitting on the rear spoiler is still there, pressing the back tyres into the road, and that it hasn't wandered off to eat some bark.

I have no idea at this stage whether it will be faster than the Ferrari or the Porsche around the spaghetti-shaped racetrack here in southern Portugal. That test doesn't happen until after this newspaper has gone to bed.

But whatever the outcome, we are now in the future. It certainly feels that way from where I've been sitting all day.

11 October 2015

Yabba-dabba-doo! T Rex is snarling in evolution's face

Lamborghini Aventador

One day, many years ago, a penguin must have landed in the frozen wastelands of Antarctica and thought: 'Hmm. It's a bit cold but there are no polar bears trying to eat me and the sea is full of fish, so I reckon I'll stick around.'

Now if we are to believe the teachings of the baby Jesus, he'd have lasted about five minutes before freezing to death. Or he'd have jumped into the sea, where he'd have immediately become a tasty frozen snack for a hungry leopard seal.

Luckily, however, there's such a thing as evolution, which arrived in the snowy wilderness and with a heavy but loving, parental sigh took charge of the situation, giving Mr Penguin bigger lungs and a fat tummy and turning his wings into flippers.

We see this kindly benevolence everywhere. When people started to live below sea level in what we now know as the Netherlands, evolution arrived and quietly made sure they grew to be very tall so they'd be OK when the place flooded.

Then there's Australia. It was designed to be a faraway dustbin for all the animals that were really too dangerous to live anywhere else, so evolution had to make sure that when people decided to live there, too, they'd become hardy souls with a belief that anyone who has tear ducts must be a Pom.

I like to think that evolution lives on something a bit like Tracy Island, waiting to drop everything and help out when a tortoise decides it wants to live in the sea, or when people decide they want to keep dogs as pets. Secretly, it thinks: 'Why would you want to do that, you imbeciles? Dogs are dangerous carnivores.' But it rocks up anyway and turns what's basically a wolf into a spaniel with floppy ears and a cute, waggly tail.

We see evolution at work in the world of cars too. When we were all called Terry and June, we were happy to drive around in four-door saloons, but one day we woke up, started naming ourselves after various white wines and decided we would only be happy if our car was 15 feet off the ground and called an SUV.

One day, everyone wanted a hot hatchback. We liked them. We thought they made a great deal of sense. And then we decided for no reason at all that we didn't want to go quickly any more. We wanted to save fuel. We are worse than otters, which, of course, started out as fish, then decided they liked the land and then decided, just after evolution had turned their scales into fur, that actually they wanted to be fish again.

But despite our otterishness, the car industry has kept up, giving us what we want with remarkable speed.

However, occasionally evolution is caught out. Thanks to the teachings of the great American scientist Michael Bay, we now know the dinosaurs were wiped out by a giant meteorite, which means that one day they were walking through the woods thinking: 'These plants are awfully dusty today.' And the next they were sitting there thinking: 'Why am I so dead?'

Evolution didn't even have a chance to put down the crossword and slip into its *Thunderbird* suit before the whole planet was carpeted with decaying carcasses. And we are seeing a similar sort of thing today in the world of supercars.

Back in the mid-1960s, Lamborghini decided to put an

enormous engine in the middle of a car that was about the same height as a piece of paper. It called its creation the Miura and the supercar was born.

There have been many imitations over the years, but they've all adhered to the same basic recipe: dramatic looks, enormous power and, er, that's it.

Now, however, Porsche, Ferrari and McLaren have taken the unusual step of using hybrid technology to get even more power from their road rockets. The combination of electricity and petrol is as potent as it sounds. These new cars are phenomenally fast and have therefore arrived in the supercar arena like three extinction-event meteorites.

Honda is next with a hybrid all-wheel-drive NSX, which I hope will be more successful than its efforts in Formula One. And BMW is said to have an improved i8 in the wings. And that takes us back to where the whole genre began: Lamborghini.

Lamborghini is a division of Volkswagen, which because of this ludicrous emissions saga will not be spraying much cash around in the foreseeable future. Which means Lambo will have no funds to develop a hybrid supercar of its own. Which means it will be stuck with what it's got now for quite a while.

Which in many ways is no bad thing, because what it has got now is the best car it has yet made: the Aventador.

Oh sure, even by dinosaur standards, it's not the best supercar to drive. It feels big and heavy. And if you go for a hot lap of a racetrack, you'd better not even think about doing another, because the brakes will fade and then fail. It's all very well saying that this cannot happen because they are carbon ceramic, but I know it does.

There's more. Inside, an Aventador is very dramatic, with

a starter button that hides under the sort of red flap that you normally find over the Fire Missile button in the cockpit of a fighter jet. But if you actually look at all the stuff carefully, you'll notice it's been lifted straight from an Audi TT.

And who cares? Because – let's be honest, shall we? – nobody has ever bought a supercar because they want to get round the Nürburgring in four seconds. Supercars are capable of going at 200mph, but they're bought mainly for doing 1 per cent of that speed in Knightsbridge. And when it comes to prowling, nothing looks quite as good as the big Lambo. It's a masterpiece.

And why are you bothered about the 'I started wi' nowt' Audi underpinnings? What would you prefer? Italian electrics?

Yes, it's soundly beaten both in a straight line and round a corner by the new breed of hybrid hypercars, but, while they make a range of unusual noises, they can't compete with the raw, visceral bellow of the T Rex that lives under the Aventador's engine cover. Ungodly. That's how it sounds.

And another thing. The new McLaren P1 is very difficult to drive fast. If you make even a tiny mistake, it will kill you. The Lamborghini isn't like that. Thanks to its four-wheel-drive system and the fact that it's more for show than go, it's on your side when the outside world gets blurry.

I love this car. I love its clunky, old-school manners and its honest-to-God, shepherd's-pie approach to the business of getting down low and going quickly.

Will it die in the face of the modern competition? Well, look at it this way. When steam power came along, horses were no longer necessary. But instead of melting them down – which is what I'd have done – we turned them into pets.

And that's what I hope happens with the big old Lambo:

that after the meteorite of hybrid power has struck, people will continue to want it precisely because it suddenly appears to be lumbering and old-fashioned.

Certainly, if I were given the choice of any supercar, this is the one I'd buy. I respect and admire the P1. But which would you rather have as a pet: a clever and sophisticated electronic robot? Or a bloody great brontosaurus?

My case rests.

25 October 2015

Fetch Fiona Bruce: I've found the world's fastest antique

Ford Focus ST Estate

Back in 2010 the Conservatives announced that there would be no more idiotic bus lanes on the M4 and that speed cameras would be switched off. New Labour's thirteen-year war on the motorist, they declared, was over.

Sadly, they were lying. Because today, if you have to get from, let's say, west London to Luton airport, you are monitored by hidden speed cameras on the motorways and average-speed cameras everywhere else. You cannot stray over the limit even once. Compared with Tony Blair's puny war on the motorist, this is nuclear.

Smug speed-camera enthusiasts will argue through their muesli-stained teeth that the new blanket coverage means that no one can ever break the law. But I have a couple of points on that.

No. 1. In a modern car with good brakes and airbags on a good, well-designed road where pedestrians and traffic are kept apart by railings, it is absurd to impose a 40mph limit. Forty is just a number plucked from the sky by a fool who knows nothing. There's no science or sense to it at all.

If you want total safety, make the speed limit 1mph. But if you accept that casualties are inevitable, then balance the need for safety with the need for speed. And on a dual carriageway that means a limit of 70mph. As it always used to be when the country was run by sensible people, not ill-informed morons.

No. 2. And this is more important. Just because we now

have the ability to prevent speeding of any kind everywhere, that does not mean we should use it. Hey, why not implant everyone in the country with a tracking device so the police can keep an eye on their movements until the day they die? Why not take a DNA sample from every newborn baby? We could do that easily, and if fighting crime were our priority we would. But it isn't.

No. 3. Speed cameras do not cut accident numbers. In fact, when they were switched off in Oxfordshire recently – they're back on again now, by the way – the number of casualties showed no noticeable increase. We all know they are a tool for raising money. So why can't the government admit it? Why can't it say: 'They are a tax on people who want to go quickly.' I wouldn't mind that because, if I were late for a flight, I could make the choice: do I pay the speed tax and catch it, or do 40mph and get the next one?

The only thing ministers would have to do to make this work is drop the penalty-point system. Because that's the real problem. The fact is that on one journey from London to Luton it is now possible to amass enough points to mean that you arrive without a driving licence.

Of course, that's not going to happen. So I guarantee that we will reach a stage very soon where it will be impossible to get away with speeding on any road anywhere. And there will be no point hiding from the law in a bothy in Scotland because there will be a tracking device in your head and Plod will send attack choppers to hunt you down.

This is something you should bear in mind when choosing your next car. Because what's the point of having a 500 brake horsepower engine when all you need to reach 40mph is just one actual horse? Certainly that would make more sense than the car I am writing about today.

It's called the Ford Focus ST and it's wilfully set in about 1984. There are extra dials above the dashboard to keep you informed about temperatures and pressures, which is important in a 1940s fighter plane but less so in a modern car; there are illuminated Essex disco motifs in the kick plates, body-hugging seats and – what's this? – yes, it's a manual gearbox that you operate with a stick on the floor.

Oh, and let's not forget the name. ST. Doubtless, Ford will tell you this stands for 'Sports Technologies', but we all know what it really means, don't we, ladies? And now it's available as a diesel. So that's an STD. Excellent. I haven't been able to make jokes along those lines since Citroën's Project VD.

I'm trying at the moment to work out who would want to buy a practical estate car that's named after a feminine hygiene product and comes with Wayne and Kev styling, a Dickensian gearbox and enough power to put you on a speed-awareness course every time you go into third. Nobody is springing to mind at the moment. Is there someone perhaps from Dexys Midnight Runners who has a dog that's only really happy when it's doing 150mph?

I'll be honest: I'm partial to a fast Ford. I go all gooey about a 3-litre Capri, I spent most of the 1990s in an Escort RS Cosworth, my first car was a Cortina 1600E, I adore the GT40 and there's no doubt in my mind that for sheer fun there is no better car on the market today than the Fiesta ST. But I dunno – this Focus ST estate seems a bit weird.

Partly this is because I know it's a fluffer designed to warm us up for the all-wheel-drive 345bhp Focus RS. And partly it's because I was in London most of last week and the manual gearbox made my teeth itch with rage. Using your leg to change gear in 2015 feels as old-fashioned as using the phone on the hall table.

However, I must say that when I got out of London it did what all fast Fords do: it put a big smile on my face. Yes, there is a huge amount of torque steer when you accelerate hard in second or third gear – you don't drive this car so much as hang on for dear life. But the engine is a gem, the ride is nicely judged, the seats are epic and my dogs appreciated all that space in the back. It covers a lot of bases, this car. And it appears to be good value as well.

But while it comes with a lot of toys, many don't work as well as you might hope. There is the option of headlights, for instance, that dip automatically when a car is coming the other way, which is handy. But they also dip when you are approaching a reflective warning sign, which means you are suddenly no longer able to see either the sign or whatever it was warning you about.

Then there's the satnav screen. Mostly, it all works very well, except that in an effort to look snazzy Ford has completely overdone the amount of information that's being conveyed. At any given point you have thirty-three features on the screen, and that's not including the map.

This has always been a Ford thing. Its kit is a bit like supermarket own-brand baked beans. It looks the same as the real thing. But it isn't.

And that's never really bothered me because, all things considered, fast Fords were bloody good fun. They still are. But, because of the jackbooted Tory Stasi with their surveillance cameras, you struggle to enjoy that fun on the road any more.

Which means that, today, this car only really works as a wistful cameo on the *Antiques Roadshow*. Not as something you'd realistically want to buy.

1 November 2015

So smooth, Hank could perform eye surgery in the back

Lincoln Town Car

Because I now have my own production company, I have had to learn how to behave like a businessman when travelling. It's the little things that set them apart: the wheeled suitcase that fits precisely into the overhead locker, the laptop that never runs out of battery. And the maroon polo shirt that's tucked into a pair of bad jeans.

When travelling, a businessman deliberately wears jeans that don't fit properly because it tells everyone that he spends most of his life in meetings or on a golf course, where the denim trouser is frowned upon. It is important, therefore, when wearing jeans to look as uncomfortable and as stupid as possible. Like a fish in a hat.

A businessman never uses any of the business facilities in an airport lounge because hooking up to the airline's services implies that he does not have the right equipment to do this for himself and, worse, that his business is so unimportant he doesn't mind if his conversations are broadcast over an unsecure server.

You see someone in one of those airline lounge business booths and you can be assured he is a business foetus. A new boy. And you are thus at liberty to pull his hair.

On the aeroplane, a businessman never has a drink because this suggests to other people in this cabin that he is an alcoholic. No true businessman drinks. Ever. Neither does he watch any of the films that are on offer because he gets all the stimulation he needs from a spreadsheet. He is in his inflight pyjamas, horizontal and fast asleep six seconds after the seatbelt light is turned off. Eating? That's for wimps. Relaxing? That's what you do when you're dead – something he hopes to become when he is fifty-seven.

When the seatbelt light comes back on, he is immediately bolt upright and dressed in the suit that was somehow concealed in his locker-sized suitcase. He then either whips out his laptop that's been on for six years and still has 42 per cent of its battery life remaining. Or he watches a businessmen-friendly half-hour episode of *Curb Your Enthusiasm*, just to show everyone else in the cabin that he is so well organized he doesn't need to check the spreadsheets one more time.

Four minutes after the wheels chirp into the runway, he's outside the airport, in the back of the Mercedes S-class and on his way to grease the wheels of the world.

I have to admit I'm pretty hopeless at all of this. I watch films on planes, my suitcase is too big and I don't have a suit. But I do have a grasp of the wheels you need at journey's end. And I know that the S-class is wrong. It would be the correct choice in Europe or Asia, but any businessmen on a trip to one of those places is saying that he's second tier.

Really, the only place to do proper business is America and, if you're going there, you don't want to be picked up in a Kraut-Tank. Which is why last weekend, on a quick trip to Seattle, I was picked up in a Lincoln Town Car.

Sadly, this will soon be a problem because Ford stopped making it four years ago, which means that, eventually, the current crop being used to transfer businessmen to their downtown hotels will sigh for one last time, then die. And then what? Because there is simply no other car quite like it on sale today.

First of all, it is enormous. Until 2003, in fact, it was the largest car in the western hemisphere. If you could make a Town Car float – and you can't because it's made from the heaviest metals known to man – you could use it as an air-craft carrier.

Happily, this size means the interior is slightly larger than most branches of Walmart. Fitted with bench seating, it can handle a driver and five businessmen (or three Americans), and the boot is so vast that not even the Beckhams would be able to fill it with luggage. Apparently, it will take four sets of golf clubs, which I understand is impressive. And a golf buggy as well, probably.

But the best thing about a Town Car is not the size, or the loungeability of the rear quarters, it's the comfort.

European and Japanese cars are always made with one eye on the Nürburgring. We can't help ourselves. Deep down, we think that handling is more important than safety, price, fuel consumption, world peace, the global economy or God Himself. But the problem is that, if you build a car that's designed to cling and scrabble on a high Alpine pass, com-fort will inevitably play second fiddle.

In America, it's different. Many think the steering wheel is nothing more than a handy place to rest a laptop. Going round a corner at more than 2mph would cause your bucket of coffee to fall over. So why bother?

Lincoln definitely understood this when it was designing the Town Car back in 1876. Of course, it's changed since then – it now has a cigarette lighter and the leather is ruched – but the recipe is basically the same. You get a body bolted on to a chassis, a live rear axle and a V8 engine that produces 7 horsepower but lasts for 1,000 million years.

Then there's the suspension, which can iron out, completely, even the most savage pothole in New York. You could drive a Town Car through a recently bombed city while doing eye surgery and the patient would be fine. I once parked a 1980s Town Car outside a shop in Detroit and when I returned an hour later it was still rocking. It's probably still rocking now.

Of course, this does have an effect on the way it goes round corners. And we know how it does this because the Lincoln's sister car – the Ford Crown Victoria – is used by many of America's police forces. And we've all seen what happens when they get involved in a chase. Even though they have beefed-up suspension they usually end up in a ditch, with hilarious consequences.

But here's the thing. When you emerge into the world after nine hours in an air-free, overheated tube, which would you rather have transport you through the inevitable jams and into the city centre: a car that can get round Silverstone in ninety seconds? Or something comfy?

There are other things too. Because the interior of a Town Car is made from DVD-box plastic and DFS furniture, and because it has nineteenth-century railroad underpinnings, it cost, when it went out of production, 16p. And because the engine turns over at no more than 2rpm, it only has to be serviced once every million years.

The Town Car was everything a limo should be. Spacious, well equipped, comfortable and cheap for its operator to buy and run. Apart from the lemon-fresh smell from the inevitable air freshener, it was a lovely place to be. A little taste of America before you actually got there, if you see what I mean.

But now it's been replaced by something called the MKT, which looks like a Citroën. No businessman would be seen dead in it. Which is why you won't be reading a review of it from me any time soon.

8 November 2015

Ahoy, Captain Ahab – they've put quad exhausts on Moby-Dick

Volkswagen Golf R Estate

Choosing what car you are going to buy is always ten times more enjoyable than actually buying it. So when I decided I needed a Volkswagen Golf GTI in my life, I spent many hours on the company's configurator, examining colours and options and working out whether the aesthetic appeal of the bigger wheels would compensate for the inevitable loss of comfort.

Eventually, of course, I had to give up the delicious procrastination and place my order. It wasn't easy. One dealer laughed in my face and said I'd have to wait six months. Another said I'd never get the car I wanted at all but he had a very nice Scirocco R that I could have instead. 'I'm sure you also have a potted plant,' I said, 'but I don't want that either.'

In the end, I gave up with the telephone and drove to my nearest dealership, which, it turned out, is shut on a Saturday. How did it make that one work in a business plan? And then it turned out not to be a dealership at all.

I could have given up and bought something else, but my heart was set on a GTI. I'd had enough of driving flash cars because they cause other motorists to take pictures on their cameraphones. Constantly. I wanted something that would attract no attention. Something grey. And I'd always wanted a GTI, ever since 1980. It was a dull, unfulfilled ache, but when the Mk 7 version came along a few years ago it became an all-consuming need. It's really, really good, that car, and I wanted one a lot.

My persistence was eventually rewarded – though when I say 'persistence', what I actually mean is 'contacts at VW's head office' – and in September a brand-new car arrived at my house on the back of a lorry. I was very excited and was tempted to jump up and down clutching my tinkle, until I noticed that the car had five doors. Two more than I'd wanted. With a five-door car you can't drive along with your arm out of the window because the B-pillar is in the way. I'd thought about that a lot while choosing the car. But then I'd forgotten to tick the right box on the form, and that was that.

There was another problem too. On holiday in France this year I used a Golf R, which is a bit like the GTI only it has 78 more brake horsepower and four-wheel drive and the wheels look less lost in the arches. I liked it enormously. And you would too. I don't care what you drive now: I can pretty much guarantee that, if you took an R out for a test drive, you'd want it in your life immediately.

However, to convince myself that the GTI is still better, I've told myself over and over that the R is a bit knowing, a bit anoraky, a bit Subaru-ish. And then last week an R estate came to my house . . .

Commentators have observed that this is a silly car because in basic rental spec it costs upwards of £33,000 and that is too much for a Golf. I sympathize with this argument because I'm well aware you should never buy the most expensive house in the street.

However, let's just look for a moment at what you're getting. First, it is an estate car and so, with the back seats folded down, there's space in the back for a small horse and all the paraphernalia that goes with it.

And then at the front you have the GTI engine, which has better pistons and valves and a whizzier turbocharger, so it churns out as near as makes no difference 300bhp. This is allied to a double-clutch gearbox that features a launch-control system, though I strongly advise you not to use this facility if you do in fact have a small horse in the back because it will fall over. Ooh, it's brisk.

In between the horse and the horsepower, you have the bit where you live, and this is perhaps the best part because not only is it all screwed together to a standard way beyond what you could reasonably expect, but also, if you choose your options carefully, you want for nothing at all.

This is a car that can read out text messages, help you stay in lane on the motorway, apply the brakes if it thinks you're going to crash and a million other things.

What we have here, then, is a commodious, fast, comfortable, quiet and very well-equipped four-wheel-drive car. Which brings me on to the Range Rover.

Round where I live in Chipping Norton, my friends all used to have Range Rovers. But now you get the impression that absolutely everybody has one. I was at the local farm shop last weekend and in the car park I counted thirty-seven of the damn things. And I'm not talking about Evoques. I'm talking about the big, 100-grand jobs.

The Range Rover has become a uniform, and I'm sorry, but when I'm presented with a dress code, I'm consumed by an overwhelming need to wear something else. I love the Range Rover. It's magnificent, but here's the thing: is it better than a Golf R estate? Look at the figures. No, actually, don't bother, because of course they come from Volkswagen, which means they're probably plucked from the sky. Ja, it does 1 million miles an hour und 40,000 miles to ze gallon.

It doesn't, but it is very, very fast and very beautiful to drive. The compromise between ride and handling is judged perfectly, and so's the noise. It's quiet most of the time, but when you accelerate hard it produces a snarly bark that makes you go all tingly. And, best of all, if you crash into a tree it's cheap to repair because most of the panels are the same as they are on a Golf diesel.

All things considered, then, this is a five-star car – except for one rather enormous problem. The styling. VW decided R-spec cars should not be showy in any way. They wouldn't even get the little red flashes that you find on a GTI. They'd look to the untrained eye like a run-of-the-mill model. I approve of that. I like a Q-car.

It's a philosophy that works well for the hatch because that's a good-looking vehicle in the first place. The estate, however, isn't. It's dumpy and bulbous. And in the R spec it looks stupid because it's dumpy and bulbous but there are four exhaust pipes sticking out of the back. Which make it look like some kind of weird turbocharged whale.

So there we are. A very impressive car. Ruined.

15 November 2015

When the traffic stops, the love-life turbocharger starts to whir

Fiat 500

If you are thinking of coming to London for some festive shopping, I have a suggestion: have you thought about going to Peterborough instead? Or Swindon?

I've wondered for many years how a city that wasn't designed at all hundreds of years ago manages to cope with the demands placed on it today. Because asking it to deal with the daily transport needs of more than 8 million inhabitants is a bit like asking your landline telephone to take a photograph.

Somehow, though, it has always just about managed to cling on, like a grand old battleship: shot to pieces, with a broken rudder, but still in the fight.

Today, though, the bridge seems to have been taken over by a bunch of slightly panicky monkeys. Of course, London's transport system has always been managed by idealists and lunatics, because how else would you arrive at the concept of a bus lane? 'Right, comrades. London's streets are higgledy-piggledy and were designed as gaps in which people could leave a dead horse. They are not wide enough for the motorcar, so let's take half the available space and turn it into a special lane so that old ladies can get to the post office more easily.'

Then along came the bicycle. 'Right, comrades. Let's make special lanes for these wheezing old communists. And better still, let's make a little space for them to sit in front of the cars when the traffic lights are red.'

Someone in the meeting must have put his hand up at this point and said: 'But cyclists don't stop for red lights.' And? Well, your guess is as good as mine. He's probably in a correctional facility now, in a wing for the mentally impaired.

And there's more. When Ken Livingstone was in the hot seat, he put down his newts for a moment and decided to model the phasing of the traffic lights on the passage of the sun. Red and orange for fourteen hours, with a brief green flash in the evening.

And then there's the issue with parking. They decided that cars causing an obstruction should be clamped. So they continued to cause an obstruction for many more hours. Or that they should be towed away by a fleet of lorries that would cause even more of an obstruction in the process.

Next, they decided that every single one of the 4 million people who'd arrived on the underside of a Eurostar train after a long and difficult journey from North Africa or the Middle East should be given a Toyota Prius, a smartphone with Uber on it and a licence. To kill. And yet, despite all this pedestrianized, camera-monitored idiocy, the capital continued to grow and flourish.

Now the maniacs have come up with a new wheeze. It's a biggie. They've decided that every single road in London should be dug up simultaneously. It's so far beyond a joke that it's actually funny.

Every residential street is clogged by someone digging out a basement. Every side road is having calming features installed. And every main road is subject to traffic control so that Crossrail can be built. They've even shut half the

Embankment so they can install a new cycle way. Honestly, they have. If this lot were doctors, their solution to a dangerously clogged pulmonary artery would be to open it up for six months so that it could be filled up with Chris Hoy.

This time, they really have scored a blinder, because even I have reached the bottom of the pit of despair. I view the onset of every meeting with a crushing sense of dread. And I lie in bed at night seething about how much time I've wasted by sitting in a completely unnecessary jam.

And I feel so powerless. I can't use a bus because I don't like being murdered. I can't cycle because it's too cold and wet at this time of year. I can't go on the Underground because . . . just because. And that brings me neatly on to the Fiat 500. This, you may think, is the solution. Something small. Something that can make its own lane. Something that will fit into even the tiniest parking space. Surely this is the antidote to the panicky monkeys on the bridge.

Hmm. This may well be true in a city such as Rome, where any piece of ground that isn't occupied by a structure can be viewed as a parking space. But here in London it doesn't work that way. Parking spaces are all marked clearly and are big enough for a Range Rover. So using something titchy makes no difference.

Then there's the business of lanes. Yes, in a small car you can make new and exciting lanes in European cities, but not here. On a road such as, say, Holland Park Avenue, in west London, there are two. And if you try to make a third you're going to get looked at. And being looked at in Britain is worse than being eaten.

So there's no point driving a very small car in London, because you're going to be just as stuck as if you were driving something much larger. The only real difference is that in a small car such as the Fiat you are more likely to be injured in a crash. Unless you are in the back, in which case you can be injured without a crash being involved. Ooh, it's a squash.

So the only reason for buying the little Fiat is that you like it. And I get that. The version I drove had a matt-black flower pattern stuck on to the shiny black paint, and green ears. This was a good look – even as a £460 option.

Under the bonnet it had the clever twin-cylinder 0.9-litre engine, which, thanks to all sorts of jiggery-pokery and witchcraft, produces 103bhp. That's not far short of what you got in the original Golf GTI.

There is a fair bit of turbo lag, which is annoying, because just as the blower has fully girded its loins and the fun's about to begin, you run into a set of roadworks and have to stop again. Only once in a week did I get the full shove, but it was worth the wait. There was a tremendous wallop and a whizzy racket from the clackety-clack engine, and for a moment it felt as though I were inside a mad, flowery, home-made go-kart.

It's a hoot, this car. It's nicely equipped and electronically savvy. Many of the details will be a bit beyond the elderly, but anyone under twelve will be quite content with all of the submenus in the submenus. It will give them something to do in the jams.

Me? I just sat there thinking two things: that I'd quite like to peel the people responsible. And that if I'm going to be stuck for two hours, I'd rather be in a Fiat 500 than something bland and anodyne from the Pacific Rim. Because sitting in a car such as the Fiat is like walking through the park on a sunny day with a cute dog. Sooner or later someone is going to lean out of their window and say: 'I love your little car's green ears.' And who knows where that might end up?

That's what this car is, really. Tinder. With windscreen wipers.

22 November 2015

Not coming to a young boy's bedroom wall near you . . .

Renault Kadjar

As you know, I try every Sunday morning to brighten your day with some frivolous and not-at-all important observations about the car I've been driving the previous week. But today is different. Today I need to be a bit serious.

Right now, all the world's big car-makers are engaged in a mad dash to replace the petrol engine with something more in tune with the times. Honda and Hyundai are rushing towards hydrogen fuel cells, and BMW is looking at electric propulsion with small generators to keep the batteries charged. Elsewhere, there are pure electric cars, plug-in hybrids and ultra-low-emission diesels.

It all sounds very interesting, but it's pointless, I'm afraid, because in ten or twenty years the three biggest car-makers in the world will not be Toyota, Volkswagen and General Motors. They will be Google, Apple and Uber. That's because they have come to understand something more important than what goes under the bonnet. They've come to understand that you don't need a car. But you do need one tomorrow morning, at about ten past eight. And on Thursday afternoon for a couple of hours.

Think about it. This morning your car is parked outside your house doing nothing except costing money. You probably won't use it at all until tomorrow morning, when you'll be forced to drive through all the roadworks and all the jams so that you can leave it outside your office all day. Where it will probably be keyed, or broken into.

Life will go on like this for months until, one day, it needs a service, or it breaks down, and that'll be a nuisance because then you'll have to make alternative travel arrangements, which will be a chore. You're paying thousands of pounds a year, then, for something that you use for – what? – 5 per cent of the time? Two per cent?

The car, therefore, has become like a fondue set. You have one because that's the done thing. But if you actually stop for a moment you can't for the life of you work out why.

It's the same story with your fridge. Why do you have one today, taking up a corner of your kitchen and making noises, when you can have milk and butter delivered every day and there's a supermarket on every street corner? Why not let Waitrose pay the electricity bills to keep your food fresh?

It really is the same story with your car. Wouldn't it be better if you had access to some wheels only when you needed them? Of course it would, and that's what Google and Apple and Uber have grasped. We won't buy their cars. We will share them.

So if you decide on a whim to visit your parents one afternoon, you tap a few passwords into your phone and, in minutes, a car arrives. Maybe it will have a driver. Maybe it will be driven by nobody at all. Maybe it will run on electricity from the mains or electricity created by hydrogen fuel cells. All you care is that a) it will get you where you're going and b) when you've finished with it, it will cost nothing at all.

Never again will you have to look for a parking space, or

worry about the meter running out, or pay for insurance, or book an MoT test, or break out the bucket and sponge on a Sunday morning.

If I were running one of today's big car companies, I'd be worried sick about all this, because the whole business model on which their empires are founded is daft. They're making us pay thousands and thousands of pounds to buy something that we won't use 95 per cent of the time.

And that in the remaining 5 per cent is a bloody nuisance, because of the jams and the buses and the cyclists and the Gatso cameras and the CCTV-monitored junctions and the speed-awareness courses and the 20mph limits that are being imposed because every council is now being run by a bunch of frizzy-haired lunatics.

Of course, in our minds, the car is still glamorous and exciting. It's a big Healey sweeping through the lanes at 100mph. It's an Alfa Romeo on the Amalfi coast with a young woman in a headscarf in the passenger seat. It's a growl and a roar.

But it isn't. Peel away the history, put down the rose-tinted spectacles and you'll see very clearly that it's just a tool. And that because it's just a tool, it's vulnerable to pressure from a newer tool that makes personal mobility cheaper and easier.

The only way today's big car companies can fight off this new pressure is to make their cars more glamorous and more exciting than ever before. They need to accept that, on a practical level, they can't compete with Google's silent igloo and must inject their new models with the sort of pizzazz that will make a grown man drool. They need to rekindle the spirit of the big Healey and the convertible Alfa Romeo.

Watchmakers did it when Casio came along. Restaurants did it with the dawn of fast food. Airlines and supermarkets are trying to do it now to fend off budget alternatives. But car-makers are not doing it. They are so obsessed with eco-twaddle and new propulsion systems that they are forgetting about the one thing that will keep us buying their products: excitement.

You get none from the car I am writing about today. It started out in life as the perfectly sensible but dreary Nissan Kumquat and was then turned, for accountancy reasons, into a Renault Kadjar. A name dreamed up by an agency when all the other names have gone.

No one is going to yearn for the day they own a Kadjar. No one is going to spend hours on a configurator, seeing what it would look like in orange or with bigger wheels. No one will search for it on YouTube. It will never be seen in a *Fast and Furious* film. It'll never be an option in the *Forza Motorsport* video game. It'll never be a poster on a small boy's bedroom wall. There will never be a Renault Kadjar Airfix model, or a fast 'R' version that will sweep to victory on a racetrack or in a rally stage.

The Kadjar offers absolutely nothing that would make you buy one if you could use a Google Igloo instead. Both are soulless tools. But one is much, much cheaper.

I've singled out the Kadjar because that's what I've been driving for the past week. But the same thing is true with the majority of cars you can buy these days. They're just an expensive, awkward hassle that you can do without.

Of course, the car as we know it will survive. Niche manufacturers such as Ferrari and Bentley will soldier on, perhaps making luxury or speedy versions of the Igloo. And you'll still be able to buy classics.

But I can assure you of one thing: many, many years from now, when people gather at a racetrack to give their old self-drive, self-owned, petrol-driven 'cars' a bit of a blast, no one will turn up with a Renault Kadjar.

29 November 2015

Et voilà! School-run mum slips into her thigh boots

Peugeot 308 GTi

You were supposed to be reading about some kind of new Mitsubishi pick-up. But at the last minute a chap from the company called to say he would not be lending it to me because a workaday car such as that with its good turning circle for builders' yards would not be of much interest to the readers of the *Sunday Times*.

In his mind, then, builders and plumbers and gamekeepers read the *Daily Mirror* and are too busy lamenting the demise of *Nuts* magazine to be thinking about buying a new pick-up any time soon. Which will surprise the builders and chippies who are currently making noises in my sitting room because they all read the *Sunday Times* and they all drive vans and pick-ups.

To make matters worse, the chap from Mitsubishi also says that my booking to drive some kind of electric car in a few weeks has been cancelled as well. 'Dom Joly has already written about it in the *Sunday Times*,' he says by way of explanation.

I'm not sure that argument stacks up. Film companies do not ban Claudia Winkleman from reviewing a movie because Camilla Long has already written about it in the *Sunday Times*. Restaurants do not ban A. A. Gill because Giles Coren has already done a piece in *The Times*. Of course, he gets banned for lots of reasons, but not that one.

I think it's fairly obvious what's happened. The man from

Mitsubishi is peeved about the firm-but-fair review I wrote about his Outlander PHEV plug-in electric vehicle last year and I've been cast into the wilderness as a result.

That's his right. And I don't mind. Secretly, I'm rather proud. It shows I'm doing my job properly. And certainly I'm not going to wake up every morning from now on thinking, 'Oh no. I won't be driving a Mitsubishi today. I shall have to make do with a Mercedes-AMG GT instead.'

It's not even much of a professional bother because if I really do need to test a Mitsubishi, I shall simply rent it. Or if I need it for the new Amazon show, buy it.

Over the years, I've been banned at various times from driving Toyotas for saying the Corolla was about as interesting as a fridge-freezer, Vauxhalls for refusing to say anything at all about the Vectra, and BMW for saying its cars were driven by cocks. Weirdly, however, I have never been banned by Peugeot.

I've not had a kind word to say about any of its products for many years. I even devoted a large chunk of *Top Gear* last year to ridiculing its customers. And yet still the PR department keeps on coming back from more. Secretly, I think its press fleet manager is Anastasia Steele.

Perhaps in an attempt to suffer more pain and humiliation, the company last week sent round its new 308 GTi, which was red at the front and black at the back. Instantly, this aroused the eye-rolling cynic that lives in my head. 'The only reason it would do that,' it said, 'is to take your mind off all its shortcomings.'

Inside, there was more. The steering wheel is about the size of a shirt button and sits below all the dials in the instrument binnacle. Until you raise it so that it's no longer between your knees, at which point it sits right in front of all the dials in the instrument binnacle. Revs? Speed? Fuel level? No idea.

'It's done this on purpose,' said the eye-rolling cynic. 'Because if you're focused on the invisibility of the dials and the two-tone paint, you won't notice that the door mirror has fallen off and that the radio's broken.'

The thing is, though, nothing did break. In fact, everything felt a lot more solid and well made than is normal in a modern-day Peugeot. By which I mean any car the company has made since 1971.

There's more. Most of the functions are now controlled by the centrally mounted screen, which is a triumph of common sense. Except for the Sport button that makes the car more zingy. That sits in the centre console and, when you press it, all of the dials in the instrument binnacle turn red. Apparently. All I could see was the steering wheel.

And it was annoying me because the actual system it controls isn't that brilliant. There's no real feel. It gives no sense that it's concentrating on the job in hand. It's fine around town but when you're zooming along it delivers no real joy, which is a shame because the rest of the package delivers it in spades.

It may have only a 1.6-litre engine – most of its rivals come with 2 litres – but there's no shortage of oomph. And it may come with an old-fashioned manual rather than a flappy-paddle system, which can be a chore sometimes, but ooh, it's fun.

Finally, it seems, Peugeot has managed to recapture some of the magic that made the 205 GTI such a monster hit back in *The Official Sloane Ranger Handbook* days of Mrs Thatcher.

This is a car you want to drive. It's a car you will find an excuse to drive. Yes, it's practical and sensible on the school run but, on the way home, after you've dropped off the kids, it pulls off the traditional hot-hatch trick of slipping out of its slippers and into a pair of PVC thigh-high boots. It becomes a raunchy, up-for-it playmate.

Weirdly, you can buy the new car with less power and a less sophisticated limited-slip differential, but I really can't see why you would want to do that. Because it's not like the full-fat version is expensive. Compared with its rivals from Volkswagen and Ford, it's very good value indeed. But all things considered, is it as good?

Ah, that's the big one, isn't it? I have a Golf GTI for several reasons. My mum always had Beetles. I want to support Volkswagen in the emissions saga. And it reminds me of the good old days in the White Horse in Fulham when everyone had one, with Val d'Isère mud up the side and an army cap in the boot.

It's possible – probable, even – that none of these things matters to you. Maybe you're a working-class boy done good, in which case you'll want the Ford Focus ST. You see it as a metal embodiment of yourself. A blue-collar car with humble origins that can mix it with the blue bloods. Bruce Springsteen with windscreen wipers.

We all have our reasons for wanting to buy one brand more than another. My son has a Fiat because he likes Italian football. I used to have a Mercedes because it annoyed Richard Hammond. My grandfather had a Bentley to irritate those with Rolls-Royces. Some people choose Mitsubishis because, er, I can't help you with that one at the moment. Sorry.

And then we have those people who want to buy a French car because, in these troubled times, they want to be supportive. They fancy a Peugeot because back in the day they had a 205 1.9 GTI and they reckon its modern-day equivalent would help rekindle some of their lost youthfulness.

Well, the good news is that, today, for the first time in ages, you can. You can follow your heart, buy a 308 GTi and not spend the next couple of years regretting it.

6 December 2015

Think hard before you hit the throttle in the camber gambler

Nissan GT-R Track Edition

In my most recent review of the Nissan GT-R I said it was pretty much perfect in every way and declared at the end that it's not a five-star car. It's *the* five-star car. I stand by that. If you want to go fast, in any weather, on any road, there is simply nothing else that even gets close.

You know the Space Shuttle. The pictures would suggest that it lumbered off the launchpad as though it were getting out of bed after a heavy night, but nothing could be further from the truth. When the restraining bolts were released and those 37m-horsepower engines could do their thing, it exploded upwards so vigorously that it was doing 120mph before its tail had cleared the gantry.

Anyone familiar with the Nissan GT-R would call that 'a bit pedestrian'. Maybe on a sweeping ribbon of tarmac in the Scottish Highlands on a dry, hot, sticky day the McLaren P1 could just about keep up. But it's doubtful. And what makes this so extraordinary is that the Nissan has four seats and a big boot and to the casual observer appears to be 'just a car'.

I have no idea why Nissan makes it. It costs a little over £78,000, so the margins must be small. So is the volume. Which means the company probably makes more money each year from its factory-floor vending machines. And it's not as though the GT-R creates any form of meaningful halo for Nissan's other cars. Nobody in the world has ever said: 'Ooh, I admire the GT-R's ability to get round the Nür-burgring in four seconds so I shall buy a Juke immediately.' The GT-R sits in the Nissan line-up in the same way as a Fabergé egg would sit on the shelves of your local Lidl.

I suspect Nissan makes the GT-R primarily to keep its engineers awake and loyal. Most companies put photographs of their employees of the month on a wall in reception. But at Nissan, if you do good work on the rear-light cluster of the dreary Kumquat SUV, you are allowed to develop a differential for the GT-R.

That's great, but how do you reward your brightest and best when there will be no new GT-R for at least five years? Simple. You let them make the existing car even better.

This recently resulted in the Nismo version. I have not driven it but I gather from speaking to the hollowed-out, mumbling wrecks who have that it's almost stupid in its ability to bend, break and then eat the laws of physics.

I'm also told that while it works extremely well on a track, it's far too raw to work on a road. Think of it, then, as a scuba suit. You need it if you want to look at a turtle, but it doesn't really work on the Tube or in meetings with clients.

So now Nissan has come up with the Track Edition, which is supposed to be a halfway house. You get the standard car's V6 twin-turbo engine and the standard car's interior fixtures and fittings. But you get the Nismo's handling tweaks. Which include this: glue to supplement the spot-welds and make the body even stiffer.

This is the sort of thing that makes an enthusiast of the brand need to repair to the lavatory for a little 'me time'. To the people who populate GT-R internet forums a car that uses glue as well as spot-welds for added stiffness is way beyond Angelina Jolie and Scarlett Johansson in a bath of warm milk.

This is all part of the GT-R legend. It's a car that is built in a hermetically sealed factory and has tyres full of nitrogen because normal air is too unpredictable. It uses an engine that's built by one man and is mounted out of kilter to the transmission so that when you accelerate and the torque causes it to rock backwards, all is in perfect harmony. No one can tell if any of this stuff actually makes any difference. But knowing the car was built this way makes its fans priapic.

There's a problem, though. Because the body is now so stiff and the suspension is so unforgiving, the car is completely undriveable on the road. It's so bad that after one run from London to Oxford and back I parked it in my garage and have not even looked at it since.

There is no give. At all. Drive over a manhole cover and you get some idea of what it might be like to be involved in a plane crash. You actually feel the top of your spine bouncing off the inside of your skull.

Jimmy Carr was in the passenger seat and after less than half a mile he asked if the satnav was programmed only to take the occupants to the nearest chiropractor.

But I wasn't really listening because the Track Edition was serving up another unwanted party piece: any minor camber change in the road surface causes it to veer violently left or right. I'm always hesitant to say that a car is dangerous, because it's a legal minefield, but this one gets bloody close. Twice in just an hour I very nearly had an accident because of the sudden and unexpected changes in direction.

It wouldn't have been a big accident because it happens mostly at slow speed but it would have been annoying and embarrassing explaining to the driver whose car I'd hit why I'd suddenly driven into his door for no reason.

Naturally, you'd expect that on a track there would be some upside to these issues – but I can't answer that because driving this car to a racing circuit to find out would be too uncomfortable and too fraught with danger.

One American magazine found that the standard car can generate 0.97g in a corner and the Track Edition 1.02g. That's not much of an improvement, and when you factor in the fact that the track was stickier when it tested the new car, it's not really an improvement at all.

It's no faster in a straight line either because it has the same engine. In fact, it may even be slower over a quarter of a mile because it will spend most of its time veering left and right. The normal GT-R can and will go from A to B on a drag strip in the shortest possible distance. Which is a straight line.

Still, you might imagine that because the Track Edition is compromised so badly, it will be cheaper. Not so, I'm afraid. It is in fact about £10,500 more expensive.

So we are left here with a rather tragic conclusion. The standard GT-R is a five-star car. It is one of the very, very best cars in the world. And yet this track-day abomination gets no stars at all. Because it's pretty much useless.

I'll sign off, then, with a simple message to Nissan. If you feel the need to tinker with your masterpiece again, stick to the styling. Because that's the one area where a little bit of TLC wouldn't go amiss. Everything else: leave it alone.

20 December 2015

I was ready to wrestle a fire-breathing raver, not an IT geek

Audi R8 V10 Plus

In Italy, or Spain, or America, or anywhere but here, really, when you fill an expensive and fast car with petrol you are approached by people who want to tell you how lovely it is. They smile and they purr and then ask if it'd be all right for the children to have their pictures taken in the driving seat.

Things are rather different in 'It's all right for some' Britain, where some bloke invariably says: 'I bet you don't get many miles to the gallon out of that.' Or 'I can get more in the boot of my Austin Maestro,' or – and this is the one I've always hated most of all – 'Where the hell can you ever drive a car like that?'

The answer is: 'Well, I'm very rich, obviously, so I can hire a racetrack.' But instead we smile sweetly and try our hardest not to put the nozzle down his trousers and set him on fire.

He is quite right, though. You can't really open up a super-car these days because the bitter and twisted, mealy-mouthed Maestro-driving caravan and cycling enthusiasts have taken over the town halls. I was up in Staffordshire last weekend tootling about in my old stomping ground and, on the A515, which goes from nowhere in particular to nowhere at all via various places that only mean anything to me, there were regular speed cameras in all the villages and average-speed cameras on the bits in between.

And to make matters worse, this fast and really rather good road is now governed by a 50mph speed limit. A speed that Isambard Kingdom Brunel would have designated as pathetic. He'd have been right. It is pathetic: 50mph is for animals.

This ridiculous attitude to speed is catching on all around the world. Even the French have completely lost their sense of humour about a bit of flat-out screamery on the auto-routes. And I haven't found a stretch of derestricted autobahn for years.

Which brings us back to our friend in the cardigan-and-Maestro combination and his question: 'What's the point of a 1,000 brake horsepower, mid-engined, fire-breathing rip-snorter when you are forced to travel at the same speed as a dog or a rabbit?'

He is completely missing the point because supercars are not supposed to be driven at 5,000 miles an hour round the Nürburgring. That's what a Subaru or a Volkswagen Golf R is for. Supercars are for doing 3mph round Harrods.

If you try to go any faster than this, you will crash. Which is why, when you fire up YouTube and ask it to find some amusing supercar crashes, they invariably show a Ferrari or a Lamborghini whizzing into a bus stop or a lamppost or some other bit of urban street furniture.

You don't see them crashing into trees and hedges because they're to be found in the countryside, and in the country-side no one's looking. And if no one's looking, what's the point of putting your foot down in a supercar? Or even driv-ing one in the first place?

Supercars are tricky little sods. If you put your foot all the way to the floor in a normal hatchback, it will pick up speed. If you put your foot all the way to the floor in a supercar, it will spear into a bus stop. The acceleration these days is very vivid indeed.

That's why my current favourite supercar is the Lamborghini Aventador. It may not be the best for going round Stowe Corner and it may not have the best brakes in the world, but for snarling round Knightsbridge at two in the morning it's fantastic. It's just so amazing to behold. And that is the whole point.

The Audi R8 isn't amazing to behold. It's an odd one, this. It's a mid-engined two-seater with 1 million brake horsepower, a V10 and four-wheel drive. It really is a Lamborghini underneath. And yet Audi, which owns Lamborghini, has done everything in its power to make it sober and refined and comfortable.

Mostly, it's done a very good job. In the socialist boroughs of London, where the worker johnnies only repair potholes with speed humps, it rides like a Lincoln Town Car from the 1970s. It's also roomy, for two people, and quiet.

There are some issues, though. No one looks at it. And if no one is looking at it and you can't drive it quickly, why put up with the tiny boot? Because it will appreciate in value? No, it won't. The last R8, albeit with a V8 engine, had the same problem and is now about £40,000.

The biggest issue, however, is the tech. I commend Audi for trying something new; the instrument binnacle is a computer screen. I commend it also for nearly making it work. But everything else is just too complex. It's a big problem with cars these days. How do you make all the electronic add-ons intuitive and intelligible? RAF pilots train for years before they are allowed in a Eurofighter and, let me tell you, there's way more stuff to learn in an R8. Way more.

I'd learn how to shuffle tracks on my iPod or answer the

phone or input a satnav address and then, after I learned some more things, such as how to change the interior lighting, I'd forget the first stuff again. This meant I spent most of my time behind the wheel wearing my reading glasses to peer at the screen and swearing gently when I got it all wrong.

The satnav is an issue too. It's set up in a widescreen layout, which means you can see where Wales is, and New York, but not how to get to the street that is half a mile to the north.

In other words, Audi has tried hard to make the R8 an every-day car – it even has cup-holders – but it hasn't quite succeeded. The suspension isn't quite right either. No matter what setting you choose, the car has a curious vertical bouncing gait, which is a bit annoying. Oh, and on the motorway it would sometimes have an electronic burp and make what felt like a botched gear change. If I wanted gremlins, I'd buy a Lamborghini, thank you very much.

Which is pretty much how I feel about the Audi. If I wanted a supercar, I'd buy its virtually identical brother: the Lamborghini Huracán. In lime green. With orange seats.

I can see what Audi's tried to do with the R8 and it'd be a clever trick if it had pulled it off: a car that can corner at 2 million miles an hour, go from 0 to 100,000 in a quarter of a second and then become a Golf for the ride home. But it hasn't quite managed it.

And even if it had, I'm not sure anyone would be interested because what we really want from a supercar are lasers and photon torpedoes. Not cup-holders and a Comfort setting on the suspension menu.

27 December 2015

Remember the rolling Robins? Well, I've a confession to make

Reliant Robin

To judge from the letters I get and the remarks in the street, it seems the most memorable thing I did on *Top Gear* was a short segment about the Reliant Robin. You may remember: I drove it around Sheffield and it kept falling over.

Well, now's the time to come clean. A normal Reliant Robin will not roll unless a drunken rugby team is on hand. Or it's windy. But in a headlong drive to amuse and entertain, I'd asked the backroom boys to play around with the differential so that the poor little thing rolled over every time I turned the steering wheel.

Naturally, the health-and-safety department was very worried about this and insisted that the car be fitted with a small hammer that I could use, in case I was trapped after the roll, to break what was left of the glass. Not the best idea ever, because I distinctly remember seeing the hammer in question travelling past my face at about 2,000mph during the first roll. After that I invited the health-and-safety man to eff off home, with the hammer in his bottom.

Since then, I've used similarly doctored and similarly hammer-free Reliant Robins in countless games of car football during our live shows. And as a result, there's probably no one on the planet who's rolled a car quite as much as I have.

It makes me sad, if I'm honest, because rolling a Reliant Robin on purpose is a bit like putting a tortoise on its back.

It's an act of wanton cruelty. When you see it lying there with its three little wheels whizzing round helplessly, you are compelled to rush over and put it the right way up.

I feel similarly aggrieved when people – and everyone does this – calls it a Robin Reliant. That's like saying you worship Christ Jesus or that you drive an Acclaim Triumph. Or that your favourite Fifa presidential hopeful is Sexwale Tokyo.

I'll be honest with you. I really like the Reliant Robin. I know that Del Boy did his best to turn three-wheelers into a national joke. And I know Jasper Carrott went even further – the bastard. But the truth is that the Reliant Robin has a rorty-sounding 848cc engine and the sort of snickety gearbox that makes you lament the passing of the proper manual.

Plus, it's an absolute hoot to drive, partly because it's light and nimble and partly because passers-by are genuinely fond of it. It's like going about your business in one of the Queen's corgis. Mostly, though, it's a hoot to drive because you know, if something goes wrong, you will be killed immediately. There'll be no lingering and agonizing spell in hospital. No priest with his last rites. One minute you'll be bouncing up and down wearing a childlike grin and the next you'll be meat.

In fact, I like the Reliant Robin so much that when Richard Hammond, James May, Andy Wilman and I formed our new production company, I rushed out immediately and bought one as a company car. Interestingly, the other three did exactly the same thing. So now we have a fleet sitting in the executive car-parking spaces at our offices and we love them very much. Especially the fact that they cost us less than £15,000. That's £15,000 for four cars.

Of course, they've all been fettled to suit our tastes. May's is an ivory-white estate model that is standard in every way, right down to the chromed overriders. Hammond's is a lovely chocolate brown with whitewall tyres. Wilman's is finished in racing green and inside is fitted with a wooden dashboard and lambswool seat covers – as befits, he says, the chairman of our enterprise. Mine – a coupé, naturally – is finished in winner blue and fitted with an Alcantara dash and quad tailpipes. Minilite wheels complete the vision of sportiness.

A lot of people think we have bought the cars purely as some kind of weird publicity stunt but, actually, nothing could be further from the truth. Because we really do use them on a daily basis. Or, to be honest, we try to use them . . .

My first attempt had to be abandoned, because the engine decided that tickover should be about 5,500rpm. Which meant that in fourth gear I was doing about 80mph without putting my foot on the accelerator. I say 'about', because the speedometer wasn't working. For an accurate reading I'll have to wait for a letter from the speed-camera people.

Hammond's has no functioning fuel gauge and he would therefore like to apologize to everyone on London's Cromwell Road for running out of petrol the other night while turning right into Earls Court Road. Apparently, the chaos he caused was quite spectacular.

Wilman's hasn't actually gone anywhere at all because, as he tried to put it into reverse, the gear lever came off in his hand. I'm not sure what's wrong with May's. He tried to explain but after four hours I nodded off slightly.

We didn't give up, though. And the other night I went all the way from our old offices in Notting Hill to our new offices, appropriately enough, in Power Road, in Chiswick, west London, and then – get this – all the way back to a party in Chelsea. Where the car spent the night, because its starter motor had broken.

Hammond said he'd come to the rescue but, annoyingly, his

ignition barrel came out as he turned the key, and Wilman was of no use because the gear lever popped out again when he went for first. So I rang May, who turned up in his Ferrari.

Anyway, on my trek across London I learned many things about my Reliant Robin. First of all, to get my right shoulder inside, I have to drive with the window down, which makes life a bit chilly. And there's not much I can do to rectify that issue, because while there is a knob on the dash that says 'Heater', it doesn't seem to do anything. The only other knob says 'Choke'. Pull that and immediately the whole car fills with petrol fumes.

But despite the cold and the likelihood of it suddenly becoming very hot, the Reliant Robin is brilliant to drive. The steering is extremely light, possibly because there's only one front wheel to turn, the acceleration is great, for anyone who's used to, say, a horse, and in a typical London parking bay it's so small and looks so lost and lonely you are tempted to give it a carrot or some other treat.

This is what makes the Reliant Robin such a joy. My Volkswagen Golf is a car. The Porsche Cayenne I used over Christmas and will review next week is a car. You drive a car. But the Reliant Robin is not a car. It's not even three-quarters of a car. It's more than that.

It's sitting in its parking space outside the office now, in the rain. And I'm worried about it. I hope it's OK and isn't missing me. Owning a Reliant Robin is like having a family pet. Yes, it's a nuisance sometimes, and, yes, it can be stubborn and unreliable, but it scampers when you go out together and, if you play with its differential, it will even roll over so you can tickle its tummy.

10 January 2016

The turbocharged mammoth stampedes away from extinction

Porsche Cayenne Turbo S

I have driven a Bentley Continental many times, and at no point have I ever thought, 'Hmm, I like the opulence and the strange sensations of cultured thuggery but I wish I could buy a version of this car that has a slightly lower top speed and is a lot less wieldy and considerably more expensive.'

Bentley has recently launched a large SUV that covers all those bases. It's called the Bentayga and, in essence, it is a Continental that's been ruined. It's also a little bit ugly, and yet I guarantee that it will sell by the bucketload. In the Christian Louboutin and Chanel part of town you won't be able to move for the damn things.

Lamborghini, too, is said to be working on a jacked-up supercar. It will, I understand, look like an Aventador on stilts, which means it'll be like an Aventador, only slower, less economical and worse round the corners. That'll sell as well.

The demand for leather-lined SUVs has gone berserk. I was at the Soho Farmhouse in Oxfordshire last weekend and the car park was hysterical. Everyone looked at me arriving in my Volkswagen Golf with open-mouthed wonderment. 'How did you get here in that?' they exclaimed.

Almost everyone else had turned up in a black Range Rover. Indeed the Range Rover is now so popular that Land Rover's sister company, Jaguar, has a rival — the F-Pace — arriving on forecourts this spring. It'll be ideal, I should imagine, for all those who choose not to buy the Maserati Levante, another SUV, which will make its debut at the Geneva motor show in March.

It's easy to see why all these car-makers are so keen to make SUVs. The profit margins are huge, because you're selling farmyard technology at farm-shop prices. And when I say 'farm shop', I mean Daylesford.

A saloon car has to be fast and comfortable and refined, and all of this stuff costs millions of pounds to develop. An SUV just needs to be big and full of buttons. That costs 8p. For an extreme example of this in action, peer underneath America's offerings. They're just pick-ups with tinted windows. Rationally, then, SUVs make no sense. And yet . . .

I know that driving along in an SUV is like inviting all the poor people in your village to watch you build a bonfire out of tenners. I know SUVs are ridiculous and that they simply arm those who want us to go to work in a Google Igloo. But I must admit that my inner nine-year-old rather enjoys being at the wheel of a massive and turbocharged Tonka toy.

Which is why I was pleased when Porsche said I could use a Cayenne Turbo S over the Christmas holidays.

The Cayenne is an old car now. There is a city named after it in French Guiana. And a pepper. They've even found prehistoric cave drawings of it in various parts of the world.

In 2014 there was a small facelift that included the fitting of LED daytime running lights, but as soon as you step inside you know it's old. The satnav screen, for instance, in most modern cars, is 16 feet across, whereas in the Cayenne it's the size of a stamp. And get this: to start the engine you have to put a key in a slot and then turn it. That's as quaint as Anne Hathaway's cottage.

The other thing that hasn't really changed over the years is the styling, and that's a bad thing. This is not a looker, and age has not improved matters one bit. It still appears as though the stylists were consumed by the idea of making the front look like a 911 and then had a tantrum and gave up completely with the rest of the car when their efforts failed.

However, there is no getting away from the fact that in one important respect the Porsche feels bang up to date. It is extremely fast. Bonkers. Insane. Eye-swivelling.

Under the bonnet is a 4.8-litre twin-turbo V8 that produces 562bhp. And that makes it – since the 918 Spyder is sold out – just about the most powerful car Porsche builds. It's so powerful, it holds the SUV lap record at the Nürburgring, having smashed the Range Rover Sport SVR's time by almost fifteen seconds.

It's not just fast for an SUV, either. In a straight line to 62mph it'll embarrass the driver of an Aston Martin V8 Vantage. Flat out, it'll be doing as near as makes no difference 180mph.

My test car was fitted with the optional sports exhaust system, which produces the sort of deep, crackling rumble that frightens dogs. And it also helps to mask the sound of the fuel pumps, which, I presume, are a bit like a bank of firemen's hoses.

To try to keep all this weight and all this power in some kind of check there are many buttons, all of which when pressed make the experience a bit less comfortable. I went for the softest setting, and – I'll be honest – it wasn't bad. Of course, even in sporty mode, it's no 911 – it's too high up for that – but then at least you aren't sitting there thinking, 'Oh no. I'm going to crash at any moment.' And that's the best you can hope for, really, in a car such as this.

Bigger stopping distances. Lower cornering speeds. Thirst.

These are the prices you pay for all the extra . . . um . . . er . . . height? Ground clearance? Off-road traction?

Well, yes, you get all that and a lot of clever electronic trickery, but the truth of the matter is that a car this big and this heavy is going to get stuck on a wet, grassy hill. The only way round that is to fit it with off-road tyres and, if you do that, it'll be a noisy, wayward nightmare on the way home.

Which brings us right back to the beginning. Why spend almost £120,000 on a Cayenne Turbo S – and that much again if you want it to have doors and a steering wheel and a radio – when it won't work in the sort of off-road conditions that we get in Britain? Why not buy a Panamera instead? Or a BMW 530d? Or a Golf R or a Toyota Hilux?

Admit it. You want a big SUV because it's part of today's uniform. It tells people that you have a second home in the country and that you shoot. It says that money's not a worry. All of this is human nature. It's silly, but it's how we are.

The question is, however: having made the decision to buy a large SUV, should you buy a Cayenne Turbo S, with its quaint key slot and stamp-sized satnav screen?

Well, yes, if you want the fastest SUV on the road. But bear in mind that, within a year or so, once Bentley and Lamborghini are offering rivals, it won't be.

17 January 2016

Oh, you're good, Audi, but I bet you can't give it vertical take-off

Audi A4 Quattro

Towards the end of the eighteenth century a chef in the Italian city of Naples decided that he'd like to invent an easy way for the locals to eat their food when there was no cutlery to hand. Presumably, he had encountered a haggis and decided that, while the idea was sound, the execution wasn't.

So then he looked at the pasty, which, he'd heard, could be eaten even by people with sooty hands in a mine. But there was a problem with that too. A meat pie would work in a country where there was rain and flabby people who would be happy later on to drive around in a Morris Marina. But it would not work, he reckoned, in a country that had given the world Rome and the Renaissance and would go on to provide it with Ferrari and Alfa Romeo.

Having looked at a burger and decided it was far too American, he came up with the pizza. And I presume that, having created the base, he experimented for several years before deciding that the topping should be made from cheese and tomatoes. In the next 200 years every chef would refine and hone our Neapolitan friend's original design until, one day, someone came up with the American Hot, and that was that. The pizza was finished. Perfect. Unimprovable. Move on.

But people didn't move on. They kept coming up with new designs and new toppings. Adding leaves and weeds and lumps of buffalo garnished with guillemot. They went for cheeses that have no place outside the fridge of Blur's bassist and cooked them in ovens that filled the restaurant with the pungent smell of a forest fire.

They invented the pizza-delivery man, who would go on to star in a million low-rent porn films. They added sultanas and lentils and beans. And the customers came and their shoulders sagged because all they wanted was an American Hot. Because that's what a pizza is.

The American Hot is pretty much where we've got to in the world of cars with the new Audi A4. The idea of personalized mobility using internal combustion was dreamt up by Karl Benz, and for the past 130 years everyone's been fiddling around with his original concept until we've arrived at the point where there's nothing left to do. Except think of a new concept.

It's almost impossible to review the A4, because there's almost nothing to say. The boot is big enough for your suitcases, the doors don't fall off when you go over a bump, the dashboard is laid out to look like a dashboard and the 3-litre turbodiesel engine in my test car hummed like a contented monk. You may think that the engines in all modern saloon cars hum like contented monks, but the humming in this Audi seems to be coming from very far away. It is remarkably refined. Astonishingly so, in fact.

Audi had obviously been paying attention to the weather forecast and supplied the car on skinny and knobbly winter tyres that until recently would have sat in the mix in the same way as a large turd would have sat on your American Hot. But not any more. They were quiet and grippy, even when the weather was nowhere near as frosty as the overexcitable Met Office had predicted.

Because the snow terror and the ice chaos never arrived,

I had a good whizz about in the Audi and can report that, even though it is whisper quiet, it's startlingly fast. Not that long ago BMW M5s had such performance figures. And it's a diesel.

It handles nicely too. The Quattro badge may have begun in the forests and on the icy tracks of the world rally calendar, but it quickly became nothing more than a marketing tool, a handle that sounded cool and interesting but actually gave your car handling that was woollier than a Swede's jumper. Not any more. Thanks to all sorts of clever-clever electronics, the Quattro now feels how a Quattro should feel. And never has.

It's the same story with the comfort. As recently as five or six years ago Audis didn't ride properly. They jiggled and pittered and pattered. A road that in most cars was billiard-table smooth was a ploughed field in an Audi. But not any more. Now, you glide.

This car is so magic-carpetish that you may nod off, but that's OK because up to 37mph in a city there is an option that lets it drive itself. Outside the city it can steer itself down the motorway and stop if the car in front stops, and all while you're sending a text. It also knows where it's going and, because the monk up front runs on diesel, you'll be able to get from London to Scotland and back without stopping for fuel.

Niggles? It's as hard, really, as niggling about your Pizza Express American Hot. Only people who write on Trip-Advisor could do that. And that lot are so mean and bitter, they'd even find fault, publicly, with their wife's breasts.

I could tell you the satnav graphics are a bit Mothercare and I don't need a warning buzzer to tell me that the door is open. I know it's open because I just opened it. And, er, that really is pretty much all.

The only genuine gripe is the price. A base-level 3-litre TDI A4 Quattro is knocking on the door of £36,000, which is a lot for a car that, let's not forget, started out in life – in the form of the 80 – as a rival for the Ford Cortina. I can't say for sure because life's too short to work it out, but I reckon the car I drove, which was fitted with quite a few choice extras, would cost in excess of £50,000.

This may cause you to wonder if perhaps you would be better off with a BMW or a Mercedes or a Jaguar instead. Well, that's up to you. Because the truth is that their mid-sized saloon cars are all pretty good as well. The Jaguar XE especially. It's surprisingly excellent, that thing.

Or maybe you want to wait and see what Alfa Romeo's Giulia will be like. That's the car I'm most looking forward to driving this year. Mostly because I just know there will be loads to say about it.

And that really is the Audi's biggest problem. There isn't. It's a car, filtered and refined and honed so that every last little foible and idiosyncrasy is gone. It's everything a car can be and should be and, as a result, it's a little bit dull. There's no flair, no pizzazz, no wow factor. It's as characterful as a toaster.

What we need now, then, is no more development of the original idea. We've done that. We've achieved peak pizza. What we need now is new thinking, new means of propulsion.

Our man in Naples didn't look at the pasty and think: 'Oh, well, that's that, then. It's been done.' He started a new idea from scratch. It's time for the car-makers to do the same thing.

24 January 2016

It could swallow a horse and forty-seven other things. Anyone with forty-eight must get a lorry

Volkswagen Touran 2.0 TDI

After a long and dreary drive down the M1 last weekend, the satnav said I had just 6 miles to go. And even though it would be 6 miles across London, I figured that in half an hour I would be kicking off my shoes and sitting back to spend the rest of the day watching television and eating chocolate.

So would you like to guess how long it actually took to cover those 6 miles? No, I'm sorry, but you're not even close. It was two hours and thirty-five minutes.

I have never seen so many roadworks and cones and temporary traffic lights and buses on diversion. And in every single one of the endless snarl-ups there'd be an Uber driver in his infernal Toyota Prius making everything worse. Or a senior citizen in a Peugeot. And every single rat run I took was festooned with speed humps and width restrictions and dead ends and more Uber drivers pootling about while under the influence of God knows what. Not speed, though, that's for sure.

It's a fairly typical story these days. Everywhere you go, the roads are being turned into cycle ways and bus lanes and pedestrian zones. Which means you are being inconvenienced while the council builds something to inconvenience you for ever. And last week that made me stare with barely concealed contempt at the gear lever in my Volkswagen Touran test car.

'Why,' I wailed inwardly, 'would anyone ever buy a car with a manual gearbox these days?' It's like saying: 'I don't need a television with a remote control. I'm perfectly capable of walking over to it and changing the channel myself.'

Yes, on a racetrack or a deserted switchback road in the Atlas Mountains, a manual gearbox is sublime. Snapping it up a cog when you reach the red line and double declutching on the way back down . . . ooh, it makes me go all tingly.

But we don't drive on racetracks or in the Atlas Mountains. We drive on the Oxford ring road, where there are narrow lanes and signs saying you are not allowed to overtake cyclists. And here, a car with a manual gearbox is just annoying.

I had it in my mind as I sat in the Touran, fuming, that these days – with flappy-paddle gearboxes and automatics being fairly cheap and easy – the only people who would buy an old-fashioned gearstick manual are the sort who choose not to have a washing machine because they prefer to clean their clothes in the local river.

It seems, however, that I'm wrong. Yes, automatics in whatever form are becoming more popular but, even so, more than 70 per cent of all cars sold in Britain have manual gearboxes. That means more than 70 per cent of Britain's car drivers are mad.

There was a time when automatics chewed fuel, weighed a ton and cost about the same as a house. And there was a time, too, when the halfway-house arrangement – usually a manual gearbox operated without a clutch pedal via flappy paddles on the steering column – was jerky and complicated and completely incapable of setting off without making more smoke than a First World War battleship. Those days are gone. Flappy-paddle gearboxes now are sublime. Fast. Easy. Rewarding. Nice.

But there I was in the Touran, pumping away at the clutch and manually moving the sort of lever that would be familiar to any Victorian signalman. And I felt like one of those people who won't have a mobile phone because they've a perfectly good Bakelite landline device at home.

Before we get on to a road test of the actual car, I should make one point. If you pass your driving test in a vehicle with a flappy-paddle set-up, which is technically a manual, you are only permitted to drive automatics on the road. Which means, of course, you can drive a car with flappy paddles. Even though – as I just said – it's technically a manual. Odd, eh?

Anyway, the car. Well, it may be called a Touran and it may be billed as a people carrier – it comes with three rows of seats – but when all is said and done it's a Golf. So you get all the Golf features, including eco-tips that flash up on the dash asking you to maybe think about driving more eco-logically, to which you can now reply: 'If I wanted to drive ecologically, I wouldn't have bought an effing Volkswagen diesel, would I?'

You also get a satnav system that sometimes turns itself off. A quick check on Google says this is a common fault and the cure is to stop the car, get out, lock it, unlock it, get back in and start the engine again. In other words, it's the same as your Sky box and your phone and your laptop. You turn it off and on again.

And that's about it so far as faults are concerned. Even the styling is right, chiefly because there isn't any. It's modelled, from what I can see, on the box in which chest freezers are delivered, and that's exactly how it should be, because any-one who needs three rows of seats has plainly done the children thing and no longer has any need for sleek curves and a barking, snarling exhaust. Or they are a taxi driver. In which case, the same thing applies.

Inside, the seats can be moved about so easily that even I managed it without swearing once. And when they are folded away, the boot is more than 700 litres bigger than the boot in a Golf. It's so big, in fact, that you could transport a medium-sized horse, no problem at all.

And get this: there are forty-seven cubbyholes. Which means it's no use at all for someone who needs forty-eight places to store stuff. But for everyone else it's great. My test car also had a glass roof. Which was nice, for no reason that I can think of.

Other touches include an optional system with an app called Cam-Connect that, when used in conjunction with a GoPro Hero4 camcorder, feeds an image or – if you're stationary or driving slowly – footage of what's happening in the back to the screen on the dash. I thought at first this might be some kind of porn-based feature, but it's so you don't have to turn round to see if the children are fighting.

And you don't have to shout at them either because your voice is picked up by the hands-free unit and fed via the speakers to the people in the back. VW really has thought this one through.

To drive? Well, apart from the manual gearbox, it was pretty good. Perhaps it's not quite as comfy over the bumps as a Renault Scénic, but the upside of this is that the people in the back are less likely to become vomity should you ever find yourself on a switchback road in the Atlas Mountains.

I've said for many years that the only people carrier worth buying is Volvo's XC90, but the new one is very big – and pricy. I also used to quite like the Vauxhall Zafira, which had a clever seating arrangement, but I see from the tabloid newspapers that these days Vauxhalls are even more likely to burst into flames than hoverboards.

And so, if you've given up on life, you've got children and you just need a sensible family car to move you around while you wait to die, the Touran is probably your best bet.

7 February 2016

A sporty number . . . for Terry and June

Suzuki Vitara S

Back in the 1950s, when James May was an old man and everyone on the radio sounded like the Queen, Hillman launched a two-tone version of its Minx saloon called the Gay Look. *Autocar* magazine was very impressed and put it on the cover, under the headline 'Go gay with Hillman'.

I'm not sure why I've brought that up. Perhaps it's because I've been thinking about the old Suzuki jeep. Actually, Jeep is a registered trademark, so we can't call it that. And we can't call it gay either. But you know the car I mean: the SJ410. That sit-up-and-beg run-about that was popular with hairdressers and airline stewards in Brighton in the 1980s. God, it was terrible. Putting the roof on was more complicated than building a circus marquee, and it never quite fitted properly, which meant that if you actually wanted the poppers – oo-er – to do up, you had to use your fingernails to stretch the fabric until they all came out.

So then you'd have no fingernails and you'd think life couldn't possibly be worse, but it was, because then you'd have to get inside and go for a drive. Except you didn't drive a Suzuki SJ. You bounced. It was fitted with the same suspension – and I mean exactly the same – as you would find on a medieval ox cart.

This meant that it was simply a system for suspending the body. And that's all it did. It had less give than a dining-room table so, if you ran over a speed hump at anything more than 15mph, you took off. And then you bounced down the road with blood pouring from your ruined fingers until you hit the next speed hump. Or a manhole cover. Or a small piece of gravel. Which would cause you to bounce into a parked car, or a lamppost.

On a motorway things were extremely scary, because in an accident the car could bounce and then land sideways, which would cause it to roll over. And because it was a convertible, your head would come off and then you'd be gouting blood from your severed neck as well.

Happily, the top speed was very low. Or at least I think it was. It's hard to say for sure because, once you got above about 40mph, the noise from the 1-litre engine was so enormous that your ears would start to bleed.

And then we get to the steering. There was a wheel, which gave you hope, but any attempt to use it as some kind of directional control device was pointless. Because when you are bouncing, the wheels are mostly off the ground and, as a result, you have no real say in where you're going. Once, I drove a Suzuki SJ and ended up at Spurn Point in East Yorkshire.

And the prospect of driving back to London and possibly ending up by mistake in Paignton was so awful that I seriously considered staying there for ever. A lifetime in Hull? It's better than three hours on a motorway in an SJ.

Weirdly, however, on holiday I would often rent an SJ. It was a cheap way of putting some wind in my hair. And around town, on a sunny day, it was an unusual and rather endearing alternative to the hatchback norm. It was cheaper, too.

If I'd had a farm, or a shoot, or some kind of agricultural job back then, I'd have had an SJ, because it had four-wheel drive and it was fitted with nothing other than four seats and a couple of windscreen wipers. So there was nothing to break. That car? It was horrid. But it was honest.

Today, the spirit of the SJ lives on. The modern Suzuki Jimny is certainly safer. But it has a permanent roof, so the main appeal of the original is gone. Shame.

There are glimmers of the spirit in the larger Vitara, too. But even in the apparently sporty 1.4 S model I drove, they are buried beneath a Terry-and-June suet pudding of bland, inoffensive, dreary, lacklustre, unimaginative pigswill. This car is wilfully boring. They've painted the wheels black and the air vents nail-varnish pink in a desperate, last-minute bid to give it some soul, but it hasn't worked. Partly because the exterior of my test car was red. And red and pink work together only in the mind of the Queen's interior designer.

I pretty much hate all the small SUVs. The Nissan Juke. That Renault thing. The Ford with the sliding doors. There's a Vauxhall, too. No idea what it's called. I hate the fakery, the way they seem to suggest they are rugged and sensible four-wheel-drive off-roaders that will work at a gymkhana but, actually, they're just expensive, ugly hatchbacks.

The Vitara has another problem. It feels quite astonishingly flimsy and cheap. The rear doors couldn't weigh less if they'd been made from tracing paper, and the dash has less of a robust feel than a supermarket carrier bag.

However, there's an upside to this. Because there's no substance at all to any of the components in this car, it weighs a bit less than a mouse. And that means it is more fuel efficient, and faster, than it would be if it felt heavy and durable.

And there's more. My car came with a reasonably sophisticated four-wheel-drive system, so it actually could go into gymkhana car parks. And then come out again.

A little more digging reveals that, for the money, you get quite a few toys as standard. There's DAB radio, which cuts out if you're near a building, and all sorts of 'connectivity', whatever that is. You even get a system that beeps if it thinks you are going to run into the car in front. That sounds tremendous, but it was plainly set up by the winner of last year's butter-side-down award, because, ooh, it was pessimistic. 'Beeeeep,' it would shriek, as you joined the A1 in London. Because, in its mind, you were definitely on a collision course with Edinburgh Castle.

Other issues. Well, getting in and out's not easy, because the roof line is too low – it's worse, apparently, if you have the panoramic sunroof. And putting just about all the controls on the central screen may have sounded a good idea in a meeting but, in practice, it doesn't work at all. When a nasty song comes on the radio, it takes you a long time to find your spectacles, and even longer then to find the volume graphic.

There's plenty, then, to not like in this car. It's very boring to look at, it feels more flimsy than pretty much anything on the road and there are some practical annoyances. But hidden beneath all this is an honest little car, and one that is quite likeable. It drives well, zooms along and is made in Hungary, which is a byword for good quality.

If you have a not-very-successful fencing-repair business, it might be just the job.

14 February 2016

The beancounters' gift to box-haulers

BMW X1 xDrive 25d xLine

John Terry is the lion-hearted soul and backbone of Chelsea Football Club. If he leaves at the end of the season, as has been reported, and is carted off to a home for used footballers, he will be replaced by someone called Schmitt or Ng or Aspuertoli-Detomaso-Gorva-Didivichlaboueff. And then will Chelsea be Chelsea any more?

What will give the team their character? How will they be different from Arsenal or Manchester United, or any of the other clubs that, behind the chanting, will be just businesses that employ the best people?

At present, my son argues pretty much all the time with his mates about football. He loves Chelsea. His mates don't. But how will they be able to stoke up that level of passion when their clubs become like Sainsbury's and Tesco and Lidl? Because nobody gets into all-night debates about which of those does the best sandwiches.

I worry about this sort of thing with car manufacturers, too, because all of them earned their reputations back at a time when their products were designed and engineered and built by people from a specific area. An Alfa Romeo felt Italian. An Austin really didn't. That was important.

But, today, car-makers have to keep that spirit and that heritage alive when it isn't second nature to the people who work there. The Germans who run Rolls-Royce have to guess what a British engineer would do. The Italians who run Jeep have to think American. And the Indians who run Jaguar have to read in history books what a Jag should be like. (And sometimes I wish they'd pay more attention.)

Look at Citroën. Its design offices will be more international than Arsenal's Christmas party, but somehow it's got to make a product that feels French and quirky and odd. You can see this in the products, this desperation. And you can feel it, too – a sense that it has built an ordinary, global car and then given it some silly design touches that it hopes will cause customers to imagine they are driving around in President Charles de Gaulle.

That's a bit like replacing John Terry with an Argentinian and then asking him to call everyone 'geezer' at post-match press conferences. We won't be fooled.

Amazingly, though, we are mostly fooled by cars. The Suzuki I reviewed last week is built in Hungary, but it still feels Japanese. A Bentley is built largely from Volkswagen components, but at no point when you are driving a Continental GT do you think: 'Mmmm. It's as if I'm in a bar in Baden-Baden.'

And the Alfa Romeo 4C? Not once when you're behind the wheel do you ever think: 'I wonder. Is this Australian?'

Then there's BMW. Its cars are made from the same components that you find in any other vehicle, and I don't doubt the design team is fully international, and yet they all feel as though they were conceived and built by a team that started the day with a few star jumps and then went to work wearing raspberry- or mustard-coloured jackets and extremely clean shoes. They feel utterly German.

Except for the horrible old X1. You got the distinct impression that BMW's engineers – quite rightly, in my view – didn't want to build a so-called crossover. They felt such cars were all right for Renault and Chrysler and Terry and June, but not for a company that had spent fifty years building a reputation for finesse and driving pleasure. BMW making a hatchback on stilts? That's like Rolls-Royce making a van.

So they had it made in factories in India, China and Russia, and it felt like it. In fact, it felt like a cement mixer. It was rough, impractical, ugly and slow. No crossover car is particularly nice, but this one? Ooh, this one missed the bar by about 40 miles.

Unfortunately for the BMW purists, it was a huge sales success, so the company had to make a newer version. And with this it has really thrown away not just the bathwater and the baby but the bath as well. It has a BMW badge, but it doesn't feel, sound or drive like any Beemer I've been in.

I'd love to have been a fly on the wall when the accountants met the engineers for the weekly catch-up. 'Look, you lot. We are in business and, to survive, we must make this car. It's what customers want these days, so stop cocking about and do it properly.'

Well, they didn't. They simply decided to mount the new car on the same platform as the Mini. Which means the engine is mounted sideways – that goes against the grain for BMW – and in some models it drives the front wheels, which is the devil's work so far as they're concerned. The styling? I think they did that with the lights off.

They've even fitted the gear-lever surround with a shiny plastic that reflects everything you drive under. So when you go down a motorway you can see out of the corner of your eye the lampposts speeding by. After a few miles this will give you an epileptic fit.

BMW says that, despite the way it looks and the people it's

aimed at – caravanists, basically – it's still pretty fast. But the range-topping TwinPower 2-litre diesel that I drove didn't feel speedy. In fact, it left the line about as enthusiastically as its designer got out of bed in the morning. With a plaintive cry of: 'Must I?'

My test car was fitted with four-wheel drive, so you might think it'd be able to deal with a bit of muddy ground. Nope. On a short piece of level grass it was skidding about all over the place.

Comfort? Well, the suspension's not bad, but the seats put me in mind of my old school desk. And while the boot is quite long, it's not very wide. I suppose it'd be all right if you had to transport a coffin. Or me. The only other thing of note back there is how you open the boot. You wave your foot about as if you're doing some kind of *Riverdance* routine and it pops up.

I'd love to be able to say at this point that because the X1 is so meh – that's the first time I've used this word – and because it's based on the Mini, it is at least priced keenly. But compared with its rival from Nissan, it's actually quite expensive.

I suppose that, all things considered, it's not a bad car. It doesn't crash all the time, or explode. If it were a Kia or a car from one of those weird Chinese companies, you'd say it was quite nice. But because it says 'BMW' on the back, and because you know just how good BMW can be, you expect something better.

21 February 2016

I did not expect the wandering hands

BMW 730Ld M Sport

If you are the Austrian finance minister, or an African dictator, or the managing director of a successful carpet business in West Yorkshire, then you will have a chauffeur-driven S-class Mercedes. And it's easy to see why.

Mercedes tests every new invention to see if it really offers any benefit. And if it does, Mercedes fits it to the S-class. So this was the first car in the world to have airbags. The first with seatbelt pre-tensioners; the first with crumple zones. This means it's always ahead of the pack. It's always the yardstick.

But BMW has come up with a cunning plan for its new 7-series. The company has looked at what you get in the S-class and then it's added a bit more. Let me give you an example. Mercedes fits the S-class with a system that monitors the driver's face. If it thinks he's getting drowsy, it sounds a gentle bong and suggests he pull over for a cup of coffee.

BMW has gone further, so that with its system the driver can choose what level of drowsiness he must achieve before the bong sounds. Seriously. You can tell the monitors to leave you alone if you are just having forty winks but wake you if you fall into deep REM sleep. Can you see why this would be useful? No? Me neither.

Then you get an optional system that means you can

remotely park the car. I kid you not. You can pull up. Get out. And tell the car to park itself. That's fantastic, but Mercedes would have said: 'Why would someone want to be outside the car, in the rain, while it parks?' And it's a good question, if I'm honest.

BMW has also reinvented the ignition key. It's now a sort of mini iPad, and it will tell you how many miles your car can go before it needs refuelling and when it requires servicing. You can even use it to start the air-conditioning. Lovely. But the key is so big, it sits in your pocket like a brick.

By far the worst feature of the car, however, is the rear seating, which is fitted with a massage facility. We've seen this before, of course, but BMW has gone berserk by offering a whole range of massages, none of which comes with a happy ending.

There's one that comes close, though. It gives you the sensation of someone fondling your buttocks. I found it vaguely horrifying. I needed to turn it off and reached for the central command screen, which is located in the armrest. I turned it on and it said it needed to receive a system update. Crying with the shame and humiliation, I waited until the update was complete, dived into the menu, found the seat controls and stabbed at the massage button, only to be told this feature needed a system update too.

Eventually, I realized that you can turn the massaging off with an old-fashioned button but, when I did that, one of the little bags that inflate and deflate remained pumped up, so it felt as if I were sitting on a snooker ball.

And even when I did manage to get the seat to be just a seat, it wasn't very comfortable, and there was an annoying rattle, possibly from the rear privacy blind or possibly from the fridge.

After that, I sat playing with the voice-activated system, which, it turns out, understands what you're on about only if you impersonate Donald Sinden. You need to roll your 'r's and enunciate as if you're the over-eager lead in an am-dram production of *The Corn is Green*.

Because this is tiresome, you may be inclined to use the touchpad. On this, you simply trace the letters of, say, the town you want to go to. But it is in the centre console, so you must use your left hand. Which means that if you're not left-handed, the car thinks you're a drooling infant.

If you don't want to write like a three-year-old or talk like Donald Sinden, you can use gesture control. Seriously: if you wave your index finger like Robert Duvall summoning a chopper evac from a Vietnam battlefield, the volume on the stereo goes up. Which is tremendously clever. But it does cause people in cars alongside to think you have taken leave of your senses.

It's worse, though, if you want to skip to the next track, because then you must flick a V at the stereo. And because it won't register the first time, you have to do it again. And then, usually, again.

That's exactly what I was doing one evening last week when my rear-view mirror filled with blue lights. It seems that while I was telling my car to eff off over and over again, I'd driven past a government camera that had noted the 7-series was uninsured.

While calls were made and checks done, I stood with one of the officers, laughing about the technology that had made the mistake. 'You don't need a camera linked to a central database to find uninsured cars,' I said. He agreed, and at that moment a six-year-old Škoda Superb minicab went by. We both laughed because, of course, the point was made.

You sense the same issues in the new 7-series. It uses the satnav, for example, to decide what sort of road surface and what sort of bend lie ahead, and then it sets up the air suspension to provide the right balance between comfort and handling. I can't even begin to imagine how much software code is needed to do this. But I do suspect that a boffin in a brown store coat could achieve better results using a spring.

The Comfort Plus mode does make the ride almost unbelievably soft, but in high winds on a motorway it felt as if the damn thing was chine walking.

Also, the 7-series is confused by potholes and it's not quite as quiet as you might imagine. You sense that there was a dilemma in the early stages of this car's design: should it be a BMW with inherent sportiness, or should it be an out-and-out limo? The result is a car that's sort of neither.

That said, the interior design is lovely – far nicer than in the Mercedes. And because there's so much stuff to play with, you will never get bored in a traffic jam.

But I think the main reason you'd buy the 7-series is that everyone else has an S-class. It's a reasonable point, except the reason everyone else has an S-class is: it's a better car.

28 February 2016

Sit back and let it torque the torque

Lexus GS F

When the Lexus first arrived at my house, I decided I liked it. And when it went away a week later, I liked it even more. Even though it had been annoying.

I think one of the reasons I like it is that I like most small-ish, fast saloon cars. They seem to make sense, because you don't really need 6 acres of room in the back. The rear seats are for children, and after a party they're happy to sleep on the floor, so they certainly won't mind being squashed for a few minutes.

And it is only ever a few minutes. It's not as though you take them to the Kamchatka Peninsula every morning, so they're not going to develop gangrene or anything like that.

No, a smallish saloon the size of a BMW 3-series is all you really need. Which of course brings us on to the father figure and trailblazer of the 3-series range. The M3. The latest incarnation is not perfect. If you put the steering in anything other than Comfort mode, it feels lifeless and twitchy at the same time.

Also, its engine is turbocharged. There used to be a time when turbocharging meant that you put your foot down and nothing happened while the exhaust gases spooled up the fan. Then everything happened all in a big rush and you careered into a tree.

That doesn't happen any more. There is no discernible lag at all in an M3, but all the time you know the power is coming from witchcraft and that, if it weren't for various pie-in-the-sky EU emission regulations, BMW would not be using forced induction. It's effective. But it's not proper. It is to engineering what cornflour is to cooking. A cheat.

The engine in the Lexus GS F is not turbocharged. It's a 5-litre 32-valve double-overhead-camshaft V8. It's old-school. It's a roux. And I liked it a very lot. I especially liked the noise.

In the mid-ranges – up to, say, 4,500rpm – it sounds baleful and hollow, like a lonely wolf. But if you keep your foot planted in the carpet and go up past 6,000rpm, it starts to sound as though it's angry about being a hollow wolf. It sounds – and this is the highest praise you can lavish on any car – like a Ferrari 458 Italia.

It doesn't develop as much torque as a BMW M3, but at no point do you ever think: 'Hmm. This is a bit slow.' Because it isn't. And it isn't fitted with a speed limiter either, which means that, flat out, you'll be knocking on the door of 170mph.

If anything, it stops even better than it goes, thanks to enormous Brembo brakes, and because it's fitted with an eight-speed gearbox – which I thought was completely unnecessary when Lexus announced it – you're never in a torque hole. Not that the holes from a 5-litre V8 are likely to be that deep anyway.

I've got to heap praise at this point on the comfort. Yes, this is a stiff car, and, yes, the suspension is firm. But even at slow speeds on Boris's ploughed roads in London, it's never harsh or wince-inducing.

The only fly, really, in the driving ointment is the steering, which at low speeds feels as if it would rather be doing something else. It's always fidgeting, as though it just wants class to end so it can go home. At higher speeds, however, I've no complaints at all.

I read a road test of this car in one of the 'oversteer is everything' car magazines recently, and the writer said that he preferred it to the AMG Mercedes and the BMW M3. And, thinking of it as a driving tool, I'm with him. It really is that good.

But, oh deary me, it doesn't half try its hardest to make you hate it. First of all, if I put anyone in the passenger seat, the brakes squeaked, and every time anyone tried to retrieve a can of zesty drink from the cup-holders, the satnav immediately decided it wanted to go to Pinner.

The problem is, Lexus decided several years ago that a computer-style trackpad was the best way to operate the central command and control system. Time has taught everyone else that it isn't, because it's too fiddly and too sensitive and the trackpad itself is mounted right next to the cup-holders.

Lexus, however, will not be deterred, so instead of enjoying the braking or the old-fashioned V8 power, what you're actually doing most of the time is concentrating, with the tip of your tongue out, on getting the little arrow over the icon you want and then swearing when you miss and end up going to Pinner again.

Oh, and once it's decided it's going to Pinner, then that's where it's going. There is no changing its mind. And to make everything worse, it tells you every fifteen seconds that it has found a new route, and would you like to accept it? I learned eventually just to say yes and let it get on with its trip to the

London suburbs while I used signposts and common sense instead.

Other things? Plenty. The wiper stalk is on upside down; there are several million buttons on the steering wheel that all retune the stereo system to Radio 3; and just about the only knob of interest is the big silver one on the centre console that ruins everything. It changes the settings of the car to either Eco, which isn't interesting, or Sport S, which is bumpy, or Sport S+, which would work only at the Nürburgring. But you're not at the Nürburgring, because you've just reached for your can of refreshing orange pop and now you're going to Pinner again.

I'd love to tell you that the problem is that the GS F is too clever for its own good but, actually, there are almost no gimmicks at all. There's no voice activation or wi-fi connectivity or any of the stuff you see these days on even fairly humble Fords. It can't even park itself, for crying out loud. And my Golf GTI can do that.

I assumed that this back-to-basics approach would mean that the Lexus sat at the bargain-basement end of the spectrum. But no. I damn nearly fell off my chair when I found out it costs, as near as makes no difference, £70,000. That's BMW M5 money.

And then I fell off my chair again when I found that, while it feels small and nimble like an M3, it's actually – give or take 5 millimetres – the same length as the 5-series. It's uncanny. And it's another tick in the box, because a car that shrinks around you is a good thing.

This is the best Lexus I've driven since the LFA, which is also riddled with annoying details but remains my all-time favourite car.

I wouldn't blame you at all if you went off and bought a BMW M3 or M5 instead. They're both tremendous. But don't assume they're the best of breed. Because, in my book, this flawed old-school charmer has them beat.

6 March 2016

Bubbling with ideas for inventors to pinch

Suzuki Swift 1.2 SZ2

I'm baffled by the car industry's apparent reluctance to think more seriously about hydrogen as a replacement for petrol and diesel. Hydrogen is the most abundant element in the universe, so we wouldn't run out of it for about a billion years, and it's clean too. A car powered by hydrogen fuel cells produces nothing from its tailpipe but water.

Right now, we have the technology to make hydrogen-powered vehicles, and yet, by and large, the car industry is sitting on its hands. Several years ago, with a fanfare provided by a lone bugler on a distant hillside, Honda leased out a handful of test examples in California, but then the bugler stopped playing and went home. And we've heard very little since.

Like everyone else, Honda is now making hybrids that use two motors to combat the problem of overconsumption. And the demand for hydrogen is so low that, in the whole of the UK, only four public filling stations stock it.

Rather gamely, a small Welsh company called Riversimple is swimming against the tide and has developed a hydrogen car called the Rasa. It's clever because it uses electricity garnered from braking to provide acceleration and electricity from hydrogen fuel cells to provide a gentle cruise.

But while the Rasa is made from all sorts of exotic materials, the company has given the poor little thing styling that Riley would have dismissed for being rather old-fashioned, and then added tyres that W. O. Bentley would have called 'a bit thin'. Any normal person would look at it and think: 'You know what – I think I'll stick with my Ford Fiesta.'

This is what the modern-day pioneers of future propulsion systems must remember: we know how a car should look, and we simply won't take the plunge if it looks odd in any way.

It's like houses. We may swoon over the cleverness of modern architecture in magazines but, when push comes to shove, we all want to live in something that looks as though it was designed by a Georgian.

This is where Riversimple is going wrong. It's no good saying that the Rasa weighs about the same as a mouse, uses almost none of the world's resources to move about, produces only water and could be used at night, silently, to provide electricity for a whole street. Which it could. Because no one is going to drive a car that causes other people to laugh at them.

Extreme petrolheads crave the extraordinary and will even drive a car that has no windscreen if they think it will deliver one more mile an hour, but everyone else craves the ordinary. They want to blend. And going to the shops in a Rasa would be like going to a funeral in a scuba suit. You wouldn't blend at all.

Talking of scuba suits, I recently needed one when I was filming in Barbados for my new Amazon Prime motoring show.

I also required some wheels for this important work, and that was a problem, because every single hire car on the entire island had been rented to someone else. Which turned out to be good news, because all these people had drunk far too many rum punches to know what a car was, or that they'd rented one, or where it was, which meant I could nick it.

The car I decided to nick was a small Japanese saloon with black wheels and extremely squeaky brakes. Each time I tried to slow down it sounded as if I was lowering a cement mixer on to a cat. Oh, and the steering wheel was loose. And the engine was so gutless that, every time I tried to speed up, literally nothing happened.

Barbados is not a mountainous country – it can in no way be confused with, say, Bhutan or Switzerland – but there are a few gentle hills and all of them flummoxed my small, white Japanese saloon car. I'd row away desperately at the gear lever, but it was futile. The only way of getting up even the smallest incline (I nearly said 'slope' then) was to arrive at it doing about 100 miles an hour.

However, on the fourth day I grew to rather like it. And I didn't work out why until the fifth day, when I realized that I'd somehow got into another small Japanese car and was using that by mistake. This one was different from the first one, partly because it was blue and partly because it had a bullet hole in the door. But mostly because it was excellent. So excellent that I went round the back to see what it was. And – surprise, surprise – it was a Suzuki Swift.

I know this car well. We used Swifts when playing games of car football on the Clarkson, Hammond and May world tour, so I know they are nippy and that they have a great turning circle, especially if you use the handbrake. I can also tell you, because car football is quite a violent contact sport, that they are good in a crash.

I have crashed a Suzuki Swift probably 500 times in the past few years, so I know they can take an enormous impact without breaking. The only real problem is that the washer bottle can burst if you slam the front-left corner into James May's door while doing about 70mph.

I've even driven a Swift on the road. It was the Sport model and I seem to recall I gave it four stars. I can't recall why I didn't give it five, because it was fast and fun and extremely good value for money.

The car I drove in Barbados was not the Sport version. It was the cooking model, and I should imagine that it therefore represents even better value. You could probably buy the car I had for about £1. Mainly because of the bullet hole.

As you probably know, my every-day car is a Volkswagen Golf GTI. I drive one because it costs less than £30,000 and does everything you could reasonably expect from a car today. Well, the Swift does everything for less than £10,000. So that makes it even better, in my book.

It has whizzy acceleration, a smooth ride, space in the back for grown-ups, a decent boot, fun handling and excellent fuel economy. No, it can't park itself, there's no wi-fi hub and you have to use a map if you want to know where you're going. But it has a fuel gauge and electric windows, and that's all you need, really.

Best of all, though, you don't stand out. It's a plain-Jane, ordinary box – 12.5 feet of car. It's the shortest poppy in the field. And it should therefore be the shape that all the future-fuel start-up businesses adopt.

Because if a car looked like this, produced only water and could power our house at night, we'd buy it. And then the motor industry would stop fiddling about with its pointless batteries and its hybrid-drive systems and get on the only road where there is actually a future for personal mobility. The hydrogen road.

13 March 2016

Mix iron, wood and little boys' dreams

Ford Mustang Fastback 5.0 V8 GT Auto

Plainly, someone at Ford in Detroit was given an atlas for Christmas because, after fifty years or so of making the Ford Mustang, the company has decided to put the steering wheel on the correct side of the car and to sell it in the hitherto unknown Great Britainland.

Many of us on this side of the Pond have known about the Mustang for years. We've seen it in lots of films and when we go on holiday to California it's what we rent to drive up the Pacific Coast Highway. Of course it is. You can hire cars for less, but the Mustang brings out our inner line dancer. And for a couple of weeks that's not such a bad thing.

Because of the films and the fond memories we have of rumbling through Monterey with 'The Boys of Summer' on the CD player, we like the Mustang. However, just because something works when we are on holiday, it won't necessarily work on a miserable Tuesday morning in November in Leamington Spa.

I've always harboured a concern that the Mustang is a bit like a Greek fishing-boat captain. In Greece, after a couple of hundred retsinas, it seems perfectly natural to take him to your bed. But would you want to bring him home and introduce him to your mother?

Or food. I was once invited by the owner of a restaurant in Hanoi to suck out the still-warm brains of a dead sparrow, and I must admit I enjoyed the experience very much. They were delicious. But in the office, when I have only a couple of minutes for lunch, I'd rather have a cheese-and-pickle sandwich.

So this is the question I must answer. The Mustang: is it a viable proposition in Britain? Or is it nothing more than a come-hither poster boy for Hertz?

Well, first of all, we must take a long, hard look at the price. And you'll need to sit down for this, because the 5-litre V8 Fastback GT auto coupé I've been using is £35,995.

This means it costs less than half what Jaguar makes you pay for a superficially similar F-type. More incredibly, this 410bhp, 155mph American icon costs less than I paid for a Volkswagen Golf GTI. I do not know of any car that appears to offer such good value for money.

It's not as if you just get an engine and four seats either. Because it comes as standard with a limited-slip differential (yeah), selectable driving modes, dual-zone air-conditioning, a rear-view camera, DAB radio, and so on.

Confused by the price tag and the sheer amount of stuff you get free, I plunged into the cabin with a raised eyebrow, looking for where Ford had cut corners. It doesn't take long to find them. Lada would describe the plastics under the steering wheel and around the glovebox as 'a bit cheap', and I suspect the seat leather came from a polyurethane cow. But that, really, is it.

All things considered, I'd say that I prefer the look of the Mustang's dash to the rather dreary affair Jaguar fits to the F-type. It's more exciting. Let me give you an example. On the speedo it says, 'Ground speed'. How delightfully child-like is that?

And there's more. On the bonnet are two massive ridges

that reflect the glare of the sun directly into the driver's eyes. Now, Ford's engineers must have noticed this when they tested the car in the vast, unending blueness of the Arizona Desert. And they must have said afterwards: 'Hank. We can't see where we are going because of those ridges.'

And then there will have been a meeting at which someone must have stood up and said: 'We take your point, Bud, but those ridges look good, so they're staying.'

I like that attitude. Style over practicality. And you see it everywhere. The speeding-horse symbols that are projected by down lighting on to the ground under the door mirrors. It's as though Ford only employed designers who were ten. Which is as it should be. Ground speed. I love that. I'm only amazed it doesn't have space lasers.

So far, then, so American. But now it's time to fire up the surprisingly quiet V8 and see how it copes with the Hammersmith Bridge width restrictions and the M3 roadworks and doing a three-point turn in Monmouth Road, west London.

Straight away, there's an issue. In America, the Mustang is a small car. But in the UK, it is ginormous. And it has the turning circle of Jupiter. Which means that a three-point turn in Monmouth Road is actually a seventy-two-point turn with much swearing.

It also feels a heavy car. After just a yard you start to understand why the Jag costs so much more: because it's made of exotic materials. The Mustang is made from steel and iron and, possibly, wood.

It's billed as a sports car, but that's like calling the *Flying Scotsman* a 'sports train'. It just isn't. It's too heavy. What it is, is a muscle car. And you sense that in the second yard. This is a machine that wants to turn its tyres into smoke and go round every corner sideways. You've seen the film *Bullitt*. Well, it's that.

This is emphatically not a criticism, because who wants to go round the Nürburgring in forty seconds when you can go round slowly, sideways and smiling?

It doesn't have to be this way, of course, because for more than fifty years the Mustang has been built as a starting point. Only rental companies buy one and then leave it alone. Everyone else buys one and then employs a tuning company to turn it into something else. That's what I'd do with this model: buy it and then give the money I'd saved by not buying something else to Hennessey or Roush. Those guys can make a Mustang fly.

Don't get me wrong. The Mustang as it is can be driven quite normally. It moves around quite a lot on poor surfaces, indicating that it has fairly rudimentary underpinnings, but for the most part it's quiet, docile and rather unassuming. Too unassuming, perhaps. Because, despite the flamboyant touches, the actual shape is a bit ho-hum. It's not the worst-looking Mustang — that accolade rests with the post-oil-crisis box — but it's not the best either. Not by a long way.

Certainly, it doesn't turn many heads. But I liked the reaction it caused among those who did notice it: they smiled.

Which brings me to Ford's recent advertising campaign. In the meeting at which this was dreamed up, the company will have decided to shake off its Mondeo Man image and tell everyone it now makes exciting cars. So it is showing us pictures that include the new Focus RS, the Mustang and some kind of snazzy SUV and urging us to 'unlearn'.

Well, if I 'unlearn' what I remember about Ford's past, I'll have to forget about the Lotus Cortina, the GT40 and the

Escort RS Cosworth. I'll have to forget about everything that makes people smile when they see the Mustang go by.

If I were to sum it up as a car, I'd give it four stars, because a big V8 coupé for £36,000 is remarkable. But because it's a Mustang, because of Steve McQueen: well, that makes people yearn to own one. And now you can. And there's no earthly reason why you should not.

20 March 2016

It's a blast . . . until you look for the brakes

Zenos E10 S

In the past two weeks I've been to Barbados, India, Turkey and Morocco. And having studied these places in some depth, I'm forced to ask an important question: why doesn't anyone buy sports cars any more?

By and large, driving is extremely boring. You sit there listening to the engine moaning out its one long song, with your face in neutral and your mind turned off. Just look at the faces of people when they are at the wheel and tell me this: when do you ever see people look like that in normal life? Gormless. Like fish.

When you are mowing the lawn or buying washing-up powder or having breakfast with the children, you are animated. You are thinking about stuff. But when you are driving a car, the dopamine and the serotonin and all the fun drugs that normally course through your body just dry up. You become the undead. You become a zombie.

Unless you are driving a sports car. A sports car is exciting when it's parked in a multistorey and you're in a meeting. A sports car is even exciting when it's November and it's raining and you're on your way to a funeral. Because in a sports car you are living the dream that gives 'the car' all of its appeal.

Remember 'The Ballad of Lucy Jordan'? She was sad because she'd realized at the age of thirty-seven that she'd never drive through Paris in a sports car with the warm wind in her hair. To me, that's what cars are all about. Nobody dreams of driving through Paris in a Hyundai with the warm wind in their hair.

Think of all the hundreds of thousands of people who design cars for a living. Not one of them joined up so they could design a saloon car or an SUV or a pick-up. They signed up so they could design sports cars. Because sports cars are fantastic. They fizz and they pop and they bang and they talk to you and they make you smile. Sports cars make you happy.

But I've noticed on my recent travels that people are giving up. In Barbados, everyone has a Suzuki Swift. In India, they buy whatever has the most amount of legroom in the back. In Italy, it's nothing but small grey hatchbacks. The car is being bought as a tool, not as a dream.

Remember the film *Battle of Britain*, when Christopher Plummer set off from his base to meet Susannah York for a bit of inter-sortie rumpy-pumpy? He had an MG. Of course he did. He was a Spitfire pilot. Whereas, today, I can pretty much guarantee he'd have a Nissan Juke.

I met an astronaut once. He'd been to *Top Gun* school. He could handle an F-14 on combat power. And he had been the first man to dock a Space Shuttle that was travelling at 17,500mph. And yet he drove a Toyota Camry. It was tragic.

And at this point I should explain what I mean by a sports car. It's not simply something with no roof. A Lamborghini Aventador convertible, for example, is not a sports car. It's a supercar. And neither is a Mercedes SL. Or a Bentley Continental GT.

A sports car must be little and light. It should have a small, revvy engine and no more than two seats. The Mazda MX-5 is a sports car — and a bloody good one. It's fast enough. It handles beautifully. The roof folds in a jiffy. It's also well made, reliable and prices start at just £18,495. It is the obvious choice and yet, all over Britain, there are people who wake up of a morning and think, 'If I borrow some money from the bank and get a shed, I could make a sports car that is even better.'

The latest offering comes from Norfolk. It's called the Zenos and it's a sports car unplugged. Its designers have looked at every detail of what isn't needed and simply thrown it away. Which means it has no doors, no windows, no sun visors, no radio, no carpets and no roof of any kind. I have encountered better-equipped pencils.

The result is a car that weighs just 725 kilograms. That is ridiculously light. A Triumph Herald weighed about the same and that was made from tinfoil and hope. And a Triumph Herald was not fitted with the 2-litre turbocharged engine from a Ford Focus ST. The Zenos is. Which means it has a Looney Tunes power-to-weight ratio. And that means it's bloody fast.

To drive? Well, you climb over the side, hunker down into the unpadded seat, attach the steering wheel and then do up the optional four-point harness, by which time the chap in the Mazda MX-5 – which has a fixed steering wheel and inertia-reel belts – is back from his lap of the track, talking about what fun he's had.

You're going to have more – eventually. Because when you are fastened in place and the wheel is on, the Zenos is a hoot. It's more than just a track car fitted with indicators and lights to make it road-legal. And yet you know the track is where it belongs, really.

It's good when the going is smooth and there's nothing coming the other way. It feels balanced, as it should with the engine in the middle. And as you jink this way and that, you think that maybe your commands are being sent to the four corners of the car using telepathy.

However, on the road, where I mostly drove it, the noise was fun for about a minute and then not fun at all thereafter. The exhaust bark is tremendous, but all you can hear really is the wastegate, which sounds like a fat man who's using Victorian plumbing to flush away the after-effects of a particularly enormous dinner.

The steering became wearing, too, because it's unassisted and very fidgety. It's not as bad as the set-up in an Alfa Romeo 4C, but it's quite draining nevertheless.

And then, I'm afraid, we come to what might fairly be described as the turd in the swimming pool. The brakes. In a car with not much weight at the sharp end, the front wheels have a tendency to lock up. See the original Lancia Montecarlo for details.

To get round this, the Zenos boffins have backed off on the brake force to the point where the pedal feels like it's connected to not much at all. This causes you to push it more firmly, which causes the fronts to lock up anyway.

An antilock system would solve all that, but the whole point of the Zenos is that you get no driver aids of any kind. I like that philosophy, when I'm on a sofa and someone else is doing the driving in a race, on the television. But I'll be honest, I like it a bit less when I'm heading towards a tree in a cloud of my own tyre smoke.

At a time like that, you tend to think that maybe you would have been better off in one of the other low-volume British sports cars that have the same amount of go as a Zenos. But can stop as well.

27 March 2016

For comfort and looks, a camel wins

Hyundai i800 SE Manual

The road from Marrakesh to Ouarzazate should be right up there with the best of them. It has everything. You start in the desert and then you climb through pine forests in the foothills of the Atlas Mountains up to the snow line, where it's hairpin after hairpin and drop after vertical drop.

After you crest the highest point, which is about 6,000 feet above sea level, the road surface becomes foreign-aid smooth and, as you drop down into the Sahara proper, the corners turn into third- and fourth-gear sweepers.

This is the section Tom Cruise chose to use for the bike chase in his most recent *Mission: Impossible* outing, and I can see why. It's fast and it's dangerous and I loved every inch of it. Especially because it was 85 degrees Fahrenheit and I was at the wheel of an Alfa Romeo 4C and the roof was off.

However, the road does come with one or two issues, chief among which is 'drivers going the other way', who are never really sure which side of the road they should be on. Or maybe it's because they are mostly at the wheel of ancient Renault 12s that have never been serviced and are therefore impossible to steer with any accuracy.

On one long stretch a chap going the other way pulled out to overtake a lorry and I assumed foolishly that he would see me approaching and immediately pull back on to his side of the road. So I didn't brake. And I should have done, because he kept coming for such a long time that I was able to register the fact that his face was rather gormless.

Anyway, I reversed back out of the desert and, when the dust had settled and I'd stopped swearing, I got back on the road, and 2 miles later the same thing happened again. I think there must be a rule in Morocco that states overtaking vehicles have the right of way.

It's not just the locals who cause a bit of buttock-clenching because, as Morocco is now the only country in all northern Africa that we can visit, it's become a favourite among Europe's classic-car clubs. Which means that when you are not swerving round Mr Gormless in his spit-and-Kleenex Renault, you are presented with an out-of-control E-type Jaguar with an enormous Belgian at the wheel.

I haven't even got to the biggest hazard of all yet: the roadside vendors who walk out in front of your car, even when you're doing 90mph, to see if you'd like to buy their rock. That's all they sell: rocks. I think everyone in this remote place has a rock that has been passed down for generations.

'My grandfather didn't sell this rock before he was mown down by a German in a big Healey. My father didn't sell it before he was squashed by someone in a Renault 14. And now it's my turn not to sell it either.'

Someone ought to explain to these people that tourists are unlikely to buy rocks, as there are many that can be had free at the side of the road. And indeed in their own gardens back at home. And they should certainly be told that the stopping distance of an Alfa Romeo 4C when it's travelling at, ahem, 50mph is not '1 inch'.

The fact is, though, that I didn't crash into an oncoming Renault or a speeding Chevrolet Corvette. And I didn't run over any roadside vendors and, despite a couple of near-misses, I arrived in Ouarzazate with a burnt face, hair as solid as a breeze block and a smile the size of Cheshire on my face. It had been four hours of unalloyed joy, a reminder of what it was that made me fall in love with cars in the first place.

But then two days later I had to drive back to Marrakesh on the same road, and the Alfa Romeo was not available. Which meant I had to hitch a ride with my colleagues James May and Richard Hammond in the back of a Hyundai i800 people carrier. This would provide a rather different experience.

First of all, there was the seating. I was sitting in the middle, on what Hyundai probably bills in the brochure as an airline seat. But 'church pew' is nearer the mark. And to make life even less comfortable, the bench in the back wouldn't anchor properly, so every time our driver touched the brakes, Richard Hammond clattered into my spine.

Then there was the view. I love a desert. A man can get in touch with himself in the vastness. But when you're in the back of a Hyundai i800, it feels as though you're watching the world go by from inside a police van. You don't even get wind-down windows; just a sliding flap that would be familiar to owners of the original Mini. Which brings me on to the air-conditioning. Or lack of it.

So I was hot and feeling like a criminal, and Richard Hammond had just clattered into the back of my head again, and then I realized this journey was not going to pass quickly because the engine under the Hyundai's bonnet was producing what appeared to be no more than 4 brake horsepower.

It's not as if it was heavily laden. We were only five up. And since one of the five was Richard Hammond, it was more like four up and a packet of biscuits. But even so, there simply wasn't enough grunt on even the longest straight to pass even the slowest lorry.

We tried to tell the driver that it was the job of oncoming drivers to get out of our way, but he didn't believe us, which meant that we wouldn't be getting to Marrakesh any time soon. Thank God I don't get car sick.

After what felt about a month I began to think that we had accidentally encountered the world's worst car. But Richard Hammond disagreed. 'It is not the worst car in the world,' he said. 'It is the worst thing in the world.'

And I think he may have been right. It's worse than that parasite that burrows into children's eyes. It's worse than the cubicle on a hot army base with a D&V outbreak. It's worse than trying on trousers, even. I would rather apply sun cream to James May's back than do that journey again in a Hyundai i800. It was, I think, the worst four hours of my life.

It's annoying. Hyundai knows how to make a decent car. But with the i800 it has chosen to make one that is boring and slow and ugly and awful. Because it probably figured there was no point trying with a car that was only going to be bought by African taxi drivers and European Catholics who'd had too many children and were consequently too exhausted to notice that they were going at only 6mph.

I will never go in one again. Even if it's three in the morning and it's raining and I just want to get home and it's what the taxi driver happens to be driving. Because I'd rather sleep on a bench and catch flu.

10 April 2016

Thor's family chariot can race a Ferrari

Volvo XC90

The Range Rover is an excellent car: fast, luxurious, well made and capable of bumping smoothly over a grouse moor. It's so excellent, in fact, that shortly after you take delivery, it will be stolen.

The problem has reached such epidemic proportions that whenever the police in London are not investigating former MPs and army officers for no reason at all, they are apparently under orders to pull over every Range Rover they see. Because chances are the man at the wheel is on his way to Albania.

I suspect this would take the sheen off the ownership experience, coming out of your house in the morning to find your car isn't there. Or finding it is there and being pulled over every 100 yards by a policeman who will assume you are rich and that therefore you must at some point have done some inappropriate touching.

So if you are not going to buy a Range Rover, what other choices do you have? Well, only one, I'm afraid. And it's the new Volvo XC90. And now your shoulders have sagged and you are thinking that, if that's the only other option, you may as well commit suicide.

I get that. As a small boy, you didn't lie in bed at night dreaming of the day you could own a Volvo. It's something you buy for practical reasons, like a pair of gardening gloves. It's what you do when you are old and everything stops working down there. It's just somewhere to sit while you wait for the Grim Reaper to pop his head round the corner and say: 'Ready?'

The old XC90 was a little different and in some ways even worse because this was a car you bought because it was a safe and practical space for your children. Which meant that it was always bought with just a hint of resentment. You weren't old enough for a Volvo. You still had fire in your loins. You could still ski and scuba dive and, at parties, women still found you attractive. You wanted a BMW M3.

But you had to have a Volvo because you needed seven seats for your kids. And it was the most practical seven-seater of them all. And it had to be a diesel, really.

The new XC90, however, is different. Yes, it's still a Volvo and, yes, it's still the most practical and sensible seven-seater of them all. But, oh my God, it's a nice place to sit. It feels like you're lounging around in one of those Scandinavian furniture shops where everything is beautiful and pale and a chair costs £2,500.

There's a diamond-cut starter button and a crystal-glass gear lever and detailing on the dials that makes the detailing on an IWC watch look like something you'd find on a proud parent's fridge door. The central command screen is like an iPad and the roof is glass and it's protected by a cool and crisp electric sunshade made from what looks like white calico.

Every other car in the world feels like the inside of a German's washbag. They're all a symphony of dark greys with red detailing. The Volvo is not like that at all. It's better. This side of a Rolls-Royce Phantom, it's the nicest interior you'll find anywhere.

And unlike a Danish chair, it's not that expensive. Prices for the entry-level all-wheel-drive diesel start at less than £47,000. And so that's that then. Or is it?

Because the car I am writing about today is a new version of the XC90. It has the same enormous body and the same spacious and wonderful interior. But this one, says Volvo, can do 134.5 miles to the gallon.

That's not a misprint. It is actually claiming that this car, which is almost 5 yards long and weighs 2.5 tons, can travel from London to Nottingham on less than 8 pints of petrol. And that's not a misprint either. Petrol. Not diesel.

Oh, and just in case you are thinking that it must be fitted with the sort of engine that you'd normally expect to find in a tin opener, consider this: it'll do 0 to 62mph in 5.6 seconds. It's as fast off the line, therefore, as a Ferrari 348.

So what we have here is a large and sensible seven-seater estate car, with an excellent Scandi interior, that can keep up with a Ferrari but do 134.5mpg. Drooling yet?

Well, obviously, there are a few things I need to point out before you rush off to the Volvo dealer. First of all, it can only do 134.5mpg in theory. You'll never manage that figure in real life. And certainly not if you go from 0 to 62mph in 5.6 seconds. Oh, and the car I tested, which had a few extras fitted, costs more than £75,000.

The design is called the T8 Twin Engine, and I like that. Most car companies use the term 'hybrid', which is another word for 'mongrel', but Volvo has been honest and told us what's what. The car has two engines.

There's a 316bhp turbocharged and supercharged 2-litre 4-cylinder petrol engine at the front that drives the front wheels. And then at the back, driving the rear wheels, there's an 86bhp electric motor. In between, where you'd expect to find a prop shaft, is where the batteries live.

This car can be charged from the mains, or by the petrol engine as you drive along. Either way, it is not going to be a vehicle you can service at home. Even if you have the Haynes manual.

There's a button on the centre console that allows you to choose whether you'd like to use power made at a power station by burning Russian gas, or power made by crushed prawns to produce oil. Most of the time I used both.

Volvo says you can travel about 27 miles on electric power, but I didn't get that far. I engaged silent drive while in the multistorey car park at Selfridges and I'd only gone down one level before a woman ran out of the shop and right in front of me. She simply hadn't heard me coming. I decided after that to use the petrol engine as well. Because that's the thing about petrol, it's not only brilliant and ecological but safe too.

Other things? Well, sitting on the optional air suspension the ride was smooth, the stereo was beyond brilliant, the seats were comfortable, the handling was better than I expected and, while I didn't understand all the read-outs on the dash, I did enjoy looking at the graphics.

Drawbacks? A couple. The petrol engine is not what you'd call refined. It sounds like a diesel and this is a sound that has no place in a £75,000 car. And the gear lever has to be nudged twice before it engages a gear.

And the size, I'll be honest, can be a nuisance. It'd be fine in Houston, which is what Sven and Thor were thinking about when they said to one another: 'Let's make it enormous.' But it can be a bloody nuisance in Britain.

You'd have this issue with a Range Rover, too, of course.

And that brings me back to the original question. Which is best? Well, for refinement and imperiousness, the Range Rover, of course. But in every other way, it has to be the Volvo. Especially the way it will always be where you left it. Because who in their right mind would ever want to steal it?

17 April 2016

It's devilishly good at rattling Mr Normal

Ferrari 488 GTB

We British like to think of ourselves as being well mannered and cultured, with a great sense of humour and a steely resolve that manifests itself in the shape of a stiff upper lip. But when you drive a Ferrari through this green and pleasant land, you realize quite quickly that, actually, we are mealy-mouthed, bitter and racked with envy and hate.

If I drive a normal car to work, I pull up to the junction at the end of my street and people let me into the slow-moving crawl on the main road. But when I'm in a Ferrari, they don't. And it's the same story on a motorway. People pull over to let a normal car overtake. But when I'm in a Ferrari, they just sit in the outside lane for ever.

In Britain, Mr Normal sees a Ferrari as a reminder that his life hasn't worked out quite as well as he had hoped. And he sees its driver as a living embodiment of the good-looking kid at school who got the girls, and the sixth-former who nicked his packed lunch on a field trip.

He believes that if he can inconvenience a Ferrari driver, just for a moment, it's one in the eye for the rich and the privileged. It's 'score one' for the little man.

Then you have the cyclists. Many, as we know, use their bicycles to wage a class war. They see all car drivers as an unholy cross between Margaret Thatcher and Hitler, so they

spit and they yell and they put footage of you on their bicyc-
ling websites when they get home.

If, however, you are in a Ferrari, they go berserk because
now you are an ambassador for the devil himself. You used
child labour to make your money. You were responsible for
Bhopal. You may even be a Tory. So it is their duty as a com-
rade to bang on your roof and scream obscenities.

Even the moderately well off can't cope with a Ferrari. It
upsets their inner zebra. Last week, in one of those towns
outside London that's exactly the same as all the others, I
encountered the owner of a hunkered-down, souped-up
BMW M3. This was his patch. He was the alpha male in this
manor. He probably owned a wine bar. And he really didn't
take kindly to someone turning up with what was very obviously a bigger member. So he came alongside and he roared
his exhausts and he danced and skittered to make me go
away. Which I did.

You simply do not get any of these responses in other
countries. A Ferrari in America is a spur, a reminder that you
need to get up earlier in the morning and try harder. In Italy,
it's a thing of beauty to be admired. Elsewhere, it's a dream
made real. But in Britain, it causes everyone to say: 'It's all
right for some.' Which is the most depressing phrase in the
English language.

And it means that for every minute of enjoyment you get
from your Ferrari, you have to endure ten minutes of abuse
and hate. This means you need a thick skin to drive one.
Unless you encounter me on your travels. Because when I
see someone driving a Ferrari these days, I want to run over
and embrace them and offer to have their babies.

The problem is capital-gains tax. Because there isn't any

on most cars, they have become a zero-rated currency. You buy something rare, then you put it in a garage, in cotton wool, and then you sell it and trouser 100 per cent of the increase in value. George Osborne gets not one penny.

This means it's your nest egg. It's your pension. It's an ISA with windscreen wipers. And so, obviously, you're not going to drive it anywhere. The risk is too great.

That saddens me because all of the world's wonderful cars are now locked away in dehumidified cellars, which means they aren't on the road, where they belong. If I were chancellor of the exchequer, I'd introduce capital-gains tax on cars tomorrow. And I'd make it retrospective. It would be a vote winner among the mealy-mouthed and the bitter. And because rare cars are now changing hands for millions, it would net enough to pay for a kiddie's iron lung or something. And, best of all, it would get all of these wonderful cars back into public view where we can enjoy looking at them.

Certainly, if I owned the Ferrari I was driving last week, I'd use it to go everywhere. I would take it on unnecessary journeys. I would volunteer to run errands for friends. And I would be happy when one of the children rang at three in the morning to say they had no money and couldn't get home. Because I could go and pick them up.

There are those who say that a 488 is not a proper Ferrari because it's turbocharged. And that turbocharging has no place on such a thoroughbred. They argue that it's turbocharged only so that it can meet EU emission regulations and that sticking to the letter of the law flies in the face of the Ferrari ethos. A Ferrari is about freedom and adrenaline and speed and passion and beauty and soul. It's not about carbon dioxide and bureaucracy.

Yes. I get that. But let's not forget that Gilles Villeneuve's

Ferrari race car was turbocharged or that the best Ferrari of them all – the F40 – used forced induction. And also let's not forget that, thanks to modern engine-management systems, you simply don't know that witchcraft is being used to pump fuel and air into the V8. It doesn't even sound turbocharged. It sounds like a Ferrari. It sounds baleful. It sounds wonderful.

And, oh my God, it's lovely to drive. You can potter about with the gearbox in automatic and it's not uncomfortable or difficult in any way. That is probably Ferrari's greatest achievement with the 488. To take something so highly tuned and highly strung and powerful and make it feel like a pussy cat.

It's so docile that you get the impression it can't possibly work when you put your foot down. But it just does. I know of no mid-engined car that feels so friendly. So on your side. There's no understeer at all and there's no suddenness from the back end either. The old 458 was not as good as a McLaren 12C. But this new car puts the prancing horse back on top. As a driving machine, it's – there's no other word – perfect.

I still hate the dashboard, though. Putting all the controls for the lights and indicators and wipers on the steering wheel is silly. And so is the satnav and radio, which can be operated only by the driver.

I suppose you'd get used to it if you used the car a lot. And that's the best thing about the 488. Because you can. James May recently bought the old 458 Speciale, which, because the car market is mad, has rocketed in value to such an extent that he hardly ever uses it.

The 488, because it's not a limited-edition special, will not make you any money. So you can, and you may as well, use it as a car.

Yes, it'll cause everyone else on the road to become Arthur Scargill. But look at it this way. When you're filling it with fuel and you're being sneered at by the man at the next pump, give him a real reason to dislike you. Saunter over and point out that, if you didn't have a Ferrari, it would make no difference to his life.

He'd still be on his way to a useless garden centre, in his crummy Citroën with his ugly wife and his two gormless children.

24 April 2016

The superbarge gets a rocket up its rear

Mercedes-AMG C 63

Right. Let's be clear on one thing straight away. If you have a BMW 3-series, or a Mercedes C-class, or an Audi A4, then you are driving the wrong car. Because what you should have is a Jaguar XE.

It may appear to be an ordinary four-door saloon, but actually, if you stand back for a moment and look at it properly, you will notice that it is extremely handsome. The body appears to have been stretched over the wheels, which gives the impression that it's ripped, that it's barely containing its internal organs.

And that's just the start of it. I was bombing about last week in the V6 version, and, oh my word, what an engine. It doesn't move the needle very much when it comes to power or torque. It delivers what you were expecting. No more. No less. But the noise it makes when you accelerate is sublime. Not since the Alfa Romeo GTV6 have I heard such a muted, mellifluous sound. And it seems to be coming from the engine itself, not electronic trickery in the exhaust system.

There's more. Even though it is fitted with 35 per cent profile tyres that sit on the wheels like a coat of paint and have about as much give as elm, the car is not busy or crashy in any way. Life gets a bit hectic if you put it in Dynamic mode, so I didn't bother. I left it in Normal and settled back into a perfectly crafted seat to let it waft along in the way a Jaguar should. And the diesel version I tried a few months ago – which has taller tyres – was even better.

If I had to find a criticism, I'd say the dashboard is a bit dreary. All the buttons are small and hutched up in a corner, leaving vast swathes of plastic. I've seen more interesting-looking tabletops. And the graphics on the dials are a bit Lada circa 1974. But that's not a good-enough reason to not buy this car. Not by a long way.

The only reason you might buy something else is that you don't want an engine under the bonnet. You want a howling, fire-breathing monster. Jaguar will offer such a thing in the future, but for now it doesn't. That means if you want a superheated, medium-sized saloon car today, it comes down to a choice between the BMW M3 and the Mercedes-AMG C 63.

This is not a good-looking car. The back looks as if it's melted, and there are way too many flashy styling details. It seems as though it's crashed into an Abu Dhabi interior design shop and everything has just sort of stuck.

Inside, the news is better. It feels special. And beautifully put-together and interesting. When I had the Jag, I accidentally removed the satnav data card, and when I put it back I was told via a message on the screen that I had to turn the car off and then on again so the system could reboot. You just know that this wouldn't happen in a Mercedes. And that if it did, the man responsible would be sent into the desert with a shovel and a service revolver.

Then of course there's the engine. Gone are the days when AMG Mercs had massive, charismatic 6.2-litre V8s. Because of emission regulations, you must now make do with four litres. Sure, a brace of turbochargers means you get even more power than before, but the bellow has gone. And the crackle. Now it's just loud.

Not as loud as the tyres, though. God, they make a racket. I went to Bray in Berkshire for lunch, and when I arrived, all I wanted to eat was a handful of Nurofen.

I was also extremely uncomfortable. One of the things I used to like about AMG cars was that no real concession had been made to handling or Nürburgring lap times or any of that stuff. They were fast in a straight line and sideways in the corners. This made them fun and comfy.

But obviously someone at Mercedes has decided that AMG cars must corner flat and fast, which means the suspension has been beefed up, which means they can go round the corners more quickly, which means they have become frightening and bumpy.

Very bumpy. I know my car was running on the optional 19in wheels, which will have made things worse, but the ride really was far too stiff.

On the upside of all this, the car doesn't half shift. The mid-range acceleration is mesmerizing, and it really does cling on in the bends.

You'd imagine, then, that because the company has gone all serious and decided to change the character of the AMG from a sort of European muscle car – a Ford Mustang in lederhosen – to a finely balanced and fast road racer, it would have fitted a twin-clutch flappy-paddle gearbox. Weirdly, though, it hasn't. You still get a slushmatic that, even more weirdly, is operated via a Cadillac-style column-mounted stalk.

Regular readers of this column will know that I've been a fan of AMG Mercs for many years. I've even owned three. But the love affair is waning slightly. They're becoming too chintzy. And unsure of what they're supposed to be, which is smile-a-minute battleships. Not fast and agile motor torpedo boats.

Because if it's a fast and agile motor torpedo boat you want, you're way better off with the BMW M3. As a driver's tool, it knocks the Mercedes into a cocked hat. And it looks better. And it's easier to live with. But, that said, it too is far from perfect. The steering is weird and it feels heavy. If I were to write a school report on this car, I'd say: 'BMW can do better.'

Frankly, if I were in the market for a fast, medium-sized saloon, I'd wait six months and buy the new Alfa Romeo Giulia Quadrifoglio, which has 503bhp and rear-wheel drive and is an Alfa. But you probably don't want to wait that long for a car that you sort of know won't quite live up to its on-paper promise. 'Twas ever thus with Alfa.

Which brings us right back to the beginning. Because that Jaguar V6 is not exactly a slouch. It does 155mph, accelerates to 62mph before you've had a chance to look at the speed-ometer and corners beautifully. And it's cheaper to buy than its German rivals, costs less to run and is better-looking.

Right now, then, as I wait for the Alfa because I'm daft in the head, you should buy the Jag. Because if it's your head you're using, it's the obvious choice.

1 May 2016

The secret sex robot has testers in a fever

BMW M2

Two recently launched cars have sent the specialist motoring press into a squeaking frenzy of tinkle-clutching ecstasy. One is the Ford Focus RS, which, they say, is as good as a Nissan GT-R, for less than half the money. And the other is the BMW M2.

I'll be honest. I've yawned through their eulogies, thinking: 'I'm sure the Ford is very good . . . but only for people who can't actually afford a Nissan GT-R. And the BMW M2 is only very good for people who can't afford an M4.'

Seriously. Who in their right mind is going to wake up one morning and think: 'Yes. I have the money to pay for an M4, but I shall buy something smaller, less good-looking and with less power and less equipment instead'? That's like saying: 'I can afford to take my holiday this year on a superyacht in the Caribbean. But I've decided to rent a cottage in Margate instead. Because that'll be better.'

The problem is that not-very-well-paid road-testers are like Brummies, endlessly banging on about how Birmingham is so much better than London, when everyone else in the entire world knows it just isn't. Unless you have only £7.50 to spend on a house.

I'll be honest, then. As I climbed behind the wheel of the M2, my hackles were up. I wanted to scoff and scorn, and happily there was plenty to be disappointed about. The steering wheel was too big, the plastics were horrid, there's some kind of eco-readout on the dash and the seat was so high I felt as if I was sitting on the car rather than in it.

And, yes, while it costs considerably less than the M4, it's still a whopping £44,070, which is a lot for what is only a jumped-up, pumped-up version of the 1-series. Which is basically a BMW Golf.

But then, about an hour later, I was in a secret-squirrel car park near Stamford Bridge, on my way to that dismal Chelsea game against Manchester City. It was chock-full of Aston Martins and Range Rovers, as you'd imagine, and yet somehow the little BMW didn't look out of place at all. It may be only a 1-series in a muscle-man suit, but thanks to its flared wheelarches and the way the tyres seem to be stretched to breaking point to fit over the huge rims, it looks kinda cool. I liked it.

And then three hours after that, I was on the A1, going round a long left-hander at 70mph, and I thought: 'Hang on a minute. This steering is absolutely bleeding fantastic.' I wasn't taxing the car in any way at all; a Reliant Robin could have taken that bend at 70mph with ease. And yet I could feel that the steering was weighted perfectly and that it was talking to me in a gentle whisper.

And what makes that even more astonishing is that the power assistance is electric. Which means that the sensations were all artificial. If BMW ever makes a sex robot, you should buy one immediately, because it'll be indistinguishable from going to bed with an actual person.

Later I was overtaken by a Porsche 911 GTS that was travelling at about a million. And then, before I'd had a chance to think, 'Golly, that was quick', my world was rocked by an Aston Martin DB9 that tore by at a million and one. It's been a while since I've seen two cars really going for it on the public highway. It's a hobby I thought had been killed off by speed cameras. But plainly, up there in the flatlands of eastern England, there's nothing else to do once the turnips are planted, so the locals are still at it.

I didn't join in. Well, not much. But, coming off one roundabout, I may have put my foot down a bit, into the overboost zone of the M2's turbocharged torque lake, and there's no getting round the fact that it was faster than both of the way more expensive GT cars.

At first I thought the M2 simply felt fast because from behind the wheel it's as if you're in a low-rent hatchback. So you're not expecting much of a shove in the back. But, actually, it's fast no matter what yardstick you use. Round the Hockenheim racetrack in Germany it's faster, apparently, than its bigger brothers.

And that's because it's not just fast in a straight line. It's also fast through the corners. And not just fast, but a complete delight.

It's worth remembering at this point that while the M4 is extremely good, it is not perfect. It has a lot of electronic jiggery-pokery in the steering and suspension systems that in the M2 is gone. BMW's engineers set it up to be as good as it can be, and you aren't given buttons to change anything. That's why the M2 is cheaper than the M4: because it's less complicated. And because it's less complicated, it is a better drive. Much better. It's so good that in a few bends I was actually dribbling with joy.

Thanks to a clever electromechanical differential, it can corner with its tail out like a Looney Tunes muscle car, or right on the raggedy edge of adhesion like a proper racer. It's brilliant at both disciplines. And you want to know the best bit? It's not in the least bit uncomfortable. Sure, it's stiff, so it's a bit bumpy on poor road surfaces, but it never jars.

My only concern is that in the last small BMW M car – the 1M – I suffered the biggest and most sudden spin in my entire road-testing career. It hit a puddle while travelling in a straight line and swapped ends in an instant. Will the M2 do that? I don't know. It wasn't raining.

Away from the performance stuff, you get seats in the back that can be used by humans and a large boot. And now it's time to get back to the performance stuff, with news that the M2 comes with a launch control system that permits what are called 'smoky burnout' starts. Utterly pointless. You'll never use it. But it's fun to know you could.

There have been many M cars over the years. The lineage stretches back to 1986 and the original toe-in-the-water, left-hand-drive-only M3, which many still regard as the best. I disagree. It was too racy. Too serious. And in the wrong hands – mine, at the time – a twitching nightmare.

I like the M3 before the present model – the one with the V8 – and I adore the current M6 Gran Coupé. And then there was the original, 286bhp M5: the ultimate Q-car. It looked like the sort of box that your chest freezer was delivered in but it went like a spaceship. That's always been my favourite M car. Until now.

The road-testers were right. The M2 is a lot cheaper than the M4. And a lot better as well. It's a fabulous little car, and now I'm looking forward to getting my hands on a Focus RS. Which, apparently, is even better.

8 May 2016

It'll give Geoff all the fares he can carry

Škoda Superb estate

At school, after committing some trivial misdemeanour – hopping through the memorial garden or putting Polyfilla in all the classroom locks; I can't remember which – I was made to write a thousand-word essay about the inside of a ping-pong ball.

It was tough, but the practice was useful later, on the *Rotherham Advertiser*, where I was regularly made to file a report on what had happened at the previous evening's meeting of Brinsworth parish council. That meant coming up with six or seven paragraphs about absolutely nothing at all.

Today, though, I face my biggest challenge yet, because I must write a 1,200-word report on the Škoda Superb diesel estate, which has headlamps, a steering wheel and some seats – and that's it. Except that isn't it, because I still have a lot of space to fill.

This hasn't happened before. Not once in more than twenty years of writing this column have I sat for quite such a long time, watching the cursor blinking impatiently as it waits for me to write something down. Four times the screen has gone to sleep. I've done much the same thing twice.

I was going to explain that a Škoda Superb is a cheap way of buying a Volkswagen Passat because that's what it is, under the skin. But the truth is, you're not going to be very interested in reading about a Volkswagen Passat either. It's not a car that keeps anyone awake at night. And being told that there's a cheap way of buying one is like being told there's a cheap way of flying to Dortmund. Who cares?

I became so desperate for inspiration that I even turned to Škoda's brochure, where I discovered you can buy a Superb with a system that downloads the car's data to your iPad so you can analyse your day's driving style over supper with the family.

'Hey, kids, I pulled 0.4g on the roundabout this afternoon and hit 3200rpm at one point.' Who'd want to do that? No Škoda driver I've ever met, that's for sure.

I've met a lot of Škoda drivers over the years. They are called Geoff, and life hasn't been kind to any of them. They all had reasonable jobs, as timber salesmen or line managers, but the company they worked for was driven out of business by Chinese competition, so they ended up at home all day, eating biscuits and slowly coming to realize that they neither liked nor fancied their wife any more. To get out, they bought Škoda Octavias and set themselves up as provincial minicab drivers. Which means they now spend their evenings mopping up sick, which is better than watching *Downton Abbey* with fat women who hate them.

What they really want, of course, is to give up the late-night runs full of drunken provincial agri-yobs and get some of the airport work, because then, instead of watching *Downton* with a fat woman or clearing up sick, they can stand around in Arrivals at terminal 3 in an actual suit while waiting to pick up a businessman. And run the lucky bastard home.

And that, I guess, is where the Superb estate comes in, because it's not only cheaper than a Passat but also bigger. Much bigger. Geoff could get three adults in the back easily and every single one of their belongings in the boot. Even if they were all compulsive hoarders. It is the biggest car you can buy for £20,000.

And never mind what it says on the steering wheel about it being a Škoda. It isn't. It has a Volkswagen engine, a Volkswagen gearbox and Volkswagen electronics, and it was built by Volkswagen robots. It even has Volkswagen economy: the manufacturer claims it will average 67.3mpg. Ha-ha-ha-ha-ha.

The only trouble is that while the Superb estate is a great minicab, Geoff is unwilling to take the plunge, because he knows that as soon as he does, Uber will open in his town and he'll be back at home with his enormous wife, his place on the cab rank taken by a small man in an anorak and a Toyota Prius.

All of which means that no one is interested in the car I'm reviewing this morning. No one. Not even the minicabbers who bought its predecessor. And I still have 500 words to go.

But bear with me because I've been having a think recently about the star rating system that's used in these reviews. The Škoda Superb estate is a five-star car. It's nigh-on impossible to fault. It is beautifully made. It is equipped with everything you could reasonably expect. The 148 brake horsepower diesel engine is quiet and powerful. It is extremely good value for money. It's really rather good-looking. It is spacious and – try not to laugh – it does nearly 70mpg. Oh, go on then. Ha-ha-ha-ha-ha.

And yet it just isn't a five-star car, is it, because it has the same amount of soul as a fridge freezer. It's the sort of car that you'd buy by the foot.

'Hello. I'd like five-and-a-bit yards of car, please.'

'Certainly, Geoff. Let me show you the Superb.'

At no point when you are driving a Superb do you think, 'Eugh.' But you never think, 'Wow,' either. And that's not good enough. If you spend thousands of pounds on a holiday, you want the view and the service to take your breath away. And it should be the same thing when you buy a car. It should dazzle you.

There should be a handful of small touches here and there that are absolutely brilliant, and I'm not talking about being able to download your drive home on to a tablet. I'm talking about styling touches and finishes and noises.

I drove for 200 miles up the M1 the other morning, and it was an endless procession of cars such as the Superb. Some were Hyundais. Some were Kias. Many were Vauxhalls and Fords. And they all suffered from the same problem. They were all average. And so, in the past, they'd have got three stars in a review such as this. Because 2½ is hard to illustrate.

Well, that's going to stop. From now on, if a car is dull, no matter how competent it may be, it is not going to get more than two stars. Because unless the car companies start to let their creative juices flow, people will simply stop buying cars and go for something more convenient instead. Such as an Uber app or the number of their nearest minicab driver.

Which I guess is good news for Geoff. Cars such as the Superb are going to cause people to wonder why they bother with the hassle or the expense of car ownership when the car itself offers nothing in return. Which means there will be lots of business to go round.

So go ahead, Geoff. Buy the Superb. Because as a tool, which is what you want, after all, it's impossible to better. And, thanks to the design philosophy that created it, there's a lot of work coming your way very soon.

15 May 2016

The attack bunny has hearts thumping

Mazda MX-5

I've said it before and I'm going to say it here again, now. Nothing brilliant has ever resulted from a meeting. A meeting, by its very nature, is bound to produce a consensus. And a consensus is never going to have any peaks or troughs. Margarine came from a meeting. Butter didn't.

I once worked with a television director who let everyone argue about what we'd do next. And then he put up his hand and said, quietly but firmly: 'Right. We are going to have a meeting where only I speak and then something happens.' So that's what we did, and everything worked out well.

Gravity didn't come from a meeting. Neither did the Spitfire. But most cars today do come from meetings, and as a result they're almost all yawn-mobiles. The engineers compromise their position to accommodate the whims of the stylists, who have to compromise their views to keep the rule makers happy, who in turn must satisfy the wishes of the accountants, who are ratty because they had the engineers on the phone last night arguing about the need for multilink suspension.

And now, to make everything more complicated, you have the electronics nerds, who baffle everyone with their weird science and seem always to get their way. Probably because no one knows what they're on about. They sit talking to people who can't tell an iPhone from a fax machine about how they can use ones and noughts to change characteristics of the car as it goes along. And that sounds brilliant to a layman.

'Wow. You can make the suspension soft or medium or hard? You can change the feel of the steering, and even how much power the engine is producing?'

You can see why the board of directors and the marketing departments would go for something like that. But actually it means the way the car feels is down to the customer, who, as the IT manager for a building supply company, doesn't know one end of a shock absorber from the other.

Let me put it this way. When you buy a really good amp that's been built by a brilliant acoustic engineer, it has two buttons: one to turn it off and on, and one to adjust the volume. When you buy a really bad amp, it comes with a graphic equalizer.

And so we get to the new Mazda MX-5. The old model has been the world's bestselling sports car for about twenty-five years, thanks to a combination of low price, ease of use and a smile-a-minute factor that's up there alongside a game of naked Twister with Scarlett Johansson and Cameron Diaz.

When they were deciding what the new version should be like, the electronics people must have been there, jumping up and down and saying they had the technology to change the shape of the boot lid and make the headlights see round corners. And it must have been very tempting. But I'm glad to my core that they were told to shut up and get out.

This is a car that has been set up by engineers just the way they like it. You can't change it as you drive along. And after about a hundredth of a second you think: 'Why would I want to? Because it's completely perfect.'

Actually, that's not exactly what I thought. What I thought

was: 'God, I'm getting fat.' I didn't really struggle to fit into the old model, but in this new one I felt as though I was the corned beef and it was the tin. Passers-by could see my jowls and maybe an ear pressed against the side window, and the windscreen was just a mass of strained shirt and eyes.

To reach the main controls, located behind the gear lever, I had to dislocate my shoulder. You need to be a T Rex to turn the stereo up a notch, and getting something from the storage compartment, which is located behind your left shoulder? Forget it. I had to stop the car, get out and come in head first to retrieve my phone. And even then I put my back out.

I resolved, as I was pushed back into the driver's seat by friends, that I must go on a diet. But then I read when I got home that in fact the new MX-5 is a little shorter than its predecessor. So that's great. It's not my fault that I didn't fit. Break out the biscuits.

If you aren't an actual giant, you will be snug, but you'll fit just fine. And it's the same story in the boot, which is exactly the right size for two overnight bags.

Not that you'll want to stay the night anywhere because, ooh, this is a lovely little car to drive. Because it's so organic and raw and simple, it feels how a sports car should. It sings and fizzes and jumps about. It always feels eager and sprightly, and that makes you feel eager and sprightly too. It's a cure for depression, this car, it really is. You just can't be in a bad mood when you're driving it.

And I like the way the new model looks just a bit more serious than its predecessor. That was always a bit chumpish, really, and soft. This one looks as if it means business. It's an attack rabbit.

It's a cure for depression, this car. You just can't be in a bad mood when you're driving it.

Maybe, if you really, really concentrate when going round a long bend at about 60mph, you can feel a small dead spot in the steering. But why concentrate on that when there is 93 million miles of headroom and the sun's out and Steve Harley's on the radio and you've dropped it down to third on the sweetest little gearbox and now the engine is singing as well?

I tried the 2-litre version, which was excellent, but I'm told by others whose opinion I respect that the cheaper 1.5-litre is even better. Only one thing made me a bit cross. The satnav was, I presume, designed by the electronics nerds who weren't allowed to practise their dark arts on the suspension. So as a sort of payback they've designed a system that makes you lost. Do I deduct a star for that? Not really, because being lost in an MX-5 means you spend more time driving it, and that's no hardship.

The only thing I didn't like about the old model was a lack of personality. I drove one all the way from northern Iraq through Turkey, Syria and Jordan to Israel once, and it didn't really worm its way into my heart. The new one, though, thanks to the styling changes that make it look more serious? It probably would.

So, yeah, by not really changing much of anything at all, and by avoiding the latest trends for more complicated electronics, Mazda has once again come up with a full-on five-star gem.

22 May 2016

Gary, son of God, *v* the bean-counters

Ford Focus RS

Journalists who were invited by Ford to sample the new Focus RS at its official launch in Spain have been saying that it's certainly the greatest car yet made and that possibly it's even more than that. Quietly, using nuance and subtle phrase-making, they've been hinting that perhaps it's the new baby Jesus.

They speak of a £31,000 car that can go round corners at a million miles an hour and a five-door family hatchback that comes with a Drift mode. They say it is capable of immense speed and great comfort, and after a thousand words the reader is starting to get the picture: nobody has yet let on what form the Second Coming might take, so who's to say God's new emissary won't arrive on earth with windscreen wipers?

Hype, however, is a dangerous thing. I was told by critics that *12 Years a Slave* was an absolutely tremendous film, and it wasn't. They did the same with *Dallas Buyers Club*, and halfway through I found myself thinking: 'This is just a very long advertisement for whatever slimming pills Matthew McConaughey has been taking.'

I didn't even agree with their assessment of the new *Batman v Superman* film. They said it was terrible, and it just isn't. It's way worse than that.

Hype, then, is a nuisance for film makers. Because instead

of leaving the cinema thinking, 'That was very enjoyable,' audiences tend to leave thinking, 'That wasn't as good as the critics said.' And on that note we arrive back at the Ford Focus RS.

I may have touched on this before, but it bears repeating here for those who can't remember – namely, people such as me who are in their fifties. Ford has been running an advertising campaign recently urging people to 'unlearn' what they know about the brand. The company is of course talking to the Mondeo Man generation. But there's a dangerous downside to this. Because when it asks people of my age to 'unlearn' all they know about Ford, that means forgetting about the Escort Mexico and the Lotus Cortina and the Essex-engined 3-litre Capri and the RS200 and the GT40 and the Sierra RS Cosworth and the Cortina 1600E and the XR3i. It means forgetting that Ford has made more truly great cars in its history than any other company. Including Ferrari.

In the early 1990s I had an Escort RS Cosworth, and that car would go into anyone's list of all-time greats. It wasn't so much the wallop from its turbocharged engine or the grip from its four-wheel-drive system or even the preposterousness of its enormous rear spoiler that made this car so endearing; no, it was more the fact it was a working-class hero, a blue-collar bruiser that could mix it with the blue-bloods. A Ford that could keep up with, and then overtake, supercars that cost five or six times more.

After the Cossie was dropped, though, Ford rather lost its way. With the exception of the GT and the wonderful Fiesta ST, it stopped making great cars and began to believe good was good enough.

But it isn't. Every car firm needs to make the occasional loss-leading halo. Manufacturers need to accept that not one of the designers or engineers they employ joined up so they could work on the new rear-light cluster for a hatchback. They joined up so they could get their teeth into something that would cause the world to stagger.

Oh, Ford had a couple of attempts with the Focus over the years. It put a powerful engine under the bonnet and told us four-wheel drive was unnecessary because it had developed a differential or a new type of knuckle joint in the suspension that would keep the torque steer at bay. But the cars failed to ignite any passion in the enthusiast, because we knew the real reason they didn't have four-wheel drive. It would mean redesigning the whole underside of the vehicle, and that would mean new tooling at the factory. And that would be too expensive.

Well, with the new Focus RS, Ford has bitten the bullet. It has locked the accountants in a cupboard and bought the tooling. It has fitted four-wheel drive, and you know after about 100 yards that it has created something very special. Even at James May speeds, on a roundabout in Hounslow, this car feels cleverer than is normal. It feels like a Nissan GT-R.

That's because it's not just an off-the-shelf four-wheel-drive system. It's one of the most advanced active asymmetrical systems fitted to any car at any price. Somewhere in a cupboard an accountant is screaming.

The engine is less amazing. It's a so-called 2.3-litre Eco-Boost unit, lifted from Ford's hire-spec Mustang in America and beefed up in Europe so you get 345 brake horsepower. That isn't as much as you get from the hot Mercedes-AMG A 45, but, remember, that thing is a lot more expensive.

And, anyway, 345bhp is enough to provide a meaty shove in the back when you accelerate and a growly forty-a-day rumble from under the bonnet. Put it in Sport mode and you get some spitting from the exhaust as well. If this car could talk, you suspect, it would sound like John Terry.

Interestingly, given the sophistication of the four-wheel-drive system, you get a straightforward six-speed manual. Old skool. And a proper handbrake lever that you can use to do bird-pulling skid turns in a car park.

Put all of this lot together and what you get is, as the critics have been saying, something really quite inspirational. A genuine half-price GT-R. However, whereas the critics on the launch went off to play with the Drift mode, which allows even those with fingers of butter and fists of ham to power-slide round corners, I started to think about what else you get with this car.

Even in Normal mode there's a choppy vertical bouncing motion that is a bit annoying. You also get seats that are mounted on the car rather than in it – they're far too high. Then there's a range of only 250 miles and wipers that judder. Oh, and there's a slot for your iPhone in the dash, which is great. But if you accelerate hard, it shoots out and goes on to the floor.

Furthermore, only one colour is available as standard. It's a matt grey that Ford calls Stealth. Yeah, right. There is nothing stealthy about this car. It's so loud and so festooned with spoilers that many potential customers will say, 'No, thanks,' and buy the much more subtle Volkswagen Golf R instead.

That might be a wise decision, because while the Golf doesn't have a Drift feature or quite such fearsome cornering ability, it won't throw your phone on the floor every time you accelerate and it won't cause your friends to call you Gary.

I like to think, then, that what I've provided here is a balanced review of the baby Jesus. I've explained that it has a few flaws and that you may be better off with something else.

Because, that way, your test drive in an RS won't be burdened with hype, and you'll emerge from the driver's seat after ten minutes thinking: 'I have got to get me one of these.'

29 May 2016

Ahh, sauerkraut sushi soup. Looks delicious

Infiniti Q30

Once, when I worked for the BBC's Midlands division, I was invited to the opening of what was billed in the promotional pamphlet as 'Birmingham's biggest restaurant'.

And I remember thinking: 'Hmmm. I've heard of people saying they'd like to go out in the evening for an Italian or a Chinese. I've heard people say they'd like to eat somewhere intimate or cosy. But I have never heard anyone say, "What I fancy tonight is eating out in a restaurant that's really big."'

All of which brings me to the Infiniti Q30. Which is going to be at the top of anyone's list if they're after a Mercedes A-class that is built in Britain, badged as an upmarket Nissan and fitted with the diesel engine from a Renault.

I'm not sure, however, I've met anyone who has this list of criteria when they're choosing a new vehicle. A safe car, yes. Or a fast car. Or a car that's green. But never has anyone ever said to me: 'Jeremy. I want a Mercedes, but I'd like it to be a bit more Japanesey with a clattery French heart. Oh, and can it be built in Sunderland?'

The Infiniti sounds a complete mess: a car that's been hurled together by the marketing and accounting departments from various companies in Yokohama, Stuttgart and Paris. And that works about as well as a starter made from sauerkraut, a few bits of sushi and some powerful *bouilla-baisse*. But who knows? Maybe it's brilliant.

Or maybe it isn't . . . The Infiniti brand has not been what you'd call a runaway success. It was designed as a halo for Nissan in the same way as Lexus is a halo for Toyota and Acura is a halo for Honda in many parts, and while the idea is sound, the cars have always been ho-hum and have been sold only to people in America who were too interested in food and the baby Jesus to notice that their shiny new set of wheels was a tarted-up, half-arsed Datsun.

To try to boost the name a little bit, Nissan got its partners at Renault to slap the Infiniti brand on the Red Bull Formula One car – Renault made its engine – but that was desperate and tragic. A car company advertising itself on the side of a car . . . that it hadn't designed in any way.

I really did think that, after this, Infiniti had been quietly shelved, but no. I came out of the office last week, and there in the car park was the all-new Q30. So I decided to see what it was like.

The first problem was trying to decide what it was. One magazine calls it an 'active hatch', but I don't know what that means. And, anyway, it's not really a hatchback at all, and even though it has the option of four-wheel drive, it's not an off-roader or a crossover or an estate car either. What I can tell you is that it sits on the chassis from an A-class. And I think it's fair to say that the worst thing about the A-class is . . . drum roll . . . its chassis.

I'm sure Infiniti has done its best to iron out the inherent problems, and for the most part it rides and handles quite well. But sometimes you run over a smallish pothole, and then you think: 'No, wait – it doesn't.'

It's the same story with the 2.2-litre diesel engine. It moves you along and it doesn't appear to have an alarming thirst for fuel, so that's fine. But it sounds like a canal boat when it's cold. It's so loud that it has to be fitted with noise-cancelling technology.

I think that's what the engine does, in fact: turn diesel into sound. Because it sure as hell doesn't turn it into large lumps of power. Every time I pulled out to overtake a caravan, I had to pull in again because there wasn't quite enough grunt. So, all things considered, that's not fine either.

The interior is a different story. In the back it's a bit cramped and hard to get through the door if you're bigger than an ant. But up front the picture is much more rosy. The seats are tremendously comfortable and the quality of the materials is exemplary. I know a fair bit about stitching, having sewn up Paddington Bears for ten years, and I can tell you that the cottonwork on the dash of the Q30 is up there in Elizabeth Keckley's* league.

The Wearsiders and their neighbours from up north may be hopeless at football these days but they really can put a car together.

This is no good either. Because who is sitting at home thinking: 'I don't care what my next car is like, just as long as it has a tasteful interior that has been stitched together by former dockers'?

But there is one thing that does cause people to lose any sense of reason and buy something that is not safe, fast, economical, green or any of the things that really matter, and that's styling.

* *Keckley was an American former slave and seamstress who became the confidante and modiste of Abraham Lincoln's wife in the White House.*

You don't have to be a motoring ignoramus to fall foul of this one. You go into town, see a car you like the look of, come home, search for it on the internet, find you can afford it and buy it without stopping for a moment to wonder if it's in any way suitable.

On that basis the Q30 is going to be a quiet success, because, ooh, it's a looker. This is a car that is needlessly curvy and fitted with all sorts of styling touches that are in no way necessary. And yet it doesn't look fake or idiotic at all. It looks – and there's no other word – fantastic.

All of the alternatives are dreary and bland to behold, except the Range Rover Evoque, which is a bit common these days. The Q30 is not dreary or bland and, with only fourteen dealers in the UK, it's never going to be common either.

Which gives you a bit of a choice to make. You can drive a genuinely interesting-looking car that isn't really very good at all. Or you can buy a good car that is a bit boring to behold. I guess you have to ask yourself a question: do you want a mistress or a wife?

5 June 2016

I need a screensaver – and this ain't it

Vauxhall Astra SRi

I've just had the editor on the phone, wondering why I haven't responded to his emails and whether I'm going to send him my road-test report on the Vauxhall Astra SRi – because I'm way past the deadline.

I'm not procrastinating, I promise. I really do have a two-fold problem. First of all, I can't think of anything interesting to say about the Astra, and, second, I have spent the past two days with a mobile telephone that works perfectly, except the screen, which doesn't work at all.

I spent most of yesterday morning holding down various buttons for various periods of time until I realized that, of course, it's electronic, which means its problems can be resolved by turning it off and then on again.

But this made everything worse, because when an iPhone has been turned off, you can't use a thumbprint to bring it to life: you must put in your passcode. Which I couldn't do because the screen wasn't working.

I decided that all would be well if I plugged it into its home laptop and ordered a system restore.

How foolish of me. The computer said it could perform the task only if I unlocked the screen. Which I couldn't do.

That meant I had to find someone else with an iPhone 6 and copy his screen on to a piece of tracing paper, which I then laid over my own, dead screen. Clever, eh? Sadly not, because the screen needs direct human contact. It won't work if there's a tracing-paper interface.

So I broke out a ruler and marked where the numbers would be, using sugar granules. This simple act of genius worked. The computer hooked up with the phone, and I was about to press the Restore button when the friend whose iPhone I'd borrowed to use as a map said: 'You know if you do that you'll lose everything on your phone, don't you?'

Actually, I'd only lose everything since the last backup, which I noticed had been in February. So that's the number of everyone I've met since then and all the pictures I took in India and Jordan and Namibia and the ones of my daughter doing her first triathlon.

And all the while the incoming-email buzzer was sounding and I knew it'd be the editor, wondering why I hadn't sent him news of the Vauxhall. 'Because there are more important things in life,' I seethed inwardly. 'Such as killing everyone at Apple with a shovel.'

There was another problem I had with the Vauxhall. I'd driven it only once, from Holland Park to Chiswick, in rush hour. I was supposed to have taken it to the country at the weekend, but on Friday night Richard Hammond announced that he didn't like the colour of the Aston Martin Vanquish Volante he was supposed to be driving and went home in his own car.

I did like the colour – it was a sort of pearly metallic white – and I much preferred the idea of tooling around in a convertible Aston for the weekend to bumbling about in a mildly speedy Vauxhall. It was unprofessional, I know, but . . .

While I was in the Aston I decided I'd write about that instead, about how useless its satnav is and how you can get your right foot stuck under the brake pedal, which makes slowing down a bit tricky, and how the steering judders at low speeds and how annoying it was to have a convertible on a beautiful sunny day and not be able to take the roof down because I'm fat and fifty-six and I'd look stupid.

I was going to put all this in my column. But then I discovered I'd already reviewed the Vanquish Volante and had said much the same sort of thing. So I'd have to cobble together some thoughts on the Vauxhall. Which was hard because a) I didn't have any and b) on my laptop screen iTunes had just flashed up a message saying it had suffered a 'catastrophic' failure and was closing, which meant the sync with my phone wasn't working.

This happened six times. And on the seventh attempt at syncing I decided I didn't want to kill everyone at Apple with a shovel. I wanted to use a cocktail stick.

However, the seventh attempt was at least successful. The sync was done. So finally I could restore my phone to see if that would bring the screen back to life. However, being a cautious soul, I thought I'd just check everything had been transferred, and guess what. It hadn't. So I had to start all over again, and I couldn't because iTunes announced once again that it had stopped working and would be closing.

It's incredible how all-consuming this sort of problem becomes. I knew I must write my column on the Vauxhall. I knew I must send out a tweet saying our Amazon show's big tent was to be transported round the world by our new sponsor, DHL, and I knew I must sort out the kitchen cabinets for my cottage. And yet all those things were still sitting in the in-tray because getting my phone to work properly had become even more important than taking my next breath.

Then it rang. It actually rang. So I took a guess at where on the screen the Answer button might be and took the call. It was the editor. Wondering in a tone that was polite and pleading but also laced with a hint of menace where my column might be. 'I'm doing it. I'm doing it,' I replied impatiently, before going back to the telephone issue.

They say a Dutch bargee can swear without hesitation, repetition or deviation for two minutes and that no other language offers such a rich vein of opportunity for fans of the expletive. Well, that's rubbish. When the iTunes program shut down for, I think, the twelfth time, I swore constantly for thirty-six minutes and at such a volume that the walls of my office were bulging.

Fearing I might be on the verge of a sizeable coronary – I'd love to know how many heart attacks have been caused by malfunctioning mobile phones – the office staff broke off from their important work to call for assistance. And half an hour later a man arrived to make everything better.

I felt for him. Because, as a mobile phone consultant, he never in his working life meets anyone who's calm and rational. Nobody thinks: 'Hmm. It's a lovely day. I think I'll call Gary at Ezee iPhone Solutions to see how he is.' The only people he meets are bright red and shouting.

Anyway, he's in a nearby office now, sorting everything out, which means finally I can get on with my review of the Astra.

It had a 4G wi-fi hotspot facility, which would have been useful if my phone had been working. But, as I may have mentioned, it wasn't.

Other than that, it was red and turbocharged and would be fine for anyone who needs four wheels and a place to sit down when moving about. And now I'm out of space, which is probably a good thing, because I have nothing else to say about it, really.

19 June 2016

Raving in slippers with General Franco

Seat Ibiza Cupra

Most of the world's car companies were started by someone who had a vision. Sir Henry Royce, Sir William Lyons, Louis Chevrolet, Nicola Romeo, Soichiro Honda, Enzo Ferrari, Brian Hyundai. I may have made that last one up.

All these men saw what everyone else was doing and decided they could do something different, something better. They had a dream and they decided to live it. Seat, however, is different.

Shortly after the Spanish Civil War had reduced Spain to a smouldering ruin, a committee of serious-faced bankers and industrialists was formed, and after a couple of meetings these men decided that if their country was to be hauled out of the mire, the population would need cars. And to stop people spending what little money they had on imports, they reckoned the country should make its own. Siat was born.

At the time, the Spanish were extremely good at shooting one another and throwing donkeys off tower blocks but extremely not good at making anything as complicated as a car. They would therefore need a foreign partner, and they set off into Europe to find one.

Sadly it was 1942, and the rest of Europe was a bit too busy with other things to worry about how the Spanish might make a small and inexpensive family saloon. So they had to wait until 1948, when Fiat came along, explaining that no one in the world was quite so good at making sub-12bhp cars for the downtrodden masses. The Italian company was given the gig and just five years later produced a Barcelona-made family saloon that was very luxurious and expensive. It flopped.

What's more, General Franco had decided that the 'i' in the company name, which stood for Iberica, should really be an 'e', for Española. Which meant the firm wasn't thinking about exporting to any English-speaking country. Because who in their right mind would buy a car called a Seat?

Actually, strike that. In Britain we had the Humber, which was named after a sludgy brown river of turd and effluent. And in America they had the Oldsmobile. And in Russia they had the Pantry. So, in the grand scheme of things, driving around in a chair wouldn't have been the end of the world.

The new Spanish operation had bigger problems anyway. Many years of strikes, floods and industrial shenanigans followed, during which no cars of any note were made. Seriously, can you picture a Seat from the 1970s? Nope. Me neither.

At the beginning of the 1980s, though, there was a disaster. Fiat pulled out. Seat was thus forced to go it alone, and in 1982 there was a great deal of trumpetry when it announced it had made a car, all by itself. With no help from Fiat at all. None, d'you hear? None.

Yeah, right. Even people with terrible conjunctivitis could see the Seat Ronda was nothing more than a Fiat Ritmo with a new nose. Happily, however, the people at the arbitration court in Paris plainly did have terrible conjunctivitis, because when Fiat sued, they sided with Seat. Which, to celebrate this important legal victory, started making Volkswagens.

On the face of it, this didn't sound a good idea. When you

buy a Jaguar today, you like to feel it's shot through with the DNA of Sir William Lyons. It's the same story when you buy a Honda or a Ferrari. Each of these cars, even today, reflects the passion and dreams of the person who founded the company. But when you bought a Seat, you'd be getting a Volkswagen garnished with a bit of Franco, a layer of social engineering and some tiresome lawsuits.

And, anyway, who in their right mind would wake up one day and say, 'Yes. I'd like a Volkswagen, but I'd rather it weren't built by those efficient Germans. I'd like it to have been made by a Spaniard'?

Lots of people, as it turned out, because Seat later hit on the clever idea of naming its Volkswagens after pretty Mediterranean holiday hotspots. You might not get many takers for a Spanish Polo. But call it an Ibiza and every drug-loving twentysomething from Arbroath to Zurich is going to be queuing round the block.

Which brings me shuddering this morning to the door of the Seat Ibiza Cupra, a racy-looking little three-door hatchback with fat tyres, black wheels and a turbocharged 1.8-litre engine. That's quite a lump in a car that's not much bigger than an insect.

I was expecting all sorts of dawn-on-the-beach histrionics. As it has 189 brake horsepower under the bonnet, I reckoned there'd be a pulsating beat and a Eurotrash DJ endlessly inviting the party people to spray one another with foam. But no. It was more chillout than house. It was quiet and restrained and surprisingly grown up.

It's the same story with the ride. This is a hot hatch built to draw your attention to Seat's effortsin various touring car championships. It has a manual gearbox and is aimed at people who enjoy discomfort so much, they walk around with their trousers done up under their bottoms. And yet it simply glides over potholes and speed humps.

A chintzy interior, then? Something as colourful as the cocktails in Pacha? Nope. It's grey with added grey. I've seen snazzier slippers.

It is up to date, though. When you accelerate hard out of a bend, it will brake the inside wheel to stop it whirring round pointlessly, and there are adjustable dampers. More important in this day and age, it comes as standard with the ability to connect to just about every interface known to man. There's Apple CarPlay on offer and something called Android Auto. I think this means it's capable of sending pictures of your private parts to the ether, possibly through voice command.

It's a strange car, this. Make no mistake: it's very fast and it looks good in a tight, iPoddy sort of way – white paint and black wheels is a combination that works well.

Yet it's like climbing into a pair of gardening trousers. The Volkswagen Polo GTI – its identical twin mechanically – is far more lively to behold and sit in. And that's odd, because you'd expect to find that the VW was dour and sensible and the Seat was the hallucinatory alternative.

I'm not sure which I prefer, and I can't be bothered to work it out, because while both are fine, neither is anything like as good as Ford's Fiesta ST. That car is a gem. You sense Henry Ford's pile-'em-high-and-sell-'em-cheap mass production, but you can feel Ford's racing pedigree as well.

The Seat, by comparison, is just somewhere to sit down and relax while it moves you about.

3 July 2016

Merci, Bono, it's just what I'm looking for

Vauxhall Zafira Tourer

Even by my own slightly weird view of what's normal, last Sunday was a bit odd. I was on a boat – a big one – and we'd anchored off the south of France when half the people on board suddenly took leave of their senses and decided they'd like to walk up the Nietzsche path to the village of Eze for a drink.

The Nietzsche path, I should explain, is a walk the philosopher liked to do when he needed to think, but all anyone else can think when they're on it is: 'Christ, my thighs hurt.' And: 'Oh no, one of my lungs has just come out.' Steep doesn't begin to cover it. It's bloody nearly vertical and it goes on and on, up to 85,000ft, and every one of the gravelly, ankle-breaking hairpins is festooned with one of the old man's pearls of wisdom about how there was nothing he couldn't teach ya about the raising of the wrist.

As you can imagine, I thought this was very stupid but I quite liked the idea of having a drink in the Golden Goat on top of the mountain. So I said I'd use a car.

Happily, one of the people on the boat – and you need to be awake for this bit – said he knew someone who lived on the beach and that I could probably borrow a car from him. And the person he knew? Well, of course, it was Bono out of U2. Someone I met only briefly at a small dinner with the King of Jordan.

Anyway, I was taken to the shore in a little speedboat and after a lengthy and tricky walk along a slippery shingle beach, I arrived at Mr Bono's house with a bright red face and noticeably sweaty moobs. He wasn't at home so I was greeted by a shabby-looking individual who I thought must be the gardener. But he turned out to be John F. Kennedy's nephew. Only Adrian Gill can drop more names before he's started talking about what he had for supper. But that's the last, I promise.

JFK's nephew was a bit stand-offish. He'd had a garbled call from someone saying that someone else was maybe coming round to pick up some wheels but he was nervous about letting the sweaty tramp who'd arrived drive off into the evening in Bono's car. Especially as I was accompanied by a woman who looked like she'd arrived, in a time warp, from a 1967 surfing party in California.

Tentatively, he handed over a set of keys, and with a stern face, said: 'I just want to make this clear: if you bend it, you mend it.' And with that I was in the driveway, with surfer woman, clutching the keys to a car that belongs to, let's be honest, one of the coolest people on the planet.

There's no flowery way of putting this so I'll just come straight out with it. Bono drives a Vauxhall Zafira diesel.

I was quite impressed with this little seven-seater when it first came out, but then the old model tarnished its reputation somewhat by bursting into flames for no obvious reason pretty much constantly. Google 'Zafira' and 'fire' and you'll see what I mean.

I wasn't thinking about those things, though. It's quite a tricky drive and it was even trickier that night. Partly because I knew that if I had a crash, the embarrassment and the shame would live with me for ever but also because my head was spinning. Bono. Has. A. Vauxhall. Zafira. With. A. Diesel. Engine.

In my mind he'd have had something fast and expensive but not showy or vulgar. A Maserati Quattroporte. Or a BMW M6 Gran Coupé perhaps. Once, I was in a military helicopter flying over southern Iraq when someone fired a heat-seeking missile at it. I was listening to Vertigo by U2 at the time, and as we ducked and weaved in a shower of our own flares, I remember thinking how the music and the moment were so well matched. If only I'd known then that the man who actually co-wrote Vertigo has a diesel Vauxhall. I'd have had a trouser accident, that's for sure.

As we climbed up the mountain, the Zafira was very roly-poly but I found it surprisingly easy to moderate the pitching by turning the wheel gently and braking as though the pedal were made of an egg. Then I noticed how brilliant the engine was. It's an all-aluminium, turbocharged 1.6-litre unit that can apparently do more than 60mpg on a cruise and 120mph when you're in a hurry.

And then I went over a speed hump and I simply didn't feel a thing. Never in all my years in this business have I encountered any car – including the Rolls-Royce Phantom – that's quite so good at refusing to transmit road surface irregularities into the cabin. Which makes it the most comfortable car – pause – in the world.

That night, after I'd safely returned the Vauxhall to Bono's house, I looked it up online and found that *Autocar* magazine disagreed with my findings. It said that the Renault Grand Scénic rides more smoothly.

Fearful that Bono had bought a special Zafira with marsh-mallow shock absorbers and suspension units made from eiderdown, I came back to England, hired a Zafira and went for a drive. And I'm sorry, *Autocar*, but I'm right about this. The car's extraordinary.

If you have a bad back or you just want to be comfortable as you move about, you need look no further. But don't worry, because it's also very good-looking and it has a wind-screen that is bigger than the one you get on a National Express coach. It's so big that from behind the wheel you can't see any pillars or a roofline, so it feels as if you are float-ing along, powered only by magic.

The interior's top-notch as well; nicely styled, well put-together and festooned with all sorts of stuff you wouldn't expect for this kind of money. I drove a Ford S-Max later, which I've always thought was pretty good, and it felt like something from fifty years ago. Diesely. Lacklustre. Old.

It seems that after my visit, Bono telephoned JFK's nephew who explained that a tramp had come round to the house and borrowed the Zafira. Bono was apparently a bit surprised by this: 'You gave Jeremy Clarkson the Vauxhall!' It turns out I was supposed to have borrowed his BMW 6-series convertible.

But I'm glad I didn't because I would never have experi-enced something that's unique. A miserable diesel seven-seater Vauxhall that you would actually want to buy. And not only so you could tell your mates: 'Bono's got one, you know.'

10 July 2016

Joie de vivre? Not in this Brexit poster boy

Wolseley 1500 Mk 1

I feel such an idiot. For twenty-odd years I have been coming here and – foolishly, as it's turned out – talking about cars from exotic places such as Germany and Japan. I've spoken breathlessly about turbocharging and exciting new lightweight materials. And I've tried to bring to life what it's like to drive a 700bhp Ferrari on the Transfagarasan Highway in Romania.

Stupidly, I believed that you might be interested. I thought that, thanks to social media and easyJet and exotic new takeaway restaurants that can deliver exciting dishes to your door in a matter of moments, I was speaking to an audience that was sophisticated and international. Broad-minded. Global.

But it seems I was wrong. The Brexit vote has shown me and everyone else in the sneering metropolitan elite that, actually, you want to live in a black-and-white world with Terry and June on the television, pints in glasses with handles on the side, prawn cocktail crisps, powdered coffee, pineapple juice for a starter, ruddy-faced police constables, red phone boxes and no one speaking bloody Polish on the bus.

You weren't remotely interested in torque-vectoring differentials or satnav systems, because you only go to Bridlington once a year and you know the way already. So you don't need some electronic German barking orders at every roundabout and T-junction. You want it to be the 1950s all over again, because Britain was great then, apart from the lung diseases.

You certainly weren't interested in buying a Renault, because it's bloody French. And you were never going to buy a Fiat, because you need at least one of the gears in the box to not be reverse. What you've always wanted is the car I've been driving recently. The post-Brexit poster boy. The Wolseley 1500.

Compared with the modern-day equivalents from abroad, it's not very fast. It goes from 0 to 60mph in a leisurely 24.4 seconds, but the top speed is 78mph, and that's plenty because 70mph is as fast as you need to go here on this, our fair and sceptred isle.

Obviously, this kind of performance means the Wolseley would be a bit out of its depth on the German autobahn, but you don't care about that because you aren't going to Germany any time soon. Because you can't stand the buggers. The Blitz. Hitler. Battle of Britain. Best film ever made. And so on.

It must also be said that by modern standards the handling is extremely poor. The steering wheel is connected to the front wheels by what feels like a bucket full of rapidly setting cement, and there are some alarming levels of lean in the bends.

Of course, if you are bothered by such things – and why would you be, because having fun in a car is flamboyant and therefore almost certainly foreign? – you could buy the Riley One Point Five, which is basically the same car but with sportier suspension and two carburettors. Which are French, and therefore disgusting.

I began my journey with the Wolseley in Wales, which is

just about all right. Certainly it's better than Scotland, which is full of people who are possibly communist. I stayed in a hotel that served British poached eggs on toast that had been made from proper bread, which is like a wet vest and not all full of fancy bits.

Opposite, there was a dress shop selling some rather fetching one-piece bathing suits. Seeing them on the mannequins in the window made me a bit aroused, I'm sorry to say.

So I hurried to the car, which was painted in a fetching shade of grey, and climbed aboard. The seats were made from leather and the dashboard from wood, which is entirely right and proper. Around the doors were strips of red velvet, which gave a very regal feel, and that's what you want, of course, not some plastic, which is republican and therefore untrustworthy.

The car smelt of home. By which I mean it had the aroma of a headmaster's wood-panelled study. There was that familiar fustiness, caused possibly by the carpets gently rotting after they'd soaked up the tears of all those abused pupils. Those were the days. Damp days. Dismal days. Wonderful days.

The visibility all round was excellent, there was space for two children in the back, which is the number parents should have. Not seventeen, like the bloody Catholics seem to think is sensible. Bloody Pope.

I eased the MG gearbox into first, and off we set into the Brecon Beacons, which are more beautiful than anywhere else in the world. Apart from Bridlington, obviously. And soon, in my wake, there was a lengthy traffic jam, made up of various foreign vehicles such as Fendt tractors and a dustbin lorry or two.

The Wolseley is not even on nodding terms with speedy, as I've said, but that's OK, because why do you need to get anywhere quickly? That's the language of big business and global activity. Download speeds. Coffee to go. A third runway. That's not what you want at all.

And, anyway, there's so much to enjoy from behind the enormous wheel of this fine British motoring car. There's an indicator stalk with a green blinker light on the end. Not sure that green is the right colour, mind. It's a bit Muslim.

But the switchgear had that reassuring feel we crave. The wiper knob, you just know, was attached by a man with a Birmingham accent who was wearing a brown store coat and loved Harry Worth. Which is probably why it came off in my hand.

I was going to say that the 1.5-litre engine pulled well in a high gear (fourth), suggesting that it had good torque. But torque sounds French and is therefore not a word that we should be using any more.

After a couple of miles I tried to pull over in a lay-by to admire the view, but the weakness of the brakes – which are basically milk bottle tops – meant I missed it completely and ended up in a Costa Coffee car park several miles further down the road.

There I enjoyed some proper sandwiches and a sausage roll made from proper sausagemeat; none of that foreign muck with la-di-bloody-da herbs in it. And then I finished off with a banana that was bent. Like a proper British banana should be.

I wanted to listen to the Jeremy Vine show, because I agree with all its callers, but, sadly, although the Wolseley had a speaker in the middle of the dash, there was no radio. Nor was there much of a heater, come to that.

This is how life's going to be now. It's what more than half the voting public want. The country as it used to be.

And I'm sorry to have to say this, but what I wanted was what the country could have been. Which is why, next week, I shall be reviewing the Alfa Romeo Giulia Quadrifoglio.

If you're not happy about that, buy the bloody *Sunday Express* instead. Apparently it's reviewing the new Hillman.

17 July 2016

Foot down, I'm in clover

Alfa Romeo Giulia Quadrifoglio Verde

I've waited nearly three decades for this car. The Alfa Romeo Giulia Quadrifoglio Verde. An Alfa Romeo that isn't just a rebadged Fiat. An Alfa Romeo that has rear-wheel drive and serious power. An Alfa Romeo that you would actually want to buy.

Or would you? Well, for the purposes of this test I'm going to set aside my love of Alfas, which is profound. It's so profound that I even manage to love the 4C, a car so riddled with faults, it should have been called the San Andreas.

I will even defend the old 75, even though its handbrake cut your fingers off every time you used it, the electric window switches were in the roof and it had been styled by someone who had only a ruler.

Here, however, there will be no misty-eyed ramblings about Dustin Hoffman, or the engine note of the GTV6, or the days when Alfa's racing cars tore around those hay bales, making their driver's face all oily. No. I'm going to review the Giulia Quadrifoglio (four-leaf clover) in the same way as I'd review a BMW or a Mercedes. I'm going to review it simply as a car. A tool. A thing.

We shall start with its faults. And that brings us directly to the driver's door, which is either too small or in the wrong place. I can't work out which, but, whatever, getting out is like getting out of a postbox. The only way you can do it with any dignity is by pushing the steering wheel as far forward as it will go, and that's a nuisance.

This brings us on to the steering wheel, which, as is usual these days, is festooned with buttons, none of which is lit at night. So when you want to turn up the volume on the stereo, as often as not you engage the cruise control. Which you then cannot turn off without reaching for your phone and turning on the torch feature.

By which time you'll have run out of petrol. It's not an uneconomical car, especially, but it's fitted with a 58-litre tank. And 58 litres is known in scientific circles as 'not quite big enough'.

Other things? Well, for a car that'll cost just shy of £60,000, the quality of the interior fittings is not as good as you might expect. The green and white stitching is wonderful to behold, but the plastics are a bit airline cutlery and the sat-nav screen is about the size of a stamp. Also, the knobs and buttons are a bit cheap. You'd have to say this doesn't feel the sort of top-quality item you'd get from, say, Audi. The engine, for example, wobbles when you slam the door.

So it's hard to get out of, it's poorly finished, it has a small-ish range and the engine is mounted to the car with Blu-Tack. Those are the drawbacks. That's what you'd have to put up with if you bought one. But don't worry, because there are some upsides as well, most of which are stratospheric.

Let's start with the headline. This car, this four-door saloon, which is priced to take on BMW's 155mph M3, has a top speed of 191mph. That's possible because of the Alfa's smooth and magnificently sonorous 2.9-litre V6 turbo engine.

Ferrari – which is controlled by the Agnelli family behind Fiat, the owner of Alfa – is adamant that it's not the same unit it fits to the California, with two cylinders lopped off.

The fact that the two engines have the same bore, stroke and V angle is a coincidence, it says. As is the fact that in both the twin-scroll turbo is in the V of the engine, providing instant punch whenever the driver so much as twitches his little toe.

You are perhaps aware that some of the time it's not the torquiest engine in the world, which means you have to fish around rather more than you'd imagine in the clever eight-speed automatic gearbox. But to compensate, you get 503 horsepowers. This means you need to be careful when you're fishing, because, God, this car is quick. Laugh-out-loud quick.

And it's an absolute joy to drive. The steering is fast – there are only two turns lock to lock, which means you need almost no input at all to go round a roundabout. And on a sweeping A-road you can steer, really, by thought.

Then there are the brakes. My car was fitted with £5,000-worth of carbon-ceramic discs, which were tuned perfectly. You can press the pedal much harder than you think is realistic before the antilock system cuts in, and, of course, fade won't be a problem.

Naturally, there's a button that makes the car even fizzier and even a setting called Race, which turns the traction control off. I'd leave that alone on the road if I were you. On a track I had a play and was sideways constantly. A feat made ever so easy because the Quadrifogliettore has what amounts to a limited-slip differential.

The man who project-managed the Quattroformaggio cut his teeth on the Ferrari 458 Speciale. And it shows. It's not just the big flappy paddles that are fixed to the column, as they should be, or the moving spoiler at the front; it's the whole DNA of the car. If Ferrari made a mid-sized, four-door car, you suspect it would feel and go exactly like this.

Do not think, however, that it's uncivilized in any way.

Even though it sits on tiny wheels and rides close to the ground, and even if you have the suspension in 'bumpy' mode, it is remarkably smooth. Its ability to deal with potholes is uncanny. And while it makes a racket, with added gunfire on the upshifts, it is extremely quiet when you're inside.

Space? Well, the boot is fine, but the back is a squash, chiefly because my car was fitted with optional carbon front seats, which were enormous. That said, they were very comfortable. So comfortable that after a three-hour schlepp to Wales, I got out – after a bit of a struggle, I admit – and felt as though I'd just popped to the shops.

Then I went for some fun in the Brecon Beacons, and it was sublime. The fast throttle response, the fast steering and the preposterous rate at which the speedometer climbs combine to make this car feel extremely special. Maybe an M3 would last longer, and maybe fewer knobs would fall off. But the M3 has wonky steering and feels heavy compared with the Alfa and . . . I can't believe I've just written that.

What I'm saying here, in this straight, no-cocking-about road test, is that Alfa Romeo has made a car dynamically better than the BMW. And it has. It really has. This is Iceland beating England. And I couldn't be more pleased.

24 July 2016

Mr Quirky, I'm here to burst your bubble wrap

Citroën C4 Cactus

I always thought that the letters 'CV' used by Citroën for the hateful 2CV stood for Chevaux. But I learnt last week that, actually, CV stands for Chevaux-Vapeur. Which so far as I can tell means 'vaporized horses'.

And I wonder if the weird-beard vegetablist nutters who made this stupid little car their own knew that. I suspect they didn't. Because a vaporized horse is not the sort of thing that goes down well at a peace-and-love bong festival. It'd be like turning up in a Ford Mashed Badger.

The 2CV was originally designed, so the story goes, so that the French peasantry could drive across a ploughed field without breaking any eggs that happened to be on the passenger seat. It was cheap and comfortable, and with its folding roof, good fun. It was a French Fiat 500, an onionized Mini, with a stripy jumper.

Until the eco-loonies started using it as a statement to show the world they didn't believe in oil or beefburgers, I always rather liked it, with its silly gear lever sticking out of the dashboard and its golden-wedding-anniversary-at-the-village-hall seating.

It was typically Citroën, a company that had always looked at what the rest of the world was doing and then did the complete opposite. It was belligerence, really, but often it produced some truly brilliant ideas that everyone else then had to copy. Using the body as the chassis is a pretty good example of this. Swivelling headlights is another.

This sort of thinking made Citroën a uniform for people who were a bit odd. Poets and art historians drove them. The brilliant boy who excelled at school and then became a plumber. He would have one too. Stockbrokers, accountants, bank managers – they didn't. Citroën was a haven for those who were going through life the same as everyone else, but not quite.

One of my all-time favourite cars is the old Citroën CX Safari. It had a one-spoke steering wheel because every other car had two, three or four, and it had a cassette player mounted vertically between the seats because . . . why not? Actually, I'll tell you why not; because after about a month the cassette slot would be jammed up with the bits of Double Decker chocolate bar that hadn't fallen into a fold of your shirt.

Underneath, the Citroën was very different because it rode on a puddle of magic that meant no road-surface irregularities would be transmitted to the cabin. The downside of this system was a steering setup that had a mind of its own and brakes that worked like a switch. They were either fully off or fully on.

Once you became used to having a cassette player full of chocolate and a bruised nose from bumping your head into the windscreen every time you slowed down – oh, and indicators that didn't self-cancel, as they weren't operated from a stalk, because that would be too normal – you could genuinely fall in love with this car. It was just so weird.

At one point Citroën bought Maserati and made the beautiful and beguiling Bora, a supercar that mated a ton and a half of French oddballery with a healthy dollop of Italian unreliability. I'm told that when it worked – which was pretty much never – it was brilliant.

But then, bit by bit, Citroën started to be absorbed into the Peugeot empire. The silliness was phased out and the cars became nothing more than rebadged Pugs. They became boring and normal, and the only way Citroën managed to sell any at all was through the power of breathy and frantic special-offer advertising campaigns. 'Get 100 per cent off and a chance to sleep with the wife of the boss on a Tuesday.' That sort of thing.

That's why I was a little bit pleased to see it had launched a car called the C4 Cactus that had waded into the marketplace with a slab of what appeared to be bubble wrap down each side. 'Yes,' I thought. 'It's gone belligerent and stupid again.'

The news gets better when you climb inside because this really doesn't feel like any car you've seen before. The glass roof is one thing but the dash is something else. Principally because it doesn't really have one. There's a small box that tells you how fast you're going and then there's a sort of info-tainment satnav arrangement that does everything else. And I do mean everything. If you want to change any aspect of the car, you have to go into a sub-menu first. I'm amazed the company hasn't put the indicator controls in there. That'd have been a very Citroëny thing to do.

It would also have been Citroëny to design a suspension system made from sewage. But we live in straitened times where the other bottom line is king so the C4 Cactus runs on exactly the same sort of suspension that you find in every other car. However, it is tuned to give a flavour of the past. This is a comfortable car – not as comfortable as the Vauxhall Zafira – but it's a pretty nice place to be if you have a bad back.

But not if you are tall. If you are tall, you will hit your head a lot. This is because Citroën has fitted a low roof lining to house the passenger airbag. Which means you are forever banging your head into what is essentially a bomb. Not sure about that.

And then you will be infuriated by the glovebox, which is styled to look like a steamer trunk but isn't as big as a pencil case, and then you will want to turn the temperature up or change the radio channel and that will take you half an hour because you can't be bothered to read the instruction manual.

I must now moan about the driving position, which is fine if your arms and legs are exactly the same length. But mine aren't and neither are yours, which means you'll have to drive with your legs wide apart. This makes the car unsuitable for those who enjoy wearing short skirts.

At some point you will put your foot down – to join a motorway, for example. And you will be extremely surprised by what happens next. Because what happens next is nothing at all. I once drove a supertanker and it took three minutes to increase its speed from 13.8 to 13.9 knots. These are figures the C4 Cactus driver can only dream about.

Which caused me to wonder for a little while what sort of car this actually is. Underneath, it's a supermini but to look at, it's more a sort of crossover. So your eyes are telling you it'll be a snazzy performer with perhaps a soupçon of off-road ability while the rest of your head is saying that it's just a school-run 'n' supermarket car.

You can't even get much of an idea from the price because that's always 80 per cent less than Citroën says it is, thanks to that week's 'everything must go' sale.

I really was hoping that the C4 Cactus would be quirky

and odd and endearing but after a week with it, I'm afraid, it's nothing more than a hatchback with bubble wrap on the side. Pity.

7 August 2016

Yo, homey, it's an iDinosaur

Bentley Continental GT Speed

I met someone the other day who uses an old Nokia mobile telephone. 'I can make and receive calls,' he said, 'and I can send texts, and the battery lasts for days. What more could you want?' I couldn't be bothered to answer.

Using a phone that can't receive photographs or dispatch emails or store music is like living in a cave. Yes, it's dry and it's warm and it needs very little maintenance, but you'd rather live in a house with central heating and a cooker. No, don't argue. You just would.

Yes, I admit that whenever there's a week in the month, Apple drives me mad. I don't like the way I buy a film from it and then it doesn't let me watch it unless I find some wi-fi and select a new password – 'No, that's not good enough.' 'And that isn't either.' – and give my credit card details and accept its terms and conditions, which basically say it owns my soul until the end of time.

I also hate the latest music storage system, which won't let me put the damn thing on random and have it flip from the Bee Gees to the Clash. And the iCloud makes me fall to my knees and howl at the moon. Because as far as I can tell it's just an intangible soup full of nothing but poor old Jennifer Lawrence's breasts.

But despite all this I'd rather lose a lung than lose my iPhone. I'm more likely to remember to take it with me in the morning than my trousers. And every day, someone shows me a new feature or a new app that makes my life even more amazing, easy and enjoyable. If I couldn't have Snapseed to adjust my photographs, or Instagram to peek into the perfect lives of friends, or a map to show me just how much traffic is on the Oxford ring road, I'd have to commit suicide.

And that brings me neatly to the mildly tweaked Bentley Continental GT Speed I've been driving. It's been mildly tweaked because the design is getting on for fifteen years old. But it still doesn't have a USB port. My Volkswagen Golf has one. A Fiat 500 has one. But this £168,900 uber-grand tourer does not. Sure, it has Bluetooth, which Bentley probably thinks does the job just as well. But it doesn't, and, anyway, it didn't work.

My phone just sat there saying it was searching for devices with me bouncing up and down in the seat, waving it at the dashboard and shouting: 'How can you not find a Bentley, you stupid piece of junk? It's huge.' Until eventually it delivered a photograph of Jennifer Lawrence with no clothes on.

Even more amazingly, while conducting a fingertip search for the hole into which I could plug my cable, I opened the glovebox, and in there was a meaningless flex that would connect to nothing from this century, and a CD auto-changer. Which, in terms of technology, is up there with a Garrard SP25 turntable.

We all know the problem, of course. To fit the Continental with a USB port would require the whole infotainment system and the entire dash to be redesigned. That would mean refitting the production line, and that would cost about a hundred and ten hundred eleventy billion pounds.

And, you may think, what would be the point? Bentley is almost duty-bound to fit its cars with a gramophone and with a wood-burning stove instead of a heater, because the people who buy such things are old and stuck in their ways.

But in fact the average age of Bentley's customers these days is about six. The Continental has become the weapon of choice for absolutely everyone who's made it in the world of rap. Urge your fans to kill a policeman on Saturday and you're in leather-lined luxury on Monday.

'Homey, you can catch me swooping. Bentley coupé switching lanes, ha-ha!' So sang 50 Pence, apparently.

In America, Bentley is now so synonymous with the rap culture that when I went to pick up a New Yorker from the airport the other day, she climbed into the Continental and said: 'Oooh. An MFB.' In a family newspaper I can only tell you that the B stands for Bentley. You'll have to work the rest out for yourself.

But the point is clear. This is now a youthful car. A cool car. But could I drive a car that doesn't have a USB port? I guess the answer is yes, just as I could write this column on a typewriter and then send it to the *Sunday Times* in the post. I could do that. But I wouldn't want to.

There are some other issues with the car as well. It started out in life with a body that managed to be vulgar and bland at the same time. But a couple of years ago some very small styling tweaks made it extremely attractive. And now the company has gone backwards again, especially at the rear, with a boot lid that puts me in mind of a Sunbeam Rapier.

The biggest problem, though, is the enormous 6-litre twin-turbocharged W12 engine. There's nothing wrong with the power, which is immense, or the torque, which is planetary, and there's certainly nothing wrong with the noise, which is a muted, slightly frightening rumble that rises to a muted, very frightening rumble when you open the taps.

I'm not going to grumble either about the incredible speeds it can achieve, and neither am I overly fussed by the fuel consumption. No, my beef is twofold. First of all, this W12 engine simply isn't as good as the V8 that Bentley offers as a cheaper alternative. Yes, you get a dribble more oomph and a slightly higher top speed, but the downsides are pronounced. It makes the car heavy. Which means you are aware when you go round a corner that the suspension and the tyres are having to work harder than is necessary. The problem is even more obvious when you brake. It feels sometimes as if you are trying to halt the tide.

Genuinely, the less you pay for a Continental GT, the better off you are. The V8 S still feels how a Bentley should – grand and opulent – but it feels weighty without actually being heavy. And that means it's nicer to drive and more chuckable and more economical than the Speed.

It comes with pretty much the same interior and pretty much the same level of equipment. Which means it doesn't have a USB port either. This is something Bentley is going to have to deal with, whatever the cost may be.

28 August 2016

Tusk, tusk. It's like an elephant on a unicycle

Fiat 124 Spider

First things first. The Fiat 124 Spider has a Fiat engine and it says Fiat on the back, and it takes a couple of styling cues from the achingly pretty 124 Sport Spider from 1966. But, underneath, it's a Mazda MX-5.

When I heard a few years ago that Fiat had approached Mazda about making a He-Man version of the world's bestselling – and best – sports car, I was so excited I had to have a bit of a lie-down.

Here's why. Making a sports car should be simple. But then making a poached egg on toast should be too. And yet almost every hotel in the world gets it wrong. They cook the egg for too long, or they put it on the toast before they've drained the water away properly, or they smother it in weeds such as parsley, which is unnecessary.

This is what happens when car companies try to design a sports car these days. They optimize it for track use rather than the road, or they put the engine in the middle and you're left thinking: 'Look, you imbeciles. I want the engine at the front, rear-wheel drive and a canvas hood that can be thrown away when the sun's out. Don't complicate it. Just do that well.'

And that's what Mazda has got so right with the MX-5: it is simple and perfectly executed. The best poached egg on toast the world's seen. It's the perfect size. It's the perfect price. It has the right-sized engine and is fitted with only the toys you actually need. I love it.

However, there's no getting round the fact it's a bit ... how can I put this? Light in its loafers? You don't see many Sarf London gangsters in Mazdas. Guy Ritchie hasn't got one. It's not a car that would be used by the Terminator.

Which is why I was so excited about this Fiat business. The idea was simple. It would take the Mazda's architecture, which would save a fortune in development costs, and add its own styling and engine, which I figured would turn a finger of Baileys into a gallon of Bloody Mary with all the trimmings.

Hmmm. The problem is that the old 124's most distinctive and attractive feature was the way its rear wings flicked up like a frigatebird's wings from the horizontal boot lid. Fiat has tried to copy that on the new version, but the Mazda's boot lid isn't horizontal, so the result looks awkward, like amateur taxidermy.

There's more, I'm afraid, because while it's all very well making your vehicle's body bigger and more butch, it's no good if you plonk it on the underpinnings of a car that's more dainty. You end up with what looks like an elephant sitting on a unicycle. A big car with little-car wheels lost in the arches.

The front's not bad, but even here I have issues because of the twin power bulges in the bonnet. The original 124 had them because the extra clearance was needed for its twin-cam engine. Now, though, they are there for effect, like the stupid fake gills on the Range Rover, and that annoys me.

I've spent more time than usual discussing the way this car looks because that's the whole point of it. The main reason you'd buy one is that you find the MX-5 a bit weedy and you want something a bit more hirsute.

The other reason is that you want some Italian flair, and that brings me on to the engine, which in the version I tested was Fiat's 1.4-litre turbo. It's not a bad little unit, but I was hoping in the 124 Fiat might have made it sound more zingy. And it hasn't.

That's not good enough. When you are in a sports car and the sun's out and the roof is stowed away, you want to hear some induction roar and a crackle from the exhaust. Whereas what you get from the 124 is a missionary-position noise from the front and a vanilla exhaust note. It's a pity.

I have argued in the past that when the roof is down, all cars, from a super-modern Rolls-Royce Dawn to an ancient Sunbeam Alpine, feel exactly the same. There's so much noise and wind and buffeting that trying to concentrate on the finer points of the handling and exhaust note is like trying to concentrate on your surroundings when you are being eaten by a bear. But it's nice to know that if you did concentrate on such things, they'd be right.

So . . . to drive, the Fiat is softer than an MX-5, which is sort of fine, but somehow the squidginess means you get a bit of what feels like old-fashioned scuttle shake. A sense that the whole car is sort of wobbling. And that's not so fine.

And to further distance the 124 from peppier Mazdas, most versions lack a limited-slip differential, so you won't be doing any smoky drifts. It's odd. You'd expect the Fiat, being Italian and all, to be sportier and more manic than the MX-5, but actually it's quieter and less fun.

I'm told by my colleague Richard Hammond that the Abarth version – which does have a limited-slip diff – is a different kettle of fish, but I haven't tried it yet. And, anyway, it's a lot pricier. And, speaking of money, I'm afraid the news is not good. Because the Fiat I drove is more than £1,000 more expensive than the entry-level MX-5.

It sounds as if I have a downer on the 124, and I have, really, mainly because I was expecting it to be something that it isn't. But, that said, it's still a nice place to be. The roof really can be lowered and raised with one hand, without you getting out of the driver's seat. And I love that it's not electric.

I also love the brown leather seats and the equipment levels. I can connect up my iPhone and play Genesis, I have a satnav and electric windows and, er, that's it. But there is a decent-sized boot. Probably because the lid's not flat, as it should have been.

Most important of all, though, it makes me feel all warm and fuzzy to know that outside my house right now is a two-seat Italian sports car. What makes me feel a bit cold and prickly, however, is that it's simply not as good as its Japanese brother.

11 September 2016

Tweaked, but still a funometer-buster

Ford Fiesta ST200

According to the Mail Online, I've been very busy. While filming for my new *Grand Tour* series I flouted all sorts of bird-related by-laws on Beachy Head in East Sussex by flying a drone and then, when there were no more breeding peregrine falcons to mince, I headed off to a Hampshire hotel to gatecrash the wedding of someone called Danny Dyer from *EastEnders*.

A couple of things need straightening out there. I wasn't filming for *The Grand Tour*. I didn't fly a drone. It isn't falcon-breeding season. No one flouted any by-laws. I wasn't in Hampshire. I didn't gatecrash a wedding and I have no idea who Danny Dyer is because I've never seen *EastEnders*.

It got one thing right, though. I was at a hotel. And as at all swanky, country-house getaway spa retreats, the menu offered all sorts of vertical food prepared by a chef who'd trained in Southampton and could do wonderful things with weeds and seeds. But all I wanted was a prawn cocktail. In a glass, with a twist of lemon.

This often happens. I'm on my way to a restaurant, having spent the day gatecrashing weddings and sparking general fury, and I know it will offer me a choice of sautéed sheep's brains and the barely formed areola of a lightly salted baby pig, and suddenly I become overwhelmed by the urgent need for a poached egg on toast.

It's not just food, either, where I crave the simple things. Throughout the summer my Instagram feed was topped up every half-hour by friends posting pictures of themselves on beaches in Greece and on boats off Italy and in hot springs in Colorado. And then one day there was a photograph of a friend's wife and kids playing at Daymer Bay in Cornwall and I almost vomited with envy.

So it goes with cars. I spend most of my life whizzing hither and thither in exotica made from platinum and rhodium and fitted with engines that roar and bellow and spit fire. And all I want on the way home is a Ford Fiesta ST.

Over the past forty years there have been many hot versions of the Fiesta and largely they were tremendous little things – blue-collar buzz bombs with puppy-dog enthusiasm and raspy back ends. The XR2, for instance, was perfect for those whose Thames estuary vowel sounds and rust-round-the-optics drinking dens precluded them from having a slightly superior and slightly more expensive Volkswagen.

But then, four years ago, Ford gave us a hot version of the then current Fiesta. It had a turbocharged 1.6-litre engine, bucket seats and breathed-on suspension, and everyone thought it was going to be more of the same. A cheeky chappie. Up the Junction. Up the Chels. Do you want some, etc., etc., etc.

In fact it was a game-changer; the most endearing and brilliant hot hatchback the world had seen. We get all misty-eyed about the original Golf GTI and the 1.9-litre Peugeot 205 GTI, and rightly so. They were very excellent. But the little Ford Fiesta ST? That was in a different league.

On a day-to-day basis, no car – not one – was as much of a laugh. It was propelled down the road by telepathy. You thought about the corner ahead and it went round, gripping when you wanted it to and slithering about when you didn't. If there were such a thing as a funometer this little car would break it. And now Ford has tried to make it even better by launching something called the ST200.

Let me talk you through the headlines. It's a little bit more powerful than the standard car, which means it's a little bit faster. A very little bit. In fact it's only 0.2 of a second faster from 0-62mph. But it feels more urgent because it has a shorter final drive. Not good for the fuel economy. Not good for Johnny Polar Bear. But tremendous for putting a smile on your face.

You need to dart into the next lane on a slow-moving motorway. No car does it better. Any gear. Any revs. And in a blink, the move is made. I've seen less nippy water boat-men. And then there's the noise. You expect, in a car of this type, to have the 'wheee' of a Catherine wheel. But instead you get something deep and bassy. It sounds like a faraway battle. It's wonderful.

Underneath, the rear twist beam is stiffer and at the front there's a bigger anti-roll bar. This means the platform is more solid and that means Ford has been able to soften the springs and dampers. Which means you get all the compos-ure you need, and a decent ride.

The only trouble is that the tweaks have been so successful, Ford has applied them to the standard ST as well. Which means you are paying a £4,850 premium for the ST200 to shave 0.2 seconds off the cheapest ST's 0-62mph time. Hmmm.

Oh and you also get a little plaque on the centre console that says ST200 on it. If it were made from gold, or myrrh, maybe the price hike would be justified. But it isn't. It's just a fridge magnet.

Other than this, the interior is standard ST, which means

you get Recaro seats that are too high and so big they reduce legroom in the rear to the point where only Douglas Bader would fit. And a dashboard of unrivalled complexity.

I assumed when I first tried to use it that my inability to change the radio station or engage the satnav, let alone read it – the screen is the size of a stamp – was because I'm old. But no. I recently bought a standard ST for my eldest daughter and like all young people she plunged in, pushing buttons hither and thither until she, because she's a she, said: 'I'll have to read the handbook.'

We then set off and . . . disaster. One of the clever things in the ST is the MyKey feature. It means you have one key for yourself and a spare that you hand out when you are lending your car to, say, your teenage kids, or, in my daughter's case, her brother.

The idea is that you programme the spare so that when it's used to start the car, the engine produces reduced power. And the stereo has a maximum volume of about two decibels. It's actually a very, very good idea, but such is the complexity of the dash that even my tech-literate daughter somehow managed to set it up so that both keys prevent her from listening to her drum and bass at anything more than a whisper.

Anyway, back to the ST200. And . . . I'm not sure, if I'm honest. Apart from the shorter final drive, and that grown-up exhaust boom, it's pretty much the same as the standard car, only more expensive.

I would therefore buy the base model instead. And I don't mean instead of the ST200. Or instead of another hot hatchback. I mean instead of just about anything else on the road.

18 September 2016

A lesson from Audi to laptop makers

Audi S8

I'm writing this on a six-year-old laptop. It has been around the world umpteen times and is used to churn out five or six thousand words a week. The screen is fogged with spatters of coffee and mucus, the keypad is full of ash, the 'A' button has worn to a stump and the cooling fan often has hysterics. But I am in no mood to swap it for a newer model, because it would be different.

I hate different. Which means I hate Macs. You need the fingers of a gynaecologist to operate their stupid keypads, there's no right-click and nothing's where it's supposed to be.

It is of course the same story with my telephone. It's very old and sometimes it forgets what it's for. But I can't upgrade to the latest model, with a Hubble telescope for a camera and 9G capability, because it'd mean sitting down with an instruction book, and I couldn't do that, because I'm a man, so I'd just plunge straight in. Which means within an hour I'd have put a very private post on Twitter by mistake.

Strangely, however, I have no problem at all using a different car every week. They all come with different satnav systems – some are good and some are bad – but I can operate them all.

It's the same with the electric seat controls. Some companies put them in the door, some on the transmission tunnel and some down the side of the seat itself, where they can be reached only if you have fingers like a conductor's baton. But, despite this, I never squash myself against the wheel by mistake, or end up in the back, where I can't reach the pedals.

Car firms have intuitiveness down to a fine art. The Audi S8 Plus I've been driving had a head-up display that had been set up by someone who was 4in tall. I needed to lower it on the screen, so I reached out and my hand immediately alighted on the button that did just that.

It was the same with the map. It had been set by the delivery driver to rotate every time I went round a corner, and I find that annoying. So I pushed the correct button, twiddled a knob the correct number of times and pushed OK to confirm. The job was done. If the man who designed the Audi's dashboard worked for Boeing, everyone on earth could land a 747 with no problem at all.

And then things get even more impressive, because while I was driving down the M1 at 50mph, because someone in a box had decided that was the highest speed a human being could possibly manage on a road where everyone was going in the same direction, my mind started to drift off and I found myself wondering how on earth Audi managed to fit all the stuff into the car.

Many years ago, when we were allowed to do 70mph – and usually a bit more – I went to interview a chap at Rover who had a dashboard in bits on his desk and a worried look on his face. 'Not that long from now,' he said, 'people are going to want air-conditioning and CD players as standard in even the cheapest cars. And where the hell am I going to put it all?'

He did appear to have a point. The dashboard of a car is not like the inside of an aircraft hangar, and even then, in the days of the Rover 216, it was pretty much jammed full with tubes and looms and relays. So how, I wondered as I crawled along at 50mph for yet more miles, has Audi managed?

Quite apart from the head-up display and the climate control and the satnav and the passenger airbag, there were buttons to stop the engine shutting down at the lights, buttons to alter the interior lighting, buttons to turn off the traction control, buttons in fact to turn off a million things that hadn't even been invented when Johnny Rover Man was pulling his hair out.

And because I was still doing 50mph, to 'protect the workforce' that wasn't bloody there, I started to wonder about more things. The engine, for example, is a dirty great V8 that's fitted with two turbochargers. How does that go under the bonnet?

And then there's the four-wheel-drive system and the antilock braking system and the bouncy castle that inflates when you have a bump, and the parking sensors and the cameras and the system that steers the car by itself and the forward-facing radar. Why, I wondered, isn't this car bigger than the USS *Dwight D. Eisenhower*?

And then the man in the control box decided that, actually, 50mph was way too fast for this day and age, so he changed the dot-matrix signs to say we could do only 40mph. And then I began to wonder why on earth anyone in their right mind would buy a car such as the 155mph Audi.

That didn't take long to answer. Because it can do 155mph, it is barely awake at 40, which means it is supremely quiet and, if you put the suspension in Comfort mode, dreamily smooth. Honestly, I've been in noisier and less comfortable beds.

You may imagine that a car this squidgy is incapable of being exciting. And you'd be right. Even if you put everything in Sport mode – that's something else you can do – and turn off the traction control, it is stubbornly understeery. It's almost as though it's saying: 'What on earth are you playing at?'

A fair point. Driving a car such as this as though your hair's on fire is like playing rugby in a £400 pair of loafers. And that brings me on to the question of price. I don't know what it costs and I can't be bothered to look it up. This is not a car anyone will buy. It'll be leased. And the monthly bill will depend on who you are, how many A4s you're buying for your sales staff and whether the dealer is struggling to meet his yearly quotas. All I do know is that it'll be a lot less than you imagine.

Of course, exactly the same applies if you are thinking of buying a Mercedes S-class, or the Jaguar XJ, or a BMW 7-series, which are pretty much identical to the big Audi. They're all quiet and comfortable and loaded up with stuff you'll never use and power reserves you'll never need. The S8 Plus I had developed 84bhp more than the A8 on which it's based. Which meant . . . absolutely nothing at all.

What does matter is that I liked it. I've always said the 7-series is the best of the big barges. But I don't think it is any more. I think the A8 is a nicer place to be. When you're doing 40. Which you will be.

The only problem is: you currently use a Merc, don't you? And you're used to it. And you're frightened to change. Don't be.

9 October 2016

Take it away – I'm just not ready to grow up

Citroën Grand C4 Picasso

I had a bit of a discussion the other day about when men grow up. A friend explained that when he used to work in a clothes shop he would fill quieter parts of the day by carefully unwrapping the underwear. He'd then use a chocolate bar to create authentic-looking skid marks before wrapping it up again and putting it back on the shelves. 'The beauty was,' he said, 'that no one would ever bring it back to complain.'

I won't tell you his name, obviously, save to say that it begins with an A and ends in A. Gill. What I will tell you is that today he's in his sixties* but, given the chance, he said with a big smile, he'd do the exact same thing again.

I fear I'm just as bad. When I'm told by a passport person to stand behind the line, I simply cannot bring myself to do it. I always, always, always position myself so that at least some of one foot is in the forbidden zone. It's pathetic but I can't help myself.

It's why I loathe average-speed cameras. With a normal Gatso you can roar up to the box, brake as late as possible and then roar off again when the damn thing is out of range. That's sticking one to The Man. But when you are being monitored constantly, there is absolutely nothing you can do.

* *A. Gill died in December 2016.*

You are forced to just sit there being obedient, and that causes me actual physical pain.

Neatly stacked tins in a supermarket make me ill as well. I become dizzy and faint when I walk past them because the urge to knock them over is so unbelievably strong. It's one of the few things left on my bucket list.

However, I'll need to hurry up about it because I can feel myself getting old. I can sense the rebel in my soul quietening down. It's not just because I now enjoy a 'nice sit-down' more than almost anything. It's worse. It's because I can't be bothered half the time to make a nuisance of myself.

This brings me on to the business of renting a car. It's a chore. It's up there with trying on trousers or rubbing sun-cream into James May's back. You stand for hours in a queue full of terrible people, and when you finally get to the front of it, you are made to stand there while the woman behind the counter writes *War and Peace* on her computer.

Why do they always do this? I have the money and they have the car, so what's the complication? Why the need to tap away on a keyboard for three hours? They don't do that in a sweetshop or at a petrol station. But they do at the air-port rental desk. And the only upside is that when the interminable wait is over, you are given the keys to the fastest car in the world.

I have always driven hire cars as though my hair were on fire. It's just so liberating when you arrive at a road where a sign says 'Unsuitable for motors' and you think, as you floor it, 'Yes, but it's suitable for this one, because . . . yee-haw . . . it isn't mine.'

This year I rented a house in Mallorca that sat at the top of what was easily the narrowest and longest and most challen-ging drive in all of the world. In the past it wouldn't have bothered me one bit. I'd have simply ricocheted up it in the rental car, bouncing off the trees and the walls as though I was a large-scale demonstration of Brownian motion.

However, this year I found myself taking care. And amazingly at the end of the ten-day break the hire car was handed back without a scratch. It was a first, and it made me think: 'Oh shit. At the age of fifty-six I've become an adult.'

The panic, though, is over, because last week Citroën sent round the same car as I'd been using in Mallorca. It's a Grand C4 Picasso and it had the most extraordinary effect on me. I drove about the place, agreeing with all the callers on the Jeremy Vine show and missing Nigel Farage.

I scoffed at girls in ripped jeans, tutted at men with earrings and engaged the handbrake when stationary. This is a car that can accelerate from 0 to 62mph in 10.1 seconds and thunder onwards to a speed of nearly 130mph. But I never did either of those things.

What I did instead was admire some of the features, such as the comfy headrests and the passenger seat that comes with an electrically operated footrest for when the floor is just too uncomfortable. Then there are the sun visors that fold up and away to reveal a windscreen big enough for a National Express coach, and, further back, an all-glass roof.

Further back still, there's a third row of seats, and everywhere you look there are cubbyholes and storage bins. This is one of those cars that are hard to resist in the showroom. It really is jam-packed with stuff you'll want as soon as you see it.

Driving it is a different story, because there is some quirkiness. The gear lever, for instance, is a flimsy little stalk on the steering column. And just about everything else is operated by a screen in the middle of the car. That's fiddly and annoying.

Well, it would be, but you'll be too busy sticking to the speed limit to be overly worried about how you turn off the engine stop-start function. Not that you'd want to turn it off, because it saves fuel and that saves money. And saving money is the single most important thing in life. It's why Grand C4 Picasso owners do all their shopping in the sales and only go to restaurants with all-you-can-eat buffets for £4.99.

It's why they have Citroëns in the first place. Because they are cheap, long before you get to the endless everything-must-go special offers.

This is not a criticism of Citroën's customers. Each to his or her own. And it certainly isn't a criticism of the car, because if you want a seven-seater, it makes a deal of sense. You just have to remember that behind the clever design touches there's a car that's not inspiring to drive and will break down more than, say, a Toyota. And that sounds like the incoming-torpedo alert on a submarine if you leave the lights on or open the door when the engine's running.

On the upside, though, you'll never crash it. Because you'll never be going fast enough. Because a Grand C4 Picasso brings out the adult that lives in us all.

That said, just before the delivery driver came to take it away, I was tempted to create some chocolate skid marks on the seat. And say it was like that when it was delivered.

23 October 2016

The moor the merrier in our hot hatch rally

VW Golf GTI Clubsport

My television colleagues and I had to visit Whitby recently, which meant there was a debate in the office about how we'd get to North Yorkshire. If we chose something comfortable and quiet, to deal with the massively over-policed M1, it'd be no fun at all once we got past Malton and said: 'Have some of that.'

Whereas if we chose something that would be fun on that truly glorious road over Fylingdales Moor, it'd be a chore in the stop-start hell that is the M1.

In the end we decided to cheat and use a train from London to York, which is more expensive than going on a golden elephant but takes about three minutes these days. And then we'd use a car for the final leg.

But what car? The temptation, obviously, was to select something idiotic – a Lamborghini Aventador, perhaps, or the new and really rather beautiful Ferrari GTC4Lusso. But the truth is, show-off cars such as those are designed to work, mostly, in cities.

So quite quickly all three of us decided that hot hatchbacks would be perfect for the job. And this caused another debate. There's no doubt at all that the best of the bunch is the little Ford Fiesta ST. But I'd driven that, and anyway it was shotgunned immediately by Mr Hammond.

And before I could draw breath to say, 'Well, I'll have a

Ford Focus RS, then', James May put down his pipe, adjusted his slippers and shotgunned that. So I had a good long think and remembered that Volkswagen had recently smashed the front-wheel-drive lap record at the Nürburgring with a car called the Golf GTI Clubsport S.

In essence it's a GTI, but, thanks to a lot of electrical jiggery-pokery under the bonnet, it produces a colossal 306bhp. And there's more. The ride has been made priapic. The body shell has been stiffened. The back seats and the parcel shelf and various bits of carpet have been removed. And as a result it's hard and tight and light and, as we saw when it broke that lap record, very, very fast.

This is exactly the sort of car that would be terrible to live with day to day but perfect for an afternoon assault on the North York Moors. I was very happy with my choice until I received word that the Clubsport S is a limited-edition special, and that none was available.

Instead I ended up with a car built to celebrate the GTI's fortieth birthday. Called the Clubsport Edition 40, it looks like a Clubsport S but it has carpets and back seats and all the luxuries you'd expect. You can even have it with four doors, which is a very un-Clubsporty thing.

All of which means it's a GTI with some spoilers and a small amount of electrical jiggery-pokery under the bonnet. And that in turn means it's nothing more than a slightly pricier version of a car I already own.

It did have a nicer steering wheel – I'll admit that. And lovely seats. But it had a manual gearbox, which was a nuisance in York, where the traffic lights are red for about six years and then flash green in the same way as the sun does when it sinks into the sea. It took longer to get out of the city than it had taken to get there from London.

By the time I finally found the A64 to Pickering and the glory of the moors, I was far behind Hammond in his little Fiesta, but it's always possible to catch May. Even if you're on a mule with a hurty leg.

So off I set, and straight away I could tell the Clubsport Edition 40 is more than VW's present to itself. The figures suggest it has only 35 more brake horsepower than the standard GTI, but if your right foot comes into contact with the firewall, there's an overboost facility that gives you 286bhp. This makes the front wheels spin, which makes the traction control go into busybody mode. Which means that if you want this sort of power for this sort of money, you're better off with the all-wheel-drive Golf R.

However. And it's a big however. In my standard GTI – chosen because I can't be bothered to explain to people at parties what an R is – there's a definite hole in the power delivery. When you just want to go slightly faster, you put your foot down a bit and . . . nothing happens.

It's almost certainly some kind of ludicrous emission programme in the engine control unit, but it feels like turbo lag and it's annoying. However, in the Clubsport Edition 40 it doesn't happen. The movement of your foot is translated instantly into a change of pace. It makes the whole car feel more alert and alive.

I'd love to tell you that the chassis is crisper too, because it probably is. But the truth is that this car feels exactly the same as the standard GTI. Which means it is extremely clever at riding the bumps and then gripping as if it's on spikes in the corners.

VW even says that the bigger rear spoiler and the splitter at the front create actual downforce once you're going above 75mph. So in order to not crash, you just need to speed up.

Hammond will tell you — and he's right — the Fiesta ST is more fun, and May will tell you that the Focus RS is better in extremis. But as a blend of all you need, the VW is in a class of its own.

It's the same story with the interior. Everything has a top-quality feel that you just don't get in the two Fords, plus there's a lot of standard equipment provided as standard.

Of course it's not as good as the Golf R. That's a remarkable car. A brilliant car. But if you want a GTI because, well, you want a GTI, this Clubsport Edition 40 makes a deal of sense. It's my own car, with a couple of neat styling touches and the performance hole caused by bureaucrats in Brussels filled in.

Richard disagreed with this. And so did James when he finally arrived at the hotel. And we argued about that into the night. It's good to be back.

6 November 2016

Engineers – give it everything you've got

Audi SQ7

James May has decided he doesn't like Audis. I recently had to transport him in the back of the new SQ7 and he chuntered away constantly like a speedboat on tickover. Obviously, I can't be bothered to listen to his specific gripes but the thrust of his argument seems to be there's too much design and not enough engineering.

As usual, he's wrong. Because the SQ7 – the hot version of Audi's biggest SUV – is actually a lumpen-looking thing that hasn't been designed enough. But oh my God. There's more engineering in this 2.25-ton, 16.5-foot road rocket than you find in that giant arch they're building over reactor four at Chernobyl. This car? It's like the spirits of Isambard Kingdom Brunel and Steve Jobs have come together to create a mind-boggling orgy of brute force and chips.

We shall start with the engine. You'd expect, in a car that goes from 0 to 62mph in less than five seconds, and onwards to a top speed of about a million, that it'd be a monstrous V12 with petrol coursing through its injectors. But to make it even more annoying for the world's ecomentalists, it's a 4-litre V8 forced-induction diesel.

I say 'forced induction' rather than 'turbocharged' because Audi has invented a whole new way of ramming air into the cylinders. You get two turbochargers, as you'd expect these days, but downstream of the intercooler and close to the engine itself there's something the no-nonsense Germans have called an 'electrically powered compressor' (EPC). What it is is a compressor that's powered by electricity rather than exhaust gases. And it can go from rest to 70,000rpm in less than 250 milliseconds. Which is, as near as dammit, instantaneous.

In a normal turbocharged car there is always a gap between you putting your foot down and the engine delivering its full potential. This is because the turbochargers take time to spool up. In the SQ7 that gap is filled by the EPC.

What I love about this is that it's a massively complicated solution to a problem that today exists only in books about algebra. Turbo lag – as the gap is called – was pronounced and annoying when turbocharged road cars came along in the Seventies. But today it's noticeable only if you concentrate very, very hard. Which means Audi has spent a fortune exorcising something that exists only in theory. It is to be commended for this in the same way as a top-flight chef is to be commended for going the extra mile with his truffle sauce. Almost none of his customers will notice, but . . .

And that brings me on to the engine itself, specifically the cam shafts, which are profiled so that they vary the amount of valve movement. This is advanced mechanics, but what it means, Audi says, is that you get torque when you want it and economy the rest of the time. Again, you won't notice, but . . .

What you will notice in the SQ7 is that when you go round a corner it doesn't seem to roll very much. This is a big car that sits on stilts, so you'd expect its door handles to be scraping along the asphalt when you give it the beans, and yet they aren't.

This is because of yet more engineering. An electric motor and a three-stage planetary gearbox are used to operate an anti-roll system. It's designed to disengage when you're off road, so you don't get jolted too much, and then engage when you're on the road, going quickly. And when it does, it effectively props up the side of the car that should be leaning over. This is technology that was tried, and then banned, in Formula One.

I'd love to say it does all its cleverness without affecting the ride comfort, but that would be a lie. You do feel the bumps – a bit – but again I admire the way the engineers have been allowed to experiment with the boundaries. They could have just painted some snazzy stripes down the side and fitted big tyres, but they've gone further, and I like that. The SQ7 even has mild four-wheel steering.

I could go on and on about other innovations – Audi has come up with a new way of combining lightness with strength in the construction, so you get better economy from a car that doesn't fall to pieces when it hits a tree – but it's probably time now to move inside, where you get two rows of seats, plus a temporary row that rises electrically from the boot floor. You're never going to get your grandmother back there, but children will be fine.

Move further forward and you start to get to the bits that annoy May. As we know, James is a man who enjoys mending Bakelite telephones, so obviously he is going to be irritated by what he'd call unnecessary blue downlighting and what Audi calls 'horizontal' design.

I have no idea what horizontal design is, or why it's better than vertical design, but I do like the finished product. The Audi, slightly bumpy ride aside, is a nice place to be. And even though it is burdened with a million new engineering solutions, it's not like the cockpit of an experimental spaceship. It's simple and straightforward, and you're never left looking at a button, thinking: 'What the bloody hell does that thing do?'

You press a button, engage a driving mode on the surprisingly old-fashioned torque converter automatic gearbox and drive about. It's as demanding as taking a bath.

So it's fast, strong, safe, clever, innovative, interesting, spacious, very well made and, so far as I can see, completely pointless.

I've tried all week to imagine the sort of person who might want to buy such a thing – and I can't. I know people who like to drive fast cars, and certainly they will enjoy the bassy and slightly rough sound of that big diesel V8. But nobody who enjoys a car such as that will want it to have seven seats.

Then there are people who do need the practicality of seven seats for the school run. Yes, the Audi's anti-roll system will stop them being carsick, and that's good, but who needs 663 torques and half a billion horsepowers to get a bunch of kids to the playground?

It's the same story with the off-road abilities. Yes, the Audi can hoist itself up to give good ground clearance and it has four-wheel drive. But it sits on performance tyres, so if you try to get it to your peg on a shoot, it'll get stuck. So it isn't an off-road car at all, really.

This is the trouble. It's not an off-roader. It's not a sports car. It's not a sumptuous long-distance luxury car and it certainly isn't a looker. The only element likely to raise a pensive eyebrow is the price. It's less than £71,000, which is good value for this much engineering. It's actually £12,380 cheaper than a slower and less practical V8 Range Rover.

The trouble is, £71,000 is a lot for a car that you neither need nor want.

13 November 2016

Torque of the town, but quiet as a mouse

Bentley Mulsanne Speed

People who live near a busy road often moan about traffic noise, and they have my sympathy. I'd rather listen to a wounded hare than a motorway. And I'd rather live in Svalbard than near a busy roundabout.

There are many reasons why traffic makes such a din. Motorbikes are a big source, and so far as I can tell from my vantage point in west London, they're getting even louder. When I come to power, the banishment of these hideous and ugly machines from the roads will be near the top of my 'to do' list.

Buses are noisy too, and I think it would make sense to get rid of them as well. This would force poor people to use bicycles instead, and that would cause them to be less fat. Which would mean there'd be less of a drain on the National Health Service. Speaking of which – ambulances. Do they really need sirens that can be heard twenty miles away?

With cars it's a different story. With the exception of some found in extremely expensive supercars that you never really encounter, modern-day engines and exhaust systems are pretty much silent.

Bob Seger once sang about being on tour – 'You can listen to the engine moanin' out his one-note song' – but he's wide of the mark. Because in fact between 75 per cent and 90 per cent of the noise made by a car on a motorway comes from the tyres.

It's not just the sound of the rubber gripping the road; it's the sound of the air in the tread pattern being compressed, and it's all amplified because a tyre is basically a big echo chamber.

And that brings us to the Bentley Mulsanne Speed. It was delivered to my office by two earnest chaps, who were at pains to point out the various interesting features. But the one that stopped me in my tracks was the Dunlop rubber, which, they said, had been tuned for quietness.

They weren't kidding. At 70mph this car is as near as makes no difference silent. It's a huge thing, with the aerodynamic properties – and weight – of a house, but it barges its way through, and over, the elements with all the aural fuss of a butterfly alighting on a buddleia petal.

It's not just quiet for the occupants. It's quiet for everyone. So quiet that after just thirty miles on the M4 I made a mental note to make sure that when I take control of No. 10 those tyres become compulsory for all cars. They're brilliant.

And so, for exactly the same reason, is the 6.75-litre V8 engine in this automotive leviathan. Amazingly, it was designed before I was born. And, on paper, you can tell. Words such as 'single camshaft' and 'pushrod' are from a time of rationing and diphtheria.

Eighteen years ago, when Volkswagen took control of Bentley, it said this venerable old V8 would have to be discontinued in the near future because it simply couldn't be tuned to meet various emission regulations. But it was wrong.

It has fitted a couple of Mitsubishi turbochargers to

provide forced induction and added a system that shuts down half the cylinders when they're not needed to save fuel. And you'd imagine that all this tweakery would cause it to become feeble and weak. But it doesn't.

The numbers are incredible: you get 530 brake horsepower and, at just 1750rpm, a truly colossal 811 torques. There are bulldozers with less than that – 811lb/ft is planetary force. It's hysterical force. And you'd imagine that its creation would cause an almighty din. But astonishingly it doesn't.

If you really stab the throttle deep into the inch-thick carpet, there is a barely discernible hum. But at all other times it's as silent as a sleeping nun.

So this is a quiet car. And no matter what setting you choose for the air suspension, it's a comfortable car too. It's also good-looking. The aggressive new front end is especially impressive.

And it is extremely well equipped with all manner of things that you didn't even know were possible. The rear touchscreens, for instance, rise silently from the back of the front seats. And then there's the 2,200-watt stereo. That's not a misprint. The manufacturer has fitted this completely silent car with a sound system that could blow your head clean off.

However, it's precisely because of all this equipment and all these toys that I would buy a Rolls-Royce Ghost instead.

Someone at Bentley obviously believes that luxury can be measured in the number of buttons. They think that a house is palatial if you can run a bath from the garage and open the front gate using your television remote. And that is probably true – if you are a footballer. But I'm not.

I have criticized Bentleys in the past for being a bit 'last week' when it comes to electronics. The Continental GT

Speed, for example, doesn't have a USB port, and that, in this day and age, is obviously nuts.

The problem is that with the Mulsanne Speed Bentley's gone berserk. So you now have two satellite navigation screens in the front that can be operated from the dash or the steering wheel or by touching the screen itself or by using your voice.

Eventually, I'm sure, you could machete your way through the operational complexity that results, but I suspect it would take many years.

Happily, there is a USB port. But it's in a little drawer that can't be shut if you're using it. Then there's the charging point, under the central armrest, which also can't be shut if it's in use.

You get the sense that asking Bentley to fit modern-day electronics is a bit like asking David Linley to reprogramme your iPhone. Or Bill Gates to make a chest of drawers.

The result is daunting. You sit there, behind the wheel, confronted by hundreds and hundreds of buttons and switches, and you can't help thinking how much better this car would be if only it were less complicated.

And maybe a tiny bit smaller. On the A40 in west London, where there are narrow lanes to 'protect the workforce' – that's never there – I was recently unable to pass a coach for miles. Which was a bore.

It's annoying. I like the idea of a Bentley more than the idea of a Rolls-Royce. My grandfather had a Bentley R Type, and it was the first car I drove. I like the idea too of telling people I drive an 'MFB'.

But I never once drove this car as a Bentley could and should be driven. I never felt obliged to put the suspension in its Sport setting and unleash all those torques. I just wafted about in it. And if I want a large and luxurious car in which to waft, I'd rather have the simpler, airier, more tasteful Ghost.

Because when you sink into one of those, you say: 'Aaaah.' Whereas when you sink into the Mulsanne Speed, you think: 'Oh, for God's sake. Where's the button that shuts the bloody satnav woman up?'

20 November 2016

Drop this one in the bin, please, robot

Honda Jazz 1.3 i-VTec Ex Navi

Not that long ago we all used to look forward to the car ads on commercial television. We had Paula Hamilton ditching her fur coat but keeping the Volkswagen Golf GTI. We had burning cornfields, and Geoffrey Palmer dolefully talking about beating the Germans to the beach, and dancing robots and Gene Kelly, and Škodas made from cake, and 'Isn't it nice when things just work?'

Car ads were almost always better than the programmes they funded. They were cleverer. They made you want a certain type of vehicle when you had been told almost nothing about it. But then, all of a sudden, everything changed.

Today even BMW, which only used to say it made the 'ultimate driving machine', fills its commercials with all the finance deals that are available. It really is a case of: 'Here's 14 feet of car which you can have for £9.99 a week with 2 per cent APR and the value of your house could go up as well as down.'

It saddens me that cars have gone the way of takeaway food. Nobody cares about the quality or the health benefits or the company's history any more. Just how much you can get for how little.

I think the last truly great car commercial was Honda's 'The Power of Dreams' ad. Filmed in New Zealand, Argentina and Japan, it featured a magnificent-looking chap with a huge moustache and sideburns setting out from his beach-side caravan on a small Honda motorcycle, and then, to the backdrop of Andy Williams crooning 'The Impossible Dream', he is seen singing along as he flies through the scenery in just about every important product Honda has made. Racing bikes, Formula One cars, speedboats, sports cars, touring bikes, quads – the lot. It is a true epic, and you're left at the end thinking: 'I have got to have one.'

It was updated several years later, with an extended ending in which we saw Mr Moustache at the controls of a Honda jet, and in the hydrogen fuel-cell car and then arriving at a house on the coast to find the Honda robot had got the hot tub ready. It was brilliant.

But I can't help wondering: if Honda updates it again, what the bloody hell will it feature to say that the dream goes on? The current F1 campaign? Not sure that's completely on message, as the only impossible dream is finishing anywhere other than nearly last. So what about the cars? Er . . .

I once described Hondas as Alfa Romeos that start, because, really, that's what they were. This is a company that did reliable better than anyone, but it never did dull. Everything it made was a bit weird, a bit odd. A bit fabulous. The Jazz I was using last week, however, is none of those things.

Finished in what Honda calls Brilliant Sporty Blue and what everyone else calls 'blue', it was the version called the Ex Navi. I'm not sure that name works here, because ex-navvies in my experience are something completely different.

Priced £16,755, it came with a driver's seat pocket, electric windows and a cigarette-lighter socket. But no actual cigarette lighter. On the outside, Honda lists the highlights as fog lights and wheels. There is absolutely nothing to make you think: 'Wow.'

Until you put your foot down, hard, in second gear. You'll certainly say, 'Wow,' at this point because nothing of any consequence happens. This is a small car with a 101bhp 1.3-litre i-VTec engine. It should be quite peppy, and yet somehow it is the complete opposite.

If you're not really concentrating when you are driving the Jazz, you may find that your forward progress is being undone by tectonic drift. You set off to go to the shops and end up, three thousand years later, drifting backwards into Norway.

You may imagine the engine is tuned this way so that it's kind to your wallet and Johnny Polar Bear, but I'm afraid not. Compared with various other engines of this size that are available from rival manufacturers, it's uneconomical and produces quite a lot of carbon dioxides.

One of the extraordinary things is that it doesn't produce its peak torque until it's turning at 5000rpm. So to get the best out of it, you have to rev the nuts off it at all times.

I used to love Honda's engines. They were always so sweet and willing. They were like small but very well-trained Jack Russells. But the engine in that Jazz? The only dog to which it can be likened is one that's dead.

At this point I'd like to tell you about the handling, but I can't because the car won't go quickly enough for any deficiencies to be uncovered. And if we're honest, the average Jazz driver doesn't care two hoots about understeer or lift-off oversteer; they're happy just so long as there's somewhere to store their bingo pencils.

On that front, it's not bad. There are four doors, which means Peggy and Maureen will be able to get into and out of the back easily.

And there's a boot that's big enough for two tartan

shopping trolleys. But then we get to the infotainment centre, which is good and clear and clever if you are nine. But completely baffling if you grew up with rationing.

My mother used to say that all she ever wanted from a car was a heater and Classic FM. She had a first-generation Jazz and loved it because it had both things. But in this new one I guarantee she'd be flummoxed on the radio front. Partly this is because if you don't touch the screen in exactly the right place it does nothing at all.

There's more, I'm afraid. It's not a good-looking car. The wheels are 16-inchers but they look lost in the arches, and there are some swooping styling details that are unnecessary and odd.

The only good things, really, are the quality of the materials in the cabin and the space in the back, which is much greater than you'd expect from a car of this type.

If the other people in your bridge four are extremely fat, this might be enough to convince you the Jazz is a worthwhile buy, but if they aren't, you'd be better off with a Ford Fiesta or a Volkswagen Polo or a Škoda Fabia. Or an Uber app.

I can't believe I'm saying that. I can't believe Honda has sunk this low. Six years ago it was making cars and television commercials that made you dizzy with desire. And now it's making cars with engines that turn a lot of fuel into nothing at all.

As I said at the beginning, Honda used to ask in its commercials: 'Isn't it nice when things just work?'

To which the answer is: 'Yes. It was.'

4 December 2016

It's dressed to thrill with nowhere to go

Honda Civic Type R

In one of the upcoming *Grand Tour* television programmes I have a bit of a rant, saying that the world's car makers seem to have shifted into neutral and to be simply biding their time making dreary boxes until they are consumed by Uber.

I single out the Renault Kadjar SUV, which I hate very much, and I say that it will never be a poster on a young boy's bedroom wall and that no one will ever dream of the day they can buy one. I argue loudly that it is just some car, on which Renault can make a couple of quid from the finance deals.

I fear, however, I may have been a trifle hasty, because I've come to realize car makers are swimming against a tide that will eventually consume them, no matter what rabbits they pull from the hat.

There have always been people who say, 'I'm not interested in cars', but today it's not just the occasional old lady with a twin set, pearls and a Mrs Queen haircut. It's pretty much everyone, especially if they are under twenty-five.

I sit down at a party and immediately I'm told by everyone at the table that they do not wish to talk about cars. It's annoying. Because I can't imagine many of them are very interested in accountancy, but they never say to an accountant when he sits down: 'We don't want to talk about Ebit and CGT.'

I actually know a proctologist, and I've never heard anyone say to him: 'We don't want to talk about anuses.' Which has led me to believe that today people are more interested in rectums than they are in the new Ferrari GTC4Lusso.

I can see why. For twenty years they have been brainwashed by the liberal elite – the people who are now getting their arses kicked in every single election – that cars are bad for the environment and if we keep on using them to go to work and the shops, *Planet Earth* III will have to be about wasps and cockroaches because everything else will be extinct.

The constant drip-feed of eco-mental nonsense affects politicians especially. They respond by worrying about the constituent parts of the upper atmosphere and think they can sort everything out if they reduce speed limits. And then reduce them again and then stick up average-speed cameras to ensure the limits are obeyed.

Then they dig up the roads for years so they can be made narrower, and they put in speed humps and cycle lanes, and another speed camera just for good measure. The effect has been profound.

When I was growing up, I dreamt of the open road, because we had such a thing back then. Cars were something you could barely afford, but, boy, they were worth it because they represented freedom and glamour and excitement. They were something you needed, for sure. But they were something you wanted as well.

Today kids look out of the back window of the Volvo on the school run, and they see the jams and the cycle lanes and the speed cameras and think: 'Well, this isn't very exciting, is it?' So when they reach the age of seventeen and they are allowed a licence, they think: 'What's the point?'

As my son said: 'Why do I need to drive? I can use a coach

to get to London for a couple of quid, even when I've had a drink, and it has wi-fi.'

It's a good point, and that's before we get to Uber, which has realized that we don't need a car. But that we do need one at 4.15 a.m. on Tuesday.

People have started to realize that for 90 per cent of the time their car just sits on the street doing nothing except costing money. So why not get rid of it and use a man in a Toyota Prius for the 10 per cent of the time when they need to go somewhere?

Now, I know I reviewed a Honda only last week, but I then drove the Civic Type R and realized it quite neatly sums up my point. A number of years ago Honda made this model, and it revved as if it were running on nitrous, handled as though its tyres were made from glue and roared and snarled as if it were very angry about something. To this day that car is revered in some quarters as a deity.

But then, one day, Honda pulled the plug and decided to make cars exclusively for pensioners and Americans, which are the same thing.

Now, though, the Type R is back, and it's no shrinking violet. Nor does it follow the age-old hot-hatchback recipe of taking one ordinary cooking car and adding a bigger engine and bucket seats. It's way more complicated than that.

It's so complicated, in fact, that really it isn't a Civic at all. The rear suspension is different, and at the front it has a system like that of no other car at all. It's slightly similar to the RevoKnuckle arrangement on a Ford Focus RS, but better, apparently. Cleverer. More able to deal with sudden gobs of torque from the engine.

Which is necessary, because the engine in the old Civic Type R produced almost 200bhp. In the latest one you get a colossal 306bhp. That's 306 brake horsepower from a 2-litre engine. And you get 150 more torques. Crikey.

But the most striking thing about this car is the way it looks. Honda says that all the wings and the splitters have an aerodynamic point. It says that without them the Type R would not have been able to hold the front-wheel-drive Nürburgring lap record. (Until Volkswagen took it away recently with a stripped-out Golf GTI.)

Ten years ago you could have driven this car down the street, and young boys would have jumped up and down and grabbed at their tinkles. Youths would have swooned. Dads would have become wistful. Not any more. Now, pretty much everyone stands with their hands on their hips and slowly shakes their heads. It's the look you give a naughty dog.

So you need thick skin to drive a Type R. But is it worth it? Hmmm. Not sure. The engine, though undoubtedly powerful, lacks much in the way of aural excitement and is patchy in the way it delivers the grunt. Honda is a newcomer to turbocharging and it sort of shows. And the chassis is so good, it makes the car feel a little bit dull. A hot hatch should put a smile on your face. It should be like a puppy. This feels a bit serious.

Of course, if you are a serious helmsman, you will admire its ability to grip and go. And you'll love the lap times it can produce at a track. But if you are a serious helmsman, why would you buy a car with front-wheel drive?

And whoever you are, you will certainly tire very quickly of getting out of the seat when you reach journey's end. The bucket is so pronounced and the side bolsters so high, it's nigh-on impossible. I also found the interior a bit clever-clever.

Overall, then, it's not Honda's best effort. But that's OK, because the company has already announced that next year it will replace the car with a new Type R.

I'm glad that Honda is still trying. But I fear it is chasing a market that doesn't really exist any more.

11 December 2016

Pay attention, 007, this one does work

Aston Martin DB11

People like Aston Martins. And what's more, people like people who drive them. They're seen as cool and intelligent and refined. They know not to drink red wine with fish and are familiar with the Latin name for every single fish in the sea.

Astons are driven by people who find Ferraris and Porsches a bit tall-poppy vulgar, a bit Manchester United. A bit disgusting. I get that, but there's always been a problem. Aston Martins have never been much good.

The DB5, trumpeted by many as the best, most iconic Aston Martin of them all, feels pretty much like a Seddon Atkinson dustbin lorry to drive. There's a scene in the Bond film *GoldenEye* where Pierce Brosnan races his silver bin lorry through the Alpes-Maritimes against a Ferrari 355. It was supposed to be very exciting but for me it was just annoying because I was being asked to believe that if someone entered a cow into the Grand National it would be in with a shout of winning.

Later Aston Martin made a car called the Vantage. It had a supercharged V8 and excellent headrests. But to drive, it felt almost identical to Ford's Raptor pick-up. I loved the Vantage, make no mistake, but it handled and braked and gripped like it was quite drunk.

To make matters worse, Astons back then were made by

hand, which is another way of saying that nothing fitted or worked properly. And they were never really tested before they went on sale. There was a sense at the Newport Pagnell factory that early customers could find out what was wrong. That would save a lot of time, bother and expense.

This sort of thing was still going on when the company came up with the DB7. I forget now exactly what was still wrong with it when it went on sale but I'm pretty sure a tendency to fall to pieces was at the top of a long list.

The DB9 was far more sorted when it came along. You sensed it had been properly developed and well thought out. But you also sensed that behind the achingly pretty face beat a fairly ordinary heart. It was as groundbreaking as a loaf of bread. And that's been the story ever since, really. Beautiful and fairly well-made cars that under the skin were just that: cars.

Ferrari and Porsche, with big-money backing from wealthy parents, could afford to develop new technology and new ways of doing things. Aston Martin was stuck. It would change the styling and the names of the cars but underneath they were all broadly the same and they were using tech that was starting to look old-fashioned.

So I wasn't really expecting all that much from the new DB11. I figured that it would be beautiful, which it is – achingly so – but that it would be no match dynamically for what the rest of the world could offer. I was wrong.

The old V12, which sounded magnificent – but which we always knew at the back of our minds had been made by nailing two Ford Mondeo engines together – is now gone. And in its stead the DB11 is powered by an all-new 5.2-litre V12 that is fitted with two turbochargers.

When I heard that Aston Martin had developed this

engine itself, I thought: 'With what? Some loose change they found down the back of the sofa?' I figured it would be a bit old-school with lag and a lot of 'That'll do, near enough' Brummie tech. It isn't. It comes with cylinder deactivation and one turbo and intercooler per bank and all the latest tech. Also, the engine's made in Germany.

Better still, there's been a tie-up with Mercedes-Benz so the DB11 has a Mercedes satnav (current Aston Martin owners will rejoice at that news). And Mercedes electronics. And the Mercedes Comand infotainment system.

As I said when I reviewed the car on the television recently, this is a very successful Anglo-German marriage. And soon it will produce a son; an Aston with Mercedes-AMG's turbocharged V8. I'm dribbling at the thought of that.

But not as much as I'm dribbling at the memory of driving the DB11 round the Mugello racetrack in Tuscany. I've driven Astons on a track before and it's always felt as if I'm trying to ballet dance in a pair of extremely good-looking Church's brogues. You always got the sense that the car was saying: 'Really?'

The DB11 is a completely different animal. The chassis was designed by a former Lotus chap who has tuned it for comfort, yes, but not – as I quickly discovered – at the expense of everything else. Ooh, that car gripped.

As you're going along, air is funnelled into ducts behind the rear-side windows and it's then shot out of a narrow vent on the boot lid. When I was told about this invisible air rear wing I thought, 'Yeah, right', and I still do to a certain extent. But something is keeping the rear end planted so maybe it does work. Maybe Aston really has thought of something new. That'd be a first.

The traction control system isn't new. But it's tuned

beautifully so it's gentle in its restraint and progressive when it feels you're through the bend and the rear tyres are fully able to exploit the 600bhp and that mountain of torque. It's even better than the system in the McLaren 675LT, and that's saying something.

You imagine when you leave the track that something this grippy will not work on the road. But it really, really does. Put it in GT mode and it becomes quiet and smooth and very comfortable.

If you're ever in Paris, at a party at 3 a.m., and suddenly remember you are playing in a tennis tournament in Monte Carlo the next afternoon, this is the car for the job. You'd arrive feeling like you'd just got out of the bath.

The upshot of all this is that you feel, for the first time in an Aston Martin, that there's some real engineering between you and the road. That it's not just a pretty face. This is an extremely good car. Phenomenally good.

But there is a price to pay, I'm afraid. It has a horrible interior. The door linings in my test car looked like those polished marble kitchen tops that have got too many chintzy bits in them and the steering wheel was square. Who thought that was a good idea? Or did the supplier misread the name of the customer and think it was for 'Austin Martin'?

Whatever, the cockpit is not a place that you will enjoy or savour. And that's a shame because everything else about this car is absolutely delightful. It's the best Aston yet. And by a very long way.

18 December 2016

I figure it's a must for algebra fans

Mercedes E 220d

If you are an old person you will remember that in the 1970s mid-sized Mercedes-Benz saloons and estates were wilfully sensible. They were designed to never excite you, for a very long time. And that's it.

You bought one because you'd done the maths. You'd calculated the rate of depreciation, and how much one break-down a year would cost, and you'd realized that the premium price of the Benz made sense. Driving, to people such as you, was something that must be done, like ironing. The idea that it could be fun was ridiculous.

The mid-range Mercedes underwent a glacially slow development process right through the Eighties and Nineties. Each new model was a shuffle. Each incorporated fresh features, but only those that made sense and worked. Gimmickry? That was for other people. And oversteer was dangerous.

But then in 2009 something weird happened. The new mid-range Mercedes, sold as the E-class but known internally as the W212 model, arrived on the market with a curved crease in the rear wings. It served no purpose. It was a bit of pointless styling flimflam. This was like Prince Philip turning up to open a garden centre, aged sixty, with a Wayne Rooney weave.

Elsewhere in the Mercedes range, pointless styling ran amok. The chintz-ometer was in the red zone. There were flashes of chrome and radiator grilles that looked like bachelor-pad cookers. There were models that no one needed, and it was as if someone at Mercedes had won the pools. You wanted Peter Jones when you bought a Mercedes (the shop, not the gangly Dragon) but what you were getting was the duty-free shopping arcade at Dubai airport.

This is probably because the people who bought cars after doing the maths had come to realize that if they wanted low running costs, and that's it, they could buy a Hyundai.

Or it's possibly because Chinese businessmen don't want subtle and think restraint is something that belongs in either a police cell or a brothel. Whatever the cause, I was so horrified, I stopped buying Mercs and switched to Volkswagens.

But then, earlier this year, along came the new E-class mid-sized saloon (codenamed internally, and logically, W213) and, wait a minute: what's this? The rear-wing crease is gone. The artistry of the fridge door is back. It's just a car-shaped car.

Yes, the one I borrowed was fitted with AMG Line skirts and low-profile tyres, but peel away the jewellery and there's no getting round the fact. Prince Philip is bald again. Peter Jones is back.

And it gets better, because the estate version I tried has a truly enormous boot. What am I saying? The sort of people who will buy this car do not understand what's meant by 'truly enormous'. They like numbers. So let me give you some. With the rear seats folded flat, you get 1,820 litres of space in which to put your things.

The Audi A6 gives you 1,680. The BMW 5-series 1,670 and the Volvo V90 a mere 1,526. So if you are an antiques dealer, or you often take luggage-laden families to the airport, the new E-class is a clear winner.

And there's more. Next year Mercedes will offer the option of two foldaway child seats fitted into the boot. So it'll work for those who practise Catholic birth control methods as well.

My car, weirdly, was fitted with a new 2-litre turbodiesel engine, which sounds as though it might be a bit too small and weedy for a vehicle this big and this heavy. But the performance figures are respectable. And the fuel economy outstanding. Thanks in part to a new nine-speed automatic gearbox, it's entirely possible you'll average 50mpg.

The downside of course is that the environmental lobby has recently decided that diesel – which it used to like – is now terrible and should be banned from city centres. I shouldn't worry, though, because by the time it's worked out how such a move would affect its beloved buses, it'll have decided diesel's a good thing again.

Is the new E-class fun to drive? No. Not really. And that's OK, because it's a tool, remember. Your iron isn't fun to drive either. Or your lawnmower. If you want fun to drive, buy a beach buggy or a Beemer.

What it is, is quiet. Incredibly quiet. This is an engine that uses compression to force the fuel to explode (oh, OK, burn), and that normally results in a canal boat clatter. But the engine in my car just hummed. Softly, like Winnie-the-Pooh when he was thinking about something.

It's also very comfortable. Yes, the AMG wheels with the painted-on tyres did their best to ruin everything, but you could tell that without them it'd be hovercraft smooth and beanbag pliant. Which brings me on to the speed hump . . .

The road safety lobby, which is run by an offshoot of the polar bear preservation unit, used to say that these were vital tools in the fight against capitalism and McDonald's. But, as is the way with the loony left, it has changed its mind on that too and now says they must all be removed.

I'm not sure I understand its thinking, but it has something to do with the way we all slow down and speed up again when we encounter them, which is bad for the ice caps. Or is it ambulances? I'm not sure.

Anyway, councils can't afford to remove them, because they will be told that'd cost £20m per hump, and they're all idiots so they'll swallow it. Which means speed humps are here to stay.

Mostly they are located on so-called rat-run roads, which tend to be used by professional drivers in executive taxis who know their way round the jams. So here's a tip. If you're thinking of using such a service in future, make sure they send an E-class, because you'll have a much more comfortable journey.

So far, then, the new E-class has not put a foot wrong. But now we get to the interior, which is light and spacious but fronted up with a dashboard that appears, when you first clap eyes on it, to have been lifted from one of those fluorescent-lit hi-fi shops on the outskirts of any town in the Middle East.

You get two television screens, one of which tells you what you need to know about the car, and how much fuel is in the tank and how fast you are going, and the other where you're going and which of the sixty-four interior lighting settings you're on. You think when you first climb aboard that it's all too complicated for words and that you should get right back out again. But it isn't. It works beautifully.

I was similarly worried about the dash itself. It appears to be made from some kind of weird grained wood that's as black as ebony but matt rather than shiny. So you lean forwards for a feel and, whoa, it's plastic disguised to look like wood – and that's horrible.

Or is it? The upholstery in Mercs of old was made from plastic disguised to look like leather, and no one minded that.

So there we are. Mercedes is back, doing what it does best. Making tools for algebra enthusiasts. If that's you, this is a very good car.

8 January 2017

From A to bliss in the Rolls flotation tank

Rolls-Royce Wraith

I was pounced on by a gay man in a restaurant lavatory last night. He said his friend didn't know which to buy, a Porsche 911 or a Jaguar F-type. Ordinarily, I would have fixed him with a steely-eyed stare and explained that I didn't come to him for free advice on what sort of sunglasses are in this season, so why should he come to me for free advice on cars?

Instead, however, I decided to bore him to death, so I went into a lengthy spiel about how the GTS is probably the best of the standard Porsche 911s but the GT3 variants, and in particular the GT3 RS, are outstanding. I then took a perch on the sink as I explained in great detail that the F-type convertible is better-looking than the coupé and that the V6 S is by far the best bet when it comes to a combination of power, noise and handling . . .

His eyes began to glaze over at this point, so I put a comforting arm round his shoulders and said: 'Look. Your friend. The best thing he can do is buy whichever of the two cars he likes more.'

I mean this. Telling a stranger what car to buy is like telling someone what film to go and see. You can explain that *One Woman's 30-Year Search for Her Hat* is a brilliant biopic with a powerful and subtly hidden message, but if the person you are talking to turns out to be a northern bare-knuckle cage fighter, it's likely he will prefer *The Terminator* 6.

'Experts' haven't been useful in the car-buying process since Humber went west, although, with the new pure-electric cars and hybrids coming on stream, that may change in the near future. We are entering a new era, and the ghost of Raymond Baxter may be called upon.

That's then, however, and this is now, and we are talking this morning about the Rolls-Royce Wraith. No one is going to accost me in a lavatory and ask if they should buy one of those, or a Bentley instead, because that'd be like asking if you should buy an ice cream or a shotgun. The two things are very different.

Rolls-Royce may say that the Wraith is tuned with the driver in mind, but I think we are talking here about degrees. It's like saying that God tuned Mars to be more hospitable than Venus. You're not going to have much fun on either, if we're honest.

A friend of mine visited Los Angeles last month, and, because he is important, his hosts sent a chauffeured Wraith to pick him up from the airport. He was invited, as you'd expect, to sit in the back for the drive into town, but as the Wraith is a two-door coupé with limited rear space, he felt extremely silly.

And that raises a question: if the Wraith isn't really tuned for driving pleasure and it doesn't work as a limo, then what's the point?

It's a question I found myself asking as I arrived at a very beautiful pheasant shoot in the north of England the other day. I had packed, as instructed, a smoking jacket for dinner and various bits of tweed for the next day. I also had my guns, my bullets, my wellies and all the other flotsam and jetsam necessary for wasting a few birds. And the boot lid wouldn't open.

No amount of pressing or holding the remote button caused it to budge. Neither did any amount of rummaging around in the grime to try to locate an actual catch; nor did the remote switch in the cabin. It was locked shut. Dinner was due to start in fifteen minutes. I was one of only two untitled people present. And I was wearing jeans and a T-shirt.

Eventually, after I'd been through the handbook, which is available on the satnav screen, I discovered that if you disassemble the remote control locking device there's a key inside that can be used to open the boot in the old-fashioned way. So I did that and made it to dinner properly dressed – in time to hear someone say: 'Whose is that vulgar car outside?'

So there we are. An unreliable and vulgar car that doesn't work as a proper Rolls-Royce because it's been tuned to be as sporty as a 1974 Volvo. Plus it isn't very good-looking and it's extremely expensive. They say it costs about £235,000. But by the time you've added a bit of garnish, it'll be a lot more than that. Despite these not insignificant issues, though, I thought it was tremendous.

Underneath, it is fundamentally the same as the four-door Rolls-Royce Ghost, which means that, contrary to what James May told you on *The Grand Tour* recently, it is fundamentally the same as a BMW 7-series. The two cars have in essence the same platform and the same engine.

However, in the Rolls-Royce there are two bulkheads. This is important. They have not been fitted to improve structural rigidity so as to make the car corner more sweetly, and they certainly haven't been fitted for lightness. They are there simply to distance the occupants from the noise and the fuss of the engine.

This is the key to the Wraith experience: the sense that you

are just sitting there while it moves you about. There's a faint
hum to suggest that explosions are happening under the
bonnet, and there's a rustle of tyre noise. But even when you
are travelling at 150mph, that's about it.

Yes, there are 624 brake horsepowers on tap and, yes, there
is roll-cancelling air suspension and a satellite-aided system
that reads the road ahead and sets the gearbox up for the
coming corner. But you aren't aware of any of this as you
waft along. What you are aware of is the weight. Especially
when you are slowing down. You almost can't believe that a
light touch on the brake pedal is all that's needed to impede
the progress of the monster. It feels faintly amusing.

Autocar magazine tells us that if you go into the on-board
menu and turn off the traction control, the car will drift
nicely. And I'm sure it will, in the same way as you could, if
you wanted to, ice-skate in a pair of army boots.

I can't stress enough, though, that this is not a sports car
or a driver's car in the accepted sense. But it is tremendous to
drive because it feels like nothing else. If you didn't want a
chauffeur, for some reason, and you therefore didn't need a
barn-like space in the back – just some lovely wood and soft
leather, a few elegant controls and a little peace and quiet on
your drive home at night – it'd be fabulous. Completely in a
class of its own.

Aston Martins and Bentleys feel like cars. This feels as if
you're in the bath. It's not for me, obviously; I still like to do
the hairy-chested man thing when I'm driving, and I'd much
rather have a two-thirds-of-the-price DB11 or Continental
GT V8 S.

But that doesn't mean you would.

22 January 2017

Fire up DCI Hunt – the quattro's back

Audi RS 7

Even if you are in a very good mood, and you are wearing a pair of rose-tinted spectacles, you have to accept that the original Audi quattro really wasn't much good.

Yes, it thrashed all its rivals for many years on the world rally stages, and that gave it just about enough kudos to justify its fairly enormous price tag. But under the skin it was all a bit Radio Rentals.

Turbocharging wasn't new when the quattro came along – Chevrolet, BMW and Saab had been at it for years – but neither was it the perfected art that it is today. When you stamped on the accelerator in an original quattro, it was like signalling to the engine room on an ocean liner. Oily men had to get out of their chairs, boilers had to be ramped up, big doors had to be closed, Victorian levers had to be pulled, coal had to be shovelled and only after that would there be a difference in the speed you were going.

And then there was the four-wheel-drive system. That wasn't new either – Jensen had been there fourteen years earlier – and neither was it perfect. But as the rallying proved, it definitely provided extra grip in snowy or gravelly conditions.

However, in reality the traction was only just about compensating for the fact that in a quattro the heavy five-cylinder engine was mounted ahead of the front axle. This meant that, no matter what Joe Normal did with the steering wheel and the throttle, he was going to plough at fairly high speed into a tree.

Later came the 20-valve version. This meant more power, so that when you hit the tree, you were going even faster.

Nevertheless, I absolutely loved that car. It was the noise it made – an offbeat five-cylinder strum – and it was the flared wheelarches and it was the stance.

But most of all it was the idea of the thing that appealed. It may have been born in the muddy underbelly of west Wales and it may have proved its mettle in the dust of Africa and the ice of Finland but it didn't feel like a crash-bang-wallop rally car. It felt sophisticated and grown up.

The girl the late Peter Sarstedt sang about, the one who sipped her Napoleon brandy and had a racehorse she kept just for fun, for a laugh a-ha-ha-ha; she would have had an Alfa Romeo Spider. But if she'd been born ten years later, it'd have been a quattro.

This was the car that put Audi on our radar screens. Until it came along, the company had been making vehicles for German cement salesmen. But afterwards it was the giant-killing underdog, with a weapon that – in theory – could hang on to the coat-tails of a Ferrari or a Lamborghini.

And which – in theory again – could overtake even if it was raining at the time. In practice, of course, you'd hit a tree if you even tried, but we will gloss over that. Because everyone else did – me included.

What's interesting is that after creating a forerunner to the Nissan GT-R, Audi decided not to replace it with something that was similar but better. It came up with the S2, but this was just a bulbous Audi 80 coupé. It had no flared wheelarches. Its strum was subdued. It never really went rallying. And then? And then nothing.

Audi continued to use the quattro name – to indicate that the car in question had four-wheel drive – but there's never been a proper successor to that glorious, and gloriously flawed, original. Until now.

It's called the RS 7, but picked out on a grille under the front bumper in very big letters is the quattro name. Because, really, that's what this thing is.

It arrived at my office just before Christmas and sat in the car park for a couple of days until I realized that it would be mine for the whole Yuletide break and then a few more days afterwards. It'd be my companion for thousands of wet, soggy, damp and cold miles. We'd be going shooting together and to parties, and within half a mile I knew it would make me very miserable.

The suspension was absolutely intolerable. I thought the Nissan GT-R Track Edition was unforgiving, but this thing had all the give of granite. Every tiny bump was amplified and directed with pin-sharp accuracy directly into my coccyx. Westbourne Grove in Notting Hill – which is the bumpiest, most badly maintained road in the world – was completely unbearable.

But then I discovered, while weeping in pain, that the delivery driver who'd dropped the car off had – I presume for a joke – put the suspension in Dynamic mode. I switched it to Comfort, and in an instant my life was transformed.

This is not the best-looking car in the world – not by a long way – and it developed a terrible vibration as the weeks rolled by. Plus, whenever you employ full beam, there's a theatrical sweep of light that is dramatic and clever but not instantaneous. Which is what you want.

And that's it. That's my list of things I didn't like. Everything else is just brilliant. The acceleration is hilarious, the noise is a deep bellow, the fuel consumption is excellent, the seats are magnificently comfortable and you will not find a better-designed set of controls in any other car. It'll also do almost 190mph.

I loved the way it just loped down motorways, often four up with a boot full of bullets and presents and all the other flotsam and jetsam that we need to survive life over Christmas. And then, later, how it would flick and dart its way along country roads like a sports car.

Does it understeer like its great-grandfather? No idea. All I can tell you is that if you are going fast enough to find out, then either you are the Finnish rally champion Kinki Wankonnen, or you have just signed up to Exit International. Or something catastrophic has gone wrong with the throttle linkage.

What I do know is that if you pull away smartly from a T-junction there is no wheelspin or torque steer. The car just sets off as if it's been kicked by Jonny Wilkinson.

I'm never normally sad to see a test car taken away, because there's always another one coming round the corner. But I was upset to see the RS 7 go, because it had wormed its way into my heart. In much the way the Audi TT did, not long ago.

Sadly, I could never actually buy a TT – fantastic though it is – because I'm not an air hostess. But I did find myself wondering if perhaps I could have an RS 7. And I kept on wondering right up to the point when I looked up the price. I had in my mind that it'd be about £70,000, but with a few extras it's more than £100,000.

This car is very, very good. But it's not that good.

29 January 2017

Pretty, well dressed and too clever by half

Honda NSX

Back in the days when you could walk from Calais to Dover and wattle was a popular building material, Honda decided it would like to build a supercar with a V10 engine. It would, the company said, be a replacement for the old NSX, and I was very excited.

Every so often I'd call Honda to see how it was coming along, and it'd say, 'Very well', but that there'd been a bit of a delay because of the ice age, or the eruption of Krakatoa or some other geological disturbance. I seem to recall at one point it said it'd had to change the interior because modern man was a different shape from his Neanderthal predecessor.

And then there was a wobble in the Japanese economy, and the V10 engine lost its Formula One halo, so Honda announced that the new car would be some kind of hybrid with electric motors and a turbocharged V6. That sounded pretty exciting too, especially when Ferrari, McLaren and Porsche were busy demonstrating just how biblical a combination such as this could be.

I kept calling Honda to ask when I could drive its new offering and was always told the same thing. 'Soon.' It said the design and engineering team in California was 'benchmarking' the Chevrolet Corvette, and when this was done it would be ready.

A year later it said the team had decamped to Germany to

benchmark various Porsches. And then a year after that it was in Mauritius benchmarking cocktails. I began to think the new NSX was a machine that existed only in Honda's dreams and that it would never see the light of day.

But then last year, after a quick trip to Sydney to benchmark some surfboards and a stopover in Bali to benchmark a couple of beaches, the tanned and relaxed designers and engineers announced the car was finished.

And I must say it looked good. It's very low and very wide – wider than almost anything else on the road, in fact. It also appeared to be very clever, since its mid-mounted twin-turbo V6 was fitted with a 47bhp electric motor that would provide power while the turbos were drawing from the well of witchcraft but were not quite ready to deliver it.

Furthermore, each front wheel was fitted with its own 36bhp electric motor, which meant this fairly conventional-looking supercar was anything but, under the skin. Can you even begin to imagine, for instance, the computing power needed simply to keep all four wheels rotating at the same speed?

When you start to consider that, you can see why it's taken so long to get the new NSX from the doodle, 'Wouldn't it be nice?' phase and into the showrooms. Especially when you step inside and realize that despite the behind-the-scenes complexity, it comes with a normal steering wheel, normal pedals, normal paddles for the nine-speed gearbox and a normal price. I'm not being flippant. At £143,950 it's almost five times less expensive than Porsche's hybrid alternative.

On paper, then, this car looks like a genuinely realistic alternative to Ferrari's 488 GTB, Lamborghini's Huracan and whatever car McLaren has just launched. However, it isn't.

The first problem is that it's not that quick off the mark.

If you are driving in Quiet mode – which you will be most of the time, because the other settings make the car noisy, uneconomical and bumpy – and you put your foot down, there is a very noticeable moment when you just know the computing system is having a think. 'Right. Hang on. What gear should I select? Fourth? Fifth? We'll have a meeting about that, and in the meantime let's see if we can work out which wheel needs what amount of power. Front left to start with . . .' Meanwhile, the driver of the Vauxhall Vectra you were trying to overtake is at home watching *Game of Thrones*.

So all the clever-clever hybrid tech doesn't give you the power you were expecting, which would be fine if it gave extra economy, but it doesn't really do that either. Don't reckon on getting much more than 20mpg.

Then there's the handling. You'd imagine that with its weird four-wheel-drive system it'd have a ton of grip, and that's probably so. But you are never inclined to find out for sure, because you are aware this is a heavy car and nearly a ton of the weight is located in the rear end. So if you went over the limit of grip, it'd be like wrestling a grandfather clock back into line.

What's more, the steering is numb, and there's a curious wobble when the car settles into a bend, as though the suspension is having a bit of a row with itself about what it should be doing.

As a car for petrolheads, then, this is no match for its rivals from McLaren, Lamborghini and Ferrari. And then things get worse.

The sun visors are the size of stamps and feel as though they've been lifted from a Soviet bread van, the horn sounds as if it's from a Toys R Us pedal car and the satnav is woeful.

I suspect it's the same unit you get in a Honda Jazz or Civic, so on the upside it could probably find the nearest beetle drive or bingo hall, but on the downside it's a touchscreen, which doesn't work in any car, and the software appears to have been written by Alistair MacLean or some other author of fiction. Twice it told me the road ahead was closed. And it just bloody wasn't.

Then there's the stereo, which sounds like Radio Caroline did in the early 1970s, and I wouldn't mind but the engine doesn't compensate for this. In the old NSX there was an intoxicating induction roar when you accelerated; in the new one there's just some gravelly noise. Which you aren't really hearing, because you're busy seeing if the carpet is stuck under the throttle pedal.

Worst of all is the fuel gauge. I don't have OCD, as anyone who has seen my desk will testify, but the needle isn't centred, so it always looks cock-eyed. And that drove me mad.

You are left, once you've lived with an NSX for a few days, with a sense that the engineers have beavered away at the difficulties of making a high-performance hybrid and then just garnished it with parts from the factory floor. Everything you touch and look at feels either low rent or annoying.

On a recent television programme my colleague James May said he liked the NSX because he found it interesting. Later he told me that the car's lack of apparent acceleration has something to do with Newton metres per inch and that the linear nature of electric motor delivery . . . I'm afraid I nodded off at this point.

He is right, though. This car is interesting. And it is pretty. But that, I'm afraid, is the full extent of its repertoire.

12 February 2017

Whatever you ask, this isn't the answer

Seat Ateca

Whenever someone leans across a dinner table and asks me what car they should buy, I always say 'a Ferrari F40'.

Then they look a bit exasperated and explain they need something sensible, so I say 'a 1986 Lada Riva shooting brake'. This normally does the trick and they go back to talking about something that is more interesting, such as accountancy or ornithology.

However, at dinner the other day, the man opposite really was quite insistent. He didn't want a Ferrari F40 or a 1986 Lada Riva shooting brake and demanded that I came up with another alternative. 'A Bugatti EB 110,' I said, hoping that would shut him up. But it didn't.

'Come on,' he said, 'I'm being serious.' So I told him to buy a Cadillac Escalade.

I hate being asked about cars as much as doctors hate being asked about ailments. They can't possibly determine, when they've had two bottles of agreeable red, what's wrong with someone who's fully clothed and on the opposite side of the table, any more than I can tell someone what car to buy when I don't know what they need it for and how much they have to spend and if they have any prejudice towards the French or the Japanese.

'Are you a racist?' I asked the man on the opposite side of the table. And, before he could answer, 'Is your wife extremely fat?' These are the things that matter when it comes to choosing a car. There's more too. If your children are prone to explosive car sickness, you don't want cloth seats. And if you have only one arm, you don't want a flappy paddle gearbox.

I went through a full range of weird questions with Mr Persistent, including, 'Will you be having sex on the back seat with your secretary?' and then told him the best car he could possibly buy was a Vauxhall Astra van.

It turned out, however, that he actually wanted an Audi Q5. 'Well, get one of those, then.'

'Are they any good?' he asked. 'No,' I replied.

I don't like the Audi Q5 or any car of that type because they seem too pointless. You get the same amount of interior space as you would in a normal hatchback but because of the extra weight and tallness, you get less performance and terrible fuel economy. It's not swings and roundabouts here. It's swings and falling off the roundabout into a pile of dog-dirt-encrusted broken glass.

I explained all this to my dinner companion but he was most insistent. He said he liked a car that gave him a commanding view of the road and didn't have any truck with my argument that a hatchback and a cushion would do the trick. So I told him to buy the Q5 and started talking to the woman on my right.

'What car should I buy?' she asked . . . I then went to the lavatory and drank all the Domestos.

The trouble is that, these days, absolutely everyone wants a hatchback on stilts. They all want a commanding view of the road. And they don't realize that soon it won't be commanding at all, because everyone will be at the same height. Which means cars will have to keep on getting taller and taller until you need a ladder to get inside. And instead of airbags, you'll have a parachute.

The other problem is that crossover mini SUVs, or whatever it is they're called, are all extremely dreary to drive. And look at. And be near. I really genuinely hate them and, as a result, I was not looking forward to spending an entire week with something called a Seat Ateca.

I mean, quite apart from anything else, you just know Ateca is one of those names that's been plucked by the marketing department from a bag of Scrabble tiles, because trademark infringement problems mean that every other actual word has been registered. This means you end up with a name that sounds like it could be an insurance company or an antifungal cream.

Everybody wanted a Cortina. It may have been named after a small café on the King's Road, but it sounded exotic. Nobody wants an Ateca in their life. Unless they've got thrush.

Seat claims Ateca is a town in Spain and that it's named it after that. But this doesn't wash. Because if you're going to name it after a town in Spain, why not pick one we've heard of? It'd be like Rolls-Royce launching a car called the Pontefract.

Anyway, it arrived, and in essence it's a Volkswagen Tiguan, which means that when all is said and done, it's a jacked-up Golf. Same basic platform. Similar range of engines. Only slower and less economical and more expensive and less fun to drive and no more practical.

Actually, because this is a Golf designed by Spaniards and built in the Czech Republic, it's cheaper than its sister car, the Tiguan, which is a Golf that was designed by Germans and that is built in Germany, Russia or Mexico, depending on which model you choose. I don't get that thinking either.

Whatever, it has doors so that you can get inside, and a

boot lid that is operated by electricity so that you have to stand in the rain to make sure it closes properly.

Inside, there are some chairs so that you can sit down, but it should be noted that all of them seem to be fitted much lower than you'd expect. As you peer over the dashboard at the road ahead, it feels as if you're moving around in a wheelie bin. And I don't get the thinking here either. Because if you want a car with a commanding driving position, why would you buy one with seats that are so low?

Other things. Well, it's quite quiet, which is nice. But then it was also a bit bumpy, which wasn't. And the boot was big enough for a footstool I'd bought.

My test car had a 1.4-litre Golf engine, which provided no discernible performance at all. Put your foot down in sixth gear, at 70mph on the motorway, and absolutely nothing happens. My kitchen table is faster. Economy, however, is what you would expect – around 50mpg – and it produces 123 carbon dioxides. But these are Volkswagen figures, so they probably mean very little.

On the face of it, then, you'd struggle to think of a single reason why you'd buy this car rather than one of the many alternatives. But my car was fitted with orange wheels and matching door mirrors. And that'd clinch it for me.

On normal wheels, it's just another way of wasting £24,440, but those snazzy rims, teamed with some plastic roo bars, give the Ateca a visual leg-up. And as a result it'd be my choice if I were being forced at gunpoint to buy a car like this. But I'm not, which is why I would buy a Ferrari F40. Which is much better.

19 February 2017

Take a seat in Sarah Lund's mood room

Volvo V90

According to my television colleague James May, buying a Volvo is like going to the dentist's. It's something you have to do one day, so you might as well get it over with.

This was certainly the case in the olden days, where James lives, because back then Volvos were bought by people in hats, whose unpredictability was their only predictability. If they were indicating left, the only thing you knew for sure was that they were not about to turn left. Since then, though, much has happened. Volvo went motor racing with a brace of absurd but amusing estate cars in the British touring car championship. Then it came up with the XC90, which is still by far and away the most sensible family car of them all. And then there was a spot of financial bother that resulted in the company becoming the northern division of a giant Chinese corporation.

This higgledy-piggledy spell of unjoined-up thinking played havoc with the brand. Gone were the days when you were a bad driver so you bought a Volvo because at least you'd escape fairly unscathed from the accident you were going to have. Also gone was the motor racing. Even the estate favoured by antiques dealers went west. Which meant you bought a Volvo because . . . actually, there wasn't a single reason.

But then, one day, Volvo decided to start sponsoring

drama on what it calls 'Sky Atlontic'. They made some gloomy, cool, blue-hued films, and sometimes they were better than the show that followed. The message was clear. Volvo was for people who wanted peace and quiet; people who preferred their television detectives to wear a jumper rather than a Swat outfit. And once this had been established, they had to set about making some cars to fit the image they'd created.

It's an odd way of doing things, but no matter, because the first of the Sky Atlontic cars is now with us. It's called the V90 and, ooh, it's good-looking. Really, really good-looking.

Then you step inside and, frankly, you're going to get straight back out again and sign on the dotted line. Because this side of a Rolls-Royce Phantom you will find no finer car interior. The combination of wood, aluminium and leather is sublime, and the way it all works is even better.

Just about everything is controlled by what is, to all intents and purposes, an upended iPad. This means there are very few buttons or knobs on the dash, which makes it a) cheaper to produce and b) more calm and relaxing. It's like being inside Sarah Lund's mood room.

My sister once asked why it always feels, in any car, as if you're sitting inside a man's wash bag, and she has a point. They're normally black and dark and enlivened only by some red stripes. Well, the Volvo's not like that at all. It's light and airy, and as a result it's a lovely and delightful place to sit.

However, at some point you're going to stop sitting there, feeling at one with the world, and start the engine, and straight away things are going to unravel. There will be a petrol hybrid in the fullness of time, but for now you have a choice of a 2-litre diesel or another 2-litre diesel.

The 2-litre diesel in my test car was the more powerful of

the two and it was fitted with two turbochargers along with a compressed air cylinder that shoots air into the engine when you demand more power. This sounds very clever and it certainly reduces turbo lag. But there's no getting round the fact that this is a very big car and it's being moved about by a 2-litre diesel.

An engine of this size works fine in a Golf or a small leaf blower. But it really doesn't work at all in the V90. It clatters when it is cold and constantly sounds as though it's working its arse off, even when you're trundling down the motorway. Couple this to a dim-witted eight-speed automatic that occasionally suffers from dementia and can't remember what it's supposed to be doing, and you have a car that is not remotely exciting, or even pleasant to drive.

This is not necessarily a bad thing. Some people won't notice the drone, or the gearbox taking five minutes to remember it's not a carrot. And they will be delighted by the small engine's mouse-like thirst for fuel and the tiny number of carbon dioxides coming out of the tailpipe.

They will also be delighted by the many and varied safety features that make the Volvo about as uncrashable as is technically possible these days.

And they are going to like the comfort as well. It's not a soft-riding car, but the body movement is very well controlled. They're also going to like the four-wheel-drive system, which is fitted as standard to the more powerful diesel version that I tried.

But they are going to be disappointed by the burglar alarm. My office backs on to a Volvo dealership staffed by trained Volvo technicians. And they set an alarm off at least twenty times a day. Which means that there must be a fault. Either that or the trained technicians are, in fact, morons.

They will be disappointed again when they try to put something big in the boot. Because there's no getting round the fact that there's a price to pay for those lovely lines, and the price is: even a Škoda Superb has more interior space. So do the equivalent offerings from Audi, Mercedes and BMW.

Though when I say 'equivalent', what I mean is 'cheaper'. I was staggered to notice that the car I tested, with a few options fitted, cost £56,480. That, for a 2-litre diesel, is ridiculous.

And it will seem especially ridiculous when you wake one day to find that, because you bought a diesel-powered car, either you are banned from the town centre or you are being made to pay more for your parking space.

Draconian anti-diesel measures are in place or are being planned in cities such as Paris, Madrid and Athens, and you can be fairly sure the gullible lunatics who run Britain will be leaping on to the bandwagon as soon as they realize just how much money can be made from milking the motorists who did as they were told a few years ago and bought a diesel because they thought it would be kinder to the polar bear.

One day we will learn to ignore the messages of doom from climate 'scientists', but until that happens, I certainly wouldn't buy a car powered by the dirty work of Dr Diesel. Which means I wouldn't buy the Volvo. When the petrol hybrid comes along, it may be a different story, but if the 2-litre diesel is £56,000, the hybrid will probably cost more than a stealth bomber. Which means I probably wouldn't buy that either.

26 February 2017

The Renault Scénic would be a steal – but it's plastic

Renault Scénic Dynamique

In the olden days, cars were made from steel, and that's only right and proper. Steel is as manly as Tarzan's scrotum. Horny-handed sons of toil mine the iron ore using dynamite and huge excavators, and then this is turned into steel in giant foundries that are hot, dangerous and noisy. A steel foundry is the exact opposite of Jane Austen.

Today we live in different times. Cars can no longer be manly, because it is now offensive to be in possession of a penis. Or to let it do your thinking. This means cars must be kind to the environment and economical and cheap and safe, and that means they must be made from plastic.

There was a time when we laughed at plastic cars. The Reliant Robin was plastic, and so was its big sister, the Scimitar, which was driven by Princess Anne. It is obligatory to mention this, in the same way as when someone sees a swan, he must point out it can break a man's arm.

The British firm TVR never really made it into the big league because, while its cars were fast and pretty and gruntsomely male, we all knew that behind the bellow and the leather the bodies were made from GRP. Which is plastic. Like a canoe. Or a lavatory seat.

Today, however, you will find plastic panels on almost every car made. And it's easy to see why. It's light, which means less fuel is needed to cart it around, and that means fewer emissions. What's more, it's cheaper than steel, which means greater profits for the car manufacturer, which means your pension fund is healthier. And on top of that, you never hear of plastics companies going on strike and throwing stuff at policemen, whereas steelworkers are always outside the plant, round a brazier, shouting. Which is bad for the just-in-time production techniques used at every car factory in the world.

The trouble is that you can always tell when a panel on a car is plastic. And I don't mean when you tap it; I mean when you look at it. There's something about the way it's curved or creased, and there's something too about the way it looks when painted. All of this stirs your limbic system, which says, 'That's crap.'

There was a white Toyota hybrid of some kind outside the office yesterday and its back end was a futuristic blend of shapes and creases that could never have been achieved if it had been made from steel. It put me in mind of a *Star Wars* Stormtrooper, and those Stormtrooper suits, you just know, are made from plastic and could therefore not withstand a pebble from David's sling, let alone a blast of green from a space laser gun. And that's Toyota's problem. Your eyes tell you it looks great. But your soul is saying, 'It's rubbish.'

And that brings me on to the snappily named Renault Scénic Dynamique S Nav dCi 110. Pop into your dealership, and within about five minutes, no matter how gormless and cheaply suited the salesman might be, you are going to be slack-jawed in amazement and ready to sell your children for the chance to own such a thing.

It's got a head-up display, for crying out loud. And I don't mean a system like those you find in high-end BMWs and the F/A-18 Hornet, where the information you need is projected on to the windscreen. I mean a system where a panel rises electrically from the top of the dash. You're going to be seriously excited when you first see this in operation.

Then there's a massive glass sunroof with an electric blind, an 8.7in touchscreen, DAB radio, leather upholstery, cruise control and a system that wakes you up if you're getting drowsy, along with more systems that keep you in the correct lane and ensure your lights dip automatically when a car is coming the other way. It can even recognize road signs.

You can change the colour of the interior lighting, and you get blacked-out windows in the back in case you need to give Puff Snoop a lift to a gig. And all this stuff is provided as standard for £25,445. Which, on the face of it, makes this car the bargain of the century.

Then you're going to step out of the cabin to take in the exterior styling, and you're going to like that too. As a general rule I loathe cars of this type and I've loathed the Scénic more than all the others. But this ... this is very, very attractive.

Obviously, it isn't a racing car. Yes, it has racy 20in wheels, but there's a perfectly ordinary 1.5-litre diesel engine that turns fuel into a dribble of performance; 0-62mph takes 12.4 seconds, which would have been considered woeful thirty years ago. But which today, in health-and-safety Britain, is par for the course.

Then the salesman is going to tell you it's capable of 72.4mpg. I don't doubt for a moment that this is true. In the same way as I'm capable of running the 100-metre sprint in roughly the same time as Usain Bolt. In normal use you won't get anything like 70mpg out of it, but it's still very economical.

And practical. The rear seats, I admit, are a bit of a squash if you are burly or long, but the boot's huge and the floor moves about to make it versatile as well. You can even buy a longer version that has seven seats.

So here we have a good-looking, well-equipped, practical and economical car that is exceptional value for money. Lovely.

Except it isn't. Because the more you look at it, the more you realize there's something wrong. And what's wrong is: a lot of this car is made from plastic. And somehow you know. Which means you know it's crap.

And I'm sorry, but all that equipment provided as standard? For twenty-five grand? It sounds tremendous, but it does make you wonder about the quality of it all.

And the more you wonder, the more you start to think that maybe the new Scénic is like one of those Korean music centres you could buy for £25.99 in the 1980s. They had the flashing lights and twin tape decks and graphic equalizers. But they were in no way a substitute for the mix'n'match alternatives from Garrard, Marsden Hall, Akai, Teleton and so on.

There's another problem too. Look up now and say to your family, 'I'm thinking of buying a Renault Scénic Dynamique S Nav dCi 110', and see if anyone is the slightest bit interested . . .

Thought not.

12 March 2017

Not so much wild horse as mild pony

Ford Mustang 2.3 EcoBoost

The right-hand-drive Ford Mustang has been on sale in Britain for a little while now, but I'm still always a bit surprised when I see one bumbling down the street. However, I'm even more surprised when I don't.

Every day, thousands of people take delivery of a new BMW or Audi or what have you, and I don't doubt they're very pleased. But the fact is that for a great deal less money they could have driven away in a Mustang. The American icon. Steve McQueen with numberplates.

The figures are remarkable because the Mustang costs less than two-thirds of what BMW charges for an M4. And it's not like the Ford is equipped like a cave. It has rain-sensing this and dark-sensing that and electric everything and a system that lets you spin the rear wheels and make smoke while the front brakes are locked. And spin they will, because under the bonnet is a big, American 5-litre V8. It's not the most sophisticated engine; often it feels as though it's made from rock and powered by gravel, but it delivers the goods well enough.

When you drive the Mustang, you are left scratching your head and wondering: what's going on here? Is BMW being a profiteering bastard, or is Ford paying its workers in beads? Because how can it possibly sell a 5-litre sports coupé for £36,000 when Jaguar – as another example – charges £90,000 for almost exactly the same thing?

Well, now we have the answer. Europe's independent safety testing body recently gave the Mustang a two-star rating out of five, the lowest rating for any mainstream car it's tested for nearly ten years.

It found that people in the rear would slide under their seatbelts in a frontal impact, that the airbags inflated insufficiently and that it lacked the sort of sophisticated braking system fitted to even the Fiesta these days. What's more, it noted that safety equipment available to American customers is not offered on this side of the pond. That, then, is why the all-singing, all-dancing, bells-and-whistles V8 Mustang costs so much less than any rival: it's just not as safe. So I guess you got to ask yourself one question, punk. What do you want? A system that lets you do burnouts at the lights? Or a head?

On the face of it, the answer is simple. You want a head. You want the safest car you can buy. But do you?

I smoke and drink and jaywalk. I try to mend electrical equipment myself. I jump off cliffs without testing the depth of the water. I fire firework rockets horizontally across lakes, and at work I put myself in tricky spots to get a laugh out of the audience.

And I'm not unusual. Kids go to all sorts of stupid places on their gap years and do all sorts of stupid things. YouTube is full of people falling over on ski slopes and tripping over next to swimming pools. And have you met anyone who says, 'No, let's not build a swing over that river. Let's go to the library instead because it's safer'?

Coming back to cars, the Ferrari F40 is not even on nodding terms with the concept of safety. It doesn't have antilock braking or airbags. And it was designed at a time when any sort of accident was simply the starting point for your journey through the Pearly Gates. So obviously you'd rather have a Volvo V70. Except of course you wouldn't.

Which brings me back to the Mustang. Yes, it's not going to look after you very well if you crash into a tree. So here's an idea. Don't crash into a tree.

There are two ways this could be achieved with the Mustang. Either you could concentrate the mind by replacing its airbag with an enormous spike, or you could buy the version I've been testing.

It's the £35,845 Mustang EcoBoost convertible, so called because, instead of a stone-age V8, it has a bang-up-to-date 2.3-litre turbocharged four-pot. Yes, that's right. A four-cylinder Ford Focus engine . . . in a Mustang.

The figures aren't as bad as you might expect. There are 313 horsepowers, for instance, and 319 torques. This means a top speed of 145mph and reasonably brisk acceleration. But not so brisk that you risk finding out first-hand what a two-star safety rating actually means.

What's more, you get a rear-view camera as standard, dual-zone air-conditioning, the burnout facility, keyless entry, DAB radio, USB and Bluetooth connectivity, selectable driving modes and every other whizz-bang you can think of, all for £35,845. Or £3,500 less than that if you go for the coupé.

To drive, it feels like a Mustang. Obviously, you don't have the Steve McQueen offbeat burble, but, if I'm honest, you don't really get that in the V8 either. You do get, however, a deep bassy engine sound that suits the car well.

You also get several acres of bodywork. In America this is fine, but here, especially in a city, it can be annoying. Especially as the turning circle is woeful. After a short while, you start to look enviously at bus drivers as they zip about in their far more manoeuvrable vehicles.

But then you get out of the city and the Mustang does what it does best. It lopes along, eating up the miles without any fuss. And, of course, because there are only four cylinders, you should do twice as many miles to the gallon as you would had you gone for the V8.

Best of all, though, are the admiring glances. People like Mustangs. They smile at you and let you out of junctions. And that's because we all know that behind the shouty noises, and bigness, it's a gentle giant. A pussycat that thinks it's a wild horse.

It really isn't an out-and-out racer. It leans and it wobbles and it gets awfully wayward if you ask it to behave like a Porsche. But minding this is like buying a burger and then minding that it's not a quail's egg dipped in a pinch of celery salt. If you want a quail's egg, you'll need to spend twice as much.

The only real problem, as far as I can tell, is that while there's not much in the way of exterior badging to say this is a 2.3-litre car, you always know. And a Mustang without a V8 is like a chicken korma.

Yes, it's less likely to crash, and, yes, it's cheaper and more economical, which means it's the more sensible option. But who buys a Mustang to be sensible? It's a fun car, so you absolutely have to have it with the most fun engine.

2 April 2017

Gulp! Frankenstein's been at the parts bin

Maserati Levante

As I'm sure you will have noticed, people have started wearing trousers that are deliberately torn across both knees. Does this mean that the Savile Row tailor Gieves & Hawkes has jumped on the bandwagon and is selling suits with raggedy holes in the legs?

No. It won't have even crossed the tailors' minds. They have spent hundreds of years developing and nurturing their reputation and they know it would be unwise to throw it all away in the pursuit of a fast buck.

People should stick to what they know. You don't find Mary Berry making programmes about motorcycle maintenance or Vin Diesel playing Hamlet. But in the world of car manufacturing, things are different.

There's a fad at the moment for SUVs, and, rather than sit around saying, 'That's not what we do', Aston Martin, Porsche, Bentley, Jaguar, Alfa Romeo and Lamborghini have all taken leave of their senses and thought, 'We'll have some of that, thank you very much.'

Lamborghini, I admit, has dabbled in this area before, with the fearsome LM002. Powered by the V12 from a Countach, it was a gigantic and hilarious monster. I tried to drive one once and it didn't go well because the gearbox was jammed in second. I sat in the back seat pushing the lever with my legs, while a burly chap sat on the dash using all his strength to pull it. Eventually, it gave in with an almighty crack and the burly man's arse shot through the windscreen. I laughed about that for six years.

I suspect the LM002 wasn't really built as a serious attempt to move in on the pre-Hummer military, and was just a gift from the network of Italian power to Colonel Gaddafi, who, it's said, loved it.

Lamborghini can probably get away with an SUV today. Because we know it started out as a tractor maker and all its cars have always had a certain He-Man appeal. They're built for doing 9mph in Knightsbridge, not ninety round the Nürburgring.

But Aston? Jaguar? Alfa Romeo? Bentley? Companies such as these making SUVs really is as odd as McDonald's launching a watercress and kale smoothie. And that's before we get to Maserati.

Maserati made its name in the 1950s on the grand prix circuit, and then nailed its colours to the mast in the 1960s with an impossibly beautiful succession of exotic cars that were named after the world's winds. This is a company, then, that has no place making a jumped-up Land Rover. But that's exactly what it has done.

The car in question is called the Levante, which sounds as though it ought to be some kind of soap for the sort of man who enjoys personal grooming.

Now. Had Maserati called a meeting to decide what this car should be like and decided it would go all-out to emphasize the 'S' in SUV, then it might have stood a chance. Alternatively, it could have decided to make it the last word in luxury, a car that would make the Bentley Bentayga look like a toddler's pushchair. And that might have worked too.

But instead it called a meeting and very obviously said, 'Right. Let's do this for as little as possible.'

I'll start with its clock. For as long as I can remember, Maseratis have been fitted with an elegant, oval timepiece, the sort of thing you would expect to see David Beckham advertising at Heathrow's terminal 5. Even when Maserati was basically bankrupt and making the Biturbo, it never stooped so low as to go down the Casio digital route.

In the Levante, however, you get an ordinary circular plastic clock mounted in a plastic oval. You look at it and think, 'Well, if they've cut corners there, where else have the accountants been making merry with the sandpaper?'

An answer becomes obvious when you fire up the engine. In time there will be a V6 that runs on petrol, but your only option in the UK now is a diesel. Which wouldn't be so bad if it were a modern diesel fitted with all the latest whizzbangs and gizmos to make it quiet and refined and torquey. But instead Maserati has fitted a single-turbo engine that happened to be available. And it's just not good enough in any area. It's not particularly quiet or powerful or economical or clean. It's just a tool that does a job, and in a fifty-grand Maserati, that's nowhere near good enough.

Then you move off, and immediately the whole car has hysterics. It's so big and so wide, its impact warning sensors are constantly convinced you're going to have a crash. Even when you are in slow-moving traffic on the A4 coming into London, it's screeching and squealing about the proximity of the barrier to your right and the bus to your left.

When you're parking, it goes berserk, insisting you stop reversing when there's enough space between you and the car behind to build a £7m house.

There's another problem with the Levante's size. It doesn't

translate into actual interior space. The boot isn't that big, the back isn't really big enough for three adults and in the front you feel hemmed in and claustrophobic. And deaf, because it's just seen a tree that you are definitely going to hit.

You may imagine, of course, that all these quibbles melt away when you leave the city and find yourself a nice piece of open road.

Nope. Like all purists, I was delighted when I heard the Levante wouldn't just be a leather-lined Jeep – Chrysler, which makes Jeeps, and Maserati both belong to Fiat – but instead would be a Ghibli on air-sprung stilts. But this isn't much better, really, because the Ghibli is actually based on the old Chrysler 300C. Which in turn was based on the Mercedes E-class taxi from about thirty years ago. So the Levante is basically a taxi with a crap clock.

You see evidence of the parts-bin mentality all over the interior. Yes, there's a lot of leather, and that's nice, but many of the buttons are lifted straight from the old Yank tank.

There are many, many people of my age who would dearly love to own a Maserati. Lying in bed at night, knowing that you had one in your garage, would make you all warm and gooey. But not the Levante. It doesn't look or feel or drive like the image you have in your head.

And, to make things worse, it doesn't even feel or look or drive as well as its rivals. To put it simply, BMW, Mercedes, Audi and Land Rover can offer you something better. Much better.

I'm willing to bet that the new Alfa Romeo Stelvio is better as well. Even though that's another car from the Fiat stable that shouldn't have been made in the first place.

9 April 2017

This nanny tucks you in, then hugs everyone outside too

BMW 530d M Sport

If a piece of technology remains fundamentally unchanged for more than a century, it's inevitable that one day it will be as perfect as it's going to get. And so it was with the most recent BMW 530d.

Every tiny lesson and shuffle forward since Karl Benz took his invention for a spin round Germany in 1888 had been incorporated. And as a consequence, the world had arrived at what might fairly be described as 'peak car'.

That thing offered an incredible blend of economy, refinement and power. It was comfortable, it handled beautifully, it was well made and easy to use and its astonishing good looks were tainted only by a deserved familiarity.

If I'd been in charge at BMW when that car was launched, I'd have asked everyone in the research and development department to go on holiday for ever because their work was done. The car, as an entity, had been perfected. And there were no more worlds to conquer.

However, the world doesn't work like that. The world demands change. So BMW was forced to come up with a new model that would, somehow, have to be even better . To try to achieve this, in a car that's still propelled down the road by the age-old principle of suck, squeeze, bang, blow, BMW turned to its laptop department, instructing it to fit the new model with all the electronic whizz bangs that had been invented since the previous model was on the drawing board. Sounds good, yes?

But perhaps it isn't. Many new cars – even my Golf – are capable of reading the road ahead and, for a few seconds, steering themselves. That's great, unless you want to change lanes on the motorway. If you indicate first, then the system knows you're doing it on purpose and shuts down, but if you don't, and frankly there's little point if traffic is light and you're moving into the middle lane to overtake a lorry, then the system tries to stop you. In some cars, you get a gentle tug at the wheel, but in the 5-series, you get a wrench. And then you end up fighting your own car, which is undignified and annoying.

Turning this facility off means plunging into the car's computer, which means you need to take your eyes off the road all the way from London to Swindon. But eventually you find the right sub-menu and then you're free to change lanes without letting the car know first.

But this puts it in a bad mood, so when you cross the white lines, it shudders and shakes, and to do something about this, you have to put on your reading glasses and go back into the menus, which is dangerous because now the car won't steer itself while you're otherwise engaged.

Mind you, it also won't crash into anything. Sensors are on hand to prevent you from getting within about 400 yards of the car in front, and if you break the speed limit, you are reminded on both the speedometer and the head-up display that you are on the wrong side of the law.

It's weird. You are driving along, with the engine ticking over at about 1500rpm. You are well within the capabilities of the car and you are a sentient being. But the electronic systems are behaving like you're armed with a sub-machinegun and you've just entered a shopping centre with a murderous look on your face.

It takes a while to turn all this stuff off and then you are left with a car that feels pretty much identical to the old 530d. The only way you can tell that the engine has diesel coursing through its veins is by driving halfway round the world and then noticing there's still enough juice in the tank to get you home.

Every single thing in the cabin works as well as is possible and there's so much space in the boot and the back that you'd have to be very fat indeed to need the bigger 7-series. Honestly, as a car – four wheels and a seat – it is impossible to fault. It's lovely when you are going quickly, and quiet and relaxing when you aren't. And it even has a party piece when you get to journey's end because you can get out, push a button on the (enormous) key fob and the car will park itself.

You'd never actually do this, of course. In the same way that you wouldn't board a plane with no pilot. You'd assume that while the electronics are capable of doing the task they'd been given, they'd go wrong, and then a human would need to be on hand to rescue the situation.

And that raises another interesting point. It's a far nicer and more relaxing car to drive with all the electronic nannies turned off, but what if I were momentarily distracted by something Jeremy Corbyn had said on the radio? Or if I'd dropped my lighter down the side of the seat? And the car crashed. And killed someone.

It's a moral maze. Do you put up with the constant interference and nagging just in case? Or do you disconnect everything and have a nicer time while hoping for the best? And does having the choice make this an even better car than its predecessor?

Or is it morally reckless to turn off all the systems that could save a child's life? Surely, you should leave them on. In which case, why would you need a car that handles so sweetly and can do 155mph? When you think about it for a while, your head starts to hurt.

So let's move on. It's not as masculine to look at as the old model. It looks less solid, less robust, more feminine. That's probably a good thing.

I don't doubt that it will be easier and therefore cheaper to make than its predecessor. And that's definitely a good thing because savings on the production line mean greater profits for BMW, which is good for the German economy. And what's good for the German economy is good for the economies of Greece, Italy and Portugal as well. Put simply, big profits on a 5-series mean fewer riots in Athens.

And of course, if more people buy a car like this – a car that forces you to indicate before moving, and obey the speed limits and not tailgate; well, that has to mean fewer fatalities.

So this is a car that hasn't moved the car itself along one jot. But it has raised the bar nevertheless because it's something you buy for the benefit of other people. That's an idea that's never really been tried before.

16 April 2017

So hot, you can cook breakfast in the boot

Renault Twingo GT

When Renault introduced its latest Twingo, many motoring journalists scoffed. They said it was slow, and that if you pushed it hard through the corners, it would understeer instead of settling into a nice, smoky drift.

Well, I'm sorry for gaping in astonishment like a wounded fish, but what were they expecting? It's a city car with a rear engine that would be dismissed by coffee lovers as too weak to grind their beans. So of course it wasn't going to be fast, and of course its tail wouldn't swing wide in the corners, because it would mostly be driven by the sort of people who'd crap themselves if it did.

Criticizing the baby Renault for not being an out-and-out racer is like buying a record player and criticizing it for not being any good at unblocking the sink.

The problem is that Renault put the engine at the back. So everyone thought, 'Well, if it's there, as it is in a Porsche 911, then it must feel like a Porsche 911.' Er, no. The engine in a small Peugeot is at the front, as it is in a Ferrari California, but the two cars feel alike only in the sense that you must sit down to drive them.

And speaking of Peugeot: a friend of mine recently bought a horrible 108 for his daughter. 'Why have you done that?' I wailed. 'You must hate her. It's a terrible car.' He listened as I droned on about how tinny it was, and how everything inside felt cheap, and then he said, 'Yes. But she gets three years' free insurance, which saves me six grand.'

This is what we tend to forget in this business. While we are looking for handling anomalies as we drift through Stowe corner at 120mph, it doesn't occur to us that most people care about safety and running costs and don't care about tread shuffle or an ability to deal smoothly with mid-corner bumps when you're at the limit.

Which brings me back to the Twingo. I didn't like it either, really, because I can't see the point of a 'city car'. Yes, it costs about 75p, but that is hardly good value if you have to leave it at home every time you want to travel more than thirty miles.

You may sneer at this. You may say that if it has an engine, it's perfectly capable of motorway travel. And who cares if it's a bit bouncy and noisy and strained? Hmmm. This argument doesn't wash, because, actually, a very small car with a very small engine is not really capable of handling a motorway.

You put your foot down on the slip road and accelerate so hard that the valves start to make dents in the bonnet, but you'll barely be doing 55mph by the time you're ready to join the motorway. Which is a problem, because your path to the inside lane is blocked by a lorry doing 56mph.

What do you do? You can't pull out, because you'll be squidged. You can't accelerate, because the engine is giving all it's got to give. And you can't slow down, because it would take too long to get back up to a reasonable speed again.

Then there's the issue of hills. In my daughter's old Fiesta, which had a 0.00001-litre engine, you'd have to start thinking about the M40 incline over the Chilterns when you were still several miles north of Banbury. And even then you'd reach the summit huffing and puffing like me when I walk to the top of the stairs.

Off the motorway things are no better, because in a small-engined small car you are forced to drive at the speed of the driver in front. If he's on a tractor, this is very annoying. It is so annoying that eventually you will attempt to overtake, and this will result in your death because you simply do not have the grunt to get past in much less than four hours.

Make no mistake, then. Cars designed to work only in the city are silly, because in the city you have Ubers and proper cabs and Tubes and buses and bicycle lanes. It's the one place you don't need a car. And in the place where you do – which is everywhere else – city cars are noisy and dangerous.

And that brings me to the Renault Twingo GT. It started in life as a city car, but it has been breathed on to give it some real-world poke. It still has a tiny, 0.9-litre three-cylinder engine, but it's turbocharged, so it produces a thrummy, off-beat 108 brake horsepower. This is a car that sounds like one of those very small dogs that growl the growl of a Great Dane. I liked it. It was amusing.

And I liked the speed too. I know 108bhp doesn't sound much, but it's what you used to get from the original Golf GTI. And no one said that was too slow for motorways.

The power delivery is a bit weird – it comes in lumps – but it's a hoot to out-accelerate most family saloons and then bomb along in a car that really belongs in a Hot Wheels set.

The way it handles is less impressive. The steering is done by guesswork – there's no feel at all – and you never have any clue that the engine's at the back. Sporty it is not. And that's fine, because this, after all, is a car designed for the city that happens to have the poke to deal with everywhere else as well.

And it looks tremendous. It's pretty anyway, and with a dinky rear air scoop to feed the turbo, and twin exhausts, it's brilliant. Mine was fitted with the optional stripes, which made it feel like a soap-box racer and me feel I was nine. It made me smile.

And that's before we get to the really impressive stuff. I went out one night with another grown-up in the front and three teenagers in the back. There was quite a lot of complaining, I admit, but the fact is that we fitted. And if I accelerated hard, the whizzy little engine drowned out the moaning.

The only problem with doing this is that the engine gets hot, which means anything you have in the boot gets hot too. This is a car that can turn your weekly shop into a delicious, piping-hot omelette before you get home.

Oh, and then there's the turning circle: it seems to be able to turn in its own length. It makes a black cab look cumbersome.

So there we are: a nifty, practical car that looks good, goes well and makes you happy. And all for £14,000. It hasn't won many fans with writers in the specialist press, because they still think it should go and handle like a 911. But I liked it a lot, because the comparison never entered my head.

23 April 2017

Something for the grizzled fur traders of Woking

Škoda Kodiaq

Most people think that despite Russia and America's wildly different political viewpoints, they have never been engaged in an actual fighty war. But that's not accurate. In the early nineteenth century Alaska was Russian and there were a lot of bouts of fisticuffs between the locals and their masters.

Today, in these troubled times, lessons can be learnt from how the dispute was solved: America simply bought the entire territory, lock, stock and no smoking barrels.

This meant that the main settlement on Kodiak Island became a thriving fishing port where people would catch salmons and halibuts, and tourists from Texas could come to shoot bears.

Kodiak means, in the local language, 'island'. So technically it's called 'Island Island'. In the 1960s it made the news because a bit of geological jiggery-pokery meant that the ground nearby suddenly rose by thirty feet. This tectonic boing and subsequent tsunami wiped out much of the fishing fleet and almost all the industry that supported it and now it exists mainly as a rugged outpost for people in checked shirts and Wrangler jeans, who I'm sure will not be best pleased that the name of their island has been nailed to the back of a Škoda people carrier.

Actually, I'll be accurate. To avoid any legal unpleasantness, Škoda has changed the final 'k' to a 'q', but the message is clear. This is a car for the great outdoors. It's for the people who know, when they're confronted by a bear, what to do. Not like you and me, who would stand there thinking, 'I know I should run if it's a grizzly and stand my ground if it isn't . . . Or is it the other way round? And what sort of bear is that anyway? And how does this gun work?'

Of course, a name on its own is not enough. You can call your son Astroflash Butch, but it's going to be no good if he grows up to have a concave chest and arms like pipe cleaners.

This is a problem for Škoda, because we all know that behind the He Man name, this car is just a stretched Volkswagen Golf on stilts. We know it's a seven-seat school-run special. We know it's as suburban as pampas grass and prosecco. It's a Volvo XC90 for women whose second-hand clothes business is not going quite as well as they'd hoped.

To try to fool us, Škoda has fitted a little button on the centre console that says 'off road'. That sits there, serving as a constant reminder that you are a person who knows how to gut a rabbit and live on a diet of nothing but your own urine. It lets your passengers know that you may have been in the special forces. You have a Kodiaq. And it's not just a glorified Golf. That little button says it can go over the Andes.

First of all, though, you have to pull away from the lights, and that's not easy in the diesel version I was driving because to make sure the engine doesn't kill any sea otters, and that it sits well inside the post-Dieselgate EU parameters of what is acceptable, the computer has been given a set of algorithms, and power is only ever a last resort.

Sensors take note of the air pressure, the incline of the road, the outside temperature, the gear that has been selected and the throttle position, and then the computer decides that, no, continuing to sit there is by far the best option for the planet.

So you put your foot down a bit more and the sensors get busy once again before deciding that moving off would cause someone to have bronchitis. So you mash your foot into the firewall, which causes the sensors to think, 'OK. He really wants to move, so I'll select seventh gear, which means it's all done nice and slowly and with minimal damage to Mother Nature.'

Happily, the EU has now changed its mind on diesels and has decided they are the work of Satan, which means taxes and parking charges for such cars will rocket. Which means in turn that if you choose to buy a Kodiaq, you'll buy one with a petrol engine. Good idea. At least that'll move occasionally.

Unless your foot slips off the throttle. I'm not quite sure how, or why, this has been achieved, but you drive a Kodiaq while sitting in the same position you adopt at a piano. And unless you have very long feet, your toes won't quite reach the throttle.

Apart from that, all is well on the inside. Well, nearly all is well. My test car had been fitted with an optional glass sunroof, which would be ideal for someone who wanted to waste £1,150. I thought sunshine roofs had been consigned to the history books, and this one serves as a reminder of why that should be so. Because when you open it, you get no air, and no sense of being outside; just a lot of extra noise.

Apart from that, though, the wood on the dash was fun, the Volkswagen infotainment satnav control module worked brilliantly and the comfort at slow speed around town was nice. This is not a car that's fazed by speed bumps.

At higher speed? I'm not sure, because every time I tried to put my foot down, the computer did some maths and reckoned acceleration wasn't climatically wise. What I can tell you is that if your foot doesn't fall off the throttle pedal and you accelerate very gently, it will reach 70mph on the motorway, where all is extremely quiet.

Handling? It's no good, but that's OK. If you wanted a car that went round corners well, you'd buy a Golf. Not a Golf on stilts.

The reason you buy this is because tucked away into the boot floor are two seats that can be used to carry very small people over very short distances. But not, at the same time, a dog.

At the weekend I went to my farm with it, as I had a number of manly jobs to do, such as padlocking the gates to stop local ruffians riding around the fields on their hateful motorcycles. The weather was extremely fine, the ground was rock hard and Chipping Norton in no way resembled the permanently wet and often icy conditions of Kodiak Island. But after just a few yards the Škoda was stuck.

And that's OK too, because if you want a farm car, you're going to buy a quad bike.

I like the idea of Škoda. It's a way of buying a new Volkswagen for less. And there is no question it makes some good cars. The Yeti is fabulous, and the Kodiaq's not bad either. It's pretending to be something it isn't, of course, with its 'Off road' button and its diamond prospector name, but when you look at it as a sensible, seven-seat school-run car, it makes a deal of sense. Especially as it costs only £35,210 – and that's the top-of-the-range model.

Just don't buy the stupid diesel. Partly because climate scientists have decided this month that diesel is bad, and partly because the only reason it gives good economy is because it's programmed not to work at all.

30 April 2017

Death it can stop. Taxes are a problem

Volvo S90

Ever since I began to write about cars, people of a Jeremy Corbyn persuasion have wondered, out loud and with a lot of spittle, why on earth anyone would want to buy one capable of speeds in excess of 70mph.

This is the main reason Mrs Thatcher was able to defeat the miners. Secondary flying pickets were so consumed by the fact that speed was the preserve of the rich, they deliberately drove Citroën 2CVs, which meant they'd arrive at the pitched battle just as the last police van was closing its doors and heading back to London.

Back then, ordinary people could do whatever speed took their fancy, because there were no cameras and the police could never catch them as most of them were too busy arresting Arthur Scargill.

Today, though, things are different. The police are still too busy – with minors, mostly, and those who may have abused them back in the day when people thought miners were the real problem – but there are electronic deterrents everywhere.

If I drive from my London flat to Luton airport – not something I do a lot, if I'm honest – I am monitored by average-speed cameras on every single inch of the journey.

I could choose, if we lived in a sensible country, to break the limit and pay a sort of speeder's tax. But for some reason the government has got it into its head that speeding is somehow a crime, and as a result I get points on my licence and the threat of actual prison time.

It's not just Britain either. It's everywhere. In Switzerland they can take away your car and put you in jail. In France they can strand young mothers at the side of the road. As a result of this idiotic, continent-wide war on speed, I'm afraid that nowadays when I'm asked why someone might want to buy a car that can do more than 70mph, I have to concede that probably there isn't much point at all.

Which brings me on to the large cars made by BMW and Mercedes and Jaguar and so on. All of them are set up to be perfectly balanced as you sweep through a lovely set of sweeping S-bends on a delightful sunlit A-road at 125mph.

Which means you are paying thousands of pounds for something that you can only do if you're prepared to spend the next six months playing mummies and daddies in a cell with Big Vern.

And that brings me neatly to the S90 from Volvo Sponsors Sky Atlantic.

Volvo Sponsors Sky Atlantic – which I think is its actual name these days – announced that by 2020 no one need die while driving one of its products.

Yup. If you have cancer or cerebral malaria or meningitis, simply climb into a Volvo and you'll live for ever.

And don't worry if you are driving it around and have a crash, because the other big announcement is that no Volvo engine will in future have more than four cylinders. So you'll never be going fast enough to get an injury that is remotely life-threatening.

To hammer the point home still further, the S90 you see here is not even available in the UK with a petrol engine.

You can only have it as a diesel, which of course is a terrible mistake, because these days the government has got it into its head that people who drive diesel cars are mass murderers and must pay £500 a minute every time they want to pop to the shops for a pint of milk.

It's not as if it's a very good diesel engine. It clatters like a canal boat at tickover, and it's even less powerful than the Liberal Democrats.

Volvo will naturally have to reverse its 'diesel only' decision very soon. There's a petrol-electric hybrid in the pipeline, which will make the S90 worth considering, because, ooh, it's a nice car to use in these speed-conscious days.

Handling? No idea. Doesn't matter. Steering feel? Irrelevant. All I can tell you is that when you turn the wheel, the car goes round the corner. Is front-wheel drive a handicap? At the sort of speed you'll be going, you'll never notice.

What I can tell you is that it rides nicely. It's very comfortable. And it's big on the outside. Nearly too big. But that's OK, because the size translates into acres of space on the inside. And it's space full of light and air, thanks to cleverly chosen materials.

Sitting in a Beemer or a Merc is like being in a well-groomed man's washbag. It's all leather and stripes and secret pockets for condoms and what-have-you. Sitting in an S90 is like sitting in a field. It's probably the best interior of any mainstream car on sale today.

One of the reasons is that just about everything is controlled from a generous iPad-type screen on the dash. Often I'm baffled by tech of this nature, but after just two days I was skipping round it without even having to take my eyes off the road for more than a couple of minutes.

And that's OK, because the S90 is fitted with all sorts of

radar-guided this and satellite-guided that to ensure you can't veer out of your lane and you can't crash into the car in front. And even if all of that breaks and you have climbed into the back for a snooze, it's still no bother, because the woeful diesel will have ensured you were going at only 2mph when you hit the bridge parapet. You'll probably just grunt a bit, turn over and go back to sleep.

The other good thing about driving the S90 is that it makes you feel more grown-up than the BMW Lynx and the Mercedes Brut. It's a car for the man or woman who's confident about themselves, their age and whatever physical deformities have been visited upon them by the passage of time.

No one who buys a car such as this – saloon or estate – will have had a teeth-whitening trip to the dentist or a tummy tuck or a breast enlargement.

Obviously you cannot buy one now. Its diesel engine is nasty, and because of various government taxation proposals on what it has labelled the fuel of Satan, the S90 will have a resale value, after two days, of about £0.

But it's worth waiting for Volvo Sponsors Sky Atlantic to launch the hybrid and start offering petrol-powered options. Because this a good-looking, comfortable and pleasant car that's just waiting for a heart transplant.

21 May 2017

Fat and silent, like a biscuit-loving ninja

Mercedes E-class coupé

At around this time of year my colleagues and I sit down in our television production company and try to work out which cars will be subjected to a sideways, smoking-tyres track test in the next series. Normally this begins with Richard Hammond saying: 'Well, there's a new 911 . . .'

That is followed by my shoulders sagging to a point just below my navel, because what can you say about a Porsche 911 that hasn't been said a billion times already? 'The engine's in the wrong place. It drives well. No one will let you out of side turnings. The end.'

Oh, sure, Porsche will explain in great detail that the new model is 4.5 per cent stiffer than the previous one and 5.8 grams lighter because it has titanium wheel nuts, but those are not the sorts of fact that work well when you are competing for viewers with *House of Cards* and *Billions* and a lot of grunting sex on Sky Atlantic.

I'm afraid it's the same story with any AMG Mercedes. It may be a tiny bit quicker from zero to 62mph than the previous model, and the Comand system may allow you to check how economically you've driven over the past 30.8 miles. But all of this is overshadowed by the thunderous noise and the massive wiggly back end. Points you've made several thousand times. Honestly, reviewing a car such as this is like being in Groundhog Day.

And so it was with some despair that I looked on the wall chart the other day and noted that a new Mercedes would be arriving for me to write about. Oh no, I thought. It'll be an AMG and I'll have to think of another long-winded simile to describe the noise it makes. 'God gargling with gravel.' Done that. 'Thor treading on a bit of Lego.' Done that. 'Tom Jones bending over to pick up the soap in a Strangeways shower.' A. A. Gill did that. And it'll never be beaten. Apart from when he described the wet V8 burble of a TVR as sounding like two lesbians in a bucket.

As it turned out I needn't have worried, because the car that turned up was not a thundering AMG (don't be fooled by the 'AMG Line' trim, which denotes sporty seats and floor mats with 'AMG' on them, not a snorting engine souped up by Mercedes' skunkworks department). It was something called an E 400 4Matic coupé. Which in English means that it's a four-wheel-drive, two-door version of your luxury Uber driver's E-class saloon.

Mercedes has gone down this route because it fancied having a pop at BMW's fabulous 6-series coupé. It explains, with a serious face, that its car has 14mm more rear legroom than you get in the Beemer and that it's also available with a four-cylinder engine. And then it sits back like a smug lawyer who's delivered his killer point. But, I'm sorry, Mercedes is missing the point.

Nobody cares two hoots about rear legroom in a coupé. If they did, they'd buy the four-door saloon. The whole point of a coupé is its looks, and on that front BMW has the market covered because, ooh, that's a handsome car. And the E 400 isn't. It looks as if it used to be good-looking before it found the biscuit tin. It looks, and there's no kind way of saying this, a bit fat. And was it beyond the wit of man to do away with that funny-looking rear quarterlight?

Inside, things are much better. You get air vents that resemble the plasma drive systems from a spaceship and, in the version I tested, a giant council-house flatscreen TV that tells you where you are, where you're going and how quickly you'll get there. As well as how much fuel there is in the tank and everything else in between.

And, yes, it does allow you to choose the colour of the interior lighting. I went for purple. Even though it clashed badly with the exterior, which was the exact same colour as a placenta.

To drive? Well, the friend who was using it to pick me up from the airport had a few choice words to say about that. As I landed, I noticed on my Find My Friends app that she was still in Chelsea, so I called to ask why. There was a lot of swearing, but the gist of it went: 'How do I make the engine begin?'

And then, after I'd explained there was a button hidden away behind the steering wheel, another call to say: 'Where's the effing gear lever?' I had to explain that it sticks out of the steering column and looks like the stalk that would operate the wipers on a normal car.

So it doesn't begin or get going like a normal car, and this, it turns out, is the E-class coupé's party piece. Because it doesn't feel normal when you're driving along either. You have a nine-speed gearbox, but you'd never know that it's constantly swapping cogs and that the power from the engine is being sent to whichever of the four wheels is best able to handle it.

Ah, yes, the engine. It's a 3-litre V6 that produces hundreds of horsepower and a mountain of torque. And yet somehow it makes no noise at all. Unusually for a Mercedes, then, I'm having to think of a whole new simile. It's like a Trappist monk who's dead in a room made entirely from kapok. Only quieter.

The drawback is that when you look down at the council-house flatscreen, you'll note you are doing 130mph. Which is against the law.

You're not even being jiggled around that much. Well, not by the suspension, at least. You could drive this thing through the broken streets of Palmyra and it'd feel as if you were in Austria at the end of a national competition to find the country's best roadworker.

However, there are many electrical systems on hand to stop you crashing, and they are a bit panicky. Time and time again, the car's on-board brain decided I was definitely on the verge of a huge accident and took control of the brakes and the steering.

This is a heart-stopping surprise, and I was tempted to turn the systems off. But if you do that and you get a text and crash, and you have to spend the rest of your life communicating with a head wand, you're going to feel a right Charlie.

Mercedes needs to turn the intervention down a bit. To make it gentler and less alarming. Because, as it stands, it's a good-enough reason not to buy this car. So is the styling.

I know BMW's 6-series is more expensive and has 14mm less legroom in the back and can't be ordered with four-wheel drive. But turning that down and buying the Mercedes instead is like turning down Uma Thurman for the woman at the post office. Because she's so good at ironing.

4 June 2017

They say it's new, but thank heavens it's not

Volkswagen Golf GTI

One of the problems with running a car company is that no department actually finishes what it's working on. Which makes launching a new car extremely difficult.

Think about it. You're the boss and you call the styling department. You ask if it has completed the way the new car will look and it says: 'Give us two more weeks.' So you give it two more weeks and then you call the engine department, which says it wants another week. So you agree to that, which causes the styling department to embark on the set of changes that somehow takes three weeks to implement. And when that's done, the suspension people call to say: 'Look, give us twenty-four hours.'

And so it goes on until eventually you, as the boss, have to turn on the factory PA system and say: 'All of you. Step away from the Cad-Cam equipment. Give us what you have now and we will build that.' Which means the car you and I buy is invariably made up completely of parts that aren't quite as good as they could have been if only there'd been a bit more time.

The problem for Volkswagen is doubly difficult because of Dieselgate. So much money has been put aside to compensate customers who were sold a better car than would have been the case if it had complied with the regulations, that there is only £2.75 left in the petty cash tin for research and development.

Which brings us on to the new Golf GTI. Well, VW says it's new – in reality it's a facelift of the current Mk 7 – in the hope that existing owners will feel compelled to sell their old model and sign on the dotted line of whatever nonsensical finance arrangement the beancounters have come up with this time.

I am one of these existing owners. The Golf GTI is what I use as my daily driver. It is an extremely good car, apart from the fact it's permanently convinced it has a puncture when it hasn't. I get in it in the morning, start it up and it says: 'You have a puncture.' So I push the button saying: 'No, I haven't.' And then, when I get back into it to go home from work it says: 'You have a puncture.' And I start to foam at the mouth.

I've taken it to a dealership, which reset the computer. And ensured all the tyres contained exactly the same amount of air. And the next morning it says: 'You have a puncture.'

Today I have solved the problem by sticking duct tape to the dash so I can no longer see the message. Oh, and a flannel between the passenger seat and centre console to solve the rattle it somehow doesn't seem to know it's got.

Apart from these things, it's a wonderful car. It's equipped like a Bentley, it goes like a Ferrari and in traffic, because it's just a Golf and it's grey, no one takes my picture. Which is what happens, constantly, when I'm in anything more flash. Which is everything.

Anyway, my car has done only 15,000 miles so it'd take quite a lot to convince me I should take the resale hit and buy the new model. But I'm open to suggestion so VW dropped one off at the office.

I looked at it for a very long time. Then I looked at my car. And then I looked at the new one again and after a lot of doing this I realized that while my car was a sort of gunmetal grey the new one was definitely white. I also noticed after a lot more looking that the new model had slightly different trim in the headlights and some styling tweaks to the wheels. I then stepped inside and straight away saw that the rather attractive speedometer and rev counter in the old model had been replaced by some less attractive instruments in the new one.

Also, instead of a button to start the car, I had to put the key in a slot and twist it. I haven't had to do that since someone worked out that in an accident an ignition key protruding from the steering column can play havoc with a driver's kneecaps.

And then I noticed the gear lever. And the clutch pedal. And I thought: 'No. I'm sorry. It's pouring with rain. The traffic is going to be dreadful and life is too short to be using my left leg every time I want to set off.' So I climbed out of the new car and into my own, which has a flappy paddle system. 'You have a puncture,' it said from behind the duct tape.

It's strange. Not that long ago, I was very much in the manuals-are-for-men camp. I saw the automatic and the double-clutch alternatives as a sign of weakness. In my mind they were a way of saying that you were a functionary, that you were willing to relinquish control to an algorithm. 'Alexander the Great would never have ordered a car with an automatic gearbox,' I would thunder at people who had.

Now, though, I reckon buying a manual is like buying a television that has no remote control. Who says: 'I like getting out of my chair to change the channel'?

Maybe it's because I'm getting old. But more likely it's because the modern flappy paddle can change cogs far more quickly than any human being. And your left leg is free to tap along to the radio.

Much later in the week, of course, I had to park my prejudice and my bone idleness and take the new car for a drive. I'd been told its 2-litre turbocharged engine had 10bhp more than the old model and that this equated to a top speed that's 2mph higher. Which sounded great. But actually all VW has done is fitted the old performance pack as standard. Which means that the updated car has exactly the same amount of power and performance as mine.

Everything else. The steering. The suspension. And even the option of a clever limited-slip front differential is the same as well. And that's a good thing, if I'm honest. Because the old Golf GTI was the world's best hot hatch. And the new one is as well. Partly because it isn't new at all. But mainly it doesn't think it has a puncture.

11 June 2017

An SUV poster boy at last. Yes, it's Italian

Alfa Romeo Stelvio

I have driven the latest Audi Q5 and can think of absolutely nothing interesting to say about it. It's a well-made box that costs some money and produces some emissions and, frankly, I'd rather use Uber.

No, really. Who's going to wake up in the morning, sweating like a dyslexic in a spelling test, because their new Q5 is arriving that day? What child is going to stick a poster of a car such as this on its bedroom wall? Who's going to think how hard they'll have to work to pay for the damn thing and reckon it's worth the sweat? No one is. You buy a car like this in the way you buy washing-up liquid. And who wants to read 1,200 words about a mildly updated bottle of Fairy Liquid?

What I can tell you before I move on is that I hated its engine. Volkswagen's post-Dieselgate 2-litre turbo is possibly the most boring power unit fitted to any car at any time. It's about as exciting as the motor in your washing machine. By which I mean, you only really notice it if it goes wrong. Which you hope it will in the Audi, because then you can call an Uber. At least that'll smell interesting. And come with some unusual opinions.

I'll be honest with you. I loathe all the current crop of so-called SUVs, except those I dislike intensely. I cannot see the point of driving around in a car that's slower, more expensive and thirstier than a normal saloon or estate. It just seems idiotic.

But then I had to make a brief trip to Tuscany recently, and once I'd negotiated a path through Alan Yentob and Polly Toynbee and Melvyn Bragg and emerged into Pisa airport's car park, I found a man offering me the keys to Alfa Romeo's new Stelvio.

Named after a remote Alpine pass in northern Italy, this is a direct rival of the Q5 and all the other mid-range jacked-up estates whose names I can't be bothered to remember. In short, it's a Giulia saloon on stilts, and I was determined to hate every bit of it.

The man was very keen to have his photograph taken with me and to say how much he enjoyed a programme called *Top Gear*, but I wasn't listening. I was thinking: 'What in the name of all that's holy was Alfa Romeo thinking of?'

If you have a heritage as glamorous and as achingly cool as Alfa's, why would you want to make a bloody school-run car? That is like Armani deciding to make carrier bags.

Alfa's engineers are at pains to explain that, while it may look like an SUV, it doesn't feel like one to drive. They say all the power from the engine is sent to the rear wheels, but then, if traction is lost, up to half the power is sent instantly to the front. They also speak about carbon-fibre prop shafts and much lightweight aluminium in the body, and I stood there thinking: 'Yes, but it's still a bloody carrier bag.'

I had much the same sense of teeth-gnashing rage when I first encountered Maserati's Levante, and that turned out to be just as bad as I'd feared. But as the man brought over more friends for more selfies, I started to gaze more carefully at the Stelvio, and there was no getting round the fact that, actually, it's quite good-looking.

Eventually, after I'd posed with all the police force, every-one in border security and 3,000 taxi drivers, all of whom loved *Top Gear*, it was time to step into the Stelvio, and there was also no getting round the fact it was a nice place to sit. Way, way nicer than the Audi.

There's some genuine sculpture in there. You get the impression in a Q5 that the dash was built with all the care of a kitchen worktop. It's just a housing for the dials and the switches. Alfa has made its one something worth looking at. I suppose it's an Italian thing. It's why Siena is a better place to sit and people-watch than Dortmund.

Setting the satnav, however, was a challenge. This is because every town in Italy has 5,000 letters in its name, and then, when you finally manage to type it in, the satnav asks which Santa Lucia del Menolata di Christoponte you would like to set as the destination. And it turns out there are 5,000 towns with that name.

Eventually, though, as Alan and Melvyn and Polly were returning to the airport from their week of brainstorming, I had the right town and fired up the engine. The diesel engine. Oh, dear Lord. A diesel Alfa Romeo SUV.

The funny thing is, though, that because everyone in Italy has a diesel-powered car, it didn't feel all that weird to be clattering out of the car park. And then it felt fine, because soon I was on the racetrack known as an autostrada, where it felt very powerful. The figures say it'll go from 0 to 62mph in 6.6 seconds, which is good, but it's the mid-range surge that impresses most of all. It's a surge you just don't get from Audi's Q5. And it means you can always break free from the walnut-faced peasant who has affixed his aged Fiat Ritmo to your back bumper at 100mph.

And it's not as if you're leaving a trail of death in your

wake because, despite the power and the torque, this engine is considerably cleaner than the diesel Porsche puts in its Macan. And Alfa says it'll do almost 60mpg.

So it's as fast as the badge would suggest, but does it handle as well as Alfa promises? Well, obviously, as it's more than 7 inches higher than the saloon and has longer springs, it's squidgier, which would be fine if Alfa hadn't given it the same superfast steering setup.

The tiniest movement of the wheel causes a big change of direction, which is great when you are on a track in a low-riding 'car', but when you are on the autostrada, on stilts, with a Ritmo up your chuff and a lorry up front that has suddenly decided to wander into your lane because the driver is watching pornography on his phone rather than the road ahead, it can be a bit alarming.

It takes time to learn to think your way round corners, but when you get there, I must say this is a genuinely exciting car to drive. It doesn't feel as cumbersome as all the other SUVs, and you get the impression it was engineered by people who were involved because they wanted to be. Not because they'd done something wrong.

And because of that – because it's a big, practical car with a huge boot and folding seats and lots of cubbyholes that's also an Alfa Romeo – it's the only SUV that's quite tempting. It may even be irresistible when Alfa launches the version with the 500-horsepower petrol engine.

18 June 2017

Well, we did tell Richard Hammond to fire it up

Clarkson on the Hamster's crash . . . and the new Range Rover

A few years ago Richard Hammond was asked to drive a car down a runway, and somehow he ended up on his head and then in a coma for a few weeks.

And now, having established he can't drive in a straight line, he has proved he can't drive round corners either. All he had to do was drive a small electric car up a Swiss hill, which he managed, but then somehow, on a left-hand bend after the finish line, he lost control, rolled down a bank and ended up in a hospital. Again.

At this rate he will get to the point where he forgets how to get undressed at night. He'll put his clothes on in the morning and then assume they will be cut off by paramedics at some point later in the day.

Seriously, I'm struggling to think of any racetrack in the world that Hammond hasn't crashed on at some point. At Imola he binned a Noble, at Virginia International Raceway in America it was a Porsche, at Mugello he bent a Jaguar and at Silverstone, in a twenty-four-hour race, he doomed our efforts in the middle of the night by stuffing a BMW into pretty much everything that was solid. Maybe it's because he can't see over the steering wheel. Who knows?

What troubles me most of all, now that we know he will be OK, is the charred mess he left at the bottom of the hill in Switzerland. It had started out that morning as something called the Rimac Concept One. And, frankly, it was amazing.

There are a few very rich people in the world who will talk sagely about the work Tesla is doing with electric propulsion, and a handful of fanatics who insist on telling us how their G-Wiz is ideal for the city centre, but most normal people think of electricity as something that powers a toaster or a washing machine. The idea of buying an electrical vehicle, unless you're a milkman, is just as daft as buying a petrol-powered food blender.

The Rimac could change all that. I had only a brief time behind the wheel and simply could not believe how fast it accelerated. We are not talking here about a car that's as fast as a Lamborghini Aventador. It's massively faster than that. It's faster than anything else I've driven, by a huge, huge margin.

It has four electric motors, one at each wheel, which together produce a simply staggering 1,200 horsepower. In the time it takes you to work out how fast it accelerates from 0 to 60, it's doing 120. And there's still a hundred miles an hour to go.

You might imagine that, with power like this, its battery pack would go flat every 3½ seconds. But, as Hammond proved on that fateful day in Switzerland, this isn't the case. Even if you drive as though you are mad, you'll get 120 miles between charges.

I've never been a fan of electric cars. Comparing them to those with a normal engine has always been a bit like comparing microwaved food to stuff that's been in the Aga for a few hours. But that Rimac changed my mind. It was – there's no other word – brilliant.

Hammond loved it. He will probably love it even more now he knows you can roll it down a hill at 120mph and still get out before some kind of electrical issue causes it to become an inferno. And doubtless we will hear more when he talks about it in the next series of *The Grand Tour*. Unless James May and I have kicked him to death by then.

In the meantime I've been having a bit of a pen-sucking, leaning-back-in-the-chair moment about what will power our cars in a few years' time.

As you may remember, the world's environmentalists declared several years ago that petrol engines were extremely bad for the planet and that we must all buy diesels instead. They scoffed and rolled their eyes at people like me who said this was nonsense. They called us climate change 'deniers' and said we could not argue with cold, hard facts.

As a result, the then chancellor, Gordon Brown, changed all the rules to make buying diesel cars cheaper, and millions of people took advantage. Only to be told earlier this year that the cold, hard facts may not have been entirely accurate and that petrol is a much cleaner fuel after all.

So now all of the people who have diesel cars are being told that they must in future pay £700 to refuel them and £9m to park them and £5000m if they wish to drive them into central London. Which means they are all trying to sell. And what they're getting is 5p. If you're in that boat, I'd send a bill for the losses to Greenpeace and Friends of the Earth. Maybe it'd make them think twice next time they have some cold, hard facts they'd like to share.

I run a diesel. It's an old Range Rover. The first of the TDV8s. And it works well. After I've filled the tank, the trip computer tells me I have a range of 500 miles before I need to fill up again. Which is good if you like shooting. You can get to Yorkshire and back without having to face the ridicule of walking into Leicester Forest East services in a pair of tweed shorts.

All sensible Range Rover owners have diesels. But, thanks to our friends in the Green Party, you'll think twice about that next time round. And so, for the first time in years, I spent last week tootling about in a petrol-powered SVAutobiography.

There's nothing I can say about this car that hasn't been said a million times already. It's in a class of its own. It has no rivals. And, with the SV engine under the bonnet, it's ludicrously fast. Hilariously fast. It's like being in the British Museum while falling down a cliff, and yet, incredibly, you still have control over where you're going. Only Richard Hammond could crash this thing.

The problem was that after 150 miles the petrol gauge was into the red zone. It's not the money: if you can afford a car like this, the cost of refuelling isn't important. No, it's the fact that, unless you are very good at fuel-light bingo, you can't get from London to Leeds on one tank.

So what's to be done? Well, there's now a hybrid Range Rover, but that's part electrical and part diesel, so it doesn't really get round the anti-derv nonsense.

The only solution, really, is to use pure electrical power. It'd work too. Near-silent cruising when you're on the road and immense torque when you aren't.

I'd like to suggest Land Rover consult the boffins at Rimac about how such technology could be employed. But I fear that, thanks to Hammond, they're going to be a bit busy for the next few weeks building a replacement car.

25 June 2017

I've done fast and silly fast, but this is flaming ridiculous

The Bugatti Chiron

Several years ago I reviewed the Bugatti Veyron in the *Sunday Times* and was a bit gushing. I talked about the sheer complexity of making a car feel stable and poised when it was travelling at 240mph-plus, and how dangerous and annoying the air can be at such speeds.

A 240mph wind would knock over every building in New York. It would devastate and destroy everything in its path. And yet the Veyron had to be able to deal with wind speeds this high while being driven by someone whose only qualification was an ability to reverse round a corner and recognize a 'Give way' sign.

I marvelled at the engineering in that car – it had ten radiators to keep it cool – and reckoned that, because of the relentless war on speed and internal combustion, we would never see its like again. There just wouldn't be the appetite to make a replacement. It would be just too difficult, not just politically, but also from an engineering standpoint.

And it turned out to be doubly difficult, given that Bugatti's parent company, Volkswagen, is spending every penny it has on dealing with Dieselgate.

But despite all the odds, Bugatti has come up with a replacement. It costs £2.5m, it's called the Chiron and somehow it is even faster than the Veyron. It has a top speed of 261mph, which means it's covering more than 125 yards a second. You know the Apache helicopter gunship? It's faster than that.

The 8-litre engine is partly the reason for this almost unbelievable pace. It has sixteen cylinders arranged in a 'W' formation and it's force-fed by four turbochargers. The result is a say-that-again 1,479 brake horsepower. Yup, 1,479 brake horsepower.

But equally important is the body and the way it lowers itself and changes its angle of attack the faster you go. You don't know this is going on from behind the wheel. Because you are too busy watching the road ahead and thinking, with very wide eyes: 'This is f****** ridiculous.'

Last week I drove the Chiron, not just for a couple of laps round a racetrack under the watchful gaze of a minder, but all the way from St Tropez to the border with Switzerland and then to Turin. I got to know it well and I still haven't stopped fizzing. The speed is beyond anything you can even possibly imagine.

At one point on the French autoroute I became mixed up in one of those rallies where young men take their Audi R8s and their Aston DB11s and their Oakley wraparound sunglasses on a tour of chateaux and racetracks in the sunshine. They kept drawing alongside and roaring off in the hope I'd put my foot down. So after a while I did. And even from half a mile in front, which is where I ended up after mere seconds, I could feel their penises shrinking in disbelief and embarrassment.

There is nothing made by any mainstream car maker that could hold a candle to the Chiron. A McLaren P1 doesn't even get close. It's like comparing me as a drummer with Ginger Baker.

And it's not just the speed in a straight line that leaves

you breathless and scared. It's the pace coming out of the corners. Plant your foot into the carpet in first gear emerging from a hairpin, and every single one of the horse-powers you've engaged and every single pound foot of torque is transferred with no fuss, and no wheelspin, directly into forward motion. It's acceleration and G-force so vivid, you can actually feel your face coming off. It's speed that hurts.

There's a secret button that you really don't want the police to know about. But if you push it, the digital air-conditioning readouts will quietly inform you what speed you've been averaging. Often I'd sneak a look. And often it came up with a figure over 120mph. That's an average. On a mountain road (which was closed to the public, since you ask). Like I said. It's ridiculous.

But it's never difficult. Oh, I'm sure Richard Hammond could roll it down a hill, but for the rest of us it's a doddle. There are no histrionics. The exhaust system doesn't pop and bang. The engine doesn't shriek. There are no aural gim-micks at all. And everything you touch is either leather or metal. Unless it's the badge. That's sterling silver.

If Rolls-Royce were to make a mid-engined supercar, it would feel something like this, I suspect. It's never hard or jarring. It doesn't pitter-patter even on cobbles. And it has a boot into which you can fit, um, a grapefruit.

The downside of this comfort and luxury is that it doesn't really behave like a mid-engined supercar. It doesn't flow. There's no delicacy. It just launches itself out of a corner, and then immediately you're braking for the next one. Pro-gress is staccato, not legato. Mainly because in a car this powerful there's no such thing as a straight. It eats them before you have a chance to notice. Which means there's no place to sort out your mind. There's no peace. It's all action.

Most mid-engined supercars dance. And the Chiron does too, but it's not a waltz or a tango. It's as if it's in a punk club in 1979, listening to Sham 69.

This, then, is not a car for serious drivers. It feels heavy, and that's because it is. It feels as if it's volcanic. You could liken a McLaren P1 to a hummingbird and marvel at its ability to dart hither and thither in a blur. Whereas when you're driving a Chiron, it feels as though you're coming up through the spout of Vesuvius, propelled by lava, convection and pressure.

It doesn't even look like a traditional mid-engined super-car. It looks important and statesmanlike. From some angles – the back, especially – it appears ugly.

Then there's that Brunelian radiator snout at the front. It's there because Bugatti tradition dictates that it should be there. And you can't help marvelling at it, because for this car to go so quickly, every tiny aerodynamic detail had to be examined and scrapped and built again.

Look at what happens to a Formula One car when it loses one of its little winglets. It crashes immediately into a barrier. And those things rarely reach 200mph. The Bugatti is way faster than that, which means that snout must have been a nightmare to fit into the mix, but the engineers managed it somehow.

And that's what this car is all about. It's not driving pleasure. It's not aesthetics. It's just man looking at nature, rolling up his sleeves and saying: 'Do you want some?'

This car doesn't challenge the laws of physics. It bludgeons them. It is an engineering marvel, because like all other engineering marvels it's an affront to God.

It's also an affront to Friends of the Earth, Greenpeace and all the other Jeremy Corbyn enthusiasts who say it's time to put away our toys and live more responsibly.

We have to love it for that, too, and applaud Volkswagen for saying: 'Not just yet, beardy.'

9 July 2017

Big roar, waggly tail: that's my kind of lion

Audi RS 5

Back in the Eighties, BMW came up with the idea of making an innocuous-looking saloon that was very fast and utterly beautiful to drive. It was called the M5 and it earned a reputation for being one of the world's great cars.

All the other manufacturers could see straight away that BMW had created something of a masterpiece, so they decided to not respond in any way at all. And that's weird. It's like all the country's football teams looking at what Chelsea did last year and thinking: 'We can't possibly match that, so let's not bother trying.'

Eventually, after BMW had had the market all to itself for years and years, Mercedes joined forces with the tuning company AMG to create a high-performace range of cars, but these weren't really direct rivals for the fast Beemers. They were big and smoky and loud and quite soft. They were muscle cars, really, in Hugo Boss suits.

And Audi? Well, it started to fit quite powerful engines to its four-wheel-drive models to create the RS line-up, but, again, they didn't have the magic of BMW's M cars – the delicacy.

If you really knew your motoring onions – if you really knew how to trail-brake and feel the limit of adhesion – you were never going to be satisfied with a nose-heavy Audi or a wayward Mercedes. If you were a proper driver, you'd always go for the BMW.

However, in recent months the BMW bandwagon has sort of fallen over. There is no M5 on sale at the moment, and while the M2 is a joy, its bigger and better-known brother the M3 is a bit of a dog. The steering is actually fairly terrible. And an M car with terrible steering? That's like an omelette made with rancid eggs.

And to make life even more difficult for BMW, other rivals have finally woken up. Alfa Romeo can sell you the Giulia Quadrifoglio, which has three-quarters of a Ferrari engine and an exhaust note to stir the soul. It would be my choice.

Then you have Mercedes, which has just produced something called the E 63 S. Its styling is a bit in-your-face for my taste – and for yours, too, unless you live in Dubai – but it's not like any AMG we've seen before. It has the power, but it's harnessed into a proper package. That's a serious car for serious people, make no mistake.

And then there's Audi, which has just launched the car you see in the photographs this morning. It's called the RS 5 coupé, it costs £62,900 and it's borderline sensational.

I was hoping Audi would have fitted it with the 394 brake horsepower five-cylinder engine from the TT RS, because when historians look back at what they'll call the 'petrol age', they will describe that as one of the all-time greats.

But Audi has gone for a twin-turbocharged 2.9-litre V6. Which gives 444 brake horsepowers. And 600 Eurotorques, or 442lb/ft. That's a lot in a car of this type.

But the bald figures of 0–62mph in 3.9 seconds and a top speed of 155mph – or 174mph with the optional Dynamic package – tell only half the story. To get the other half, you have to go behind the wheel and open it up. And, ooh, you'll be grinning. Actually, to start with, you won't be grinning. You'll be looking as though a lion has just come into your kitchen, because, God, it's alarmingly quick off the line. I once saw someone put a mustard-covered hot dog up a police horse's bottom. Well, the Audi sets off like that.

Of course, there have previously been Audis that were fast in a straight line. But that's all they could do: go in a straight line. You would be sitting there, sawing away at the wheel and shouting, 'Turn, you bastard, turn', but they rarely did. A nose-heavy layout and four-wheel drive saw to that.

The RS 5 is different. It has a bitey front and a waggly tail that is just what the enthusiastic driver wants. Oh, and while the ride is definitely firm, it doesn't pitter-patter like Audis of old. This, rest assured, is a properly sorted, well-engineered and really quite well-priced car.

It's also good-looking. The wheels are worthy of a spot in Tate Modern, the rear side windows are a nod to the Nissan GT-R – a comparable car, in fact – and the space isn't bad either for a two-door coupé.

So there we are. Another kick in the teeth for BMW's M division. A car you can drive, safe in the knowledge that the cognoscenti will give you a discreet nod at the lights – a recognition that you've made a wise choice.

And there's more. I was in Knightsbridge the other night, having dinner on the pavement (not like a homeless person – I was at the Enterprise, which is a pub, not a spaceship. Well, it was a pub. It's a bar and restaurant now.) Anyway, every third word I tried to say was drowned out by the bangs from wealthy young gentlemen's anti-lag systems echoing off the walls like a firefight for the centre of Homs.

They went round and round the area in their hotted-up supercars until even I was pissed off. So you can imagine how my fellow diners felt. Which is why they will vote for anyone who makes petrol illegal.

I sense this everywhere these days. People are fed up with owning cars. They use Ubers and trains. And those who maintain their interest in all things automotive are treated with the sort of scorn and disdain that I reserve for golfers and freemasons.

So if you're going to buy a really quick car that you can enjoy when no one is looking, it needs to be discreet. And the Audi is.

There is, however, a problem. If you're the sort of keen driver who might be interested in this car, the chances are that the vehicle you currently drive doesn't have four rings on the grille.

Which means you will have no idea how the Audi's sat-nav-multimedia-connectivity system works. You will stab away at various buttons and then mutter something under your breath and push a few more, and eventually you'll get out of your test vehicle, slam the door and buy the new version of the car you drive now.

This is becoming a serious problem. I write on a PC and cannot change to a Mac because I can't be bothered to waste my life learning my way around its systems. I use an iPhone because it's familiar, so when someone says Google's latest effort is better, I don't care, because I don't know how it works.

It's increasingly the same story with cars. I understand how to silence the satnav woman in my Volkswagen Golf and how to make Apple CarPlay work. I know how to reset the trip computer and to engage the self-parking system. But when I get into a BMW, or a Mercedes, I do not know straight away how to do any of that.

The days when a car was three pedals and a steering wheel are over. They're electronic now, and much of their appeal is their ability to steer round jams and stop before an accident happens and play the music from our phone.

And in the Audi all this stuff is bloody difficult. So you won't buy one. And that's a shame.

30 July 2017

Better hold on really tight, queasy rider

Mercedes-AMG GT C roadster

Because I'm extremely middle class, my children's prep school organized exchange trips with pupils at a school in Tokyo. This meant that my kids got to spend a couple of weeks eating fish that were still alive and later they got to host little Japanese people who had no clue what to do with a spoon.

I picked one of these kids up from Heathrow and it quickly became obvious the poor little thing spoke no English at all. So she wandered into the arrivals hall after an eleven-hour flight, jet-lagged all to hell, and she was met by a man who was bigger and fatter than anyone she'd seen in her whole life. And he communicated in what to her must have sounded like the grunts of a farmyard animal. Bewildering didn't begin to cover it.

I loaded her luggage into the boot of the family Volvo – I said I was middle class – and she climbed into the back clutching what at the time was a completely amazing translation machine. The idea was that she spoke into it and it then spoke to me in English.

Shortly after we joined the M25 I could see in the rearview mirror that my microscopic guest was trying to turn the machine on. And by the time we joined the M40 she was starting to get desperate because plainly she was having some difficulty.

Much later, on the twisting and lovely A44, I heard the telltale beep to say she'd been successful and quickly she garbled something in Japanese into the electronic wonder box. She then held it next to my ear while it said with an electronic Stephen Hawking lilt: 'Car sick.'

During her two-week stay she was sick after eating tinned tuna, mashed potato, ice cream and pretty much everything that was dead.

But I bet that if you ask her now to define the low point of her stay she'd say it was that moment on the A44, being hugged by a 6 foot 5 inch monster as she vomited the contents of her stomach into the roadside undergrowth.

Motion sickness is hideous. You really do want to die. I saw a man once lying on the floor in a cross-Channel ferry's lavatory. The voyage had been as rough as any I can remember and everyone had been sick so violently it was a lake of vomit in there. And it was swilling over the poor man who, as I entered, opened one eye and said simply: 'Kill me.'

I felt his pain. I'd been on a boat in the south of France once when the gentle rocking brought about a malaise so intense that I invited my friends to murder me. I meant it. I even told them where the knives were kept and where on my rib cage they should stab.

All of which brings me conveniently to the Mercedes-AMG GT. I thought when I first saw this car that it was a toned-down, more realistic version of the mad old SLS AMG with its bonkers soundtrack and its gullwing doors. I assumed therefore that it too would be a headline-grabbing one-off.

But no. Mercedes has turned it into an entire range that's now so complex you are able to choose how many brake horsepower you'd like and what shade you'd prefer for the seats. Naturally you can also decide whether you'd like a roof or not. And what colour you'd like that to be.

Well, as I've already driven the super-hard and bellowy GT R coupé, which I'm not sure about, I thought – it being summer and all – I should try out the slightly less powerful but still pretty nuts GT C roadster.

Like the 'I'm a racing car, I am' GT R, it's fitted with four-wheel steering. And that, if you are going for a record round the Nürburgring – something the GT R holds for rear-wheel-drive production cars, incidentally – is tremendous. When you drive a car that steers with all four wheels you are always amazed by just how readily it changes direction.

However, I was not on the Nürburgring. I was in Oxfordshire and I was not driving particularly quickly when my passenger invited me to stop. Because she felt car sick. And the last time this happened was when I was driving her in a Porsche 911. Which also had four-wheel steering.

The problem is that when you move the steering wheel even a tiny bit, the car darts. It's very sudden and if you're a passenger you have no time to brace or send a signal to your stomach to hold on. You, the driver, may like this sensation a lot. But I think it may be a deal breaker for whoever's in the passenger seat.

Pity, because there's a lot to like in this car. It looks like a traditional AMG product. Big, lairy and heavy. But, actually, it's lighter than you might think, thanks to a chassis that's made from helium and a boot lid made from witchcraft. There's even some magnesium in there as well.

All of which means that the big turbocharged V8, which responds as quickly as the steering, has much less to lug around than you might think. Which means this car is properly fast. Knocking-on-the-door-of-200mph fast. It also does a fabulous bonnet-up, squatted-back-end lunge when you stamp on the throttle.

I'd like to say this speed is surprising but you know from the moment you fire up the engine and the exhausts wake everyone in a twelve-mile radius that it's going to be mental. What is surprising, however, is that you can enjoy quite a lot of the speed with the roof down. It really is calm and unruffled in there.

And it's a nice place to sit. Sure, the gear lever is mounted nearer to the boot than your hand and, yes, there are a lot of buttons to confuse you. I once turned off what I thought was the stop-start feature and then spent the whole day in third because I'd actually changed the seven-speed automatic box into a manual.

My only real gripe is the bumpiness of the ride. It really is firm – too firm – and that's unnecessary because this isn't a track-day car. It's a handsome, look-at-me boulevard cruiser. Or a devourer of motorways and interstates. It should be softer. And it really could do without that four-wheel steering.

Mercedes shouldn't try to make sports cars. That's Porsche's job. What it should do instead is take this vehicle back to the drawing board and turn what's very nearly there back into an AMG Mercedes. Then it would be absolutely brilliant.

6 August 2017

My hop to the beach became a cliffhanger

Porsche Panamera Turbo

Jeremy Clarkson is away. That's what it should say at the bottom of the page this week. Because I am away. I'm in Mallorca, sitting in the darkened confines of the villa's dining room, looking at the sunshine streaming through the windows and listening to the children playing in the pool, wondering how on earth I came to be writing a column, and hitting the keys on my laptop slightly more viciously than usual.

I love my summer holidays. Sitting at the breakfast table with my children, who've been reduced to green-faced wrecks by whatever it was they did the night before. And trying to amuse them by dreaming up new and interesting ways of killing the wasps.

Everyone has their own technique, all of them learnt from some pool boy in Corfu or Crete. 'They don't like cigarette smoke.' 'Burn coffee grounds; that keeps them away.' My idea is better. Attract them with a plate of bacon and then squirt them with a jet of fire from a catering-sized tin of wasp killer.

'Look, children,' I shriek excitedly. But it's no good. They're too green and too right-on to be impressed by animal cruelty, even in Spain. And anyway they're not paying attention because they're adhering to standard operating procedure for all teenagers around a dining table: looking at Michael McIntyre clips on YouTube.

Later, when I've seen Michael's take on wasps, which is very funny, and after I've smeared myself in cream, except the bit under my stomach which will burn later, I lower myself on to a bed by the pool and immediately the people in the next villa start to play, loudly, whatever's doing the rounds on the Europop scene this summer. It seems to be something called *Despacito*. Which is better than *Who Let the Dogs Out?*, but not much.

Then you have the strimmers. And then the gardener turns up with his leaf blower. Even though it's August and there are no leaves to blow, just huge clouds of dust.

Later you go for lunch with people you'd never dream of seeing at home, but who are suddenly your besties because they happen to be renting a villa a few miles away. And you smile as they tell you in great detail exactly where it is, as though that makes any difference. In Mallorca, it's all based on how far you are from the restaurant where they filmed *The Night Manager*.

This is all standard holiday stuff. The chats with friends about who's had the worst budget airline experience, and who's got the best cure for mosquito bites, and endless calls to taxi companies who say their driver is as near to the house as he can get, which turns out to be two miles away in the car park of a tapas restaurant where he's sitting in the sun, hoping to God we don't find him.

Transport is always a tricky holiday issue. You rent a car, which means you have to spend the first six days of your holiday at the airport, waiting as the girl at the counter writes *War and Peace* on her computer. And then you are given the keys to something that you can never drive because you're always too drunk.

This year I was given a seven-seat, two-wheel-drive

Nissan X-Trail, which, fully loaded and then loaded a bit more, simply would not climb the road to the villa. I had a choice from the driver's seat. I could either spin the front wheels, which made a terrible noise, or spin the clutch, which made a terrible smell.

This explains why I'm stabbing at this laptop and not having a holiday, even though I'm away. The editor of the *Sunday Times* Driving section had called and he doesn't take no for an answer. 'I'm on holiday,' I said, firmly. 'Yes,' he replied, as though I hadn't spoken, 'but would you write a column if I got you a car?'

I peered over the hedge at the ruined X-Trail and thought: 'Oh what the hell.' So, two days later, a man turned up with a Porsche Panamera Turbo that he'd driven from Stuttgart. It was exactly the same car I drove at home a couple of months ago. Back then, I thought it was tremendous, powerful and smooth and fitted with an interior that's sublime. It remains a car I would happily use on a day-to-day basis in the UK.

However, it's not what I'd call a first-choice machine here on the sun-kissed island of Mallorca. First of all, it's quite wide. It's so wide in fact that it goes up the road to our villa with, in places, just half an inch of clearance on either side. That requires immense concentration, and that's hard because its parking sensors and collision warning system are in meltdown and the interior sounds like that nuclear plant in *The China Syndrome*. All of this stuff can be turned off, of course, but not when one wheel is dangling over a cliff, one door mirror is half an inch from a stone post and you have two teenagers in the back saying they feel sick. I've had the car for four days now and the fastest I've been is 6mph.

Yesterday, we went to the beach where they filmed *The Night Manager*, which, and I know this is showing off, is at the bottom of our drive. And it took nearly two hours. I arrived a nervous wreck and couldn't have a refreshing drink because later in the day I'd have to drive back.

That was even harder because we got stuck behind some Spanish Doobie Brothers in a Ford who, when they met something coming the other way, were consumed with the need for some peace and love and reversed. Which meant I and about 200 other cars had to do the same thing.

After a while, I resorted to the horn and some rude gestures, and they responded in kind, emerging from the smoky interior to let me know that it was hard enough to drive a car on that road at the best of times, but it was especially difficult when all of them thought they were being attacked by a Klingon Bird-of-Prey.

It was at this point that I realized the Porsche was fitted with the single most important thing that could be fitted to any hire car, anywhere in the world: German plates. It meant as we finally got past the erratic Ford, using a dribble of smooth turbo power, we could hear the passenger muttering to his mates: 'Malditos Alemanes!'

13 August 2017

Jeremy Clarkson wrote this article before being admitted to hospital in Mallorca and treated for pneumonia.

From second fiddle to rock guitar god

BMW 5-series Touring

For many years I have argued that, all things considered, the BMW 530d estate is the best car in the world. It's fast, handsome, astoundingly economical, very comfortable, reliable and genuinely good fun to drive. And now there's a new version that is supposedly better in every way. But can you, I wondered, get Alex James from Blur into the boot with one of his guitars?

And then could you get the record producer William Orbit into the middle of the back seat, and could they play 'The Chain' by Fleetwood Mac as we were driven from one party to the next?

Like any sensible chap who's looking through some beer-stained goggles at what was obviously going to be a big night, I made sure a driver was on hand to deal with the business of moving me about. The trouble is that these days a driver is a bit like a packet of cigarettes at a party: round about 10 p.m. everyone suddenly decides they'd like to help themselves.

So that's why, as we left dinner, Alex and his wife asked if they could cadge a lift. That would make four of us plus a driver, and that's no problem at all in the big Beemer. But then I noticed Mr Orbit looking a bit crestfallen, so he had to come too. And for some reason that isn't clear, both he and Alex had guitars. 'It's OK,' said Alex. 'I'll go in the boot.'

Having wedged himself in, he then decided he'd quite like

to play us a tune. But this was tricky since he was upside down and could access only about half of his fretboard. To make matters worse, Mr Orbit was stuck between me, who's quite long, and my girlfriend, who's even longer. And yet after just five miles they had it cracked. And so we were whizzing through the lanes of Oxfordshire, with live music to keep us entertained. It was a happy night.

Of course there are other large cars in which a brace of musicians could perform – many, in fact, if they are built like the Rolling Stones – but very few are so good at everything else as well.

Let me give you an example. When you fill the tank in a normal car, you are informed by a readout on the dash that you have a range of . . . what? Three hundred miles? Three hundred and fifty? Well, after you fill the tank in the 530d, you're told you can go 550 miles before you need to stop again. And that, if you hate filling stations as much as I do, is enough of a reason to sign on the dotted line.

But there's more. The head restraints in most cars are designed to be just that. Restraints. Tools to prevent you from becoming an insurance fraudster by complaining that you have whiplash. But in the BMW they are also headrests: big soft pillows into which you can nuzzle when Alex and William are serenading you with a gentle ballad.

Or what about the satnav system? In your car you have to sit there twiddling a knob to spell out where it is you'd like to go. You can do that in the BMW if you like living in the past. Or you can write it out longhand on the so-called touchpad – it works better if you are left-handed – or you can just say where you'd like to go. Three alternatives to do one thing.

It's the same with quite a few of the controls. You can

either push a button or you can make a gesture. Seriously, you just wave your hand about and something happens. This car, then, has all the best tech to be found anywhere.

In other cars you often find this blanket of electrical engineering sitting there like a distracting shroud to smother and blind the owner from some fairly ho-hum mechanical engineering – a hot sauce to mask the fact you're eating a rat – but in the BMW that is emphatically not the case.

If you turn off all the nannying systems that are on hand to stop you crashing, you find that it is the real deal. You sit there doing big, easily controlled smoky tail slides, thinking: 'Er, I'm in a big five-seat diesel estate. How can this be possible?'

And it's the same story on the road. You know it's a diesel that's powering you because you heard the familiar clatter when you started. But now you can't hear it at all. BMW has done something fancy here with the acoustics, because I'm not exaggerating. At a cruise the engine is silent.

And not because it's broken. You know this because when you put your foot down it's as if you've been caught up in a giant wave of torque. The TwinPower turbo is spinning and the six pistons are causing God knows how many explosions a minute, but all you can hear are the tyres as you lunge – and you really do lunge – towards the next bend.

And that's something you're looking forward to, because the steering is perfectly judged, the brakes haul down the speed with infinitely variable feel and, thanks to that four-wheel-drive system, there is almost never any understeer. It's all just grip. Even when the snow falls.

This has always been an Achilles heel for BMW. And no one is really sure why. But when the thermometer drops below zero, the first cars to slither into a ditch are always the

Beemers. The xDrive system answers that, and now it's available across the range, I'd tick the box, especially if I lived somewhere rural.

At the very least it'll be useful when you have a rock star in the boot and you've been directed to park in a muddy paddock.

Finally, there's the business of quality. BMW has always had to play second fiddle to Mercedes in this area, but I just don't think that's the case any more. If you push and pull all the trim in the 5-series, it feels as though you are pushing and pulling a barnacle that's been welded in place. Everything gives the impression it's there to stay. For ever.

I could go on, but there's no point, because until there is a breakthrough in what we drive and who drives it and what powers it and what controls it, this is as good as it gets. It's 130 years of development brought together in a package that's as faultless as current technology permits.

Mercedes, Audi and Jaguar can sell you cars that are similar. But they simply don't do everything quite as well as this BMW does.

20 August 2017

Hey, Hans, Miguel's done better than you

Seat Leon ST Cupra 300 4Drive

What springs to mind when you think of Spain? Well, for me, it's the excellent medical care when you have pneumonia, but for everyone else, I suspect it's a blend of things. You have those who'll conjure up images of bank robbers burying other bank robbers underneath their swimming pools in Marbella. And then you'll have those who'll think of the cathedrals, and Guernica and cooking freshly caught percebes on the untouched Atlantic beaches.

Spain is so many things. It's mountains and deserts and wearing tight trousers while you stab a bull. It's clubs that stay open until dawn, pounding the night with a pulsating beat that only makes any sense if you've ingested a bucketful of what, the other day, I mistakenly called MDF.

It's beautiful, flavoursome olive oil and it's old men sitting in white plastic chairs at the side of the road, living to be 120 because Angela Merkel pays them to not do anything all day. And then there's paella, which is made by cooking up a bag of rice and then emptying the contents of your bin into it. Prawn shells, used teabags, fag ends, the tops and the bottoms of carrots and all the rest of it. God knows how this works but it does. I love it.

Oh, then there's sport. On the one hand you have Rafael Nadal grunting his way into the hearts and (they imagine) knickers of every woman in the world and on the other you have Barcelona and Real Madrid, all-conquering power-houses of world football.

Spain's great. It's my second favourite Mediterranean peninsula. Which is odd because when it comes to cars, it's up there with Ethiopia and South Sudan. Yes, it has given the world Fernando Alonso but he now spends his time driving round at the back, making jokes over the radio. Or turning up at the wrong racetrack altogether and doing the wrong sport.

Then there's driving in Spain. I've done this many times and I'd love to tell you what it's like but I can't remember. Normally, this is because it's 4 a.m. and I'm in a hire car that pulls to the left or won't stop and I'm tired. I had a Nissan Micra, I think, this year and I hated it very much. Quite an achievement since I was too ill to drive it.

Someone, and I would like to meet him so that I can poke some cocktail sticks into his eyes, reckoned, plainly after the car had been finished, that it should have a cigarette lighter. And he decided to mount it in the passenger footwell so every time it goes round a right-handed corner, the passenger's left leg is smashed.

So what about Spain's actual car industry? Back in 1898 an outfit that became Hispano-Suiza began. But that went bankrupt in 1903 and later became French. And after that? Well, put it this way, the history of the Spanish automotive industry takes up four lines on Wikipedia. At this point, Spanish car enthusiasts – both of them – will be jumping up and down, reminding me out loud there is Seat, and they're right, of course.

Seat is Spanish. Apart from the fact that it's owned by

Volkswagen, which is German, and its cars are made in the Czech Republic, Belgium, Argentina, Portugal, Ukraine, Slovakia and, naturally, Germany.

However, this car was made in Spain. Using many of the same parts that Volkswagen uses to make the Golf R.

It's called the Seat Leon Something or Other 300 4Drive estate and when I came out of my office and saw it sitting there in a car park, my shoulders sagged as if I'd suddenly got a puncture. The Golf R estate isn't much to behold but this somehow was even worse. They should have called it the Fat Girl's Ugly Sister. It would have been an easier name to remember. And more honest.

Inside, it's a Golf, except it had been fitted with some enormous front seats that were extremely comfortable. That made me happy as I set the fiddly Golf satnav, fired up the 2-litre Golf engine, which, like the Golf's unit, has received a 10bhp uplift, engaged first on the Golf DSG gearbox and set off to the countryside.

It felt pretty much like a Golf on the motorway, apart from the excellent seats, but when I reached the Cotswolds it did something strange. Right at the top of the rev range, which is somewhere no Seat driver has been before, it made an absolutely wonderful noise.

Not from the back, which is the usual thing these days, but from the front. It wasn't electronic acoustic trickery in the exhaust pipe. It was the sound of an actual engine enjoying itself.

I liked this noise so much that I spent my entire time with this car deliberately in completely the wrong gear. And the result of this was that it did about one mile to the gallon.

It was probably even worse than that when someone

folded down the rear seats and loaded up the enormous boot with bits of furniture that needed to be moved to somewhere else. Which I did. In second, most of the time.

Other things? Well, it is more comfortable than you'd imagine, given that it has sporting pretensions, the four-wheel-drive system will be useful if you have a horse enthusiast in the family and it seemed to be fitted with all of the things you'd expect in a car of this price.

And that raises an interesting point. If you grow some troublesome adenoids and pull on the sort of jumper that all cost-conscious motorists seem to wear, you'll note that the Seat is £1,215 less expensive than the VW sister car. Unless you buy it with red paint, which for some reason adds £650 to the bill.

Ignoring the weird paint issue, this price differential makes sense. Millions of people all around the world would want a hot, fast four-wheel-drive Volkswagen estate. And the number of people who want a hot, fast four-wheel-drive Seat is about none. So there has to be a price incentive. The Seat salesman has to be able to say: 'You can have this car and a DFS sofa for the price of a Golf R.'

However, if you examine the price business more carefully, you'll notice that VW has some seriously big deals on the Golf R at the moment. Two people in our television production office drive them for that reason.

They even park them sometimes in the space reserved for my less expensive Golf GTI and I never mention the fact that they are staff and they have better cars than me and that they should learn their stations in life. Well, not often, anyway.

However, in future I will be mentioning, quite a lot, the

Seat Whatever It's Called has better seats than their cars. And makes a nicer noise. And that they've been fools for not buying Spanish.

24 September 2017

Dreaming to screaming in an instant

BMW M760Li xDrive V12

Hello? Hellooooo? Is anyone still out there? Or has everyone glossed over these pages and become engrossed in the recipes? I only ask because you could be forgiven for thinking that there are now fewer car enthusiasts in the country than there are registered ventriloquists. That means three, in case you were wondering.

Car magazine sales have dwindled to virtually nothing. *Fifth Gear* went into the outer reaches of satellite television and has now disappeared altogether. *Top Gear*'s audience figures are way down. And as far as I can tell, most of the mainstream car makers are now offering cash money for you to scrap your car and buy an Oyster card instead.

My children are fairly typical, I suspect. They couldn't care less what they drive, just as long as it does a million miles to the gallon. Speed? Handling? Style? They can't even get their heads round the idea such things could matter. My son wanted a Fiat Punto, not because of the Ferrari connection, but because the manager of Chelsea is Italian. And I bet Fiat's top brass hasn't factored that into its marketing strategies.

In the wider world we have governments saying that petrol and diesel-engined cars will be banned from the roads completely by . . . (pick a date shortly after the people making the announcement have died). And the news coverage of motoring-related issues focuses entirely on the need for lower speed limits and driverless cars.

When I go out to dinner these days, people often say: 'If you're going to talk about cars, I'll sit somewhere else.' Seriously, being a car enthusiast is like being a Tory. You just don't admit it in polite company.

And yet there are Tories out there. And plainly there are car enthusiasts too. I met one last week. He was a young removal man, who looked at the BMW M760Li xDrive V12 that I was driving and said, quietly, so his mates couldn't hear: 'Why has that got less power than the M6?'

I was staggered. So staggered that I was unable to correct him. The M760Li has 601bhp, which means it has more power than any BMW since the time of Nelson Piquet. And that raises a question. Why? Because this is a long-wheelbase, super-comfortable limousine full of soft headrests and adjustable interior lighting. So why on earth has BMW fitted it with a bonkers 6.6-litre V12 engine with TwinPower turbo?

Why has the company made it accelerate from 0 to 62mph in less than four seconds, which is faster than most Porsche 911s? Why has it given it four-wheel drive and four-wheel steering, so that on country roads you can drive as if you're in a Caterham? Surely the people who buy cars such as this ride around in the back, and any chauffeur who uses the launch control system would be sacked before he'd hit 40mph.

Ah, well, that's the thing, you see. If BMW had made it silent and smooth, above all else, what would be the point of spending even more on a Ghost from Rolls-Royce? Which is a BMW company, remember. And, let's be honest, anyone who wants a silent and smooth car in which to arrive at Heathrow is going to choose a Mercedes S-class.

BMW, then, was forced by marketing and its own history of making the 'ultimate driving machine' to come up with something different. Which is why the car I borrowed was finished in the sort of matt-black paint the drifting community love so much, and a red leather interior. And I don't mean subtle red. I mean bright red. Very bright red – 1950s-film-star-lipstick red.

It looked hilarious. And everyone who climbed inside said the same thing: 'It's fantastic.' Then they found the iPad-type thing mounted in the rear armrest that controls the rear displays, and they liked that too. And then they found the fridge and were all swooning about that when I put the car in its Sport setting and put my foot down. 'Aaaaaargh,' they all said. 'That's horrid.'

This car blows your mind with its turn of speed. Not because the turn of speed is so vivid. A Lamborghini or a McLaren is faster still. No. It blows your mind because you're just not expecting it. I'll probably get in trouble for saying this, but it reminded me of those bespectacled and rather fierce-looking women in old-fashioned porn films. You cannot believe the transformation when she takes off her specs and lets her hair down.

And neither can you believe how planted it all feels when the going gets twisty. Some of this is down to the four-wheel-drive system and some to the clever-clever suspension, but, whatever, as you sit there with your passengers vomiting into their handbags, you really are left open-mouthed by the way BMW's engineers have made a 2¼-ton limo handle, grip and go like a hot hatch.

But then, when I was leaning forward to adjust – oh, I don't know what it was: the night-vision cameras or the massage-seat facility perhaps – I accidentally hit a button and everything changed. The car slowed down. The readout from the satnav became a Toyota Prius-style diagram full of arrows and dotted lines telling me that the engine was off and I was charging the battery. And the dash? Well, that went blue and was full of stuff that I couldn't read if I wasn't wearing spectacles and that made no sense if I was.

There was a diagram of a petrol pump on the left with a symbol saying +0.6mi, and a dial that read from 90 down to 50 and then, for no reason I could work out, 16.2.

Plainly, I had put the vehicle in some kind of eco-mode. This required some investigation, so I went on to BMW's website, where I couldn't find anything about an eco-mode in the M760Li. I therefore rang the BMW PR man, using the number listed on the publicity material. But was told his number isn't listed any more.

It's all a bit of a mystery. Not just the way I activated something that doesn't seem to exist in this car. But what it's doing there anyway. Because who wants Uber-driver fuel efficiency in a turbocharged 6.6-litre supersonic boss wagon?

It's true. Using this mode would save a few pounds over the course of a year, but the fact is, anyone who's interested in not wasting money would never in a million years think about buying a big-engined, super-complicated large Beemer. Because history has taught us that they depreciate like a piano falling down a mountain. The car was supposed to be collected the other day at eight. And I suspect the reason it's still with me is that it's now worth less than the cost of sending a man to pick it up.

So there we are. A very expensive, pointless car that will, in this Uberized world of average-speed cameras and silly insurance premiums, appeal only to one removal man who can't afford it and who would rather have an M6 anyway.

But still, there's nothing like going out in a blaze of glory, is there? For what it's worth, I thought it was tremendous.

1 October 2017

All mod cons, but fifty years too late

Vauxhall Insignia Grand Sport

I remember it so vividly. I was seven years old and my dad had just announced over our evening bowl of tripe and onions that the next day he'd be taking delivery of his new company car.

I was beside myself with tinkle-clutching excitement, because what sort of Ford Cortina would it be? The old model with the CND-badge rear lights that I'd seen racing once on a friend's television? Well, I thought I'd seen it. It could have been a Mini. Or some footage from inside a beehive.

Or would it be the new Mk 2 model, which none of my friends' dads had?

The next day, after school, I raced home as quickly as possible and gobbled down my bread and dripping sandwich so that I could wait in the drive — my working-class northern roots imagery has taken a bit of a hit there — to see which one it would be. Some of me wanted it to be the Mk 1. But most of me was delighted when it turned out to be the Mk 2.

I sat in it most of the night, playing with the switches. Well, moving the heater controls back and forth. And I can still remember every detail of the dash. I can even remember the registration plate: KHY 579E.

I also know it was no ordinary model. It was a 'super', which, though I didn't know it at the time, must have meant my dad was selling more timber than had been expected by his bosses.

That's how a good performance was measured back then. Not by a pay rise or a lunch at the Berni Inn. But by a Cortina that had a clock or a rev counter. Or maybe both.

A company car was a perk, a reward, a doggy chew and a pat on the head for good behaviour. And because it was such an enormous thing – to be given an entire car by your company – it became the measure of your worth. And because of that, about 80 per cent of all new cars back then were company-bought. Which meant in essence they were either Fords, Austins or Vauxhalls.

I remember Simon Shepherd saying his dad was going to get a Sunbeam Rapier. And Nigel Thompson reckoned his dad had a BMW CSL, but these were playground myths. Nobody's dad sold that much timber.

Then, back in the 1990s, the government decided that it couldn't have companies handing out cars willy-nilly and made them part of a person's tax structure – before then only directors and the highest-paid employees paid tax on them. So while company cars still take about 60 per cent of the new-car market, they're not really perks any more.

What's more, people get to choose what they want. And what they want is an SUV or a BMW or something that tells the neighbours life is good and they're the top-performing IT specialist at Siemens Staines. What they emphatically do not want is a Ford. That's why the car giant's market share has dropped to about 12 per cent. And if they don't want a Ford, they definitely don't want a Vauxhall.

I have only once met someone who wanted one. I was doing vox pops for the old *Top Gear* – the William Woollard years – and I asked a young chap with weird Nottingham-shire hair what car he would buy if he had all the money in the world. And he said: 'A Vauxhall Calibra Turbo.'

No one else has ever said that. No one has wanted an Astra of any kind or a Cavalier or even a Senator. And it's for damn sure no one wanted a Vectra. They were given to salesmen who had sold no timber and who had goosed the boss's wife at the Christmas party.

The Vectra was Vauxhall's darkest hour. Built at a time when the company car rules were changing and people were no longer taking what they were given, it appealed to no one. Even James May, whose first car was a Cavalier, says that the Vectra was no good. It was worse than that, though. It was hateful. The last word in 'That'll do' design.

Since then Vauxhall has been making a range of extremely good-looking cars – the Astra coupé springs to mind here – but no one is paying attention. They'd rather have a Kia Sportage. Or a Boris bike. Or nothing.

The only way Vauxhall can get people to pay attention is to build an absolutely superb car and sell it for 9p. And that's nearly what it has done with the Insignia Grand Sport that I tested recently.

The SRi badge had me fooled. I dimly recall some mildly sporty Vauxhalls with that handle in the 1990s. And I dimly remember thinking that they'd be sort of all right – if they weren't Vauxhalls. But my hopes were dashed when I noticed the rev counter's dismal span of ability. Yup. It was a diesel. A diesel in running clothes. And how dreary and depressing is that? Because that's like a fat man in a tracksuit.

I was a bit miserable as I set off, especially when I noted on the first turn that the steering needs more turns than the wheel on a child's toy. You need to whirl away like a dervish to achieve even the smallest change in direction.

And then there was the performance. I had the most powerful diesel engine available – 168bhp – and Vauxhall claims this means 0 to 62mph in eight-and-a-bit seconds. That's pretty sprightly, but from where I was sitting, it didn't feel that way. 'Average' is how I'd describe it.

But then I noticed the crease in the centre of the bonnet, a styling gimmick, for sure, but it gave the front of the car a solid feel, as if it had been made from thicker metal than is actually the case. And then I saw a reflection in a shop window and I thought: 'You know what? This is not a bad-looking car.'

It's also spacious on the inside and very well laid out. You're never fumbling around like how women do when they've lost something in their handbag, saying: 'Where's the button to turn the damn parking sensors off?' Everything is where you expect it to be.

And that's quite an achievement because, ooh, there was a lot of stuff on my test car. It had its own wi-fi router and head-up display. It also had tools to make sure you didn't drift out of lane on the motorway and all the stuff that you normally find only on top-notch Mercs and Beemers.

Obviously a lot of it is listed as an option. Even the paint, which Vauxhall calls 'brilliant' but is in fact just 'red', will set you back £285. The front seats were very good, too, but then they needed to be because they add a further £1,155.

And yet, despite all this, the total cost of the car I tested, which has a base price of £23,800, was a whisker over £30,000. It'd be a whisker under that figure if Vauxhall had ditched the £160 wireless mobile phone charger.

And there's no getting round the fact that £30,000 for a roomy 140mph five-seater with all the trimmings is not bad at all. It's just a shame you don't want one. Because it's no longer 1967.

8 October 2017

Oh what a hoot to be Britain's worst driver

Audi RS 3 saloon

I saw a dead man recently, and it made me sad. He'd obviously got up as usual and had breakfast with his wife. They'd have talked casually about what they were doing that night, whether the kids would be home and maybe made some plans for the weekend. Then he'd gone out, climbed on to his motorcycle and set off for work. Except he never got there because at a busy junction, he and a Toyota Prius had a coming-together. And that was that.

Two days later I saw a stupid man cycling along the Earls Court Road in London. You could tell from his corduroy jacket and huge beard he was an ecomentalist, a point he was determined to prove by pedalling along with his three children in a flimsy, virtually invisible trailer behind his bike. I presume they were his children; it'd be worse if they weren't.

Then an hour later I saw a stupid woman who'd gone one step further. She only had one child but it was in a basket contraption mounted on the front wheel of her bicycle. Yup. She was actually using her baby as a human crumple zone. Simply to make a political point. And that is insane.

There was a time when this might have been fine. London's roads felt safe, partly because the speeds were so low but mostly because everyone sort of knew what they were doing. That certainly isn't the case any more.

The motorcyclist had been hit by a minicab. And it was a

minicab that bloody nearly wiped me out last week when I went to buy the newspapers. He was on completely the wrong side of the road.

Uber, as we know, has been told that it can't operate in London any more because it doesn't take its responsibilities seriously. I don't doubt that the company will clean up its act before the case reaches appeal. But I wonder whether the driving will get any better, because at the moment it beggars belief.

The problem is this. There's much globalization these days. The Big Mac you buy in Los Angeles is the same as the Big Mac you buy in Moscow. Coca-Cola is the same. Sunglasses are the same. Phones are the same. Cars are the same too, but the way they are driven definitely is not.

If you've been to Rome you'll know what I mean. The driving there is completely different from the driving you find in, say, Houston, or Bournemouth. Then you have Vietnam, where everyone gets into fifth gear as soon as the car is doing 3mph, which is in direct contrast to Syria, where no one drives anywhere unless the engine is turning at 6500rpm. Eastern Europe is naked aggression, Paris is belligerence and India is dithering.

And people who've learnt the skills needed to get by in their own country are now in London, in a Prius, and it doesn't work at all. Any more than it would work if you put chefs from all over the world in a single kitchen and told them to make supper. You've got the chap from India hesitating nervously, not sure what lane he should be in, behind the chap from Poland who reckons that the traffic lights signal the start of the grand prix, and both are being deafened by Johnny Syrian, who's sitting there with one foot hard down on the clutch and the other hard down on the throttle, which is actually a blessed relief because it means that no one can hear what Reg Crikey the black-cab driver is actually saying.

When the lights go green, everyone crashes into one another, except the southeast Asian man, because he's going at 4mph, in fifth, the wrong way down a one-way street, wondering what the bump he just felt was. And then is alarmed to find it was a bearded cyclist that he's just run over.

And the problem is you can't lump all minicab drivers into one pot. They all do different things all the time. The only thing you know for sure is if the Prius is in the left lane, indicating left, it doesn't mean it's going to turn left.

The upshot is that the Prius is now the worst-driven car in Britain. Or, rather, it was until I borrowed an Audi RS 3 recently. You probably heard me, because every time I started it up, the exhaust system made machine-gun noises at the sort of volume that scared birds five miles away. It was fun the first time but a bit wearing after six days. No matter. It has the same 2.5-litre five-cylinder turbo engine you get in the Audi TT RS, and that's a car I love very much.

It produces nearly 400bhp and in a car the size of the RS 3 – think Hot Wheels – that means 0 to 62mph is dealt with in about no time at all. The potential top speed is 174mph unless you want it to be 155mph. I'm not sure why the former is an option, but it is. Of course for many years there have been Audis that could travel quickly in a straight line, but in the recent past we've started to see Audis that can go round corners quickly as well. This is another. With sensors and algorithms on hand to decide which of the four wheels gets the power, the RS 3 is a car that just flies down a country lane. It's a joy.

It also feels beautifully made and, provided you leave it in

Comfort mode, it's firm but not hideously bumpy. However, there are two reasons why I could not and would not buy this car. Well, three, if you include the £45,250 price tag. That is a lot for a car of this size, no matter how much grip'n'go it's got.

But worse is the satnav system. Even when you're used to it – and I am – it's a fiddle to use. You have to take two steps backwards all the time to move one step forwards. It needs to be simplified.

And then there are the brakes, which screeched every time I went near the pedal. You may say this is a one-off and that the car cannot be dismissed because of a scratched pad or an errant pedal. True enough, but this is the third Audi RS on the trot that's come to me with the same problem.

To try to drive round it, I found myself coasting in neutral up to red lights, but this is tricky in London because a Prius usually arrives on the scene from nowhere and you have to brake to miss it. So then I adopted a last-of-the-late-brakers attitude, cruising up to the stop sign and then jamming on the brakes at the last moment.

This rarely stopped the screeching, but at least when you do a sudden emergency stop, you don't have to put up with the racket for long. It did, however, alarm quite a few other road users and I'd like to take this moment to apologize for being, for one week only, the worst driver in the country.

22 October 2017

An absolute must if you're all out of lust

Porsche Panamera Turbo

The oddest thing about getting old is that you start to lose interest in style. You look at a pair of zip-up slippers on a market stall and think: 'Mmmm. They look warm and comfy and they're only a fiver so I shall buy them.' And it never occurs to you that they are even more hideous than the tartan shopping trolley you bought the previous week.

Old people have a similar attitude to everything. They buy furniture because it's easy to get in and out of and don't seem to notice that it's upholstered in the material used to paper the walls in the local takeaway.

They see no reason to buy water with a lemon zest when they can get pretty much the same thing for a lot less from a tap. And why spend all that money on a snazzy telephone when you can talk to anyone in the world from the Bakelite set on the hall table? This is all because old people are not very interested in sex.

When a young person examines a new pair of shoes, they will not really care how much they cost or how many Vietnamese children were killed in the sweatshop where they were made, just so long as they look good. Because looking good is an essential first step on the road to procreation.

When you are choosing a book to read on a beach, you are, of course, tempted to buy the latest Jack Reacher tome. But you suspect that passers-by will clock you as a moron, so instead you choose something about ancient Rome. And when you are hanging pictures in your living room, you know that a poster of a Lamborghini Countach won't do. So you go for something curious and weird instead.

Sex is behind every single thing we choose to buy: the cigarettes we smoke, the beer we drink and certainly the cars we drive. There's a tiny bit of our brain that is constantly saying: 'Yes, I know it does five thousand miles to the gallon and only costs 10p but it'll make me look like a dork.'

All of which brings me neatly to the door of Porsche's new Panamera. Yes, I know I've driven this before, and reviewed it on these pages, in fact. But that was a review written after a two-mile drive on inappropriate roads in Mallorca while I was suffering from pneumonia. This is an actual review, written after an actual drive and while I feel well.

You open the Panamera, you step inside and immediately you are consumed by a desperate need to buy one. You are less cocooned than you were in the previous model, but you still have a sense of being hemmed in place by the extremely light door and the enormous transmission tunnel. This sense of being cocooned is one of the things that made the old Porsche 928 so desirable.

And the transmission tunnel isn't enormous just for show. It's big because it houses all sorts of interesting buttons. All of which operate with the satisfying sense that they are fully German.

Then you have a widescreen television, which allows you to operate all the things that can't be controlled with the buttons to your left. You feel, as you sit there pressing stuff, that you are Mr Sulu on the bridge of the Starship *Enterprise*. Except your hands are hotter. Much hotter.

This is because you've turned on the heated steering wheel.

You don't know how you've done this, but you know that if you don't turn it off quickly, all the skin on your hands will melt. You have a cursory glance around the cockpit for something that might shut it down, but there seems to be nothing. And then you remember saying to your mum that you can't find your shoes and her saying: 'Have you looked properly?' So you have a more careful look. You go into all the menus on the control system and you put on your reading glasses and you crawl about in the footwell.

And finally you resort to Google, where you discover the button is . . . Actually, I'm not going to tell you where it is. It's a good game to while away a couple of hours next time you're bored and passing a Porsche showroom. Get the salespeople to make you a cup of tea while you ferret about. It'll serve them right for hiding it away so thoroughly.

Eventually, the steering wheel had cooled down sufficiently for me to drive the car, and I won't beat about the bush. It was sublime. There are three engines on offer: at one end is a diesel that will give you an astonishing range of 800 miles between fill-ups but will cost you £10,000 a minute to park because various councils have changed their minds and decided diesel is the work of the devil. At the other is a bloody great V8 turbo that you can park for sixpence because somehow that's OK these days.

Strangely, it is not the very fabulous V8 that Porsche's parent company, Volkswagen, uses in the Audi A8 and the Bentley Continental. It's a completely different V8, with its turbocharging based between the cylinder banks. And it's also fabulous. Really fabulous. It's quiet and unruffled most of the time, but when you poke it a bit, it makes a deep, growly noise like a dog having a dream.

Naturally there is a great deal of power, all of which is fed to all four wheels by an ingenious arsenal of algorithms that makes sure no matter what you do, the car always feels planted and secure. It also feels sprightly, because much of it is now made from aluminium. That's why the door is so light.

All of which make the gigantic brakes look like overkill. These are the sort of discs you like to envisage being used to bring an Airbus A380 to a halt. You imagine when you lean on the pedal that you are actually altering space-time in a measurable way. And on my test car they were carbon ceramic, which meant they could go on affecting nature all day long without fading.

Make no mistake: this is a wonderful car to drive. And it doesn't feel even remotely like a large five-door hatchback with a boot big enough for a trip to the garden centre, folding rear seats and (just) enough room in the back for two adults. It even rides properly, so everyone is always comfortable.

However, there is a problem. Yes, it's better-looking than its predecessor, but that's like saying it's better-looking than a gaping wound. It's still a long, long way from being even remotely handsome or appealing. And to make things worse, my test car was painted the sort of red that speedboats go in New Zealand after they've been in the ozone-free outdoors for a couple of years. And to make things worse still, that's an optional extra for which Porsche charges almost £3,000.

No one is going to buy this car for its looks, which means it will just be bought by people for whom sex is no longer important. Which makes a change from the usual Porsche customer, I suppose.

29 October 2017

Beastly beauty needs a handsome plinth

Ferrari GTC4Lusso

I have never read the Bible. I've tried, but after a few moments I lose the will to live. It's the same story with Shakespeare. You just know that no one is going to say, 'Secure the perimeter', and that even if they did, they'd need four hours to say it. And you'd need a teacher on hand to explain what they were on about.

However, when it comes to literature that's completely impossible to understand or digest, you cannot top a Ferrari press release. Let me give you an example from one I have here. 'The sophisticated and refined cabin is designed wholly around its occupants.' Really? I thought it'd been designed partly around its occupants and partly for the tea lady's dog.

Let's move on to the vehicle dynamics. 'The 4RM Evo system is more precise than ever. Management of front torque in particular has been improved across the board, but specifically in terms of SS4-based torque vectoring . . .'

That sort of guff may work well at a conference on industrial piping, but it's a Ferrari we are talking about here. And there is no space in any of that world for dry engineering technobabble. Ferrari needs to understand this. I don't need page after page of Shakespeare doing army-speak. Because the accompanying photograph is telling me so much more.

The photograph that came with this press release was of a car so beautiful, it haunted me long into the night – or, as

Ferrari would put it: 'Beauty itself doth of itself persuade / The eyes of men without an orator.'

It's called the GTC4Lusso and it's best described as a three-door sports estate. I'm a sucker for a car such as this. There's never been a bad one. The Lancia HPE, the Volvo P1800 ES and the Reliant Scimitar (Princess Anne had one, you know). They were all tremendous, but this Ferrari trumped the lot. It was the best-looking car I'd seen.

I stuck the picture on my office wall and spent many long moments gazing at it. And I drove the production team mad by thinking up idiotic reasons why we should put it in the next series of *The Grand Tour*. The team would say we should do something on hatchbacks and I'd suggest the Ferrari. I suggested it for everything. And every time I was outvoted.

I can see why. This car is a replacement for the old FF, and that was rubbish. Or, as one Ferrari high-up said: 'Yes, it wasn't our finest hour.' I tested one once on a frozen lake in Sweden and could not believe how comprehensively it was beaten in every way by the much cheaper Bentley Continental GT.

I also couldn't believe how needlessly complicated the four-wheel-drive system was. Because the rear wheels were powered by a shaft coming out of the back of the engine and those at the front were propelled by a shaft coming out of the front. Which meant it needed two gearboxes. After the BMW Z1's doors, it was the most complex technical solution to a problem that simply didn't exist. And it didn't work.

My colleague James May knows the FF well and doesn't believe it's a four-wheel drive at all. He's even been under the car and still can't get his head round it all. He, actually, was the most determined of everyone that the FF's replacement would not be in our show. Ever.

I tried to explain that you can have the GTC4Lusso with

a V8 engine and two-wheel drive only. But it was no good. I lost the argument. And now I'm quite glad.

I borrowed the four-wheel-drive V12 version and could not wait for the day it arrived. I so wanted to see it in the flesh. To see if it was as beautiful as it had been in the picture. And I was a bit disappointed, if I'm honest, because it was parked in a small car park near my flat and I simply couldn't get far enough away from it to take in all its lines.

But that was OK. I was off to the countryside, and there'd be lots of space there to see it in all its glory. This is true. But only just. My God, this is a big car. If you want to see all of it at the same time, you need to put it in a field and walk away from it for ten minutes.

What's weird is that it has broadly the same body as the terrible old FF, but just a few clever tweaks to the grille and the front wing vents and wheels have transformed it. The interior is equally sensational, perhaps because it was designed with the occupants in mind. Yes, it's got all the usual Ferrari problems, namely the buttons for the lights, wipers and indicators are on the steering wheel, but – and I loved this – there's a second dashboard in front of the passenger. They can choose whether they want to look at the rev counter or the satnav or a million other things. It's brilliant.

And the back seats? No idea. I didn't fit. And I've never met anyone who would. But the boot is the most beautifully trimmed thing since Mr Bonsai woke up one day and thought: 'I know . . . '

Let's pause for a moment now to laugh at the price. The basic version is £230,430 – of course it is – but my test car had a few extras. Apple CarPlay for £2,400, blue brake callipers for £1,178, a carbon-fibre sill cover for £4,992 and a glass roof for – drum roll – £11,520. Ha-ha-ha-ha-ha.

So what's it like to drive? Not as exciting as you might imagine, actually. Of course, with a 6.3-litre V12 engine, it's not sluggish, and it's a Ferrari so it's not sloppy either. But it's not exceptional. It doesn't cause the hairs on the back of your neck to tingle. Ever. It doesn't even make a particularly tuneful noise.

That said, in town it's docile and quiet, unlike all the people behind you, who are angry and honking because you're having to back up again because your car's too wide to fit through anything except perhaps a desert.

I understand, naturally, that if you are a fully paid-up member of the St Moritz Eurotrash set and you need a Ferrari because it's part of the uniform, it'd be tempting to buy a GTC4Lusso. Because it has four-wheel drive. But I've never been to a ski resort where this would fit. Aspen maybe, but only just, even there.

And if you don't live in a ski resort, why would you want a four-wheel-drive system that only really works at 4mph on snow? You wouldn't. You'd have the two-wheel-drive V8 version. But that is the same size, so we are back to square one. There are few places on earth a car this big works. Dubai, Los Angeles and, er . . .

It's probably best, then, not to think of it as a car at all. But as a garden ornament. The most beautiful piece of sculpture of all time. That's what I'd do: save money on the extras and spend it instead on a plinth.

12 November 2017

This yob will make you smile and cringe

Honda Civic Type R

Fifteen years ago, when it became obvious economies of scale would cause all the small car makers to be swallowed up by the giants, I figured that in the fullness of time, only two of the then current crop would remain: Mercedes-Benz and Honda.

These were the only two that actually moved the game forward. While the rest were fitting their cars with gimmicky head-up displays to lure bored flies into their web of finance deals, Honda and Mercedes were innovating, working with hydrogen propulsion and dreaming up stuff that would make a difference. And I reckoned that ultimately this was what would keep them going in a world where big was good and bigger was better and China was the biggest of them all.

But then it looked as if Honda had just given up. It stopped making interesting, revvy little hatchbacks and exciting coupés, and intoxicating mid-engined supercars and . . . er, this is awkward, I can't actually remember what it did instead.

I seem to recall there was a little off-roader that had a completely stupid shower in the back, and my mother at this stage bought a small Jazz because it was available in pink. But then it stopped that colour so she replaced it with a Volkswagen Golf.

After this, I really haven't a clue. I drove fairly regularly past Honda's giant plant in Swindon and I could see much activity but what they were making in there? Sorry. No idea. Nothing I'd want, that's for sure. And if you're reading the motoring pages of the *Sunday Times*, I guess it's nothing you'd want either.

There was talk of Honda's best engineers working on a replacement for the much-loved NSX but every time I called to ask how it was getting along with what sounded like quite a clever hybrid drive system, I got a lot of 'ers' and 'ums', and some waffle about how the engineers were in California 'benchmarking' the Chevrolet Corvette. And some beaches probably.

Eventually the new NSX arrived in the showrooms but it caused as much of a stir as the company's efforts in Formula One. It's not a bad car by any means, but it doesn't make you go: 'Wow.' You don't take a drive and think: 'God, I've got to have one of those.'

And Honda took such a ridiculously long time developing a hot and interesting version of the Civic that by the time it came out, the company was already winding down production of the car on which it was based. So it arrived in the marketplace and before the echo of the fanfare had died down, it had been dropped.

Happily, the manufacturer has been a bit quicker off the mark with the hot version of the new Civic. And yet despite the rush job, it's like the Honda of old is back because it has created something a bit special.

The 2-litre turbocharged engine is said to be largely unchanged from the previous model but whatever small alterations Honda has made have transformed it into a big, comforting muscle. You find yourself pressing the throttle gently just to experience the beginning of a shove. It's like limbering up for an arm-wrestle with a man who builds oil rigs. You haven't felt the power yet, but you know pretty soon you're going to have a dislocated shoulder.

However, it's not the shove or the speed that impresses most with the Type R. It's the chassis. There's a wider track than on the last incarnation and a stiffer superstructure. And that sounds as if you're in for more grip, if you can tolerate the bone-shaking ride. Nope. What you get is phenomenal grip and a ride that's actually quite absorbent. It's not a Labrador puppy, obviously, but it won't shake out your fillings either.

This is a wonderful car to drive hard. Yes, it's a bit of a fatty but you're never really aware of the weight because it changes direction like an electrocuted swallow. Couple that to the 315 rampaging horsepowers, the 295 torques and the bark from a weird triple exhaust system and there's no doubt Honda is back with a car that's extremely good fun.

Is it as much fun as the Ford Fiesta ST? No, it isn't. I know of no car that is more fun on an ordinary road than the Fiesta. What's more, the Ford is little and the Honda isn't and that matters. The point of a hot hatchback – and the reason I love them so very much – is they are fast and fun and brilliant to drive but when all is said and done, they are also hatchbacks. So they are practical and sensible and cheap to mend as well.

The original Golf GTI – arguably the first of the breed – played a big part in putting MG out of business because here was a car that was more of a laugh than the little sports car but which could also take a family of five and their luggage to the seaside. It was the Seventies, remember. People went to the seaside then.

And that's where the Honda keeps on scoring because although it's a rampaging Nürburgring meister, it also has five doors and a large boot and fold-down rear seats. You don't get any of that in a Lamborghini.

What's more, it comes as standard with 20in wheels and a reversing camera and a (fiddly) satnav system and so on. Prices start at £30,995, which is surprisingly low. So that's good, as is the fuel economy, as is the depreciation. The insurance won't be funny, I'll grant you, but that aside, this will be an inexpensive car to run.

So there we are, the perfect hot hatch; fast, fun, frugal and fitted with five doors for a family of . . . God, I hate alliteration.

And I also hate the Type R because just look at it. Have you ever seen anything so wilfully yobbish? We're told all its winglets and spoilers are there for a reason and I think I know what the reason is: to tell your neighbours you are very fond of football violence and shoplifting. And you have a knife.

I know a guardsman who is thinking of getting a Type R and I just know that if he does, he will wear his bearskin back to front.

I was embarrassed to drive it. Yes, a number of people pointed, made enthusiastic noises and took photographs, but a far larger number pointed for different reasons. You could see them thinking: 'How small does your penis have to be before you'd buy a car like that?'

There's a similar problem of course with the Ford Focus RS and Mercedes-AMG A 45. Neither is as in yer face as the Honda but they both wear their street-fighting credentials on the outside. Maybe this doesn't bother you. Maybe you quite like to stir things up. But if you don't, buy a VW Golf R. It's not as much fun as the Honda and it isn't as fast at top speed. But you will look less of a knob.

26 November 2017

It goes bong but my heart goes bang

Lamborghini Huracán Performante

We are used these days to cars that beep and bong constantly. They bong when you open the door, bong when you don't immediately fasten your seatbelt, bong if you put a shopping bag on the passenger seat, bong if you try to start the engine without depressing the clutch first, bong if they think you're going to bump into a lamppost, bong if you forget to turn the lights off or even if you leave your telephone in the glove box. Some even bong if you've nodded off.

But when it comes to making irritating noises all the bloody time, for no bloody reason, nothing gets close to the Lamborghini Huracán Performante. Bong it went when I set off on a chilly London morning. This was because its TSU was malfunctioning. I had no clue what its TSU was but it malfunctioned again moments later, with another bong to alert me of the fact. And then, after a minute or so, it did it again. This might have been bearable had it been regular but it had all the rhythmic timing of a bored dog.

So I called Lamborghini, which said it was a preproduction car and that its telemetry wasn't installed properly. So I took it to a dealer, which applied a laptop and said that the bonging would now stop.

Bong, it said on the way back to the office. Once again, I reached for my spectacles to see what was wrong this time. And, according to a small message on the arcade-game electronic dash, something called the MMI had become disabled. For acronyms, this thing was worse than the British Army.

However, since the disablement of the mysterious MMI – it turned out to be the multimedia interface – was making no difference to my progress and there'd only been the one bong, I figured I could live with it.

That afternoon I left London for the country and as I joined the M25 the car bonged again. Once again, I reached for my glasses so I could read the message, which this time said that I should switch off the engine and check the oil level. It was 6 p.m. and I was on the M25 and it was drizzling, so I figured it could wait until the next services.

As I slowed for the slip road to the next services, the warning light went out. It had obviously decided that there was, after all, enough oil in the engine, so I speeded up and ten minutes later there was a bong to say the oil level was low and I should stop. Which I didn't. I was too busy trying to turn on the satnav, which wasn't working, or get information about traffic. But that system wasn't working either. And then the oil warning light went out again. And all was well.

Except, it wasn't. Because by this stage I was trying to find the windscreen wiper switch. Foolishly, Lamborghini has taken a leaf out of Ferrari's book and mounted it on the steering wheel along with the switches for every other damn thing. So each time you want to turn on the wipers you end up listening to Classic FM with your left indicator blinking.

It gets worse when you are in the countryside and you need full-beam lighting because you push the button and when you let go, the full beam goes out. So you push it again, except at this point you're going round a corner so now you've turned off the wipers.

In desperation, I fumbled away at the switches by my right knee until eventually all the lights went out. So now I'm doing 50mph, it's raining and dark and neither the lights nor the wipers are on.

Shortly after sorting all this out – by swearing – I came up behind an Audi that was being driven by a headrest, with ears, at 35mph. I desperately needed to get home by 7 p.m. so I put the Huracán in Corsa, or Race, mode, which caused the dash to become one huge rev counter, and when we encountered a short straight I put my foot down.

Well, I've never heard a noise like it. Plainly, the engine had decided it was bereft of oil, after all, and had exploded. In a panic, I abandoned the overtaking move and took my foot off the accelerator. And then I realized that, no, that's just the noise a Huracán makes when you poke it with a stick.

I finally managed to overtake the Audi but by then it was too late. I'd missed the 7 p.m. deadline and *The Archers* had started. But in the Lambo that was OK because this car is so loud you can't hear anything at all. Ever again.

The sound starts off as a jackhammer and then when you floor it, you have babies crying, improvised explosive devices going off, Krakatoa, the Grateful Dead, a space shuttle rocket test, white noise, a latter-day V10 Formula One car at full chat, a squadron of F-15 Eagles on combat power, some lions, a hunt ball and a war. All going on in your car. At the same time.

What's extraordinary is that it's not a big car. Yes, it's festooned with weird spoilers at the back and a snouty nose at the front. And my test car was a flat orange. But it's not big. Which is what makes the sound it makes faintly ludicrous.

However, as I used the sound to drown out *The Archers* on that final few miles dash home, I'm afraid I fell head over heels in love. This is a wonderful car. A brilliant car. An absolute gem.

Lambo says that because it has developed a new way of making carbon fibre, it can use it to make small intricate parts, which means the Performante is lighter than you'd expect. Which it isn't. At nearly 1.4 tons, it's still a fatty. And it still has a cumbersome four-wheel-drive system, and the 5.2-litre V10 – the last of the breed, almost certainly – is broadly the same as the engine you get in the standard car.

Somehow, though, this thing is idiotically fast. In a straight line it will leave a Ferrari 458 Special Needs for dead. And around the Nürburgring, it's faster than any of the million-quid hypercars. You won't believe this – very few test drivers that witnessed it did – but it went round in six minutes and fifty-two seconds.

And it's not just fast. It's exciting. It may be making the sound of a universe forming and your head may be pinned back against the headrest but you can still feel it blowing gently on the hairs on your arms. This is a car that roars and purrs at the same time. It's like an Italian tomato – little and bright and so full of taste sensations it makes your eyes go crossed.

Yes, it's also annoying. My preproduction test model was easily the most irritating vehicle I've driven but that's part of the charm too. That's what makes this car feel human. That's what gives it a soul. And that's what turns a good car into a great one.

3 December 2017

What you do in the woods is your affair

Land Rover Discovery

I have always hated the Land Rover Discovery. The first model was cobbled together out of some steel girders and bits and bobs from the dying embers of Austin Rover. It had a shorter wheelbase than today's Mini, looked stupid and was bought mainly by murderers.

They liked it because underneath the unreliable and ugly outer shell it had a Land Rover four-wheel-drive system, which meant it could be used to carry the bodies of those they'd killed far into the woods, where they'd never be found.

Eventually Land Rover decided that it looked too like an elephant on a unicycle to cut much mustard, and in 2004 it came up with a boxy'n'big seven-seater that for some reason had two chassis. I listened patiently to an engineer explaining why Land Rover had done this, but none of it made any sense, because the car weighed about 2½ tons. It didn't drive over obstacles so much as flatten them.

However, unlike the first incarnation, it was aimed fairly and squarely at the family woman, so while it may have had all the off-road gubbins you'd need to get a severed head up Ben Nevis, the marketing and the packaging stated that this heavyweight was intended to be a school-run car.

It wasn't any good at that sort of thing, though, because back then Land Rover's engineers wore camouflage trousers and liked mud. Most, I suspect, didn't know what children were. Which is presumably why you had to use two hands to lower the middle row of seats. And that was impossible if you were carrying a toddler. 'What's a toddler?' said someone from Land Rover at the time. 'Is it a kind of machine-gun?'

There were other issues too, such as if you raised the rear row of seats there was no boot at all. Which meant your dog had to be wafer thin and your children's heads were only a few inches from the back window. I never thought that was ideal, so when the time came for me to get a seven-seat family wagon, I bought the Volvo XC90, and today I'm on my third.

All of this, however, is ancient history, because there's now a new Discovery and the first thing you need to know is: it looks ridiculous. It's fine from the front, and if you squint, it looks quite good from the side too, but what were they thinking of at the back? The old model had an offset numberplate because the spare wheel was mounted on the outside of the tailgate. But the new model's spare is not. So why stick with the off-centre plate?

The other issue is the sheer size of the damn thing. This is one of those cars in which you spend most of your time in suburbia, sitting at one end of a side road waiting for nothing to be coming the other way because it's just too wide to squeeze by. You'd make faster progress on a cow.

That said, the new Volvo XC90 is also far too big, but at least its size translates to plenty of space on the inside. That's emphatically not the case with the Disco. I was driven to a party in the back of it, and not since the old Ford Galaxy have I been so uncomfortable in the rear of a car. The seat was too hard, the legroom was tight and the backrest adjustment offered a simple choice: bolt upright, or very nearly bolt upright. This is easyJet economy seating.

To make matters worse, the front-seat headrests look like E.T.'s head after he's been stung by a wasp. This is because, in my test car, each of them housed a television, but, hang on a minute, has no one told Land Rover these days TVs don't have to have tubes at the back? They can be thin.

Further back things get quite interesting because when you open the tailgate, you're presented with a wall of buttons such as you would find in the wi-fi router room on the Star-ship *Enterprise*. This means that the seats can be raised and lowered individually, using electricity, and that's brilliant.

However, before you can do any of this, you must put your toddler in the gutter, climb inside and remove the bar in which the boot's roller blind is stored. Oh, and you must also be careful not to push the button that makes the back of the car rear up into the sky.

Still, when you've removed the internal bar, parachuted back to earth and retrieved your child from the gutter, you do have a seven-seat car. And still, despite the external dimensions, a pathetically small boot. The only advantage to this is that children can say to their teachers: 'I haven't brought my homework in. There wasn't space in the car.'

As a practical everyday proposition, then, the Disco is soundly beaten once more by the big Volvo. And the Range Rover Sport, which is also available with seven seats.

So what's it like as an actual car? Well, it's pretty good. The diesel unit is a bit shaky at tickover, but once you're on the move, it settles down to a gentle hum, and when you put your foot down, it makes a rather endearing growly noise.

There's a fair turn of speed too, and because it has only one chassis, it doesn't weigh more than a mountain, meaning it's reasonably economical. Plus, of course, it has every toy from Land Rover's extensive off-road box of tricks, which will allow it to get further into the woods than the constabulary's BMW X5s.

But, apart from the nation's murderers, who cares about that? Farmers all use Mitsubishi and Nissan pick-ups now, and rightly so. They go anywhere, and you can fill them with sheep and not care.

City boys wouldn't be seen dead in a Disco. It says they've had a bad year and can't afford a proper Range Rover. And school mums are better off with a Volvo.

If you are a casual off-roader – the odd gymkhana and a bit of light tree-felling at weekends – the old Disco made a bit of sense, but this new one's too plush and too fragile. And if your heart is set on a Land Rover, there's the Range Rover Evoque, the incredibly good-looking and very appealing Range Rover Velar and the proper and still brilliant Range Rover.

With all that lot dotted around the showroom, who's going to say, 'Mmmm, yes, I'd like the stupid-looking Discovery, please'?

I can think of only one man. Britain's most famous Discovery owner. Kenneth Noye. Who happens to be in jail for murder.

10 December 2017

The appliance of Travelodge science

McLaren 720S

By and large, it's a fact that when Ferrari is making excellent road cars, its Formula One racers are slithering about, and then breaking down or coming fourth. And, conversely, when it's making terrible road cars, its racers are cruising to victory without breaking a sweat.

All through the early Noughties, Ferrari was totally dominant on the track. It won the world championship five years on the trot. And the road cars it was making? Well, there was the 550, which was sort of quite nice, and the 360, which wasn't even that.

But then in 2009 along came the brilliant 458 Italia and a range of front-engined GT cars that cause grown men to go weak at the knees. And it hasn't won the F1 title since.

It's not just Ferrari that suffers from this problem. McLaren was pretty much always a top three team. But then it decided to start making road cars and now its F1 racers drive around at the back for a couple of laps and conk out.

Many commentators blame the Honda engine for this lack of pace and unreliability and I'm sure it's partly to blame. But think about it. If you're trying to get a road-car division up and running, you're going to put your best people on that. You just are.

And it must be said, they did do a good job. The fresh-out-of-the-box McLaren MP4-12C wasn't the most exciting-looking car and in some ways it felt as though it had been engineered by someone who cuts his lawn with nail scissors. It was all very obsessive compulsive. But, ooh, it was clever and fast.

And then the range expanded and the excitement started to come and eventually we got the P1, which, I still maintain, is the most bonkers car I've yet driven. It was swivel-eyed and mad. An insane bastardization of Elon Musk's vision, the way it used battery tech to create more speed. It really was, as I said at the time, a weaponized wind farm. I adored it.

Now, with the F1 team still in disarray, it has come up with a new road car that doesn't have the P1's hybrid drive system but somehow manages to be, as near as makes no difference, just as fast. Let me put that in figures. A P1 will do the standing quarter-mile in 10.2 seconds. And the 720S? You'll need 10.4 seconds. That's not a big gap.

And in the corners you'll make up for that lost fraction. It took me a long time to master the P1. But when I did, I found that, in extremis, it will understeer. The 720S will too but to nothing like the same degree. Which means that round a track the straightforward dinosaur will be quicker than the rainbow warrior.

There are all sorts of extremely dreary reasons for this, all of which have to do with weight and electronics. Let me put it this way. You can download data from your 720S so that after supper you can analyse how it and you managed on your journey home from work. This is a nerd car.

It may look brilliant – mine was brown and I still thought it was a sensation – but you cannot get round the fact that it simply doesn't have the soul of a Ferrari. It'll kick a Fezza's arse in any race, anywhere, anytime, but you can't help feeling it's a car built after a meeting in a Travelodge with a flip chart. And not while casually doodling over a bottle of wine.

And I'm afraid that, from this point on, things get a bit bad. There's a lot of talk about how it's 5.548 per cent stiffer than the old 650S and how the engine has 195 more cubic centimetres because of the increased stroke and how there's been a rethink in the design of the carbon fibre tub. And I don't doubt all this engineering pays dividends at the limit through Eau Rouge at the Spa-Francorchamps circuit in Belgium. But the downside is that when you run over a man-hole cover on the M40, you'll wince.

The party piece of all McLarens is the way they combine brilliant handling with a supple ride. Well, the 720S doesn't. It's too firm.

And the brake pedal is wrong. When you first push it, nothing happens, which means you have a bit of a panic and push harder, which causes the car to stand on its nose. I found that even when I had my foot on the brake pedal, the car would still creep forwards. You really have to give it a shove.

There's nothing wrong with the brakes. It's the pedal. And I'm not the only one to notice this. *Autocar* did too. And so did James May. It's an issue that needs resolving.

One that can't be resolved so easily, though, is the way the interior works. It's all done on purpose and it's too complicated. The electric seat adjustment is a case in point. There's no logic to it, and the same applies with the immensely complex Track, Comfort and Sport settings. Then there's the satnav, which is way better than it's been in any McLaren to date and is actually better than the system you get in a Ferrari, but it's still not as good as the setup you get in a Volkswagen Golf.

This then is a tricky car to sum up. Yes, it is mind-blowingly fast. It's a direct competitor for the Ferrari 488 but in terms of what they both set out to do, it's not a competitor at all.

They're in a different league altogether. I even think the Big Mac is better-looking and that's saying something because the little Ferrari is like a dreamy mix of Alicia Vikander and something I just thought of.

But the ride is too firm, and the controls are too hard to use and that brake pedal is an issue as well. And then there's the really big problem. You sense this car was designed by really, really clever people who live and breathe yaw, slip angles and various other engineering conundrums. People who really would be more gainfully employed in the company's race team, where such things matter.

For the 720S to blow my frock up, it needs some P1 fairy dust. It needs a bit of humanity in the mix, a bit of childlike fun.

In short, this car would have been better if it had been designed not in a Travelodge, but in the pub.

17 December 2017

Pistol-packing agent hiding in a hat box

Hyundai i30 N

I was driving along in a dreary, ugly and unnecessary Mini Countryman the other day when an important message flashed up on the dashboard. And, after I'd ferreted about in my pockets to find my spectacles so I could read what it said, I was a bit alarmed.

I don't recall the exact wording but, in essence, it said there was a fault with the steering system and that as a result, I should drive 'moderately'.

I wonder what that means. Because Lewis Hamilton's idea of 'moderately' is rather different from James May's. And anyway, if there's a fault with the steering, surely it'd be better to say: 'Stop immediately and flee.'

Losing your ability to steer is worse than losing your ability to stop. I know this because I once drove a brake-free lorry across Burma and I just about managed. But when the steering locked while I was in a Renault A610, I crashed almost immediately.

The problem is, of course, that to save the polar bear, the Mini Countryman has electric power steering. And when something is electrical, you can be certain that one day it will break and you'll have to turn it off then on again to mend it. That's not so bad when it's a wi-fi router but the steering on a car? When you're driving? Hmmm.

Charles Babbage, the father of the computer, talked once

about the unerring certainty of machinery. But we don't use machinery any more because we've got it into our heads that circuit boards and ones and noughts can do the job better.

They can't. A point proved by the Countryman, and by a feature you'll see in the current series of *The Grand Tour*. We took some fun-sized SUVs to Canada, where they failed to do anything very well. And when we asked them to do some actual four-wheel-drive work, they responded by not working at all. The electronics simply couldn't cope.

And that brings me on to the subject of this morning's missive, the Hyundai i30 N, which has two speedometers. I don't know why. One is analogue and one is digital. And at no time could they agree on how fast I was going. There was always a 3mph difference. And if they'd both been connected to the wheels with an actual cable, rather than some nerd's wet dream, this wouldn't have happened.

There was another issue I had with this new hot hatch. Its name: i30 N. There are certain letters that work well on the boot lid of a car. G, T, V, R, I and S are fine; B, D, U, J and L are not. But the worst letter of them all is N. I know Hyundai will say it used an N because the car was developed at the Nürburgring but we don't need reminding. We can tell.

Hyundai – which has never made a hot hatchback before – has bought a book called *How to Copy a Golf GTI* and stuck rigidly to the recipe. It's taken its ordinary five-door hatchback – the sort of car that's bought by people who wear hats – lowered it, given it a 2-litre turbocharged engine and added some red styling details and hey presto. One hot hatch . . . that no one wants because they'd rather have a VW Golf, thanks very much, or a Renault, or a Ford.

There's more, I'm afraid, because instead of going to suppliers that know what they're doing, Hyundai has got everything it needs to make this car – brakes, suspension and so on – from Korean firms no one has heard of. And that's like having a Korean shotgun or a Korean watch.

The only way you'd be tempted is by a very low price. And on the face of it, you don't even get that. However, if you look carefully, you will notice it includes all sorts of things that are options with a Golf GTI. Furthermore, this car was developed, in fifteen months incidentally, by one of the men responsible for all BMW's M models in recent years. He's a man who knows what he's doing and that shows because this car, despite its on-paper problems and an inability to work out how fast it's going, is utterly delightful.

On an ordinary day, on an ordinary road, it's beautifully understated. It's quiet and comfortable and there are many toys to keep you amused. My favourite was the button that makes the exhaust go all noisy. Because then you do get people looking. And what they're thinking is: 'Why is that hat transportation device making such a rumbly sound? And why is it barking every time it's asked to change gear?'

It's like looking at a Secret Service agent. He's wearing a nice suit and has a neat haircut and he could be a Wall Street functionary. Except, if you look, you can see the earpiece and if you listen hard, you can hear his controller talking about shooty stuff.

The Hyundai is very good at shooty stuff. It's provided with an electronic system – which will break, obviously – that allows you to choose from a whopping 1,944 setups. There's Sport and Sport+ and all sorts of individual custom programs that allow the driver to tailor each aspect to his or her personal preference, and it doesn't matter what you do, this is a car that just works.

Maybe, if I were to pick nits, I'd argue that a hot Renault is a bit more feelsome and that a Golf GTI with a front diff is a bit more sticky in an uphill, tight, first-gear bend but as an overall package, the i30 N is a sweetheart. Even in Nutter Bastard mode, it's not even remotely bumpy or unpleasant.

I especially like the rev match function. It was first seen on the Nissan 370Z and I've always wondered why more car makers haven't copied the idea because what it does, as you change down, is rev the engine so the gear change is smooth. It's double declutching for you. And it's doing this mechanically, so it'll still be working long after the Apple CarPlay and satnav system have gone haywire.

Some say the bite on the clutch pedal is too high and that they wouldn't buy this car because they kept stalling it. But that can be adjusted in about five seconds. Because it too is mechanical. And then it would be fine.

As I see it, there are only a couple of reasons why you would not consider the N if you wanted a five-door, family hatchback with a folding rear seat at the back and plenty of ponies at the front. First, you'd have to tell people that you'd bought a Hyundai, which, despite its successes in rallying, is a bit like saying your bladder has broken.

And then there's the problem of Kim Jong-un, whose wobbly rockets may well affect your warranty one day. If you think all is well on that front, because Donald Trump would be on hand with a calm, measured response, then the i30 N makes a deal of sense. It's come out of nowhere, this car, and is immediately a force to be reckoned with.

31 December 2017

E.T., phone home and ask: just what is this?

Volkswagen Arteon

Elon Musk says he is going to blast one of his old Tesla electric roadsters into a Mars orbit so that one day it can be found by aliens. Maybe, while he's at it, he could also fill the spaceship with other things that seem to serve no obvious purpose. The Ronco Buttoneer, Sir Sinclair's C5, the BSB squarial, Tom Watson . . . oh, and perhaps the new Volkswagen Arteon.

It's one of those cars that crept up on the market like a special forces sniper. Ordinarily, we tend to know which company's working on what and roughly when the finished product will go on sale, but with the Arteon it wasn't there, then with a whizz and distant kaboom, I came out of the office one night and it was.

It isn't a replacement for the four-door Passat coupé that I figured had been dropped from the range because Volkswagen had had a forehead-slapping moment and thought: 'Hang on a minute. What were we thinking of? Nobody's going to want a sleek and stylish version of a car we build for not-very-good cement salesmen. It'd be like making Crocs with tassels. Pointless.'

Nor is it a replacement for the Phaeton. That was a bubble-and-squeak, made-from-leftovers car. VW had paid a fortune to develop the then new Bentley Continental GT and thought: 'Why not use its big engine and four-wheel-drive system in a car of our own?'

It was brilliant but it turned out that captains of industry don't like to hide their light under a bushel. They didn't want a brilliant car unless it looked brilliant as well and had a brilliant badge. So the only person who actually ran a Phaeton was the director-general of the BBC – the only boss in Britain who needs a low profile.

So the Arteon, then, is a car that replaces nothing. A new entry, as they used to say on the Top 40 chart show, at 40 grand.

And, ooh, it's a looker. Usually, when I come out of the office, I'm in a rush and I'm distracted by whatever small annoyance James May has created that day, so I don't spend a lot of time walking round whatever car's turned up, stroking my chin. I just drive off.

But with the Arteon, my shoes made a comedic squeaking noise as I came to an abrupt halt. It quite literally stops you in your tracks, not because of the wide grille that makes the car look lower and more ground-hugging than is the case, or the four pillarless doors, or the in-your-face mustard paint job. No. It's the way all these things line up behind a big Beastie Boys VW badge. This, then, is not Crocs with tassels. It's Crocs made from the softest Swedish leather, and fitted with diamonds and pearls.

And there's more. It's huge. I put my shoulder bag in the boot and it was like putting a mouse in Nasa's Vertical Assembly Building. I didn't try it, but I bet if you put your head in there and shouted, there'd be an echo.

It's the same story moving forwards. Providing you can get your head under the sleek – low – roofline, the space in the rear is Mercedes S-class-generous. You really can stretch out back there.

Now, I don't want to be racist but there's a curious reason

for this. The Chinese. China's an important market these days for all car makers but for VW it accounts for a large proportion of its sales. This means that every engineer is wondering as he designs a new car: 'What would the Chinese think?' And that's why the Arteon has such a massive amount of space in the back. Because weirdly for a country where the average male is about 5 feet 6 inches tall and the average female just over 5ft, this is the most important buying consideration. They don't care about fuel consumption or speed or handling – just space in the back.

This is great news in our neck of the woods because the bigger the back of a car, the happier our increasingly strapping children will be. Which means less fighting over who sits in the middle and a far more pleasant environment.

So, the Arteon, then. Very good-looking and very spacious. And beautifully made and entirely logical to use. But first I have to get my seat in the right place and, wait a minute, what's this? A lever? Like you'd find in a Victorian signal box. How can a car such as this not have buttons and motors?

And then you fire up the engine and no matter how much you spend, it's going to be an ordinary, bread-and-butter four-cylinder rumble. There's no V6, and certainly no W12 like you could have in the old Phaeton.

Naturally, there are some diesels but no one will buy those because they're this week's bad news, so I tested a petrol-powered car that also had four-wheel drive and had an R-Line trim. Which means big wheels and a sporty stance. It was all very confusing.

Normally when I'm testing a car, I know what sort of person would be interested in such a thing and review it with them in mind. There's no point saying the boot on a Lamborghini Huracán isn't big enough if you have a painting and decorating business and nor is there any point lambasting a Fiat Punto because it won't do 200mph.

But I simply couldn't think of anyone I've met, or even seen, who might want a good-looking four-door coupé that's huge in the back and ordinary at the front. Someone who wants pop-to-the-shop economy from a four- cylinder engine and four-wheel drive. A VW badge and a 40 grand bill. Sticking with my earlier shoe simile, this car is like a Tod's loafer and a wellington boot that come in the same box.

And before you sign on the dotted line you've got to think: 'No, I don't want a Mercedes CLS or a BMW 4-series or an Audi A5 Sportback. I want that sort of thing but with a VW badge at the front and a boot the size of the Blue John Cavern at the back.'

It's a perfectly nice car. It does everything very competently and rides nicely as well. Also, you have a sense as you push a button or move the seat that the button and the lever will continue to work for many years and that this is a car that, as my grandfather used to say of his suits, 'will see me out'.

And yet, I wouldn't buy one and neither will you because it satisfies a demand that doesn't exist. It is, then, the modern-day equivalent, as I said at the start, of Musk's electric Lotus and BSB's squarial. It should be put into space so that in a million years an alien can spend a pleasant hour or two trying to work it out. I hope they have more success than me.

21 January 2018

Perfect . . . if you want a new life of lease

Audi A8

Is there anything on God's green earth quite so drool-inducingly dreary as leasing? James May recently visited an exhibition on plywood and I think that's up there. So is Jane Austen. And so are the BBC's regional news programmes. But leasing? That's in a class of its own.

I spoke the other day to a man who has leased his new car. He was explaining how he doesn't have to pay for new tyres and how it's an unlimited-mileage deal and when I woke up several hours later he was still telling me how he simply hands his car in one day and gets another. And here's the kicker. When I asked him what car it was, he didn't even know.

Sometimes, I get the impression that manufacturers these days are no longer terribly interested in the cars they make. They are just seen as three-dimensional drivers for the financing department. General Motors today? It feels to me like a mortgage broker, and the cars it makes are nothing more than giveaway ballpoints.

I've never leased a car, for two reasons. First of all, I'm from Yorkshire so I was always taught that I should never be a borrower or a lender and that I should only ever buy something when I could afford it, using money I'd earned.

Second, I wouldn't want to drive a leased car because I'd know all the time it wasn't mine. Oh, I'm sure it would make financial sense to use the capital to generate more and utilize the option of cheap money from elsewhere, but when I meet people who talk this way, I feel a sometimes irresistible urge to plunge a letter opener into their left temple.

When you take delivery of a new car that you've saved to buy and dreamt about, there is such a joyous sense of occasion. Choosing the first track you'll play on its stereo. Being careful not to use too many revs for the first few miles. Setting up the interior so it's how you like it. And then, crucially, having a sneaky over-the-shoulder glance at it after you've parked up at night. Nah. Leasing a car? It'd be like leasing a dog.

That said, I wonder what would happen if I needed to buy a large executive saloon. A captain-of-industry barge. A Mercedes S-class or the like.

The trouble with cars such as this is that the only people who can afford to run them can certainly afford to buy one new. Nobody wants to buy such a large, thirsty and complicated car second-hand. The risks of an expensive out-of-warranty failure are too great. These cars, then, depreciate like a grandfather clock that's been pushed from the back of a Hercules transport plane. You could lose maybe £50,000 in a year, and being from Yorkshire that would cause me physical pain. I'd want to plunge a letter opener into my own left temple.

The only sensible solution – apart from buying a smaller car – is to lease. To let the company that made the damn thing take the financial pain. I'm told there are some very tasty deals around. Friends talk about how they've leased a BMW 7-series for 3p a year and how Jaguar is now giving away XJs with packets of breakfast cereal. And if that's all you're interested in, then go ahead and choose the cheapest deal.

The car you end up with will be big and comfy and full of

animal skins, and you'll be fine. What's more, the dealer will be obsequious and Uriah Heepish, which is always a joy. I love nothing more than watching a car salesman genuflect before a customer's magnificence.

However, what if you see the car as something more than an irritant in the profit-and-loss account? What if you have four-star coursing through your arterial route map and you love the smell of burning Castrol in the morning? What if you're all of that and you're forced by social niceties to have a boss-mobile, then what?

Well, that brings us neatly to the Audi A8. I had been told by the aforementioned May this was the new benchmark in Freemasonry comfort, that the pitter-patter and jiggliness of Audis in the past had been banished and replaced with a creamy brilliance.

He's wrong. It's quite comfy in the front – I can see what he means when you're sitting there – but in the back, which is more important in a car of this type, it's far too crashy, especially over potholes and those speed humps that look like rubber but aren't.

That said, it's a bloody nice place to sit. In the back you can have an optional iPad Mini-style display on which you can choose the colour of the interior lighting and so on, while in the front you have a virtually all-glass dashboard. There are almost no buttons at all. It's all touchscreen stuff and if you like that, it works very well.

I don't like it. Because the screen gets covered in greasy fingerprints and in bright sunlight you can't see a thing. So you have to keep a duster or a chamois leather in the door pocket. Which marks you out as a dullard. Never trust a man who has cleaning equipment in his car. There is something wrong with him.

To drive. Well, what can I say? It's quiet and refined and not so fast you are frightened or so slow you think it's broken. The model I tested produced 145 carbon dioxides and 282 horsepowers and the price includes half a tank of fuel. Audi doesn't give you a whole tank because it's massive. Filling it would cost about a million pounds, but on the upside, you can go more than 700 miles between trips to the pumps.

That's one USP. Another is the four-wheel-drive system. Most of the time you don't need it, in the same way that most of the time you don't need insurance cover for fire damage. But then the day arrives when you do . . .

Big rear-wheel-drive cars are hopeless when the weather's bad. The Audi isn't. And it's well made, and with its enormous new shiny mouth, it's striking too. I've always said that if I were in the market for a big business bruiser, I'd have the BMW 7-series, but I think this Audi has it beat.

I appreciate of course that you will actually pick whichever car comes with the best leasing deal because if you want a car of this type, you are in business so you'll understand what the salesman is on about. You may even become a bit aroused when he says 'APR'.

I still maintain, though, that no one who buys a vehicle of this type is that interested in cars. It'd be like going on a cruise liner because you enjoy sailing. If you do enjoy driving and you want a big car, get a BMW 530d. If you just want somewhere nice to sit after a hard day in the office, the Audi's fine.

4 February 2018

Kitten heels that claw through ice

Citroën C3 Aircross

When 'the Beast from the East' combined with Storm Emma to give the *Mail Online*'s headline writers a chance to let their hair down – 'Red lockdown chaos as beast takes complete control' or some such – I was assuming, because I have a stiff upper lip, it'd amount to nothing.

It was just a load of weathermen and weathermen women inventing new levels of danger so they could be shunted from a bulletin after the news to the news itself. And I'm sorry but Britain is in the wrong place for extreme conditions. We have heavy drizzle or light drizzle. So I went to bed that night assuming my trip to the airport the next day would be fine. This wasn't a casual trip either. The last two holidays I'd tried to take were cut short for one reason or another, so I was determined to get away for a week's rest and relaxation before another year of filming with the constant dull ache that is James May.

I should have gone to London the night before the flight. People explained that my cottage, on the top of a hill in the Cotswolds, would be first to fall victim to the 'ice blizzard killer hell'. But I said, 'Pah!' and ignored them.

This was a mistake, because when I awoke, the lane to my cottage was under five feet of snow. And so, while trying to pack with one hand, I made a panicky call to my local farmer with the other and asked if he could clear it with his tractor.

'Not much point,' he said in that cheerful, farmery way, 'because even if you could get to the village, you're not going anywhere.'

I saw this as a challenge and went to start my trusty eleven-year-old Range Rover. Which decided it didn't much fancy the idea of a steep lane under five feet of snow and developed an electrical fault. This stopped the off-road gubbins working, so all it did was slither.

My girlfriend pointed out that we also had the Supacat, a six-wheel-drive, fat-tyred army machine designed to go on to the battlefield and retrieve stranded Snatch Land Rovers. 'That'd get us out,' she said. And she was right. That thing would laugh in the face of Storm Beast, but after it got us into Chuntsworthy, then what? It has no roof or number-plates or suspension, so it wouldn't work on, say, the M40. Not at −200°C, which is what the *Mail Online* said the temperature was outside.

Happily, I had a car on loan that week from Citroën. Unhappily, it was something called an Aircross, which is a mini off-road crossover urban MPV in the same mould as the Seat Arona, the Kia Stonic, the Hyundai Kona and half a dozen others that you'd rather kill yourself than buy.

To try to make it stand out from the sea of awfulness, the Citroën has orange roof rails, chunky skid plates and tough-looking wheelarch extensions, but all this stuff is a bit like Theresa May's shoes. Zany as hell but not fooling anyone.

They certainly weren't fooling me, because under the skin the Aircross is actually a Vauxhall. And is that what you want – a Vauxhall, with Theresa May's shoes, that was built in Spain? No, me neither.

And it was definitely not what I wanted on that snowy morning as the Beast became Emma and the drifts were deep enough to drown Richard Hammond. Because, while the little Citroën looks as if it has four-wheel drive, it doesn't.

It didn't have much grunt either, because its 1.2-litre three-cylinder engine is designed for tax avoidance in Paris rather than a full-on snowstorm. Yes, thanks to some turbo-charging, it develops 128bhp, which is more than you'd expect from an engine this small, but it wasn't going to be enough.

Still, there was no alternative, so we loaded the suitcases, fiddled about with the grip control system, which I assumed was a gimmick designed to fool people into thinking this little bit of Eurotrash might actually work in places it'll never go, and set off.

As the lane to the village was out of the question, I decided to take a cross-country route. I figured that most of the snow in the drifts had been blown off the fields and that they'd be clear. I also reckoned that because it was so cold, and because this part of the country is essentially brash, there'd be no sticky stuff to bog the Citroën down.

And incredibly, given that both suppositions were formed from nothing but hope, the Aircross made good progress, bumping across the monochrome, frozen landscape like Scott of the Antarctic. Who of course died. So, with that in mind, we were prepared for the worst, wearing big coats, scarves, thick-soled shoes and thermal underwear.

Soon we reached a road buried under even more snow than the lane. It was the same story at the next road. But eventually we emerged through a hedge into the village, which was like a scene from *The Omega Man*, only quieter. Everyone had taken the advice of the *Mail Online* and stayed at home with their families to await the cold hand of death.

But there was at least no drifting on the easterly route out of the village, so off we set, and soon we made it to the next village, and then – joy of joys – the main road. It was blocked. A BMW – famously the worst snow cars in the world – had tried to climb a moderate hill and failed. This had brought out the off-roading enthusiasts, who were doing manly things with ropes.

It was amusing to watch the shrill women who moan all year about Chelsea tractors begging the drivers of such vehicles for help. Everyone laughed at the Citroën, and said even if the BMW got free, a lorry had got stuck and there was no way past that. We tried another route, but that was blocked by a slithering gritting lorry. The council was doing its best and I commend it. But it was a lost cause, and as the dashboard clock flashed away, so, it seemed, was my holiday. Chipping Norton had been cut off.

There was only one option: to head for even higher ground and a small B-road. I didn't hold out much hope, and an off-roading enthusiast flagged me down to say it was impassable. But he was reckoning without the little Citroën, which, in conditions that were stopping intercity trains, got through.

There was plenty wrong with it. The wipers made a god-awful racket, the indicator ticks were too loud and you can't shut the stop-start function without going into a sub-menu on the command and control screen. Mind you, by not fitting a button for this, or anything else, Citroën has saved a few quid, which is passed on to the customer. If you want a crappy little urban crossover MPV car, the Aircross is good value.

And while there's plenty to annoy you 362 days of the year, it's brilliant on the three days when we have snow. It is far and away the best off-roader I've driven. But because I didn't think it would be, I arrived in the Seychelles still in my tweed shooting coat. The immigration man must have thought I was mad.

18 March 2018

Supersonic, but it won't fly in Blighty

Kia Stinger GT S

I am glad I don't run an airline, because if I did, all the planes would be pretty much empty pretty much always, and it would be bankrupt in a week.

For instance, I find it amazing that in early March you can't fly non-stop from the UK to Corfu. I'd have a meeting about that, and explain to my colleagues that Corfu is a lovely spot that is very popular with the sort of middle-class families who'd pay through the nose for such a flight. And then it would turn out that all the middle-class families I was targeting were in the Alps. And didn't want to spend early March shivering on a beach, on an island that's pretty much shut.

Did you know there are thirty flights a day from London to New York? Which means that when there were twenty-nine, someone said: 'Yes, the market can take another.' That wouldn't have been me. I'd have said: 'Twenty-nine flights a day and you reckon there's a market for a thirtieth? Pah. Not a chance.' And I'd have been wrong.

I also wouldn't operate a service to Paris, because it's faster on the train. But I'd put a 747 on the London–Pisa route and go every thirty minutes because Tuscany's lovely and our rail companies don't provide an alternative.

Then there's Charlotte. I flew there not that long ago on a Tuesday morning and assumed that I'd have the plane to myself. But it was rammed. And that amazed me, because how can there possibly be 300 people a day who wake up in England and think, 'I fancy going to North Carolina today'?

Recently, I wanted to go from Bogotá in Colombia to Barbados and not one single airline boss has recognized this as a possibility. Which meant I was faced with a four-hour trip to Miami, a six-hour wait, and a near four-hour trip back to virtually where I'd started.

So I had to get a private jet, which wasn't easy because the people who operate such things are unwilling to send them to Colombia in case they are used for smuggling.

Mind you, while I'd be a useless airline boss, I think I'd be even worse if I were running a car firm. Because if I were at the helm of, say, Kia, and someone came to me saying, 'Let's make a forty grand, rear-drive, four-door coupé with a snarly V6 and many horsepowers,' I'd have shot him in the front of the head for being crazy.

To us here in Britain, Kia makes a range of hatchbacks and saloons for people who know nothing at all about cars. They are quite good-looking and I'm sure they are well made but they are really for the old and the muddled. And there's the problem. The old and the muddled don't want a many-horse-powered sports saloon and those that do don't want a Kia.

There's more. In Britain, and the rest of western Europe for that matter, the car is rapidly losing its appeal. There are too many rules and too many cameras and there's too much congestion. The car is seen as an expensive nuisance. We've been there and we've done that and now we're in an Uber waiting for Google to give us something that drives itself.

People who buy a flash car are mocked for being footballists and those who buy something fast are labelled as boy racers. The love affair with the car, here, is dying. So what's the point of Kia trying to sell a fast car such as the Stinger GT S?

Ah well. As I said, I was in Colombia recently and it's much the same as any country that's emerging from decades of strife. With a new entrepreneurial spirit causing the whole place to hum, the roads are awash with people driving about, very carefully, in brand new Kias and Dacias. To us, these cars are horrible crates made from old cassette boxes. But over there they are luxury goods to rival anything made by Fabergé. You mention the word Kia in Bogotá and people take off their hats.

I would hope, because I fell madly in love with Colombia, that its emergence from the dark side continues and that soon people will be able to make money from something other than forest products. And if that happens, the people are going to want the very best car that Kia can sell them. Because Kia to them is the same as Ford was to us back in the late Sixties. And everyone back then wanted a Cortina 1600E.

The Stinger is a very good car. It's quite hard to climb aboard because the roofline is low but when you're in, the driving position has that 'hang on a minute' feel that lets you know you're at the helm of something special.

Which it is. Thanks to a twin turbocharged 3.3-litre V6, you get 365 horsepowers and that means 0–60 in less than five seconds. But it's not the straight-line oomph that impresses most. It's the way this car feels as you go about your daily business: special.

Maybe this is because the Stinger was developed by Albert Biermann, who was poached from his previous job running things at BMW's M division. You can sense his DNA in the Stinger. Same as you can in an M3.

The steering is heavy. I don't mean it'll cause you to smell while parking. I mean, it has a meatiness and somehow you know it's guiding wheels that aren't troubled by the bothersome business of propulsion. Which means it also feels clean and pure and right.

Fearful that I may have just quoted a Meatloaf song, I'm going to move on to the comfort, which is sublime. I was expecting the ride to shake my eyes out but even in Sport+ nutter mode, it just glides. In the Comfort setting, it doesn't feel like a sports saloon at all. Jaguar should have a careful look at this car to see how it's done.

The economy is a bit better than you might expect, the equipment levels are higher than you'd imagine, and it's hard really to find fault. Maybe the interior is a bit grey and maybe the exterior isn't quite as handsome as all the other Kias. I especially didn't like the fake bonnet vents. Or how hard it was to see out of the back window.

But that really is about it. Everything else was either delightful or wonderful or better than I was expecting. If you were in the market for a BMW M3, or a fast Audi or a Mercedes-AMG, it's certain you'd be better off with the Kia. But of course you wouldn't dream of doing such a thing. A Kia? What the hell would the neighbours think?

I get that. I wouldn't want to buy one either. But our friends in Colombia and Cambodia and Rwanda? They will. I'd never have noticed that if I'd been running Kia. Luckily for the company, however, I'm not.

25 March 2018

Grown-up thrills in a light-speed La-Z-Boy

Alpina B5

If you are my age, you will remember that in the olden days nerdy petrol enthusiasts would explain that the engine in their Ford Capri had been 'blueprinted'.

The idea was simple: cars were mass-produced and the components made by men who wanted only a pint after work and a decent wage when the week was done. Which meant each engine was only a rough approximation of what its designer had wanted.

Blueprinting meant building an engine to be precisely right. This was fantastically complicated. I remember once speaking to a man who said he had had to order more than 100 pistons that were supposed to be exactly the same before he had eight that actually were. And it was the same story with the rods and the valves and every other damn thing in there.

Building such an engine would take thousands of hours and cost thousands of pounds. And would anyone be able to tell the difference when it was finished? Honestly? No, not really. But if you were a fan of perfect engineering, you'd know every time you turned the ignition key that that's exactly what you were bringing to life.

Think of it as a beautifully crafted watch. Does it tell the time better than a battery-operated Casio? No. So do you want a battery-operated Casio? No again.

And that brings me nicely to the Alpina B5 I was driving recently. It started in life as a normal BMW 5-series, which means it was built by robots that didn't want to go to the pub after work. They just did as they were told, precisely, all day long.

You could take apart their work and build it again yourself, using OCD tolerances and a forensic attention to detail. But you'd end up with something that was pretty much exactly the same as it had been before you broke out the spanners. It'd be like trying to tune an iPhone.

And then there's the design itself. BMW is a business, yes, and it has one eye on the profit-and-loss account for sure. But it's hard to spot this when you drive a normal 5-series, because it really does feel as close to perfect as any car can be at this moment in automotive time.

I've said before that, all things considered, the 5-series estate is the best car in the world right now. And yet Alpina still reckons that with a staff of about a hundred it can do better. Hmm. We'll get to that later.

There's another issue. Back in the 1960s and 1970s, BMWs were quite sporty, but there was room for a tuning company to make them faster still. That's what Alpina used to do very well. So well, it was endorsed by BMW itself. But then BMW started making its M cars. And I've never met anyone who's climbed out of an M5 and said, 'Yeah. But I wish it was a bit quicker.'

This means Alpina can't offer its customers a car that is better made or significantly faster than the car BMW will sell them. So what's the point? There's a new M5 about to come out, which will cost about the same, and we sort of know it'll be epic. So why on earth would you want to spend £89,000 on a B5? Or a lot more if you want a few toys?

Good question. Yes, my test car had some snazzy wheels and a discreet little spoiler at the back. But it looked just like a standard 5-series, really. And it was the same story on the inside. We are told the leather is better than the cow skin that BMW will sell you, but it didn't feel any different to me. I did like the blue dials, though.

To really get to the bottom of it, you need to fiddle about in the suspension menu. Because it's here you'll find a new setting. One that BMW doesn't offer. It's called Comfort Plus. And that's what this car is all about. It's designed to be as fast as anything BMW will sell you but more comfy. And if you're my age, that has got to have some appeal.

The engine is the 4.4-litre V8 from the 7-series, with two turbochargers of Alpina's design. The result is a whopping 600 brake horsepower. This is sent through a tweaked gearbox to a four-wheel-drive system tuned by Alpina so that 90 per cent of the power can go to the back.

Four-wheel drive is another key to what this car's all about. It's not designed for the racetrack. It wasn't tested at the Nürburgring. It's designed for the road; and on the road, in a 600bhp car that can do 205mph, Alpina thinks four-wheel drive is better. Alpina is right.

Its engineers have even changed the camber on the front to such an extent that new wishbones had to be designed. Maybe that's why this is the first car with four-wheel steering that didn't make my passengers queasy.

Do not, however, think that this car is all about comfort. Because, God-al-bloody-mighty, it shifts. Put your foot down in Sport Plus mode and the digital speed readout in the head-up display simply can't keep up. By the time you've had a chance to catch your breath, you're in danger of going at the sort of speed that will put you in prison.

And it's not just in a straight line either. The steering and the new suspension geometry combine to make this car flow down an A-road like a smoothie being poured into a velvet bag. This was easily the best 5-series I've driven.

Issues? Well, if you concentrate hard in slow-moving traffic, you will notice that the throttle response in Eco Pro mode is a bit tardy. And that sometimes there's a weird tendency to kangaroo. The good thing, though, is that if this is a fault, the car is covered by BMW's usual three-year warranty.

I don't for a moment believe the B5 is any faster than the new M5 will be, but, critically, it's no slower. And it makes the sort of noise that tickles the hairs on the back of your neck. Yes, I know some of this sound is artificially produced. But so was *Iron Man*, and we all loved that.

What I loved most of all, though, was the sense that every tiny component of this car had been poked and x-rayed and improved by a team of Germans who went home and, to prolong their performance in bed, thought about how perhaps it could be made better still. The whole car is like those blueprinted engines of old. Only people who truly appreciate excellent engineering would want one. The M5 will be fine for everyone else.

Unless you want an estate. BMW can't sell you a hot one of those, whereas Alpina can. And, with a top speed in excess of 200mph, it's the fastest car of its type in the world. A lot of me, because I'm my age, is very, very tempted.

8 April 2018

Its screaming abdabs are locked in the boot

Lamborghini Urus

I am not sure quite when or why all the world's rich people decided they needed four-wheel-drive monsters, but they did, and so in the next eighteen months Aston Martin, Ferrari and Rolls-Royce will launch SUVs to rival the leviathans already on offer from Bentley, Porsche and Maserati.

Needless to say, Lamborghini wasn't going to be left out of a roll call like that and has come up with the car you see this morning. It's called the Urus, which I thought was an embarrassing genito-urinary problem. 'Doctor. I've got an itch on my urus.' Turns out it is some kind of ox.

Unlike the other rap'n'footballer brands, Lamborghini has been here before. In the 1970s it decided for reasons known only to the bottom of a very big bottle of wine that Colonel Gaddafi would like an Italian pick-up for his soldiers. Amazingly, it turned out he didn't, and neither did any other army, so Lamborghini fitted the V12 engine from a Countach, lined the extremely cramped interior with leather and tried to convince the world that this is what it'd had in mind all along.

I drove one once, and it was hilariously good fun and hilariously terrible all at the same time. The lever that engaged the low-range gearbox was so stiff that it took two of us, one sitting on the dash pulling with his arms, and one on the back seat levering with his legs, to shift it. And when it did finally boing free, the man on the dash shot through the windscreen. Later the engine seized in Oxford Street. And then I took it to a petrol station, where it consumed £147-worth of petrol. Back then that was what I earned in a month.

Times, of course, have changed. Gaddafi has gone, his armed forces are rushing around the desert in Toyota pick-ups and Lamborghini is no longer run by people who get all their best ideas in the pub. It's just a small cog in the Volkswagen empire.

It's also the most exciting car maker in the world. Ferrari is so up itself these days, it's started being actively hostile to even its most loyal customers, it won't allow the press to conduct proper tests and, when it does finally relent, the car it provides is always weirdly fast.

Lambo is run by nicer people and – whisper this – it makes better cars too. The Huracán Performante is easily the best supercar on the road – it eats the Ferrari 488 for breakfast – and the Aventador remains the world's greatest head-turner. But what about the Genital Itch?

Well, the first thing you need to understand is that, while it says Lamborghini on the back, it's no such thing. The platform comes from an Audi Q7, the engine and gearbox from a Porsche Cayenne, the rear axle and suspension from a Bentley Bentayga, the dashboard screens from an Audi A8 and the electric window switches – I bet the press department hoped I wouldn't spot this – from a Mk 7 Volkswagen Golf.

None of this would matter if it sounded like a proper Lambo, but it doesn't. Not in road mode, at any rate. It sounds like the mad love-child of W. O. Bentley and Ferdinand Porsche. Only if you put it in track mode does it start to wave its arms about and have the screaming abdabs.

That is what I want from a Lamborghini. I want an eye-swivelling lunatic with an axe in one hand and a chainsaw in the other. Fee Waybill from the Tubes. With windscreen wipers.

And, yes, on a frozen lake, with the traction control off, and the sun shining, and with the settings all in nutter bastard mode, it delivered the full fireworks display while wearing a cartoon catsuit. However, the rest of the time . . .

Part of the problem is the way it looks. You tell yourself it's brilliant because it's full of sharp edges and Lambo styling details. It's also a lot lower and sleeker than the other SUVs – the Bentayga in particular. But if you force yourself to concentrate, it actually isn't that mad-looking at all.

Then you step inside and, yes, there are all the lovely Italian styling touches. But it all feels very German. And then there's the space. I didn't need to put the driver's seat fully back to get comfortable, and even when I did, there was still room for a six-footer to sit behind me. And behind him was a boot big enough for a winter week with a full-on shooting schedule.

Does it work off road? Well, yes, it has four-wheel drive, and you can raise the body to give plenty of ground clearance. So, if you have the right tyres, you can go up a ski slope. I know this because I did.

But it doesn't have manual differential locks or a low-range gearbox. You just tell it what kind of terrain you're on – snow, sand or mud – and it does its best to sort you out. I fear that for serious off-road work it'll be left far behind by a Range Rover. Although it would be quite funny turning up to a shoot in a yellow Lambo. Next season I suspect lots of people will do just that.

On the road, in ordinary going-home-from-work mode,

it's very quiet and extremely comfortable. When you put your foot down, there's a hesitation, as the turbos – the first time such things have been fitted to a Lambo – and the automatic gearbox talk to each other about who should go first. It's very polite but not what you'd expect. Or want.

After a day, I started to feel a bit sad. I'd looked forward to the Urus because I thought it would be German engineering wrapped up in some video-game idiocy. But it felt – dare I say this? – ordinary. Yes, you can use the track mode and switch off the driver aids and create some madness that way. But you never will. Not really.

Make no mistake: it's bloody fast. And it screams through the corners as if it weren't on stilts at all. But, again, you'll never do this. You'll drive it normally and it'll reward you by being normal. But if normal's what you want, save eighty grand and buy a Range Rover. Or wait for the Aston. You could wait for the Ferrari, but unless you load it up with all the extras, there's a chance you'll be pushed down dealers' waiting lists and then told that actually you can't have one at all.

In the meantime, Lamborghini has made a very good car. A car that is quiet and comfortable and fast and probably super-reliable. It's also, and I know this sounds ridiculous, quite good value for money. But, sadly, by doing all this, it hasn't made a Lamborghini. Which is what I wanted.

15 April 2018

A jihad-mobile comes a Cotswolds cropper

Toyota Hilux

Many years ago, when I was hosting *Top Gear*, I was watching the news one night and, as usual, there was much footage of various people in the Middle East shooting Americans from the backs of their Toyota pick-up trucks. And I couldn't help thinking: just how tough are those things?

So the next day we bought a Hilux and decided to see how much damage we could inflict on it before it stopped working.

I rammed it into various bits of Bristol, dropped it from a crane, set fire to it, hit it with a wrecking ball, left it under the sea for a couple of hours and then, when none of that stopped it from functioning, we put it on the top of a block of flats that were then blown up.

It was a huge risk, that film, because had the Hilux failed to recover from any of its ordeals, we'd have been forced to say, 'Well, there you are, folks. You can't leave a Toyota pick-up truck under the sea and expect it to work afterwards.' And the audience would have replied with a weary, 'You don't say.'

Worse, the next morning the *Daily Mail* would have said we'd spunked God knows how many thousands of licence-payer pounds into the Bristol Channel and the *Mirror* would have said I was the unacceptable face of Tory Britain. Then we'd have been in an oak-panelled office, looking at our shoes while we were shouted at by a sustainable panel of gender-neutral executives.

Happily for all concerned, however, the Hilux survived all the ordeals and that film is probably the best remembered item we made. I think even Toyota itself was a bit amazed with the durability of its no-nonsense workhorse because the still-functioning wreck spent some time in the reception area of its world headquarters in Japan.

A couple of years later, when it was decided that James May and I should see if we could drive to the North Pole without killing one another, there was only one car we felt would be up to the job – the latest, newest Hilux.

'Wrong,' said our ice-driving contacts in Iceland. 'It's still tremendous if we want to shoot Americans but for going across a frozen ocean, its trunnions will have to be beefed up and it'll need big Icelandic tyres, and a long-range fuel tank. And storage space for the gun you'll need if a bear comes.'

It was therefore a heavily modified car we used for the journey, but the fact still remains: the cold was so severe that our cameras packed up, my phone stopped working and so did large parts of my body. Nothing works when it's -50°C. But every morning that Hilux started and every single component on it was unaffected. Small wonder the top-of-the-range Hilux is now called the Invincible X.

There are those who say that since Land Rover pulled the plug on the Defender, and agricultural supply shops stopped selling Subarus made from corrugated iron, the nation's hard-done-by farmers have been up a bit of a gum tree.

But the truth is that they've all migrated into pick-up trucks. Jihadi John and that nice Adam Henson from *Country-file* weirdly have exactly the same requirements. Toughness, durability and value. And you get all that from Nissan,

Mitsubishi and of course Toyota. A base model Hilux is £24,155. Whereas an all-singing, all-dancing, leather-lined, four-seat Hilux with satnav, cruise control, air-conditioning, the ability to tow 3.5 tons and a load bed measurable in acres, is £37,345.

That's £37,345 for what, when all is said and done, is a Range Rover with a bigger boot.

I was using one over Easter in Oxfordshire and I cannot recall any car garnering quite so much attention. The fence-builders and gamekeepers and dry stone wallers have no time for supercars or the plush off-roaders used by weekenders. They like only pick-up trucks, and in the pick-up world, a luxury Hilux Invincible is more incredible than the Queen's golden coach. I saw one gnarled and bow-legged country-man actually stroke it as he walked by.

The next day, on my farm in Oxfordshire, seeing how many trees had been brought down by the 'Beast from the East' and how much damage the badgers had done that week, all was going well when I arrived at a small hill. Yes, it was a bit steep and yes, the ground was wet underfoot. But this is a hill my old Range Rover can do in soggy conditions with its eyes shut. It has, in fact, on many occasions. So the Hilux – which kicked the Americans out of Afghanistan and Iraq and, as we speak, is holding the Russians at bay in Syria – would have no trouble at all . . .

I didn't bother engaging any of the hardcore off-road gub-bins. But wait a minute. What's this? I'm struggling. The wheels are spinning uselessly. So I stopped, twiddled the knob to select the low-range gearbox and then pushed a but-ton to engage the rear differential. And to my utter astonishment, there was a lot of beeping and some flashing lights to tell me that neither thing was working properly.

Had the sun risen in the west, I'd have been less surprised. So I assumed I'd make a mistake, but I hadn't. It wouldn't budge. So I rolled back down the hill in reverse, turned everything off, then turned everything on and still got nothing but beeps and flashing lights. I reversed some more, as this sometimes works. But all that happened was that I got more mud on the tyres, which made progress even more difficult.

I could scarcely believe it. I was in a Toyota Hilux pick-up truck, in the gently rolling Cotswolds, and it was stuck. More incredibly, it was stuck because of a mechanical fault. Except, of course, it wasn't. It was stuck because instead of the old-fashioned levers that Toyota used to fit, the gearbox and the differential are operated by electronics, and electronics in a car designed to win wars against A-10 Warthogs and Apache gunships are as stupid as electronics on a shark defence speargun.

The worst thing about electronics is that the faults are almost always intermittent. So after turning off the Hilux, walking home and coming back with another car and a tow rope, it worked fine and hauled itself out of the mire. And then the diff lock and low range wouldn't disengage. For about fifteen minutes. Then they did. This was annoying for me; it would annoy a proper farmer even more. With Brexit coming, there's no time for a mid-lambing season breakdown. But in the Middle East, it could prove fatal.

I could go on to say that the Invincible's engine was a bit rough and that space for passengers in the rear is tight. But that's a bit like telling someone with terminal cancer that they have an ingrowing toenail.

The fact is that there is only one reason for buying a Hilux. It's going to be unbreakable. But mine broke.

22 April 2018

Oh deer – lucky it has roadkill warning

DS 7 Crossback

I was going to write this morning about the Volkswagen T-Roc, a small and rather funky-looking SUV that burst on to the market a couple of months ago. But then I saw, on the back page of *The Times*, an advertisement for the car in question. 'The new T-Roc,' it said. 'With £500 towards your deposit with Solutions PCP*.'

The asterisk was plainly the point here. Obviously, that is where I'd find the snow plough and Paula Hamilton – the pithy stuff for which VW's admen are famed. But no. It was just a load of accountancy-speak that is normally read out at high speed at the end of car ads on the radio.

So there we are. Volkswagen is making it plain that the only reason you would want to buy a T-Roc is that there's £500 on offer towards the cost of its Solutions PCP. Do you know what a PCP is? Or how a normal PCP might differ from a Solutions PCP? No. Me neither, so let's forget about the T-Roc, which is only for those with an interest in accountancy, and move on to something a lot more interesting: Citroën's new DS 7.

I called a guy at our office in Chiswick and asked him to bring it to my flat. On the way, a youth in a Subaru with an exhaust the size of a Sheffield Forgemasters supergun decided to crash into it. The Impreza was damaged badly, but the DS escaped with minor cuts and bruises. This surprised me.

What didn't surprise me, a few days later, after a visit to the sweet little Brunel museum in south London, was that the engine died. Being French, it had decided to go on strike. Citroën's press office didn't seem too concerned, so I said I'd leave it to be towed away and would go home in a cab.

But as I was waiting for one to appear, the AA turned up, saying it'd plug the car into its diagnostic laptop to see what was wrong. 'Ha-ha-ha-ha,' I said, while looking for Reg Crikey to take me home. But in just a minute the Citroën came back to life, and that was another surprise because, in my experience, trying to mend a car with a laptop is like trying to do dentistry in boxing gloves.

Later Citroën called in a bit of a panic to say that there had been nothing wrong with the car, and that a faulty battery was to blame. I don't buy that, I'm afraid, because the battery is, whether the company likes it or not, as much a part of the car as its doors, or its steering wheel. Saying the car was fine apart from a battery that wouldn't hold its charge is like saying the patient is fine apart from the fact his heart exploded.

Whatever. You'd imagine after a breakdown and a car crash I'd write the Citroën off as a haunted Friday 13th car and move on to something else.

But there's more. Hilariously, Citroën is trying to pass the DS off as a standalone brand. Even though the only people who can remember the original DS are wearing incontipanties in nursing homes.

And anyway the whole point of that car was the clever suspension that allowed you to drive with one wheel missing, over a ploughed field, at 100mph, without spilling your cognac. Whereas the new DS judders over the smallest speed hump as if its ankle just broke.

There's more bad news. The basic cost of the car I tested,

a Crossback Prestige, was £39,380. But it had been fitted with a night vision pack, an electric sunroof, big wheels and a few other options, so the actual cost was an eye-watering £44,855. Small wonder Citroën is saying it's not a Citroën.

What it definitely is, is an SUV, and, as I may have mentioned a few times (No. You've mentioned it a thousand times – Ed), I can't be doing with the damn things. They're the motoring equivalent of the short-sleeved shirt. Patio furniture with brake lights. So there's much not to like here, and yet . . .

Step inside and you will find the doors and the dashboard are coated in quilted leather, such as you would find in a Bentley or an Aston Martin. And the clock is like a footballer's watch. It doesn't tell the time very well – twenty past nine comes up as four past forty-five – but it's a thing of ostentatious beauty. I would like such a thing in my life.

Then there are the buttons. Citroën has gone for a Porsche approach by blunderbussing the transmission tunnel with big, bold switches, and the instrument binnacle is just as stylistically out there. You can choose what it says and how the information is portrayed, but it doesn't matter what you go for: it's very like being in a Lamborghini. If you are in the market for an SUV – and who isn't these days? – you'd struggle to sit in a DS and decide to buy something else. I liked it enormously.

Handling. Fuel economy. Performance. They're what you'd expect from an SUV, a type of car wilfully designed to be no good at any of those things. It has a 2-litre turbodiesel inline engine; MacPherson strut suspension at the front, multi-arm at the rear; electric power steering. It's the same recipe every bugger is using.

But on a motorway I was surprised – again – by just how

quiet and unruffled it was even at what I'd say to police was 70mph. And this was an eight-speed diesel. The petrol version you'd buy, because the government's seesaw thinking is that diesels are bad, will be even better.

I was impressed with the Apache gunship-style night vision system too. When the infrared cameras spot something organic ahead, it's ringed on the spooky black-and-white picture feed in a yellow box.

And that's what I saw as I drove down the A44 late one Saturday night. A yellow box, ringing nothing that could be made out, in a wood. Being a cautious soul, I slowed down, and moments later a deer leapt out in front of me . . . It's likely that if the car hadn't had night vision, I'd now be wearing Bambi as a big, maggoty hat.

So there is much to like about this car. But it is very expensive and it was fitted with a battery that couldn't hold its charge. Yes, it's a lovely place to sit and wait for the AA, but I'm not sure that's what people really want. So I'm afraid that overall it has to be a no.

29 April 2018

Make way – I'm in my attack sub today

Ferrari 812 Superfast

A few years ago I drove the then new Ferrari F12 in Scotland and emerged with a white face and what looked like the onset of Parkinson's. Ooh, it was a scary thing. Yes, the weather was being all Scottish and, yes, the road surface was not ideally suited to a car with a simply enormous amount of bang-and-you're-on-it power. But it was the size of the thing that worried me most of all.

It felt as though I was trying to steer an aircraft carrier with an out-of-control nuclear reactor up the Kennet and Avon canal. You didn't drive this car. On roads like that, in the rain, you hung on for dear life and whimpered like a dog on bonfire night. Some questioned my petrolhead credentials when I returned and, after some medication, said the F12 was a car with too much power. 'Too much power'?' they wailed. 'That's like saying your penis is too big. It's impossible.'

I still feel, however, that I was correct. And I reckoned that what Ferrari needed to do next was go back to basics and make a small, 2-litre car. I drew it in my head and it was very pretty. It would have about 300bhp, a fast gearbox, the lightness of touch for which Ferrari was famous and a price tag of around £100,000.

But instead what Ferrari has done is replace the F12 with a car that's even bigger and even more powerful. It's so powerful, in fact, that it's called the Superfast. And it's so big that when you emerge from a turning, you need to stick six feet of bonnet into the road before you can see if it's safe to pull out.

Let's start with the little things that are wrong with it. In the night it's as paranoid as a cokehead, because every morning it flashed up a message on the dash saying a break-in had been attempted, even though CCTV said no such thing had happened.

Then there are its seatbelts. My car was fitted with £2,000-worth of optional racing harnesses that were nearly impossible to do up properly. What's more, there were many sharp edges, which my girlfriend said, as she sat there like the star of an S&M movie, would play havoc if you were wearing a chiffon dress. I'm not sure that'd bother most customers, but you never know . . .

Of rather more concern is the turning circle, which is stupidly large, and the reflection of the yellow trim in the windscreen. Then there's an astonishingly cheap wiper switch, the usual Ferrari problem of indicator controls on the steering wheel – which means they're never where you left them – and a curious piece of string hanging into the passenger footwell. I pulled it, of course, but nothing happened. Maybe it had something to do with the imaginary burglar.

There's much to annoy, then, but there's much, when you put your foot down, to make your eyes go wide and your girlfriend say: 'As soon as I get this bondage gear off, I'm going to f****** kill you.' This is a car that can get from 0 to 62mph in 2.9 seconds. And onwards to a top speed of 211mph. It's really, really fast and really, really noisy.

Much has been done to get the weight as low as possible. Suppliers were told to shed as much as possible from every component if they didn't want to wake up in bed with a

horse's head. But this car still weighs more than 1.6 tons.
And you sense it.

You also sense the size, and the mere fact that I didn't end
up in a hedge is testimony to some brilliant engineering. The
lightness of the controls, the four-wheel steering system, the
dazzling speed of the double-clutch gear changes . . . Ferrari
has had to employ every trick in the book to make its Torrey
Canyon feel like a speedboat.

I did not drive the car in the rain, or Scotland, but I can
tell you that somehow Ferrari's managed it. It's managed to
get 789bhp from the massive, gravelly 6.5-litre naturally
aspirated V12, through the gearbox and perfectly normal
Pirelli P Zero tyres and on to the road in such a way that a
perfectly ordinary driver with no astronaut training can keep
it pointing in vaguely the right direction.

That cannot have been easy. And it will be even harder
when the time comes to design a replacement, because that
will have to be bigger and more powerful still. Which takes
me back to my point that at some stage Ferrari is going to
have to start all over again, with a car that's small and light.

Or will it? Because is that what Ferrari's customers want?
It's what Ferrari's fanbase wants: a pure-bred Italian sports
car. But the fanbase only reads about cars in magazines. The
customers? The people who write the cheques? Hmmm. I'm
not sure.

There are undoubtedly those who want the last word in
precision driving. They go to track days and they think that
I am the Antichrist for not taking stuff as seriously as they
do. They will not want a Superfast, because for what they do,
the Lotus Elise is better.

Then you have the people who want a Ferrari to impress
everyone at the lodge. They don't want a Superfast either,

because the Mondial does what they need for a tenth of the price.

The main clientele for the Superfast is the chaps who arrive in London every August with an Antonov full of purple-metal-flake Lambos and G-class wagons. They want the biggest, the brashest, the fastest and the noisiest, and for them a Superfast is ideal.

They need to know that in the right hands, on the right track, it can do what the Ferrari badge suggests it can do. But that's only because they want bragging rights during a hubble-bubble pit stop. They will never actually go faster than about 9mph.

I believe this will one day be a problem for Ferrari, which seems to be focused at the moment on the customers with the big money, the people who will buy the really expensive cars and load them up with all the expensive extras.

The trouble is that this tarnishes the brand. Because the rest of us stop thinking of a Ferrari as something with Gilles Villeneuve at the wheel and start thinking of it as something that's a bit sad. And that drives us into the arms of Lamborghini and Porsche and Aston Martin.

Let me put it this way. Do you dream about driving round and round Harrods in your car at 4 a.m.? Or do you dream about taking it along the Amalfi coast at 4 p.m., with Alicia Vikander in the passenger seat saying she can't find her bikini anywhere? Because for that, a 'humble' 488 would be better. And my small, nimble Ferrari would be better still.

As a thing, the Superfast is as brilliant as an Astute-class attack sub. Which is to say, very brilliant indeed. But it is too big and too powerful and too flashily expensive for those who simply want a very nice grand tourer.

20 May 2018

Fast and furry – a fighter jet for pet lovers

Audi RS 4 Avant

In the early 1990s on a television show watched each week by millions of people I tested the Ford Escort and said it was a joyless example of 'that'll do' engineering from a company that should know better. And it went on to become Britain's bestselling car.

Later I said the new Toyota Corolla was a characterless white good like a fridge freezer. That went on to become the world's bestselling car.

Then along came the Renault A610. 'Oooh,' I swooned. 'This is a magnificent car. Well priced, good-looking, unusual and fast.' And in Britain, in the following 12 months, the total number shifted by Renault was ... drum roll ... six.

I'm still at it. Two years ago I drove the Alfa Romeo Giulia Quattroformaggi and told anyone who'd listen that it was the Second Coming. Wheeled lightning. Thor's hammer with Italian trimmings. A car that could and would kick every other sports saloon into a ditch. And so far I haven't seen a single one.

I suspect lots of people would like such a thing on their drive. It has a Ferrari engine. It was designed by a Ferrari engineer. It makes the most glorious array of noises and it goes like a 500-horsepower bastard. There must be thousands who lie awake at night fantasising about owning such a car, but when push comes to shove, they buy something else. Usually a hot Audi of some kind.

The latest hot Audi came to my house this month, and I had to admit it looked very good. It was the RS 4 Avant. But why, I wondered, would anyone choose it instead of the Alfa? That'd be like thinking of taking your summer holiday in Tuscany and then deciding to go to Dortmund instead. Because if the bog were to go wrong, it'd be easier to find a reliable plumber.

Yes, Alfa Romeos were very unreliable. It's fair to say that on, for instance, a GTV 6 every single part is a known fault. But judging Alfa on what it did in the 1980s is like not buying a Volkswagen because it made vehicles for the German army during the war. It's time to move on. To give Alfa another chance. Or is it . . . ?

The Audi RS 4 has not been consistently good. The 2006 version was a marvellous thing with a lusty V8 and he-man flared wheelarches. But the next attempt was a bit of a dog. And a fat dog at that. Much of the magic was lost in a cloying sea of blubber.

That's what Audi has tried to address. This is a car that's been sent to the Mayr clinic and then forced to run home: 15kg has been shaved from the body, 12kg from the axles, 3.5kg from the steering system, 12.5kg from the four-wheel-drive system and 1kg from the rear differential.

Then there's the engine. That's 31kg lighter, which sounds great. But to achieve this, two of the cylinders have been replaced by a brace of centrally mounted turbochargers. Yup. The naturally aspirated V8 is gone, along with its burbling soundtrack. And in its place is a lighter, fizzier, more polar-bear-friendly blown V6.

Is that a good thing? No, of course not. Unless you are Al

Gore. That said, it's one hell of a power plant. The oomph it delivers, especially in the mid range, is strong enough to detach hair. And because it, along with everything else, is so much less fat, the speed that results makes you laugh out loud, nervously.

I can't understand why Audi charges £1,450 to lift the top speed from 155mph to 174mph. And then demands £1,200 for a sports exhaust system and £950 for better steering. It's as though it's saying, 'We've made a crap car, but don't worry. If you give us all your money, we'll make it halfway decent.'

Except 'halfway decent' doesn't begin to cover how well the RS 4 goes and stops and corners. The steering has been criticized for feeling dead, but this was by a road tester who also claimed he could feel the electronics shifting power between the axles. He's obviously superhuman. I couldn't find anything wrong with the steering. No matter what driving mode I selected, it, along with everything else, felt giddy and brilliant. And, best of all, this was the first fast Audi I'd driven in years that didn't have squeaky brakes.

And what was doubly hilarious was that I was driving a five-door estate. Which meant my dog could have enjoyed the fighter-jet G-force as well. And then been sick, probably.

The boot, however, is not terribly big. I learnt this while moving two fire pits from my Golf, into which they'd fitted perfectly well, to the Audi. Into which they also fitted. But only by tearing the roof lining to shreds.

Further forwards, it's all very well screwed together and clever. You can, for instance, turn the entire instrument binnacle into a satnav map. The downside of being in something this clever is that you spend a lot of time pushing buttons and twiddling knobs and then swearing under your breath because it won't do what you want.

Comfort? Well, in full get-out-of-my-way racing mode, there isn't any. The car bounces alarmingly if you go for this setup. But in the mode everyone will always use it's not bad. Except in the back. If you're sitting there, it's so jiggly that any text you send is gibberish.

I'm picking nits because this is one of those cars that are hard to fault. I was expecting much of the RS 4's heart to have been lost with the V8, but the V6 is better. And you have that four-wheel-drive system, which allows you to drift, and then go to Val-d'Isère and drive through one. It's a very capable car.

For sure, it is better than the current M3, which is not BMW's finest hour, but is it better than the Alfa?

No. Of course not. The Quattroformaggi is so much more charismatic. It'd come into your life like a new puppy. You'd want to take care of it and let it sit by the fire on chilly evenings. And if it did a little oil wee in the night, you'd tickle it behind its ears and understand. It is a car with a soul.

And plainly that's not what you want from a car, so you'll buy the Audi instead. And you won't regret it because, crikey, it's good. Really, really good.

27 May 2018

Stuff the price tag: it's love at first touch

Range Rover Velar

Understanding Land Rover's range of cars used to be quite simple. If you got muddy for a living, either by rearing sheep or shooting people with machine-guns, you had a Defender. If you were a duke, you had a Range Rover, and if you were a murderer, like Kenneth Noye, you had a Discovery.

But then one day the bosses realized something important. People prefer working in IT to getting muddy, there are only twenty-four non-royal dukes in Britain and most of the murderers are in jail. So they decided to branch out.

And then they kept on branching out, so now we've reached the point where it is simply impossible to work out which model is for what. You have what I call the proper Range Rover, which is now driven by everyone I know and everyone they've ever met as well. It's brilliant. There's also the long-wheelbase version, which is for those who like not being able to fit their car into a parking space.

Slightly below this auspicious duo, there's the Range Rover Sport, and lower down still you have the Evoque and the weird Evoque convertible. What that's for, I have no idea. Clay pigeon shooting on the move, maybe.

After this, things get really complicated, because you have the Discovery, which I think is for people who want their car to look as though it's had a stroke, or those who hate their children. It really does have the most uncomfortable back seats I've experienced. And then there's the Discovery Commercial, which is for people who don't want any back seats at all, and the Discovery Sport, which is smaller than the normal Discovery and is for . . . er, I have no idea.

You might imagine that when you have a line-up of four-wheel-drive vehicles as extensive as that, covering every price bracket from less than £30,000 to more than £160,000, there'd be no possibility of squeezing another one in. But Land Rover has.

It has called the car the Range Rover Velar, which is stupid because it means people like me are going to call it the Velour. And while that's a fabulous seat fabric, it's a terrible name with some terrible pleblon connotations. Also, it seems to serve no purpose. I mean, saying that you want something between an Evoque and whatever the next biggest Land Rover is these days is like saying your shoe size is 12¼.

I was going to be petulant and simply ignore the Velar, but then I saw one. I was strolling down the Embankment in London, ignoring the velvet Ferraris and lime green Lamborghinis, when it came crawling past, and it stopped me dead in my tracks because, stylistically, it's up there with the Ford Escort Mk 2. That is emphatically not an insult.

Familiarity bred indifference to that particular Escort, but if you actually looked at one while wearing a beret and sitting at an easel, you'd conclude that, while it may have been as unspecial as a Coca-Cola bottle, it was every bit as good-looking.

The Velar pulls off the same trick. Yes, it's just a five-door SUV, but look at its lines, look at its detailing, look at its proportions and its stance. And then you'll be forced to agree that it is one of the five best-looking cars ever made.

It's so good-looking that, while I was considering a

replacement for my Volkswagen Golf GTI the other day, it wouldn't leave my head. So I asked Land Rover if I could borrow one for a few days. Of course, being from Coventry, the company adopted a communistical approach and made me get into the queue behind the motoring correspondents from the *Welsh Pig Breeders' Gazette* and *The Pontefract Bugle*, but fairly soon it arrived in Byron Blue, the very colour I wanted. And, God, it looked good.

Inside, it looked even better. The seats had been made from some kind of recycled material that's kind to polar bears, and that's lovely. But what I cared about most of all was how they looked and how soft they felt. I wanted to rub my face into them. Until I remembered that the previous week the car had been driven by a pig breeder from Wales. So I didn't.

Instead I climbed aboard and touched stuff. You want to touch everything because it's all just so beautiful – the two displays, the knobs, the air vents – and then you look up and the roof is all glass and you want to touch that too. Getting back into an ordinary car afterwards is like stepping from the cockpit of a modern-day Boeing 787 Dreamliner into the nose of a Halifax bomber. That interior? I have never seen better.

I was sold, so I fired up Land Rover's configurator. First of all, I selected the 3-litre supercharged petrol engine. I know this makes no sense and diesel would be much more economical. But, having said that diesel was good, the government now says diesel is bad and that if you use it, you must give Theresa May all your money.

With the power plant selected, it was time to choose some wheels. The car I'd been sent was sitting on 21in rims, which made it as comfortable as riding a skateboard down a flight of stairs. You can go bigger, amazingly, and you can go for 18in castors. But I settled on 20in, which would allow some give in the side walls and some grip if I were in a hurry.

Inside, I went for the system that lets me choose what colour ambient lighting I'd like, privacy glass and a 'suedecloth' steering wheel. Oh, and extra power sockets. Underneath, I decided on the active rear locking differential. I am a farmer at weekends, and I figured I might need that.

I didn't bother with the rear-seat entertainment, on the basis that people have phones and iPads. And I skipped over the various things that would allow me to fix bikes to the roof and canoes to the tailgate. In fact, I skipped over most of the options, and yet, when I'd finished, the price was just shy of £80,000. I'll say that again. Eighty thousand pounds.

Anyone who pays that much for the Velour is completely mad. And in fact Land Rover has just updated the model, so you can't order it as I configured it, though you might find one on a dealer's forecourt.

And yet we all pay hundreds of pounds for an iPhone, because it's so tactile and nice to use. And people pay millions for a few swirls of paint. And that's the trick Land Rover has pulled off with the Velour. You want one no matter what the price, because after you lock it, you'll never tire of turning round for one last look before you go through the front door.

3 June 2018

Lads, let's leave it in the Italian sewers

Mini 1499 GT

When the Mini 1499 GT arrived at my office with its snazzy stripes, big black wheels and John Player Special Union Jack door mirrors, I was very excited. I knew nothing about what BMW had done to create this tremendous-looking car; only that it was tickling the small boy that still lives in my creaking outer shell of fat and hopelessness.

Plainly this car had been designed to hark back to the old Mini 1275 GT, which was not well received by the pipe-smoking motoring helmsmen of the time. They didn't like the single carburettor that was being used to feed the engine, whereas back then I didn't know what a single carburettor was. I just liked the way it looked. And I'd always liked Minis because of how well they handled the sewers of Turin.

Yes, the Cooper was probably a better car, because it had all the things the helmsmen wanted. But it didn't have stripes on the side. And the 1275 GT did, so that was that.

And so it goes today. Apart from the idiotic Countryman, I've always liked the 'new' Mini as well. I know it's not very small – it has a longer wheelbase than the old Land Rover Discovery – and I know that some of the styling is a bit knowing. But, my God, it's a lovely thing to drive and to sit in. It doesn't matter whether you go for the basic model or the full-works nutter bastard: it is joyful on country roads, economical, fun to use and practical.

The only slight drawback is the cruising speed. All cars have a speed at which the components settle into a harmonious rhythm. In a Porsche 911 it's only about 50mph, for some reason, but the speed at which a Mini will settle if you leave it to its own devices, while you sit there daydreaming, is a licence-losing 110mph. You really do have to pay attention.

I was very ready to pay attention to the 1499 GT, because it hits all the sweet spots that used to be important when my love affair with cars was blossoming. Apart from the aforementioned exterior changes, it has big, deep, rally-style front seats, stiffened suspension and a John Cooper shirt-button steering wheel.

Then I got to the really juicy bit: the engine. Because here I found what appeared to be the cleverest bit of the car's make-up. It's the same engine as you get in the base-level Mini One, a three-cylinder 1.5-litre turbo. This gives 101bhp, which is roughly what you get from a food blender, and an unknowable top speed, because nobody has enough time in their lives to sit there while this big car with its tiny engine struggles to get there. Zero to 62mph takes more than ten seconds, which is tremendously fast if you are living in 1928, but a bit ho-hum in this day and age.

And how clever is all that? Because here we have a car with rally seats and grippy Dunlop SportMaxx RT2 tyres and go-faster stripes. But that will do nearly 60mpg and be cheap to insure even if you are seventeen and have a bad temper. However, there is a problem. This is a car that does not work at all. It's hard to think of the right word. But 'horrible' is close enough.

The first problem, of many, is the stiffened suspension, which enables the car to go round corners at the sort of speed its soggy engine can only dream about. But on the downside the bumpiness beggars belief. It's so uncomfortable around town that you'd be better off walking.

And then there's the way it doesn't really move off properly. Unless you give it a bootful of revs, it pulls out of side turnings like a twig stuck in an oxbow lake. Some of this is down to ridiculously tall gearing, which creates another problem on the motorway: making it go up a hill. Unless you're prepared to stir the gear lever as though you're making scrambled eggs, you'll be confined for all of time to what Michael McIntyre always calls 'the loser lane'. And even here you'll be a nuisance to lorries.

I don't mind an underpowered car if it feels fizzy and alive and if it responds to some spirited driving, but the Mini just won't. It feels slovenly, like a fat kid on a cross-country run. He may have all the right kit and the best training shoes, but it makes no difference in the end. He's going to come last.

I can't imagine you're still reading at this point, because this is not a car you'd want to buy, but, just in case, I should also mention the satnav, because obviously, in a car costing nearly £17,000, it's going to be fitted as standard. Except it isn't. What you get instead is a clip in which to store your phone.

I know that if you squint this makes sense. I know all young people use their phones to get about and mate and so on. But I prefer a proper satnav, because if I use my phone, everyone thinks I work for Uber and people get in the back when I'm waiting at a red light and tell me to go to Hornchurch.

There's more, I'm afraid. The big front seats. Yes, they're nice to sit in, but they rob nearly all the legroom in the back. And if someone back there needs to be sick – and this is a car aimed at young people who go to festivals, so it is likely – there is no way he or she will be able to get out before the pavement pizza arrives.

Apparently, the 1499 GT is a limited-run special edition. Just 1,499 will be made. This is probably because Mini knew full well it wouldn't be a big seller. But, either way, it's going to be left with all of them when the production run ends.

The only real solution, if Mini wants to save face, is to go for the full 1970s authenticity and ask the workforce to go on strike as soon as possible.

So far as you're concerned, though, I shouldn't worry, because there are many alternatives to this woeful car. First there is the standard Mini One, which doesn't pretend to be something it isn't and won't shake your hair out and doesn't have silly seats.

Then there's the Volkswagen Up! GTI. It's not as practical as the Mini, but at £13,755 it's more than £3,000 cheaper, unless of course VW has made that price up.

Then there's the Ford Fiesta ST-Line. It has only a 1-litre engine, but that delivers 138bhp, which means it can handle gentle gradients with ease. And finally, a left-field choice: the Citroën C3 Aircross. This is a car that's much, much better than you might imagine. Sweet, too.

In short, there are many options if you want a small, sporty-looking car. The Mini 1499 GT, however, isn't one of them.

17 June 2018

Keep your powder, gin and 12-bore dry

Twisted Land Rover Defender

I have never been a fan of the Land Rover Defender and cannot understand the dewy-eyed sentimentality of fully grown beardy men who shed beery tears when it finally went out of production in 2016.

It may have been very clever and important when Land Rover copied the Willys Jeep back in the 1840s. But by the time Queen Victoria died, it was already starting to look cramped and stupid. Even the army eventually gave up on it, but still, at real ale festivals and murderer conventions in the heathery bits of Britain, people with muddy fingernails wailed and gnashed their teeth when the life support system was finally turned off.

It was, to me, the red phone box of cars. It worked only because it had always been around. But the truth is that it's better to make a call from an iPhone than from inside a draughty red box that smells of a tramp's underpants. And it's better, if you work in the countryside, to drive a pick-up than a badly made, slow, evil-handling Defender.

Well, anyway, I came to work last week and outside the office was exactly the sort of thing that would cause a member of Camra to walk into a door. It was, or rather it had once been, a Defender 110, but someone had fitted fat tyres with the complexion of the Singing Detective, massive wheels, flared arches, a light bar with the power of a collapsing sun and, to judge by the twin exhausts, some kind of weird million-horsepower engine as well.

Further investigation revealed this to be so, as, under the bonnet, instead of a wheezing boiler that ran on an unholy mixture of cider and coal, there was the unmistakeable bulk of an LS3 V8 from a Chevrolet Corvette. Not a bad engine, actually, but it had no place in what I thought was Richard Hammond's latest idiotic purchase. It was even called a Twisted, only with the 's' written backwards. And that's so him.

Unfortunately, it turned out to be my car for the week. And to make matters worse, the brochure was accompanied by a letter from the daughter of the man who owns Twisted. 'Dear Jeremy,' it said. 'This is my favourite Twisted Defender. I hope you like it too. Please look after it for my Daddy. Love from Molly, age seven and three-quarters.'

'Harrumph,' I said to myself belligerently. 'I shall not be swayed by this emotional blackmail.' Well spelt and written though it may be. Especially as I'd just noticed the price of this particular top-spec version: more than £150,000. 'Hmmm,' I thought, with my Doncaster hat on. 'This may have been made in North Yorkshire, but with that kind of price tag I can't imagine they'll sell many there.'

The next day I had to go to my cottage in the country and, as I set off, the weather was overcast and gloomy, but there was no sign of what lay on the other side of the Chilterns. We all occasionally say, 'I've never seen rain like it', but I really and truly had not. I've witnessed the monsoon in India, thunderstorms in Vietnam and the relentless downpours of southern Chile, but none of them got close to the bombardment in Oxfordshire that night. It was like driving along under a fire plane.

And there's no other way of saying this: I could not imagine a better car in those conditions than the Twisted. It just punched its way through the lakes that had formed in every dip and the rivers on every slope. Yes, its roof-mounted lights caused a white-out every time we went through really deep water, and the spray plumed out as if a nuclear sub had just exploded beneath the surface, but the tyres, and the way this thing was set up: it made even the most manly Mercedes G-wagen look like a market-stall toy.

There's more. It's often the case that people who are capable of fitting front and rear air lockers, Alcon brakes and uprated suspension to what's basically the Hay Wain are absolutely hopeless at doing interiors. Often they ask their wives to help, and while they may be just about capable of turning up a pair of trousers, they can't trim a dashboard.

Well, someone at Twisted can, because apart from the inherent lack of shoulder room, it was a beautiful place to sit. They'd even managed to find an aftermarket satnav and control system that was sensible and not full of features no one needs. The next day the rain had gone and I had a closer look at the well-trimmed monster that had head-butted its way to the hills. And in the boot there was a big and nicely made chest for sloe gin, King's Ginger liqueur and all the aiming juice that the nation's pheasant-slayers need. There were even slots for your guns. Although those aren't included in the price.

What is included is a turn of speed that beggars belief. The soundtrack tells you that there's a bit of poke under your right foot, but your head is saying that you're in a Land Rover 110 and it'd need to be a lot to move such a cumbersome old tank around at anything more than a trot.

Your head is wrong, because when you mash the throttle

into the firewall, the automatic gearbox drops a cog or two, the nose rises and, with a bellow that could stun a cow at 400 yards, it takes off with acceleration that makes you burst out laughing. It is not just fast, this thing. It is hilariously fast.

And you don't have to slow down that much for the bends. Obviously, with those knobbly Cooper tyres, it doesn't have the grip levels of, say, Bambi, but, thanks to its reworked suspension and Recaro seats that hold you in place, you can make some serious progress. The only really annoying thing was the way people in Defenders going the other way gave me a little wave as I tore by. 'We have nothing in common,' I wanted to shout.

Except now we do. I shoot, and I'm well aware that it's important to have the right car when you're on one of those days that are full of businessmen with big watches and tweed that even Rupert Bear would describe as 'garish'. A simple Range Rover, in these circumstances, is not enough.

So I'd love to turn up in this monstrous Twisted, knowing that it would get deeper into the woods and then get me home faster than anything anyone else had.

So, Molly, all is well. Even though it started out in life as a Land Rover, which I hate as much as I bet you hate some of your teachers, I did like your dad's car. And if I hadn't just bought one of the aforementioned Range Rovers, I'd be sorely tempted by it. Especially the drinks cabinet.

1 July 2018

A power pup to make you sit up and beg

Volkswagen Up! GTI

Forgive me if you've heard me say this before, but if I were charged with running an airline, I can pretty much guarantee it would be bankrupt in a week.

The main problem, after I'd organized some appropriate uniforms for the stewardesses and dealt with the strike and the public outcry that resulted, would be choosing routes.

Not that long ago I had to fly to Charlotte, North Carolina, and could not believe that British Airways had a daily direct service. I figured I'd have the whole plane to myself because there could be no way that 400-plus people, every day, would wake up and think: 'You know what? I fancy going to North Carolina.' But I was wrong. I haven't been so squashed since I once said, 'Economy, please', buying a train ticket from Mumbai to Delhi.

At the other end of the scale, we have Corfu. This is a beautiful island that is very popular among the sort of people who can afford to pay many hundreds of pounds to get away for a long weekend. And yet for some extraordinary reason it is not possible to fly there directly from the UK in the winter.

As I write, I'm trying to get to Ulan Bator and it's ridiculous. This is Mongolia's capital city and the only way I can find to get there is either on an upright seat through Moscow, which is full of football supporters and airport guards who might play silly buggers with me for being English and possibly from Salisbury, or via Hong Kong. Which would mean flying halfway round the world to come three-quarters of the way back again.

These are the issues I'd address if I ran an airline. Getting people to places they haven't necessarily heard of. It sounds great. But I'm assured by people who actually do work in the airline industry that it's the worst business idea since someone at Volkswagen said: 'Yes. But what if we just cheat?'

And speaking of the motor industry, I wouldn't be much good at running a car maker either.

Last week, I was driving around in VW's new Up! GTI. And I've been consumed by the fact that, before tax, it has a recommended retail price of £11,713. Now assuming VW is making 20 per cent, that means it is putting together a whole car for about £9,761.

How is that possible? It has the same number of wheels and seats and windows as a Rolls-Royce Phantom and that costs more than £360,000. It has an engine and a gearbox and miles of wiring. It has air-conditioning and electric front windows and electronic stability control. So how can it possibly cost only £9,761 to make? Obviously it can't, so if I were running VW, I'd tell my engineers not to bother and to concentrate instead on making Bentleys, which are a lot more profitable.

Happily, though, I'm not running VW, which means you can buy this Up! GTI – including giving Theresa May a slug of VAT – for £14,055. That's £14,055 for what is surely the spiritual successor to the old VW Golf GTI.

It's about the same size and it has the same sort of non-threatening styling. You don't quite say 'Aww' when you see it but neither do you go 'Grrrr'. It does, though, because under the bonnet there's a 1-litre three-cylinder engine. And these units are inherently unbalanced, which is why they sound so charismatic.

It must also be said that 1-litre engines are inherently unpowerful and that such a thing therefore has no place in a car that says GTI on the back. But to get round that, VW has fitted a turbocharger that boosts the power to 114bhp. That's 6bhp more than you got from the original Golf GTI.

That said, the Up! GTI is more than 200kg heavier than the Mk 1 Golf GTI, mainly because it's filled with all sorts of stuff designed to keep you alive if you skid off the road and hit a tree. And you do notice this extra weight when you are on a motorway and want to pull into the outside lane . . .

You put your foot down in sixth and not much happens. So now the BMW that was bearing down on you is flashing its lights and you can see the driver is mouthing the word 'Idiot'. And you're wishing you'd dropped it down to fourth because then everything would have been fine. Unless you're a polar bear, which you're not.

In every other respect, the Up! is completely perfect. In a city it fits into the cycle lanes and beats everything off the lights, and can slip easily into even the stingiest multistorey car parking bay. And while it doesn't come with a satnav, it has a handy clip above the dash where you can mount your phone and use that instead.

Other modern-day stuff? Well, it's got a USB port where you can dock your, er, USB and it has an interface for Android or Apple devices. I have no idea what I'm talking about here but I know these things matter to under-tewnty-fives. Me, I was more taken with the cloth-seat upholstery, which was exactly the same as it was on the old Golf GTI. And the lovely-to-hold leather steering wheel.

And I was even more impressed by how this car handled itself out of town. Pick a speed. Any speed. And then it will just do that all the time. You don't have to slow down for bumps, corners or even horses.

People don't mind when you whizz past their nag at 60mph because the car's sweet and it's making the exact same noise their bicycles used to make when they put lollipop sticks in the spokes. I imagine many think as they watch the Up! fly off into the distance: 'I must sell this horse and get one of those as soon as I get home.'

For, behind the wheel, it is tremendous. The handling and the grip and the torque combine to produce one of the funnest and funniest cars on the road today. I challenge anyone to not like it.

My mate's mum saw it and ordered one straight away. The executive producer of *The Grand Tour* saw it, had a go and is now part-exchanging his BMW M3 to get one. I have no need for such a thing but I'd love to have one in my life. In that respect, it's like a four-seater hatchback dog.

As I said, if I'd been running VW I'd have assumed no one would want such a thing and there was no money to be made on it. But there is, of course: on the finance deals everyone will make to have one.

That's the trouble with business. It's not interesting. Some of the things it makes, on the other hand . . .

8 July 2018

The Lewis Hamilton of cars #blessed

Bentley Continental GT

Because no one apart from me turns up on time these days, I spend a lot of my life sitting in restaurants or bars, scrolling through my phone, pretending to everyone else that I'm emailing friends and doing important business deals.

Mostly, though, I'm on my internet platform, *DriveTribe*, looking at hastily shot videos of Russians crashing their Lamborghinis and hilarious footage of motorcyclists slithering along the asphalt in their silly leather romper suits.

Recently I happened upon some footage of a horrific accident. Shot by a dashcam, it showed a Volvo trundling along quite normally at about 50mph and then, for no obvious reason, drifting very gently into the wrong lane and smashing head-on into a 42-ton articulated lorry.

Happily, the camera was still rolling when the utterly ruined car came to a halt, and when the dust had settled and the engine had come back to Earth after a spell in orbit, I couldn't quite believe what I was seeing. The driver was moving about. And then he calmly opened what was left of the door.

It was incredible that anyone could have survived such an impact, but not as incredible as the caption. This is what it said: 'Since it was launched in the UK fourteen years ago, no one has died in Volvo XC90. Ever.'

I find this incredible because, with the best will in the

world, Volvo XC90s tend to be driven by school-run mums who spend most of the time facing backwards and shouting at Toby to stop kicking his sister. They are the exact sort of car you'd expect to drift into the wrong lane, and yet not a single Brit has died in one. Not even of boredom.

Of course Volvo can't advertise the fact, because it would be the very definition of tempting fate. It'd be like Qantas saying it has never had a fatal crash. You just know what would happen the next day. But it does give credence to Volvo's claim, a while ago, that by 2020 no one will die in any of its cars.

So that's that, then. In a health and safety-obsessed world where every fire, electrocution and weather event must be thoroughly investigated, no matter what the cost, because no one is allowed to die, ever, of anything, it's obvious your next car just has to be a Volvo. There is no other sane choice.

Except of course there is, because while the authorities are obsessed with our safety and health – and the environment – we actually couldn't give a stuff. What we want is something that we think will make us attractive to members of the opposite sex. Or the same sex, if that's your thing. Which brings us neatly on to the Lewis Hamilton of cars. The Bentley Continental GT.

When the Continental GT was launched, in 2003, it was a rather dowdy thing that went around with its dad, being polite and happy and well mannered. Then one day and for no obvious reason it decided it didn't want to go round with its dad any more and became quite cool. And now it's got a big watch and a red jet and it's gone a bit mental on the bling front #blessed.

As a general rule I don't like bling, but I have got to be honest: the new GT's headlamps are extremely amazing.

Each one contains eighty-two LEDs, and at night they glisten like the chandelier in a rapper's man cave. And when you climb inside, you really are dazzled, especially if the sun's out, because it'll be reflecting off all the chrome and burning your retinas.

I wrote last week about how on earth Volkswagen sells the Up! GTI for £14,055 when it is essentially the same as a Bentley. They both have wheels and an engine and indicator stalks and so on. But when you actually sit in the new Continental GT, you're left in no doubt that a hell of a lot of work goes into making it feel so damn special.

As an example, you push the button marked 'Screen', and the whole centre section of the dash rotates to become a satnav map. You push it again and you get three conventional dials. And it takes a while for you to realize it's like the three-sided numberplate on James Bond's Aston Martin DB5.

Everything is completely OTT. The speaker grilles. The stalks. The vent buttons. Even the optional diamond pattern on the doors and seats, each shape of which is made up of 712 stitches. And that's before you go behind the facade and learn that the Continental has five miles of wiring, 2,300 circuits and ninety-two electronic control units.

It is also a car. Bentley's engineers are at pains to point out that behind the seen-it-before styling, everything is new. They say that the W12 engine is mounted further back and the front wheels further forwards, which improves the handling. I'm sure they're right. But it still feels very much like the old model – and that's not a criticism.

I gave it a thrash round *The Grand Tour*'s 'Eboladrome' track in Swindon and it felt big and heavy and four-wheel-driveish. Which is as it should be. If I wanted something lithe and pointy, I'd buy an Aston Martin DB11.

On the motorway it was sublime. Quiet and, even in the 'Bentley' mode on the adaptive suspension, extremely comfortable. It's fast too. Despite the weight, the car will get from 0 to 62mph in 3.7 seconds. If my friends had a machine such as this, I'd spend less time on my own, looking at people crashing.

The only slight niggle is that the adjustable steering wheel doesn't come quite far enough towards the driver. Oh, and from the driver's seat the kink in the rear wing gives you the constant impression you're being undertaken by another car.

And then there's the panicky radar system that kept jamming on the brakes to avoid an accident that wasn't going to happen anyway. These, though, are niggles. And a Volvoish attitude to my wellbeing is probably not such a bad thing, actually.

Overall, I thought this was an absolutely fabulous car. A brilliant piece of completely over-the-top styling sitting like the icing on a properly made cake. If I had to choose between this and the DB11, I'd be in what the experts call 'a right old muddle'. But as I'm pushing sixty now, I'd probably go for the Continental.

My only real gripe is with the behind-the-scenes marketing. Bentley still hangs on to that whole 'the right crowd and no crowding' Brooklands scene, and a WO mentality of: 'Let's show Johnny Foreigner what's what, eh?' Maybe that's what the Chinese want: a sense that they've bought the Bicester shopping village with windscreen wipers. But I don't.

Bentley also says the car was handcrafted from scratch at its factory in Crewe. It says that 93 per cent of the workforce is British, and I'm sure that's so. But there's no getting round the fact that the company was until recently run by a man called Wolfgang Dürheimer and that underneath all the

British stitching sits the same platform as you get in a Porsche Panamera.

So. It's time Bentley forgot about what it was and concentrated on what it is. The maker of what my American friends still call, and quite correctly, an MFB.

The 'B' stands for Bentley. I'll let you work out the rest.

15 July 2018

It's easy on the nose, but who'd pick it?

Dacia Duster

There are many things I would not like to buy second-hand. A pair of underpants. A laptop computer. A mattress. A toothbrush. Those cotton wool buds on sticks that people use to get wax out of their ears. The list goes on and on.

But what about a car? Sure, you may think that if you get a team of Albanians to make merry with the Pledge and the pine-fresh cleaning products, all traces of the previous owner and their disgusting habits can be removed, but I'm afraid it simply isn't so.

A few years ago I did a CSI-style test on the interiors of various well-valeted used cars, and the findings from the men with the ultraviolet lamps, swabs and hazmat suits were grim. All the vehicles were coated in a thin veneer of mucus, and two had large amounts of semen on the back seat. One had significant traces of faecal matter in the driver's foot-well, and another contained enough dried blood to suggest that someone had been beheaded in there. After being sick.

This is what you have to remember when you buy a used car. It may look and feel and smell factory-fresh, but behind the sheen it is not. Because everyone – even Prince Philip and Joanna Lumley – picks their nose. And everyone rolls what they find into a small ball. And everyone drops that small ball into that crack at the side of the seat into which not even the most delicate Dyson attachment can reach. So using your new second-hand car as a tool to take you to work is the same as using second-hand lavatory paper to wipe your bottom. Revolting.

All of which brings me neatly to the door of the latest new car I've been driving. The second-generation Dacia Duster.

Let's get to the point of this car straight away. It is a medium-sized, light-duties off-roader with a big boot and space in the cabin for five fully grown adults. And yet it costs less than £10,000. That's about a third cheaper than any of its rivals.

This is not good value in the way that a McDonald's Happy Meal is good value. Or this newspaper, for that matter. It is way beyond that. A brand-new car with a three-year warranty and a bogey-free interior and that new-car smell for less than 10 grand. You assume the whole thing must have been made from recycled CD boxes in a Vietnamese sweatshop by child slaves.

Not quite. In fact the Duster is made by the few people who still live in Romania, using tools and parts no longer needed by Dacia's owner, Renault. Underneath, then, the new Duster is basically an old Clio. And there's nothing wrong with that. The old Clio was quite a nice thing. Safe, too, for the time.

The engine? This is where things start to go a bit wrong, because in the car I tested it was a 1.6-litre four-cylinder petrol-powered affair that came at you from the days before turbocharging. The result is 113 brake horsepower, which doesn't sound too bad, and 115 torques, which sounds acceptable also. But it isn't.

In sixth gear, on the motorway, this car will not accelerate at all. Unless you are going downhill, but then only because of gravity. What you happen to be doing with your right foot is irrelevant. To get round the problem, you must drop down to fourth, which hands some control back to your foot, but the noise goes from being annoying to being Grateful Dead deafening.

In town the car has an even bigger problem. Mine had four-wheel drive, but instead of fitting a low-range gearbox, which would have been expensive, Dacia has tried to give a low-range feel to first and second. This means you need to be changing up into third when you're doing about 4mph.

I learnt after a little while to start in second, get it right up to the red line, until blood was spurting from my ears, and then go for third, where normal service was resumed. Fourth was normal too. But from there it made sense to go straight to sixth, which meant fifth was pointless. No one is ever going to drive a Duster smoothly. Or quietly. Or with their dignity intact. And it has the personality of a street lamp or a washing machine. Let me put it this way: no one is going to give their Duster a cute name.

I'd love to conclude by saying that if you concentrate hard, the car will zip along quite nicely, but it won't: 0 to 62mph takes 12.9 seconds, which in human time is a year. And the top speed is 105mph, which, as Dacia's elderly and adenoidal fans point out, is more than enough. I can't be bothered to argue with that. It's got a 1956 price, so I suppose I shouldn't be disappointed that it has a 1956 top speed.

For a whole week I told people this. They'd get in, still remarking unfavourably on the horrible gold paintwork, and then they'd stab away at various buttons and levers, laughing about the terribleness of it all. And then I'd shut them up by saying: 'Yes. But it's a five-seat off-road car with a three-year warranty and switchable four-wheel drive but it costs less than £10,000.'

Unfortunately, when I sat down to write this, I put on my spectacles and found that the base model with two-wheel drive is indeed less than £10,000. But the four-wheel-drive Comfort version I'd been using is £15,195. And on top of that you are expected to pay £495 for the hideous gold paint and – get this – £90 for western European mapping on the satnav. Really? So if you don't give Dacia £90 the Duster can only find its way round Latvia?

I'm digressing, and we must get back to the fact that this painfully slow, difficult to drive and not especially attractive elderly Renault in an Ilie Nastase suit is actually not far shy of £16,000. And that is ridiculous.

There are cars from Nissan and Seat and Suzuki and Kia that you can buy for this sort of money, and all of them are safer and better in every single way.

Sure, you can stick to the entry-level two-wheel-drive Duster with its single rear bench and eastern European sat-nav and five-speed gearbox. And you can boast to your friends about how you've got a brand-new car for £9,995.

But I'm sorry: I'd rather buy a used Range Rover Evoque or BMW X3 or Audi Q5 and spend the next couple of years driving to and from work on someone's turdy skid marks, with my feet nestling in a garden of their dried-up nose juice.

29 July 2018

It's the nation's Bentley and Xi's gotta have it

The Hongqi L5, China's presidential monster

When mealy-mouthed Britain was moaning about the recent warm spell, I was in the Chinese city of Chongqing, where it was a fairly toasty 48°C. And that's without the humidity, which causes the air to be actually heavy. Being outside was like being under a hot dead horse.

Chinese people will tell you that Chongqing is the furnace of China. Everyone else, meanwhile, will say, 'Chong-what?' And that's odd, because the city centre is home to about 9m people, which means it's bigger than London. If you count everyone in the metropolitan area, it's home to more than 30m, which means it's pretty much the biggest city in the world. You don't feel like a person here. You feel like a molecule.

It's a forest of skyscrapers. There are more here than in Manhattan, and every morning, when you wake up, there are two more. And another bridge over the two brown rivers that meet in the city centre.

I loved Chongqing. I loved the local delicacy, 'hot pot' – it's goose intestines, or congealed duck's blood, or cow tendon, cooked at the table in a cauldron of dynamite and napalm. This causes you to sweat profusely, which means that when you leave the air-conditioned restaurant and climb back under the dead horse, you're coated in a cooling layer of perspiration. Clever.

I loved the pace of the city too, and its hills and the way

the jungle is trying hard to take it back, growing out of every crevice and crack in the forest of steel and concrete, but soon I left on the bullet train, which is capable of 311mph. It's so punctual that if you were stepping through the door at the advertised moment of departure, half of you would be left on the platform.

When I first went to China, the train I took from Beijing to Xian was pulled by a steam locomotive, and the lavatory car was a wooden box with a hole in the floor. All the other passengers had missed it. Some by several feet. And that was only thirty years ago.

Ever heard of Anshun? Neither had I, but it's one of the most beautiful cities I've seen. Set amid some geological lunacy, it's willow-pattern Chinese with St Tropez weather – and you don't have to go there on a train.

You can drive. Before 1988 there wasn't a single motorway in the country. Now the Chinese have more than 80,000 miles of them, and since 2011 they have been adding at least 6,000 miles a year.

You can't drive on these motorways with a British licence. That's not good enough. You must take an exam first. This involves opening and closing your hands, squatting and standing up again and passing an eye test. Which I did by answering the questions in a language the examiner could not understand. Then I was able to use the smoothest, freest-flowing roads in the world. The only drawback is that every hundred yards every car is photographed, and every picture is analysed to make sure the driver is not on the phone or speeding or 'touching his passenger. Or himself.'

Thirty years ago Chinese people were not allowed to drive a car. Now they are buying more than 24 million a year. To try to force locals to buy cars made in China, vehicles manufactured in Europe cost twice as much as they do in the West. But that's not stopping the new rich. You see Ferraris, Rolls-Royces and Bentleys constantly. There are fakes of many cars. There are fakes of everything in China, but having the real deal – that's what people want. It's why Bicester shopping village is one of the top attractions for Chinese tourists in Britain.

This, however, is not much use to President Xi Jinping, because he can't turn up to a global conference in a Bentley. That'd be admitting to the world that the Chinese car industry is no good. Nor can he turn up in a Haval or a Trumpchi, because then everyone would know for sure that the Chinese car industry was no good. He needs something that causes the world to say: 'Wow.' Which is why Xi uses a Hongqi L5.

It costs £550,000. You read that correctly, and it looks like a Chrysler 300C, which is how all cars look when the designer is told to make something that looks like a Bentley. Except, to set it apart, it also has hints of the Peugeot 404 and the Austin 1100. None of which you notice, because of the red flag bonnet ornament. That's what Hongqi means: red flag. This, then, is a £550,000 symbol of communism. Chinese-style.

Getting hold of one to try was nigh-on impossible. They're made only for top officials and priced to make sure no one else buys one. So no one has, really. But eventually, using nothing but enormous amounts of cold, hard cash, I was able to get one for a day. It was delivered by a one-legged man in a vest who spoke no English and knew nothing about what the car was. But we were able to work out that it's powered by a homemade V12 engine that produces 402 brake horsepower. About what you got from a big Mercedes in the 1990s.

This would be fine, except the Hongqi – a hard word to

say on television, by the way – weighs 3.1 tons, which is more than most road-building equipment. When you open the incredibly heavy door, you see why. It's bulletproof. But when you lower the window, you see that, in fact, it isn't. It weighs that much because it's made from iron ore and granite.

This means the Hongqi is a bit slow. Actually, that's not fair. A worn-out Austin Metro is a bit slow. This is much slower than that. Hongqi won't say how quickly it gets from 0 to 62mph, mainly, I suspect, because it can't get there at all. That is a good thing, because it has no airbags.

It also has no cupholders. There is electrical adjustment for the steering wheel. But that was broken. And I didn't mind, because, ooh, it was a nice place to sit. It wasn't remotely comfortable: the seats were rock-hard, and the suspension had, I think, been made from the offcuts of whatever they'd used to create the doors, but, boy, does this thing have presence.

Nothing I've driven says, 'Pay attention to what I have to say,' more than this. You roll up in one to a meeting and you're going to get your way. It is the meanest, baddest-looking son of a bitch the world has seen.

And who cares if it does only 6mph? That's all it will ever need to do, going past the adoring crowds from the airport to the global conference. This is something built for you to get out of. Theresa May has a Jaguar. Angela Merkel has a Mercedes. Emmanuel Macron has to get out of the back of a Renault Clio.

And all of them will look feeble when Xi steps out of his Hongqi. It's a symbol that China will take over the world. Which it will.

12 August 2018

The northern lights at your fingertips

Mercedes A-class

It's often said that the Germans don't have a sense of humour. But that's obviously not true, because Mercedes has launched a 1.3-litre Volkswagen Golf-sized hatchback that has a hilarious price tag — at least in the version I drove — in excess of £30,000. Oh, and here's the punchline: it's possible you are going to want one . . .

I've never really understood why luxurious and beautifully appointed interiors are fitted to large cars only. Who says that people who want soft leather and thick carpets must also need 16 feet of legroom in the back and enough boot space to hold all of Joan Collins's hats?

Most of the time, big cars are annoying. You spend ages looking for a parking space and then, when you find one that would easily accommodate a Vauxhall, you are forced to hold up the traffic while you make a fool of yourself. And then you are forced to move on. Big cars just mean you have a longer walk to the theatre.

Then there's the issue of width restrictions. In a small car you just whizz through them without thinking, but in a big car you can only get through by squeezing your eyes and tucking your elbows into your ribcage. And even then a minor misjudgment will put a ding in one of the alloys and remove a door mirror. The only real solution is to take the long way round, which means you will miss the first act.

There's more. A big car will be heavy, which means it will be less fun to drive than a small car. And it will chew fuel, which means you will spend more of your life in a petrol station rather than at home with your children. And because of your absence they will grow up to be moped thieves or glue-sniffers.

The obvious solution, if you don't want your children to end up with boils on their noses, is to buy a small car. But if you do that you get nasty leather, a droning engine and plastic door pockets that cause your house keys and phone to make a scraping noise when you go round a corner.

Which brings us back to where we started. Why doesn't someone make a small car that has big-car luxury?

Renault tried it in the past with a version of the 5 called the Monaco. It had a bigger than necessary engine that was tuned for refinement rather than speed and an interior dominated by extremely squishy seats that were upholstered in surprisingly fine leather. It should have been a runaway success, that car, but I think the total number sold in Britain was about none.

That is because behind the luxury touches it was still a 1980s horror bag. So it broke down a lot, went rusty and wouldn't start when it was hot.

Happily, none of those things will affect the new Mercedes A-class, which is very obviously trying to pull off the same trick as the Monaco. As a result, you step inside the A 200 AMG Line version that I tested and immediately you will get out and say to the salesman or salesman woman: 'I have got to have one.'

Yes, my car had a few extras, but, God almighty, it's a nice place to sit. There's a slab of what looks like zinc on the dash, and the five circular air vents closely resemble the back end of the engines on a Lockheed SR-71 Blackbird. And get this. When they're blowing cold air they glow blue, and when it's warm they glow red.

Then there's the lighting everywhere else. You can add an option that lets you choose from literally every colour known to science, and then, when you can't make up your mind what colour you want where, you just put the system on auto and it softly changes as you drive along. It's like being in the aurora borealis and I absolutely loved it.

Then there were the two glass screens, one for the navigation system and the stereo and so on, and one for the dials, and this could also be changed to suit your mood. I spent 85 per cent of my time doing that and only 15 per cent looking where I was going.

It's strange. We cannot drive while talking on the phone or while playing with a passenger, because such things are deemed to be distracting. Yet we are allowed to drive while sitting in front of what feels like the lighting desk at a Pink Floyd gig.

I suppose at this point I should flag up that, technically, the car's not that small. It's a damn sight bigger than, say, the original A-class. That was designed, I'm told, as an electric car and had two floors so the cavity between could be used to store batteries. Eventually, however, Mercedes decided to abandon the idea of developing its own volt-mobile and invest in Tesla instead, hoping that one day the owner would go mad and Mercedes would get all his development work for nothing.

It then sold the A-class as a normal-engined car that had two floors 'for safety reasons'. Which all went wrong when it fell over during a test that simulated a driver swerving to avoid hitting an elk.

I'm digressing. The A-class has become bigger and bigger over the years, and the new model is almost the same size as a Honda Civic. Still pretty small for a Merc but big enough to handle a family of five.

Which is why that 1.3-litre engine is a surprise. A 1.3-litre unit was fine in an Austin, but in a car weighing more than 1.3 tons it sounds a bit feeble. And it is, if I'm honest. Yes, it has a turbo, and, yes, it can get the car from 0 to 62mph in eight seconds, but it sounds all the time as if it's really working for a living. And it's fixed to a seven-speed gearbox that never knows what gear's best. Progress, then, is often loud and jerky. Not that you notice, because you're too busy making the speedometer go green.

To drive? Well, the base cars have a Homebase torsion beam rear suspension, which has Mercedes purists running around waving their arms in the air. But I can't see why. It's not as if the 1.3-litre engine is going to cause any issues back there.

My car had a multilink setup, and I know I'm supposed to say that this was a good thing, but when you're sitting in the aurora borealis it's hard to pay attention to rear-end bump absorption. All I will say is that, like all modern vehicles, it's too firm. Actually, in this car – one that's going to be sold to people who care more about lighting than handling – it's way too firm.

So as a car it's no good, really. The engine, gearbox, ride comfort and price tag are all wrong. But I will quite understand if you decide you absolutely must have one, because what you get is all the sleek modern grace of a double-fronted riverside penthouse, in a shoebox.

16 September 2018

Truly lovely – until you start the engine

Volvo V60

When the army was fully engaged in the Iraq War, British soldiers at the Basra airbase who needed a new gun, or a replacement axle for a Snatch Land Rover, had to queue up at a window in the stores warehouse. It was known as 'the window of no'. This is because everything you wanted was never in stock. It was the military equivalent of Monty Python's cheese shop. Except for one thing . . .

When I visited the base, there was a mortar attack, and I was actually ushered past the window of no and into the building itself, where I discovered that while there were no guns or bullets or spare helicopter engines, there were 6,000 pairs of chef's trousers.

This is because the army is fundamentally a government operation, and everything run by the government doesn't work. The NHS is a mess. The police can't catch burglars. And we give foreign aid to countries that are richer than we are.

I sit here listening to the Brexit options and I find it hilarious, because the people attempting to reach a deal left university and thought: 'I'd like to work for the government.' Nobody with a shred of ambition or drive or common sense would say that.

Which brings me neatly to the debate on clean air. Back in 2001, a bunch of hand-wringing bicycle lobbyists got into the corridors of inactivity and managed to convince the powers-that-were that petrol was evil. As a result, Gordon Brown, who was busy selling off the country's gold at rock-bottom prices, immediately adjusted the tax rates to make diesel-powered cars more financially attractive.

Then, a decade and a half later, another bunch of hand-wringing bicycle lobbyists got into the corridors of inactivity and managed to convince those in charge that diesel was killing pensioners and everyone should use petrol-powered cars instead. And guess what. The wide-eyed, job-wary, vote-hungry, clueless imbeciles agreed.

So now all the people who bought diesels thinking they were doing the polar bear a favour have been told they must pay more company car tax and vehicle excise duty, plus, if they have an older diesel model, a surcharge of £10 a day to drive in London.

This has been going on for donkey's years. Actually, since my donkeys all die when they're eight, it's been going on for even longer than donkey's years. Margaret Thatcher's government – though not Madge herself, who preferred lean-burn technology – insisted catalytic converters be fitted to petrol cars to clean up emissions, even though a 'cat' increases the amount of carbon dioxide coming out of the tailpipe.

Then John Prescott went on a diving holiday in the Maldives and reckoned that coral was being killed by the excess carbon dioxide, and that's why Brown instigated the shift to diesel, which, we are now told, causes old ladies in the north to have breathing difficulties.

This means that Land Rover is in all sorts of trouble, because no one in their right mind would buy a petrol-powered Range Rover. And everyone thinks – wrongly – that they will be worse off if they buy one with a diesel engine.

Yes, the taxes are high and persecution of diesel enthusiasts will undoubtedly reach a point where police patrol officers will be entitled to murder anyone found to be one, but for the foreseeable future you're financially better off using a more economical diesel in a big 4x4 than a petrol-powered V8 or V6.

And if you actually think about it, they can't ever outlaw diesel or go completely berserk with the tax issues, because it's what's used by lorries and their precious buses.

I'll therefore stick my neck out and say that this diesel debate will soon quieten down before some more hand-wringing bicycle lobbyists get into the corridors of power and cause the government to change its mind again.

I bet Volvo has its fingers crossed on that one too, because as recently as three years ago it was selling practically no petrol-powered cars in Britain.

To make life doubly difficult for the Sino-Swedes, their diesel engines have never been any good. And the 187bhp 2-litre turbo unit in the Volvo V60 D4 Momentum Pro I tested recently is no exception. It is a dismal power plant: as rattly and as noisy and gutless as an Indonesian freighter that's being chased by a pirate skiff off the coast of Somalia.

Sure, Volvo says it'll do more than 60mpg, which is pretty good for a car of this size. It'll save you lots of money. But so would never going out at night. And who wants to do that? Actually, scrub that. Lots of Volvo drivers never go out at night. Nothing says your sex life has died more than a Volvo in the driveway.

There's another issue I have with the V60. Volvos are billed, in my view correctly, as the safest cars on the road. The company boasted two years ago that by 2020 no one should die in one of its cars. And figures show that, in the sixteen years since it was launched, no one has died here in an XC90 in a collision with another car.

However, in the V60 a lot of the really clever tech that's used to help avoid an accident in the first place is an optional extra. You want cross-traffic alert systems and rear-collision mitigation and a blind-spot information system and so on? Well, the package into which that lot is bundled is going to cost you an extra £1,625. This is a bit like Coca-Cola charging extra for the bubbles.

There are lots of things, in fact, that are not provided as standard. Powered rear-door child locks, metallic paint, fully electrically adjusted passenger seats, tinted windows – and even a spare wheel. So, yes, while the model starts at £31,810, the actual cost of my test car was an eye-watering £45,390. This is known to economists as 'a lot'.

Of course, it may be possible you don't mind paying a stupidly high price for a noisy, gutless car that runs on a currently unfashionable fuel, in which case you'll be interested in the upsides.

There are a few. It's a handsome thing, and it's a truly lovely place to sit. No one, apart from Rolls-Royce, makes better interiors these days. Oh, and it's extremely spacious. The boot is massive. Plus, if you buy a Volvo, you are helping to fund all those excellent dramas on Sky Atlantic. Or 'Atlontic', as the voiceover man says in his Swedish drawl.

I'm not sure, however, that this is enough to offset the drawbacks, especially as my test car also came with a rattle. You could drown it out by driving at more than 17mph or by turning up the excellent Harman Kardon stereo. But that was an £825 option.

All things considered, then, you're better off with a Beemer.

7 October 2018

Ever so clever, but it's not actually a car

Audi Q8

The Audi Q8 is also an Audi Q7, a Porsche Cayenne, a Volkswagen Touareg, a Bentley Bentayga and a Lamborghini Urus. They're all, despite the different styling and the wildly different price tags, the same car, from the same company.

But they all have different jobs. The Bentley is perfect for those who are impervious to its looks and the Lamborghini works well if you are the sort of person who wraps his car in purple velvet and goes to nightclubs full of Ukrainians.

The Porsche is for people who like to use fuel unnecessarily, the Q7 is for those who know nothing about cars and the Volkswagen is for ... actually, I have no idea who it's for. Not anyone I've ever met, that's for sure.

You may say you like the made-in-Germany stamp but, I'm sorry, it, along with the Porsche and the Q7, is assembled in Bratislava in Slovakia. The Lambo is made in Sant'Agata Bolognese in Italy and the Bentley in Crewe. They're all German cars, then, but none of them was born there.

So what of the new Q8? What's that all about? Well, it has a sloping rear end and pillarless doors and big, fat tyres, so it seems to be for people who want the purple velvet and the Ukrainians but don't quite have the funds or the balls to go fully Lambo.

This means it's a rival for the terrible BMW X6, and that

means it's for people who are mad. There are a lot of them out there, it seems. In the past ten years BMW has shifted almost half a million X6s around the world. And plainly Audi wants a slice of that action.

The car I tested sported a badge that said 50, suggesting it had a 5-litre engine – something along the lines of the big V10 VW used to put in the Toerag. But further investigation revealed this to be wrong: in fact it had a 3-litre V6 diesel unit assisted by an electric motor that together produce an unpredictable amount of power.

Put your foot down to pick up speed slightly and nothing would happen. So you'd press the accelerator a bit more and still the car would fail to respond. This is because its brain has been tuned to think only of the polar bear. Going faster would melt the tiny iceberg on which the poor creature was living. And that would be bad.

Unaware of this code in the software, you push the accelerator harder and then harder still until the brain thinks, 'Uh-oh. There's obviously an emergency,' so it drops from seventh to second and sets off like a fat man running to catch a bus. It is almost impossible to make the Q8 increase speed by 3mph. It either doesn't accelerate at all or it goes berserk.

This is basically a VW engine, and after a week of extremely jerky progress I was convinced that, instead of adhering to the EU's rules about polar bears, it'd probably be better for all concerned if the company just cheated in some way.

I'm sure it could manage this because the Q8 – in the heavily options-ladened version I tested – has a device that gently vibrates the accelerator when you should be lifting off the gas for an upcoming roundabout or junction. Incredibly, the car is reading the road ahead on its own satnav and then working out when you can lift off and coast to a halt at precisely the right spot.

It is extremely clever, this, and it works. But it's a bit like having a computer keyboard that gives you a small electric shock every time you forget to use a comma. Or if it thinks your metaphor is a bit clunky. Ow. Sorry, I meant simile.

There's more cleverness. The car is able to steer itself by following the white lines, but after a few moments the driver is told to regain control. Nothing unusual in that. Lots of cars can pull off a similar trick. But in the Audi, if you don't regain control when told to do so, it will brake the car to a gentle halt and then call the emergency services, assuming you've had a medical issue of some kind. George Michael would have liked this feature a lot.

I, however, preferred the CGI system that provides a live feed of your progress down the road. It's as though a camera is mounted in a balloon hovering 20 feet above the roof and, again, it's not unusual. Mercedes offers something similar. But in the Audi you can slide your finger over the screen to adjust the camera angle. You can have the balloon behind you, or in front, or anywhere you want.

There is absolutely no purpose to this. It's just something you do while turning round and excitedly telling people in the back what you're up to, safe in the knowledge that if a junction's coming up, the throttle pedal will issue a warning by vibrating your foot.

Now, as I said, all of this stuff is fantastically clever. Some of it is even useful, and a tiny bit will keep you safe, and none of it was ever on *Tomorrow's World*. But after a week with the Q8 I'm forced to conclude that somehow Audi has lost sight of what a car is for. There has to be some excitement. Because if there isn't any joy in driving, then people will conclude that Uber offers a better service and no one will buy a car at all.

All of this mad computer stuff is like the unnecessary features you get on a central-heating control unit. I've been in my office for three years now and still have no idea how to make it warm or cold. I stab away at the buttons and see lots of symbols and sub-menus yet the temperature never changes.

It doesn't change in the Audi either. You're always tepid because despite the all-wheel-drive system and the four-wheel steering and the driving mode that lets you choose how the steering and the air suspension 'feel', it never ever causes your heart to beat a little bit more quickly. It's a transportation device. Not a car.

And it is just about impossible to drive quickly. If you put the gearbox in manual mode and select the Dynamic setting for everything, it responds by being a tiny bit less slovenly. But that's it.

I've never really liked any of Audi's Q cars. The Q5 epitomises everything I despise about SUVs, and while the SQ7 was quite interesting from an engineering angle, it is pointless. So is the Q8. It's nowhere near as much fun to drive as its looks would suggest, and because of those looks it's not as spacious inside as it could be.

Oh, and here's the clincher. Even without all those options added, the car I tested had a price tag of £65,040. And who's going to pay that when they could have a similar VW Toerag for about £16,000 less? Like I said. Only someone who's mad.

21 October 2018

A bright spark with absolutely no point

Hyundai Kona Electric

At some point everyone has faced that moment when they know the day ahead is going to be fraught with misery, angst and swearing. They know that something has gone wrong with their laptop and that after flailing around in parts of the menu reserved only for people with body odour, they are going to have to spend the next few hours on the phone to someone who uses acronyms instead of speech.

'Where does it say Tools?' you plead. 'There is no Tools in the Options list and, no, I don't know what a bar is in this context, or rich text, or plain text, or HTML. All I know is when I send an attachment, it arrives at the other end as a file marked "winmail.dat" and that no one can open it.'

All of us have spent a morning with our arses in the air, turning the wi-fi router on and off and trying to get the bloody phone to work, and all of us at some point have wondered, out loud, if life wouldn't be better if we went back to typewriters and postmen.

And that's just so we can keep up to speed with what the lefties are saying on Twitter and how well our friends' dogs are doing on Instagram. Imagine, however, what life will be like when we face similar problems every time we want to pop to the shops for a pint of milk.

The electric car is coming. Be in no doubt about that. We've had Teslas for the past ten years and in the next two just about every mainstream manufacturer will jump on the bandwagon. Saying it won't happen is not even worthy of a metaphor. It will.

I recently borrowed an electric Hyundai Kona, which the company will not be selling in Portugal any time soon. Not with a name like that. But what about here? If you're thinking of going pure electric, is this the sort of thing you should be looking at?

Well, let's get to the problem straight away. There simply aren't enough charging points. Jaguar asked the government about this before it began work on the electric I-Pace and was told that by the time the car emerged this year, everything would have been sorted out. It hasn't. And if more people start buying electric cars, things will get worse long before they get better.

The Hyundai arrived with no cable that allowed it to be plugged into a simple domestic socket. I'm not surprised. I know someone who did that and his home caught fire. Also, the charging time from a simple domestic circuit is measurable in weeks.

Instead, I was given a cable that allowed me to plug it into one of the charging stations you see in supermarket car parks and motorway service stations. Frankly, though, I didn't think I'd need it. I mean, the Kona has a range, Hyundai says, of up to 300 miles and I was planning a round trip of barely half that.

However, the range-ometer in an electric car is a weird and speculative thing, so after I'd done a bit of pottering about in London and driven to Chipping Norton in Oxfordshire, it said there was only 130 miles left. That should have been enough to get back. But what if the motorway was closed by the Wombles? This is known as range anxiety. It's a thing with our friends electric.

I didn't want to take the risk so went to the nearby Soho Farmhouse, where six charging points are provided. One was broken and one of the spaces was occupied by a black Bentley Bentayga with a personalized registration that I won't tell you to save the owner embarrassment. In Portugal the man who left it there might be called a Kona.

Eventually, though, I was having some lunch, knowing that the batteries were being topped up nicely, which of course they weren't. An hour later, only 17 miles had been added, so I carried on with lunch until I was too drunk to drive the car anyway.

Eventually I found someone to take me home in it, and then asked him to pop to the supermarket, where the batteries could be fully charged up. He plugged it into the port, which said he must download an app that would let him pay for the electricity he used.

And this is where things go into meltdown. The app wouldn't acknowledge the existence of the charging point. And neither would anyone on the number provided. So he had to waste all the power gleaned from the Soho Farmhouse looking for an alternative.

Unfortunately, the cable would not release from the charging point, or the car. Apparently, this is so ragamuffins can't unplug your car for a laugh. Only you can do that with your app. But the app wouldn't work. He called the emergency number again to say the car was firmly tethered to the port and was told to wait with it until a maintenance team arrived. But that this wouldn't happen until the next day as the team didn't work weekends.

This is far from a unique experience. Last month we read about an author called Isabel Hardman who arrived at a literary festival late because none of the chargers on her route were working. James May went home last night in his electric BMW i3 and I notice today he's not at work.

The upshot of all this is that you cannot buy an electric car at the moment. Well, you can, but it will be very expensive – even with the government's £4,500 plug-in grant, which drops to £3,500 next month – and you won't be able to go anywhere in it, not with any certainty. Electric car fans boast on forums they've covered 500 miles in a day in their Nissan Leaf as if this is incredible. But I once drove from London to Oslo in a day – more than 1,000 miles.

One day, if charging points are as reliable and as common as petrol pumps, and top-up times have come down to minutes rather than hours, then you can make the plunge. But now? No. You'd be mad.

And that's a shame, because the Kona is an extremely likeable little car. It is completely incapable of putting its 291lb/ft of torque on to the road, which means every time you stand on the throttle, it torque-steers like a 1980s Saab Turbo. This is hilarious.

It is also bloody fast. It's not the 0 to 62mph time that impresses, or its top speed; it's the immediacy with which it takes off. One minute you're doing 40mph and then you're doing 400mph. And the steering wheel has been wrenched from your grip and you're in hysterics. And a ditch.

It's good-looking too, and for an electric car in which every joule is precious, it's very well equipped. My test car even had a heated steering wheel. You'd need a very long lunch to charge that up.

It's not quiet, though. This is because about 85 per cent of the noise it makes on the motorway comes from its tyres. And you notice it more in an electric car because you sense much of the sound-deadening has been removed to offset the weight of the batteries.

It's not horrific, however. Nothing about the Kona is. In fact, I loved a lot of it very much. It's practical, far too powerful, spacious, nicely finished, well specced and handsome. Plus, you don't have to give that halfwit Sadiq Khan any money when you drive into central London.

This, then, is a car that can run. But unfortunately this country hasn't learnt to walk yet. So like all electric cars at the moment, it's completely and utterly useless.

28 October 2018

So bouncy I daren't break the speed limit

Abarth 695 Rivale convertible

When you first clap eyes on an Abarth 695 Rivale convertible, you'll immediately think: 'Well, I've certainly got to have one of those.' It doesn't matter whether you earn a living delivering rockets to the launchpad in Kazakhstan or soil to garden centres in north Wales, you will be so consumed by its looks, you'll spend all night convincing yourself that it's just the job.

At three in the morning you'll sneak downstairs to see how much it costs, and when you learn that prices for the hatchback start at £23,380, you'll be on the phone to a dealer by eight.

I get all that. When my test car was delivered, I hadn't even climbed inside before I was thinking of exactly why I needed a small Italian runaround in my life.

You know those watches you see when you're a bit bored in an airport departure lounge? You already have a watch. It was a present, so it carries some emotional value. And it works well. So you don't need a new one. Definitely. 'But could I just have a look at it?'

So out it comes, and then you notice the price and it's far too much. You'd be better off using the money to buy a dog for a blind person, or a lifeboat. But you just like it. So you want it. And you'll probably buy it.

The 695 Rivale is like that. Painted in a nautical mix of

dark blue and metallic grey, it's supposed to pay homage to the Riva boats we all covet so much. That's why the interior has the option of a mahogany pack, to give you a sense that you're ferrying Claudia Cardinale from Le Club 55 in St Tropez to her yacht on an Aquarama.

All very clever, but if you're going to create a homage to a Riva, why call it a Rivale? That's like Aston Martin doing a special edition called a Sunseekle.

More understandable is the scorpion badge. Abarth is to Fiat, its owner, what AMG is to Mercedes. It's the skunkworks that adds the chillis. So this car looks like a Riva and goes like a scalded cock.

But you won't be thinking about any of that, because you'll have noticed that, at the touch of a button, the whole roof and the back window folds away to create what is very nearly a proper convertible. And that'll be the clincher. Even if it were called Il Duce, as a homage to Mussolini, resistance would be futile. You'll buy one.

And it'll be a terrible mistake, because, ooh, this is a horrible car. The first problem is that it's actually a Fiat 500. And that was quite cute when it was introduced to Edward VII. But the cuteness has been somewhat undermined by the knowledge that its underpinnings were also used to make the Lancia Ypsilon, the Ford Ka and the Fiat Panda.

I sometimes think that if you peeled away the body from an Iveco lorry, there'd be a Fiat 500 chassis under there.

Then there's the Fiat 124 Spider. Lovely car. Captures the spirit of Rome in the 1960s. But is, underneath, a Mazda.

You probably think that I'm being obtuse and that nothing can detract from the buzzy charm of the little 500 and especially its titchy and charismatic 2-cylinder engine.

Yeah, well, sorry to relieve myself all over your retro

bonfire, but that 2-cylinder engine was dropped a while ago because it didn't really work.

The problem was that it had been billed as a brilliant way of saving fuel – but it didn't. Not really. It didn't matter where you drove it, or how slowly: it always returned 39mpg, which in a little car such as the 500 wasn't good enough.

Today the 500 uses a 4-cylinder engine, and the 695, which is also a 500, obviously, is no exception.

It's a 1.4-litre T-jet Abarth unit, which produces a fabulous noise from its carbon-tipped exhaust system and 177 brake horsepower. That's quite a lot. It means that you'll get from 0 to 62mph in less than seven seconds and that flat-out you'll be doing about 75mph.

Abarth says it will do 140mph, but I'd like to meet the man who achieved this, because he must have testicles like solar systems. Yes, the car is fitted with big-name Koni suspension, but I found the whole thing so bouncy and frightening that I didn't dare break the motorway speed limit at all.

There's another problem. Because the metal roof is gone, there's only a strip of canvas holding the body together, and it's not enough.

In the olden days convertible cars such as the Saab 900 and the Ford Escort XR3i had what's known as scuttle shake, but modern technology means it's no longer an issue. Except in the Abarth, where it is. It genuinely feels as if the car's not connected up.

None of this will be apparent in town, so if that's what you want the car for, fine. However, there's one problem that will be an issue everywhere. The seating.

The seats look lovely and are richly upholstered in fine leather. Unfortunately, however, they offer the support and comfort of milking stools.

I know that Italians do not suffer from obesity to anything like the degree that we do in Britain, but even a size-zero clothes horse in Milan would struggle to get both her buttocks on to the squab at the same time. If you're fat, it would be like sitting on a washing line.

To recap, then, the 695 convertible is wobbly at speed, and bouncy and hard to drive unless you're used to wearing a thong. Also, when I went out one night with a male friend, we had to get the roof down and play George Michael loud on the stereo, because why fight it? It's what everyone assumes anyway.

I really didn't like this car. The company can do better, and did with the Fiat Strada Abarth back in the 1980s. That remains one of my favourite hot hatches. And what was Riva thinking of?

I met Carlo Riva once. He told me how, when he was penniless, he conned Chrysler into giving him engines for his boats, and how quality meant everything.

The Aquarama was the result of his fastidiousness, and I maintain that it's up there as just about the best-looking manmade thing ever.

I saw one once, early in the morning, coming out of the mist on Lake Iseo in Lombardy, and it was like watching the birth of a butterfly. Only with a twin V8 soundtrack.

Carlo, who died last year, used to ban fibreglass boats from marinas he ran, saying nobody should have a boat made from the material used for lavatory seats, and he sold a Riva to Gianni Agnelli, the former head of Fiat, by saying that if he could turn it over, he could have it.

And now, in 2018, Riva's name is being used as a rubbish marketing tool.

I mean it. That's what this car is. A tool. And it's what you'll look like if you drive one.

Unless you really are an Italian actress and you live in Portofino. But you aren't and you don't.

11 November 2018

Forty-nine shades of grey and one glorious red

Mazda6 Tourer

When I was growing up, everything was in black and white – the weather, the moon landings, my photo album, policemen, my television and everything on it – apart from the things that were all black, such as the Houses of Parliament and everyone's lungs.

But on the road things were different. It was a rainbow nation. Your Ford Cortina was orange or green, and your neighbour's Hillman Minx was scarlet. Your office car park was more bright and vivid than a Jimi Hendrix album cover, and Arthur Daley was tooling around in a yellow Jaguar – OK, strictly speaking, it was a Daimler Sovereign – and no one buys a yellow Jag these days. No one buys anything yellow.

I don't know when this happened, but we have arrived at a point where the only colour anyone chooses for their car is grey. If you look at the online configurator for the Range Rover, you will see that many colours are on offer but all of them aren't actually colours at all. There's Carpathian Grey, Bosphorus Grey, Windward Grey, Scafell Grey, Corris Grey and Byron Blue. Which is grey, really.

And it's not just Range Rovers. In Paris or Rome almost every single car is grey, and London is going the same way. Except in August, when the Saudis arrive.

It may have something to do with a perceived notion that

a coloured car is harder to sell. People have an opinion about lemon-zest yellow in a way they don't about grey.

Certainly this is true with interior decoration. You know you could have purple carpets and green walls and coloured glass panels in the chimney breast. You know you could paint your window surrounds magenta and your chimney pots lime green. But you fear that, if you needed to sell, potential buyers would be more interested in your neighbour's house, which is Cotswold Green and Skidmark Brown.

All of which brings me on to the Mazda6 Tourer. As you'd expect, it's available in white, black, grey, grey, grey, grey and grey. And in any of those non-colours I wouldn't have bothered organizing a road test. It'd just be 15.5 feet or so of car, and I'd conclude you'd be better off using Uber. However, it is also available in Soul Red Crystal, and this is the best colour I've seen on any car.

I'm not a fan of red cars, as a general rule. My Range Rover is grey, for example, as was the Volkswagen Golf GTI that preceded it. And the Lamborghini Gallardo before that. I think that having a red car marks you out as weird: it's like having a moustache. You're hiding something.

But Soul Red Crystal is mesmerizing. And because Mazda has been extraordinarily skilful with its use of chrome, this simply does not look like a humdrum family estate. You arrive in it and you feel special.

But what about the bit before you arrive? The journey? Well, the version I tested was the top-of-the-range 2.5-litre GT Sport Nav+. I'm not sure why Nav is part of its name. Nav is just something it has, and I thought that sort of thing was the preserve of Volvo, which used to fit cars with badges saying '5 speed' or 'Lambda sensor'.

Anyway, the Mazda does indeed have a satnav and a

million other things besides: a 360-degree camera, a little light on the dashboard that suggests a cup of coffee when you're tired and ventilated seats. You'd struggle to find anything in a Mercedes S-class you don't get in a Mazda6. Except perhaps headroom.

Getting through the door does require a bit of human origami, but once you're there, all is well. Very well in fact. Mazda has been as skilful with materials on the inside as with the chrome on the outside, so that you really do feel as if you're in a Fabergé egg. Truly, there's no way you'd guess that the car I was driving cost only £31,695. It feels like bloody good value.

To drive? Well, it's unlucky. I was sitting in it, outside a shop, when an elderly gentleman drove into the back of it. He then decided to attempt a reverse-parallel-parking manoeuvre and drove into it again. Other than that, though, it's fine.

Mazda introduced the 2.5-litre engine fairly recently, and it's easy to see why. It figures that, with diesel on the way out, it needs to offer customers as many petrol-unit choices as possible. But it may have gone too far with this one. It's not a bad engine, by any means, but the fact is you get nearly all of the oomph without the fuel-consumption hit from the 2-litre version.

That's possibly the most sensible thing I've said in a road test, but it's what happens to you in a car such as this. You feel like your dad. I have a Mazda6 and now I'm going to join a crown green bowling club. Then I shall buy a pipe and worry about fuel economy.

The fact is that the Mazda and its chief rivals – the Ford Mondeo and the VW Passat – are seen as worthy and dull. People would far rather buy an SUV of some sort.

The figures bear this out. In the past ten years SUV sales have risen in the UK from 161,000 annually to at least 817,000 last year. That's a fivefold increase. Meanwhile, the sales of four-door saloons have plummeted from a 15 per cent market share in 1999 to a miserable 6 per cent, according to data published in 2017.

And of that 6 per cent, BMW had 22.8 per cent, Audi had 17.9 per cent and Jaguar had 13.4 per cent. The Mondeo? The big boy? Well, the number actually sold last year to private buyers for cash was measurable in the hundreds.

Nobody wants a four-door saloon with a low-rent badge on the back. Not even if it's a five-door estate version. Not even if it looks nice, has tons of standard equipment, costs just £31,695 and shares its name with a lightbulb.

But I'm willing to bet that when you see the Soul Red Crystal paintwork, you'll be sorely tempted. However, here's the thing. That colour is an £800 option, which brings me on to an idea I've had . . .

The other day I bought an Alfa Romeo GTV6. It's a one-owner, low-mileage gem that is let down by just one thing. It's red. I'd already decided I was going to spray it another colour but couldn't choose between black and silver. Well, my mind is made up now: it's still going to be red. But it's going to be Soul Red Crystal.

You should do the same. Buy any car you like and then pay Mazda to make it the right colour. Because in the modern age that's the only bit you'd really want from the Mazda6, a likeable but otherwise quite grey car.

25 November 2018

A bit on the dim side, but still a total belter

Aston Martin Vantage

The owners of a restaurant near where I live in the country-side have obviously decided that many of the rural customers may be so ugly, they wouldn't want to look at one another while eating. So they've fitted extremely low-level lighting.

It works well. You can make out the vague shape of your dining companion – enough to know it's a person rather than a dolphin or some kind of dog – but you can't see any of their warts or skin diseases. However, there are drawbacks. It's so dim in there, the only reason you don't crash into all the tables while you're searching for the lavatory is that most customers are using the torches on their iPhones to read the menu.

There's a hotel in Amsterdam with a similar problem. There's just enough light to pick out the reception desk but there isn't quite enough to pick out the footstool just in front of it. 'Every-one does that,' says the receptionist as you arrive, chin-first, on her cracked and blood-speckled keyboard. In my mind there's a time and a place for darkness. When you are star gazing, for instance, or trying to get to sleep. But at all other times I like to see what I'm doing and where I'm going, especially when I'm at the wheel of Aston Martin's latest Vantage.

Sadly, this is not possible because it's the first car I've driven with 'mood' headlamps. They provide exactly the right amount of light for a candlelit bath, or if you're at the cinema, but nowhere near enough if you are coming up to a tricky left-right switchback and it's November and it's raining and it's ten o'clock at night.

And God help you if something is coming the other way because on dipped beam they give off less light than the fourth star along in the Plough.

It's been a while since I moaned about poor headlamps. It's one of those things – like wipers lifting clear of the windscreen and wind noise from door mirrors – the car industry gets right these days. But something's gone awry with the Vantage because they are abysmal.

There's another issue too. The interior is nowhere near as horrible as it is in the DB11, or the DBS, for that matter, but there's no getting away from the fact that the Mercedes switchgear and display screen are from the generation before last. And the steering wheel is still squared off, like it was on the Austin Allegro.

And that's it. I have no more bad news. Because apart from the steering wheel, a satnav that says 'There be witches ahead' and lousy headlamps, this new Aston is as heartachingly desirable as a dark chocolate Bounty when you're queuing to pay for petrol at a motorway service station. You know you don't want it. You know you don't need it. But it's sitting there winking at you.

It's the looks mainly. Not since the mid-Sixties has there been an ugly Aston and this one, this makes you actually whinny like a happy horse. Unlike the old Vantage, which was a pretty little thing, this is really quite aggressive. And it's not little either. It's just over 3in longer and 3in wider than before.

You'd never think of an Aston in the same way you do a Porsche 911. Astons have always been about looks and Porsches about going round corners quickly. But there's something about the new Vantage that says that, behind the scenes, its meat and veg have been beefed up a bit.

The meat comes in the shape of a 4-litre twin-turbocharged 503bhp AMG V8 – Mercedes is a strategic partner these days – that sits almost laughably far back. You open the bonnet and then you have to peer under the dashboard to see it. You really can think of this then as a mid-engined car. Because it is. The advantage is a perfect distribution of weight between the front and rear axles and you can feel that – so long as it's not at night when all you can feel is your way. During the day, though, this new car feels so much more alive and dainty and responsive than the old one. It feels serious.

It even has a clutch-based active torque-vectoring electronic rear differential. Quite a thing for a car company that, in living memory, was making its vehicles using hammers. And quite a thing on the road too because it makes the back end ever so playful. This car is serious then. But also fun.

And God, it goes. There seems to be some debate about how much it weighs. Maybe Aston Martin keeps the scales in a darkened room but it doesn't really matter because when you mash the throttle into the carpet, you are suddenly a long way away.

If you are in the Track setting when you do the mashing, you'll be even further away and everyone within 300 yards will be staggering around in the street with blood pouring from their ears, as deaf as you are blind at night. In 'nutter bastard' mode this car is really, really loud and it's not the familiar AMG rumble either. It's just raw, naked noise. With added snaps of ballistic popping and banging from the exhaust.

For sheer excitement the Aston is a match for the Porsche 911. And it'll get you to your destination way faster because people like Astons. They let you out of junctions in a way that just doesn't happen when you're in a Porsche.

Happily, the Vantage is not an uncouth racer all the time. In normal mode, it bumbles along quite nicely and, praise be to the Lord, it isn't even all that crashy. When I first heard that Aston was going after Nürburgring lap times and Porsche's jugular, I thought it would make something uncompromising and hard. But it hasn't. On a long run, the Vantage is a proper GT car. Two seats. Useable boot. No undue stresses and strains.

I thought this was a tremendous car. But I wonder if it isn't a bit too tremendous.

At the time of writing, Aston Martin's recent stock market float is not proving to be a great triumph. The company may be enjoying one of its most successful periods in terms of sales but the Gordon Gekkos and the Jordan Belforts seem to have a problem, and share prices are slipping.

Well, I don't understand Wall Street or the City but I do understand the world of motoring and, as I see it, the problem Aston has is that to the untrained eye, its cars are all quite similar.

To make matters worse, the most expensive model – the DBS Superleggera – is £225,000. And it doesn't feel that much better than the £157,900 DB11, which in turn doesn't feel that much better than a £120,900 Vantage.

So with the Vantage, Aston Martin has made a car that's not only better than any equivalent Porsche but also better, all things considered, than its own big brother. I'm no businessman but even I can see that's probably a mistake.

2 December 2018

A true Jag, but they forgot the engine

Jaguar i-Pace

A few years ago the people at Jaguar got it into their heads
that they wanted to part company with their rather caddish
customer base, with its gin and tonics and dodgy import-
export ventures. So Jaguar stopped making comfortable,
quiet and pretty cars and concentrated on small, shouty
sports saloons.

There must have been a reason for this. I mean, you don't
abandon an image built up over many careful years on a
whim. But whatever the reason was, it hasn't worked. Because
if someone wants a small, shouty sports saloon, they're going
to buy a BMW. And they do. The last time I looked, Jaguar
was selling about 40,000 XEs a year. While BMW was selling 100,000 more 3-series cars than that. In Europe alone.

The new Jags were lovely to drive – there's no getting
round that – but they felt and sounded wrong. Imagine going
into a McDonald's and finding linen tablecloths and a spot
of Pachelbel on the sound system. Nothing wrong with that,
but it's not what you were expecting.

In a Jag you want a wooden dashboard and soft leather
seats. You want to start the engine and then think: 'Wait a
minute. Is it broken?' That silence and smoothness is key. But
you want good looks as well. Cast your mind back to the series 3 XJ12 on pepper-pot alloys. That, for me, was peak Jag.

And now, I'm delighted to say, it's back in the shape of the i-Pace, which is very pretty and can be ordered with a wooden dashboard and squidgy leather seats. And then there's the best bit of all. It's quiet. Really quiet. This thing: it's a mouse tiptoeing over a bed of kapok, in carpet slippers.

The reason it's so quiet is that there's no engine and only one gear. And that's because the i-Pace is electric.

I wondered when this would happen. When you bought a car that suited all your needs – and it turned out to be electric. Rather than buying an electric car because you're a weirdo tree-hugger and then hoping it fitted your lifestyle.

I drove round London in the i-Pace for a few days and it was just so relaxing. It glided over potholes and speed humps and wafted down Park Lane like a swan. On a magic carpet.

Later I went out of town and found that on wet roads the four-wheel-drive grip was so leechy you end up looking like Snoopy, with both your eyes on one side of your face. On dry roads you have the confidence to put your foot down and, yup, it does that electric thing of accelerating so violently, your head feels as though it's coming away. Off the line the i-Pace is Ferrari fast. And then some.

Better than a Tesla? Yes. Definitely. The trouble with Tesla is that it's a small and new company that simply doesn't have the experience or the money to develop its cars as well as the big players. Teslas are fun and they're full of amusing features, but if you go online you'll find the message boards are full of people saying that in the rain so much water pools in the rear bumper panel that it falls off, or that in the snow the undertray gets clogged and eventually falls off as well.

If these observations are true, it demonstrates the point that Tesla doesn't do the cold-weather preproduction testing to anything like the same degree as Jaguar. Put simply, it's likely the Jag's door handles will still work when it's -10°C, whereas the Tesla's, by all accounts, don't.

The i-Pace, then, is a car you will want to buy, partly because it's pretty and comfortable and practical and sensible but mostly because the electric powertrain makes it feel so very Jaggish. And, oh, how I wish I could leave it there. But I can't.

It's claimed that the range of the Jag is almost 300 miles, and I'm sure, in a laboratory, with an electronic James May at the wheel, that's possible. But, as with car makers' fuel-usage figures, there's a big gap between what's possible and what's achievable.

I left London on a Friday afternoon with four passengers and a boot full of stuff. The range-ometer on the dash said I'd go 120 miles before a charge was necessary, and that, I figured, was easily enough to cover the 70 miles to my gaff in the country.

But as we barrelled up the M40, the readout started to tumble like the altimeter in a crashing airliner. I started to wonder if it was using a unit of distance known only to Jag's boffins. Because it sure as hell wasn't taking a mile to wipe another mile off the count.

And then there was a crash. Two cars. Six fire engines. The usual overreaction from the emergency services, and long queues. Down came the readout, and down and down, until by the time I got to Oxford there really was a danger it'd conk out before I got home.

And then we'd have to download an app and find our reading glasses and fathom out the instructions at the charging point and then sit about in the cold for 40 minutes while the battery drank from the tank of power. I was panicking about having to do that, so I put everything in Eco mode to help out.

I even turned on the system that garners battery power from braking, even though this makes the car nigh-on undriveable. Every time you lift your foot off the accelerator, it's as if you've driven into a pit of glue. But I had to put up with it because I didn't want to stop. This is a syndrome known as range anxiety. It's a thing you'll have to get used to.

By being careful I made it home with twenty-two units left on the clock. Having retrieved the cables from under the bonnet, where there is spookily no engine, I plugged the car into the power supply, and – pfff – all the lights went out. Yup. It had tripped the fuse box.

Very annoyed, I took it into town and plugged it into a friend's house, and the next morning, after eight hours of suckling from the grid, it had hoovered up enough electricity to go . . . drum roll . . . 29 miles. That's pathetic.

Now I know I could have taken it to a fast-charge point and sat while it was force-fed some joules, but I had friends staying and didn't want to waste a precious weekend off by pandering to the whim of a polar bear. So I didn't. Which meant that for the Sunday evening crawl back to London I used my old Range Rover.

Of course the Jag will work if you only commute between fast-charge points at your home and office. If that's your life, it's a great car and you should buy one immediately. If, however, you have relatives and friends who live far away, and you have rich and varied weekends, full of spontaneity and let's-go-to-the-seaside moments, it's still great. But you'll need another car as well.

9 December 2018

Crazy pantomime horsepower

Lamborghini Aventador S roadster

In the olden days nothing much happened in seven years. But now everything changes every few months: the food we eat, the way we communicate, the clothes we wear, the places we go on holiday and especially the cars we drive.

The Lamborghini Aventador is only seven years old. It was launched in 2011, and to me that feels like yesterday. But it wasn't yesterday. A point that's brought into sharp focus when the big bad Lambo tries to change gear.

In a modern car you don't really feel or hear gearchanges. The only sign that they've happened comes from the rev counter. But in the Aventador it's all very different. When it changes gear it's like you're in a butter churn that's tumbling down a hill.

All of a sudden, and with no warning, action is suspended while an electronic signalman buried deep in the software pulls one set of levers and then strolls across his electronic signal box to ram another set into place. You, meanwhile, are sitting in the driving seat wondering if something has broken.

Seven years ago the single-clutch flappy-paddle gearbox fitted to the Aventador was considered very futuristic, but since then the much smoother double-clutch system has been invented. And then discarded in favour of conventional slushmatic units that have been made to work just as well.

Today, then, the single-clutch system feels as old-fashioned as a television set that has no remote control.

There's more evidence of the Lambo's age too. The command centre screen is lifted direct from an Audi, which sounds good. But it was lifted from an Audi seven years ago. Which means it was designed maybe ten years ago, and so the satnav refers to Londinium and Persia and German West Africa, and instead of traffic reports you get warnings that ahead 'There be witches'.

Then there's the four-wheel-drive system. When it's cold, waking the front differential up is like trying to get a teenager out of bed. There's a lot of banging and thumping and bolshiness and a wilful refusal to do any sort of slow-speed manoeuvring.

The car I drove was the new S roadster, which comes with a roof that can be stowed under the bonnet. Sounds appealing, yes. But there are one or two problems, such as that there's no room there for anything else.

Worse, when it's in place, it is nearly impossible for someone of my size to get into the car. And things are even worse when you want to get out. I had to push my legs down into the footwell and then twist my arse into the passenger's face before emerging from the tiny gap head first. This meant putting my arms on the pavement for balance and then pulling myself on to my hands and knees. It's not a dignified look, if I'm honest.

Oh, and when it's raining and you crack the window for whatever reason, a great deal of water gets into the cabin, which makes everything damp, which means that the windscreen is permanently steamed up. Before setting off, you need to spend at least ten minutes sitting there with the fan on.

Eventually there's a hole big enough to see through, so

with a lot of banging and juddering from the teenage front diff, you judder out of the parking space and into the traffic. And then you wait while the gearbox rummages around looking for second, and then you're at a roundabout and you cannot see what's coming because there's not enough head-room to turn your head.

And your knee has turned off the indicators by accident. And then you go straight through a red light because one of the things you can't do when you're sitting that far from the windscreen is look up. It's like driving a postbox.

Soon I was on the motorway, where it was bucketing down. And everyone in every other car was coming along-side for a gawp, and I didn't dare accelerate because this is a car that does 0-62mph in three seconds. It's a car that does 217mph. This is not the sort of power you want to be mess-ing with when there's standing water everywhere and your other knee has just turned off the wipers.

Then the satnav screen started to flicker. No idea why. But luckily my passenger used to own an Audi in the 1970s, so she knew how to turn it off. And then we were on normal roads, and the headlights, on dipped beam, weren't good enough. I don't normally get tense in a car, but on that mis-erable November night, in that mad old dog of a car, I was nervous as hell.

And the next day it was worse, because it was -3°C and the only way round the Oxford traffic was on country lanes that weren't big enough for a car that's almost the width of a Range Rover. Which is why I left the Lambo where it was and used something else.

I haven't driven such a terrible car for years, and yet, if I had the choice of any supercar, this would be it. Because I absolutely love it.

Here's why. The modern crop of mid-engined road rockets can potter about town like hatchbacks, and when you're on the track, they're easy to hustle. Make no mistake: the McLaren Senna is a sensation and the Lamborghini Huracán Performante is even better. I don't like Ferrari very much as an entity these days – it's way too up itself – but I'll admit the 488 GTB is sublime as well.

But it's like a work of great literary merit. It's one of those plays where you are expected to stroke your chin throughout and discuss it afterwards with people in sensible clothes. And that is not, in my book, the role of a supercar.

That's why I love the Aventador. It's pantomime. You go along, it throws sweets at your head, someone yells, 'It's behind you!' and then afterwards you take your kids out for a pizza.

You're not supposed to use a supercar every day, so what does it matter if it's useless at commuting or if water comes in every time it rains or if the gearbox is rubbish in traffic? These are cars you take out on special occasions, and I'm sorry but nothing tops off the moment quite as well as an Aventador. It may not be the fastest at a track, and it's certainly not the easiest, but who cares when it has that styling? This is probably the best-looking car yet made. Nah. Forget the probably.

Yes, Lamborghini will talk at length about its four-wheel steering and its carbon-fibre this and that, but when all is said and done, you can push a button that lowers its back window. Why would you want to do that? Simple. So you can hear that V12 more clearly. Does that improve cornering speeds? No. Does it make you happy? Yes.

And there's another thing. No other mid-engined supercar has a V12 these days. They've all given in to the polar bear and gone for fewer cylinders and less capacity. Some even use hybrid drive systems or electricity only.

Lambo's chief technical officer does not want to do this. And when I asked him recently what would happen if he were forced to by his paymasters at Volkswagen, he thought for a second and said: 'I would shoot myself.'

16 December 2018

Readers, it was love at second sight

Ferrari GTC4Lusso T

I can't get the big Ferrari GTC4Lusso out of my head. It's driving me mad. I vowed nearly ten years ago I would never buy an exotic car again. I'd had a Ferrari and a Lamborghini and a Ford GT, and I'd been cured of the bug. They're called dream cars for a reason. Because they're too silly for the real world. Too noisy. Too ostentatious. Too impractical. And, well, let me put it this way. Things that have never been said to someone climbing out of a supercar include: 'Ah, welcome, professor.' And: 'Thank you for coming, Your Holiness.'

They are not cars for the bright or eminent. They are cars for the man who wants to demonstrate to his neighbours that his new carpet warehouse business is doing well. And that his next purchase will be a pair of stone lions for his drive.

And the GTC4Lusso has other problems. I reviewed it last year in the *Sunday Times* and said the four-wheel-drive setup was stupid, the V12 was unnecessary and the girth was laughable. Plus I know a man who had one and in four months he lost £50,000 on it.

Yet, despite all this, it continues to gnaw away at my soul, because I see myself using it to go to my boat in the south of France. I know this is stupid, because obviously I'd fly. Nobody likes sitting on a heavily policed motorway for ten hours, no matter what car they are using. Also, I don't have a boat.

I can't even dream sensibly about using a GTC4Lusso when I get to the south of France, because that tricky right-left through the arch by the harbour in Antibes – well, it wouldn't fit. I'd have to use park and ride. Eugh.

And yet and yet and yet . . . A Ferrari sports estate. A comfy four-seater. A quiet cruiser that barked and came alive when you poked it with a stick. And I knew if I was just a little bit patient there would be a two-wheel-drive V8 version.

Well, it is here now. And I do mean here. It's sitting outside my house. I'm looking at it. Well, some of it. To see all of it, you need to be 30 miles away.

No matter – it's here, and it's a departure from the norm. Usually customers can't choose what engine or drivetrain is fitted to a Ferrari. But with the GTC4Lusso you can. And be in no doubt: there's only one answer.

The T version of the car has a twin-turbo V8 that produces 602bhp, which is 78bhp less than the V12. But because the T is lighter, they have virtually identical performance. Yes, the V12 sounds a bit nicer at the very top of the rev range, but the V8 uses less fuel. And there's more . . .

The V12 is not an exciting car to drive. It feels – dare I say this – a bit cumbersome. It's not like trying to lift a dead fat man into the boot of a Ford Focus, but it's not like watching a feather caught in a gentle summer breeze either. Whereas the V8 is just beautiful.

Unlike the V12, it doesn't feel cumbersome. You turn the wheel and there's that immediate Ferrari delicacy, a feeling that no other car maker can match. Some of it's down, I know, to four-wheel steering, which I think is a bit silly – it makes passengers car sick while offering negligible speed gains – but some of it is down to the lack of four-wheel drive.

The front wheels can just get on with the job. I adored driving this car.

Will it drift? Will it cling on for dear life, even when it's pouring and you're driving like a madman whose trousers have caught fire? Yes, of course. I turned off the traction control and stuck its tail out on a roundabout, and although it may have looked as if I was drifting the Torrey Canyon, it was as manageable as a Subaru Impreza.

This, though, is emphatically not what the GTC4Lusso T is for. You'll never see one at a track day or tearing round Harrods at 2 a.m.. It's a fat boy car. It even has a wide window-sill on which you can rest your arm as you cruise along. And you will be cruising, because it's quiet and civilized and the ride is joyously smooth. You might even call it restful. And no one's said that of a Ferrari before.

It's also a lovely place to sit. Everything feels beautifully put together, and since you get a two-year European warranty on approved used Ferraris, it probably is. It's also fun. It's an option, but in front of the passenger Ferrari will fit a second display that can be tuned to their mood. Play music. Watch the revs. Check the speed. The only thing missing is karaoke.

The driver is similarly well catered for but sadly won't be able to use any of the features, because the controls, along with those for the dim dip, the wipers and the indicators, are all on the steering wheel. So he'll be driving along shouting, 'Where's the bloody dip button gone?' It's the silliest idea, putting buttons on the only bit of a car's interior that moves, because it means nothing is ever where you left it. And I wouldn't mind, but Ford has done exactly the same thing on its new GT supercar. Madness.

And to make things worse in the Ferrari, when you are

putting on your specs to find the right indicator, which is now on the left because you're going round a corner, you will not be watching the speed . . .

Every car has a rate at which it will settle on the motorway when you are not concentrating. A Porsche 911, for reasons known to no one, is happiest at about 55mph. A Mini Cooper is at its best at about 100mph. Whereas the Ferrari settles at 117mph. Which means you need to be awake and aware or you're going to end up on the bus.

This is a tiny thing, though. And in an enlightened country where speed is not seen as a crime, it isn't an issue at all. The only big thing I could find wrong was the brakes. Being carbon ceramic, they didn't really work when they were cold.

But I'm still not bothered because, thanks to the new and much better V8 version, the GTC4Lusso's assault on my common sense has gone up a gear. I really would love to own this car. For no reason other than this: it's wonderful.

23 December 2018